UCC Revised Articles 3 & 4

The Banker's Guide to

CHECKS, DRAFTS
AND OTHER
NEGOTIABLE INSTRUMENTS

Paul A. Carrubba

BANKERS PUBLISHING COMPANY
PROBUS PUBLISHING COMPANY
Chicago, Illinois
Cambridge, England

ISBN 1-55738-351-0

Printed in the United States of America

BC

1 2 3 4 5 6 7 8 9 0

CONTENTS

PREFACE

Articles 3 and 4 of the Uniform Commercial Code (UCC), which govern negotiable instruments and the bank collection process, were originally adopted in 1952, well before the use of automation in the banking industry. Article 3 was completely rewritten and Article 4 was substantially revised in 1990 by the National Conference of Commissioners on Uniform State Laws (NCCUSL) and the American Law Institute (ALI). Many changes have taken place in the banking and finance industries over the past 40 years and the revision of these articles was drastically needed. For example, variable rate promissory notes, which make up a large portion of notes today, were not in existence when Article 3 was written. Electronic check presentment, truncation, and image technology were unheard of and the "process of posting" was a manual process when Article 4 was written. The Expedited Funds Availability Act and Federal Reserve Board Regulation CC, which were adopted in 1988, created some inconsistencies in the laws governing the check collection process. The revisions of Articles 3 and 4 address these issues and position these laws for the future direction of the banking industry.

The purpose of this book is to help the reader gain a full understanding of the provisions of Articles 3 and 4, examine what impact the
revisions will have, and act as a guide through the various sections. The
book contains numerous examples which are based on the author's interpretation of the sections plus some case law. All citations to cases are
to the Uniform Commercial Code Reporting Service.

The book contains a subject index and a table of Article 3 and Article 4 citations to assist the reader in locating a specific topic. Both the
index and the table of citations refer to the book section. Once the book
section is determined, the reader can refer to the table of contents to
locate the page number of the section in which the subject matter is
discussed.

CHAPTER 1

GENERAL PROVISIONS OF ARTICLES 3 AND 4 AND THE REQUIREMENTS OF A NEGOTIABLE INSTRUMENT

1.0 SCOPE AND SUBJECT MATTER OF ARTICLES 3 AND 4

Article 3 is cited as Uniform Commercial Code—Negotiable Instruments. As the name implies, Article 3 applies to all types of negotiable instruments including drafts, checks, notes, and certificates of deposit. The new revisions make it clear that the article applies to money orders and traveler's checks. This article does not apply to money, payment orders subject to Article 4A, or securities governed by Article 8 according to Section 3-102(a). However, several courts have held that investment securities may be subject to Article 3 if the specific issue is not addressed by Article 8 or if this article is not inconsistent with Article 8.

Specific examples of where the courts have applied Article 3 to investment securities are as follows. The court in *E.F. Hutton & Co., Inc. v. Manufacturers National Bank of Detroit, United States District Court, 3 UCC Rep Serv 752,* held that Article 8 of the UCC is the sole source of law governing the rights of parties to a transaction involving a security. However, where an issue cannot be resolved by Article 8, it is appropriate to look to Article 3 for guidance since a bond in bearer form which is a negotiable instrument can become an investment security. The court in *Victory National Bank of Nowata v. Oklahoma State Bank of Ninita Oklahoma, Supreme Court, 13 UCC Rep Serv 898*, held that a certificate of deposit is an investment security governed by Article 8 of the UCC even though it may also meet the requirements of Article 3.

Articles 3 and 4 work in conjunction with each other. While Article 4 deals with bank deposits and collections, many issues addressed in Article 3 are also addressed in Article 4. As long as there are no inconsistencies, the provisions of Article 3 apply to Article 4; however, Article 4 governs if there are any conflicts. Likewise, according to Section 3-102(b), Article 9 governs if there are inconsistencies with Article 3. Section 3-102(c) provides that Regulations of the Board of Governors of the Federal Reserve System and operating circulars of the Federal Reserve Banks supersede any inconsistent provisions of Article 3 to the extent of the inconsistency.

Article 4 is cited in Section 4-101 as Uniform Commercial Code—Bank Deposits and Collections. Items within Article 4 that are also in Article 3 and 8 are governed by those articles. If there are inconsistencies between these articles, Section 4-102(a) states that Article 4 governs Article 3 but Article 8 governs Article 4. As Official Comment 1 to section 4-102 points out, Article 4 is also subject to certain federal laws. Specifically, Article 4 is subject to Federal Reserve Regulation CC.

1.1 VARIATION BY AGREEMENT AND THE MEASURE OF DAMAGES

Article 4 may be varied by agreement; however, Section 4-103(a) states, "the parties to the agreement cannot disclaim a bank's responsibility for its lack of good faith or failure to exercise ordinary care or limit the measure of damages for the lack or failure." Clearinghouse and similar rules and Federal Reserve regulations have the effect of agreements, even if all of the parties have not assented to the rules according to Section 4-103(b). Action or nonaction taken by a bank in accordance with the provisions of Article 4, Federal Reserve regulations and operating circulars is considered the exercise of ordinary care. Additionally, Section 4-103(c) provides that a bank is considered to have exercised ordinary care if it acts in accordance with a clearinghouse or similar rule, if it acts in accordance with "general banking usage" not inconsistent with Article 4, and if there are no special instructions requiring action to the contrary.

Section 4-103 also sets the measure of damages for failure to exercise ordinary care in the handling of an item. Ordinary care is defined and discussed in Chapter 3 of this book. The measure of damages is the amount of the item reduced by an amount that could not have been realized by the exercise of ordinary care. If there is bad faith, Section 4-103(e) provides that the bank can be liable for any other damages the party suffers as a proximate consequence of the bad faith action. An example of the application of this section was a case where a depositary bank brought an action against a paying bank for damages for improper notice of nonpayment. The court reduced the $6,000 amount of the item by the $5,175 loss that would have occurred even with the exercise of ordinary care. This same court also held that the defendant was not liable for consequential damages where the evidence did not support a finding that the paying bank acted in bad faith. Bad faith is not defined in the code and, as stated in Official Comment #6 to section 4-103, "the connotation is the absence of good faith."

(a) OTHER AGREEMENTS AFFECTING INSTRUMENT

Article 3 does not contain a provision similar to Section 4-103 allowing for the variation of the effects of the provisions of the article by agreement. However, Section 3-117 addresses agreements affecting instruments. This section allows the party obligated to pay the instrument and the person entitled to enforce the instrument to enter into an agreement to modify, supplement, or nullify the obligation of the party to pay. The agreement is effective only if the instrument were issued in reliance on the agreement or the instrument was issued as part of the same transaction giving rise to the agreement. The agreement is a defense to the obligation to the extent the obligation is modified, supplemented, or nullified. The agreement is also subject to any applicable law regarding exclusion of proof of contemporaneous or previous agreements. The agreement is effective only against the parties to the agreement or a transferee or holder that took the instrument subject to the agreement. The agreement is not enforceable against a holder in due course.

1.2 DEFINITION AND REQUIREMENTS OF A NEGOTIABLE INSTRUMENT

The applicability of Article 3 is dependent upon the classification of an item as a negotiable instrument. Whether or not an item is a negotiable instrument is more of a problem when dealing with long complicated notes than with checks or drafts. Section 3-104 defines a negotiable instrument and sets out the specific requirements that must be met for the item to be given the status of a negotiable instrument. Section 3-104(a) states that "negotiable instrument means an unconditional promise or order to pay a fixed amount of money, with or without interest or other charges described in the promise or order." The promise or order must also meet the specific requirements that it:

(1) is payable to bearer or to order at the time it is issued or first comes into possession of a holder;

(2) is payable on demand or at a definite time; and

(3) does not state any other undertaking or instruction by the person promising or ordering payment to do any act in addition to the payment of money, but the promise or order may contain (i) an undertaking or power to give, maintain, or protect collateral to secure payment, (ii) an authorization or power to the holder to confess judgement or realize on or dispose of collateral, or (iii) a waiver of the benefit of any law intended for the advantage or protection on an obligor.

At first glance, it appears that the requirement under the old version of Article 3 that a negotiable instrument must be a writing signed by the drawer or maker is no longer a requirement. This requirement still remains but is included in the definitions of "order" and "promise." The first requirement of a negotiable instrument is that it must be a promise or order. "Order" is defined in Section 3-103(a)(6) as "a written instruction to pay money signed by the person giving the instruction. The instruction may be addressed to any person, including the person giving the instruction, or to one or more persons jointly or in the alternative but not in succession. An authorization to pay is not an order unless the person authorized to pay is also instructed to pay." A "promise" is defined in Section 3-103(a)(9) as "a written undertaking to pay money signed by the person undertaking to pay. An acknowledgment of an obligation by the obligor is not a promise unless the obligor also undertakes to pay the obligation." Therefore, the requirement that the order or promise must be in writing signed by the drawer or maker is still very much a part of the requirements of a negotiable instrument.

(a) UNCONDITIONAL PROMISE OR ORDER

The promise or order must be unconditional and Section 3-106 specifically addresses this issue. According to that section, a promise or an order is unconditional unless it states an express condition to payment of the item that the promise or order is subject to or governed by another writing, or that the rights or obligations with respect to the promise or order are stated in another writing. The fact that another writing is referenced to in the promise or order does not by itself make it conditional. For example, a note that contains a statement to the effect that it is issued in accordance with an agreement of the parties is not made conditional by reference to the agreement of the parties. Section 3-106(b) further states that a promise or order is not made conditional because it refers to another writing for a statement of the rights with respect to collateral, prepayment, or accelerations or because payment is limited to resort to a particular fund or source. This section allows the issuance of a promissory note without requiring that provisions for collateral, prepayment, or acceleration be included in the note itself. Such issues may be addressed in a document referred to in the note.

As pointed out in Official Comment #1 to Section 3-106, Subsection (b)(ii) reverses the result of former Section 3-105(2)(b). "There is no cogent reason why the general credit of a legal entity must be pledged to have a negotiable instrument. Market forces determine the marketability of instruments of this kind. If potential buyers don't want promises or orders that are payable only from a particular source or fund, they won't take them, but Article 3 should apply."

Section 3-106(c) makes it clear that a traveler's check is not conditional because it requires a countersignature. That section states that a promise or order is is not made conditional because it requires, as a condition to payment, a countersignature by a person whose specimen signature appears on the promise or order. This section codifies the holding of the court in *Xanthopoulos v. Thomas Cook, Inc.*, 42 *UCC Rep Serv 883*, (1985) that traveler's checks meeting all of the requirements of a negotiable instrument are not conditional because a countersignature was required.

Section 3-106(c) goes on to say that the failure to countersign the instrument by the person whose specimen signature appears on an instrument is a defense to the obligation of the issuer. However, the failure to countersignature does not prevent a transferee of the instrument from becoming a holder of the instrument. The countersignature on a traveler's check is required for identification purposes and is not there for the purposes of an indorsement. The countersignature is not required for further negotiation of the instrument. Therefore, if the countersignature is skillfully forged, the transferee becomes a holder and if it meets all of the other requirements may become a holder in due course. Transfer through negotiation will be discussed in Chapter 4 of this book.

In certain situations, statutory or administrative law requires that a legend be placed on a promise or order to the effect that the rights of a holder or transferee are subject to claims or defenses that the issuer could assert against the original payee. Such a legend or statement does not render the promise or order conditional for the purposes of Section 3-104(a); but if the promise or order is an instrument, there cannot be a holder in due course of the instrument (Section 3-106(d)). Official Comment #3 of Section 3-106 states, "The prime example is the Federal Trade Commission Rule (16 C.F.R. Part 433) preserving consumer's claims and defenses in consumer credit sales. The intent of the FTC rule is to make it impossible for there to be a holder in due course of a note bearing the FTC legend and undoubtedly that is the result." This section's primary application is to notes and should not be an issue when dealing with other forms of negotiable instruments such as checks and drafts.

(b) FIXED AMOUNT OF MONEY

The instrument must contain a promise or order to pay a fixed amount of "money" (Section 3-104(a)). The definition of "money" in Section 1-201(24) has been amended to mean "a medium of exchange authorized or adopted by a domestic or foreign government and includes a monetary unit of account established by an intergovernmental organization or by agreement between two or more nations." The intent of this requirement that the instrument must be payable in a fixed amount of money is to make it clear that the amount of the instrument must be determined by reference to the instrument itself. If the item is not payable in money or the amount is not fixed, then the item is not a negotiable instrument. However, Section 3-104(a) provides that the instrument may contain a provision for the payment of interest or other charges described in the promise or order. This provision clears up any potential dispute that the amount is not fixed if the promise or order provides for the payment of interest or other charges.

The instrument may be payable in a foreign currency since the definition of money is not limited to United States dollars. Section 3-107 states, "Unless the instrument otherwise provides, an instrument that states the amount payable in foreign money may be paid in the foreign money or in an equivalent amount in dollars calculated by using the current bank-offered spot rate at the place of payment for the purchase of dollars on the day on which the instrument is paid." This section allows for the instrument to be paid in dollars and establishes the conversion rate if not provided for in the instrument. Application of this section to instruments payable in a foreign currency will eliminate any questions concerning the amount of the instrument or if the amount of the instrument is fixed.

(c) PAYABLE ON DEMAND OR AT A DEFINITE TIME

Another requirement of a negotiable instrument is that the instrument must be payable on demand or at a definite time.

Section 3-108(a) states when a promise or order is "payable on demand." According to that section, an instrument is payable on demand if it states that it is payable on demand or at sight. The instrument is also payable on demand if it indicates that it is payable at the will of the holder or does not state any time of payment. It is not payable on demand if it is only payable at the will of the maker or drawer.

Section 3-108(b) contains several determinations as to when a promise or order is "payable at a definite time." It is payable at a definite time if it is payable on elapse of a definite period of time after sight or acceptance. An example of this type of instrument is a draft payable 10 days after sight. It is also "payable at a definite time" if it is payable at a fixed date or dates or at a time or times readily ascertainable at the time the promise or order is issued. For example, a note payable on May 1, 1993 is payable at a definite time. The promise or order is also payable at a definite time even if it is subject to rights of prepayment, accelerations, extension at the option of the holder, or extension to a further definite time at the option of the maker or acceptor or automatically upon or after a specified act or event.

Section 3-108(c) addresses the situation of when an instrument is payable at a fixed date or upon demand before the fixed date. In this situation, the instrument is payable on demand until the fixed date. If demand for payment is not made before the fixed date, then the instrument is payable at a definite time on the fixed date. For example, if an instrument is payable upon demand before May 1, 1993, it is payable on demand up until May 1, 1993. If demand is not made before May 1, 1993, the instrument is payable at a definite time on May 1, 1993.

(d) DATE OF INSTRUMENT

Section 3-113(a) states that an instrument may be postdated or antedated and the stated date determines the time of payment if the instrument is payable at a fixed period after the date as discussed above. The old version of Article 3 stated that an instrument payable on demand is not payable before the date on the instrument and this requirement applied to all instruments without exception. The revised Article 3 notes an exception to this rule for postdated checks as provided in Section 4-401(c). Under Article 4, a bank may charge a customer's account even though payment is made before the date on the check unless the customer gives the bank notice of the postdating. Postdated checks are discussed in Chapter 11 of this book.

Section 3-113(b) addresses the situation of when an instrument is not dated. The failure to date the instrument could be intentional or unintentional. In either case, if the instrument is not dated, the date of the instrument is considered to be the date of issue. In the case of an unissued instrument, the date of the instrument is the date it first comes into the possession of the holder.

(e) PAYABLE TO BEARER OR TO ORDER

Section 3-104(a)(1) requires that the promise or order must be payable to bearer or to order. This section does not apply to an instrument that is a check defined in Section 3-104(f) as "(i) a draft, other than a documentary draft, payable on demand and drawn on a bank, or (ii) a cashiers check or teller's check. An instrument may be a check even though it is described on its face by another term, such as 'money order'." The primary reason for the requirement that the instrument states that it is payable to bearer or to order is to prevent the owner of the item from claiming that it is a negotiable instrument when it was not the intentions of the parties at the time that the instrument was issued to make the item a negotiable instrument. A check is excluded from this requirement because a check is intended to be a negotiable instrument and checks are sometimes issued payable to a payee and the word "order" is not included on the instrument when it is printed.

Section 3-109(a) states that "a promise or order is payable to bearer if it is payable to bearer or to the order of bearer or otherwise indicates that the person in possession of the promise or order is entitled to payment." Not all situations are as obvious as this. Therefore, Sections 3-109(a)(2) and (3) provide that the promise or order is also payable to bearer of it "does not state a payee" or "states that it is payable to or to the order of cash or otherwise indicates that it is not payable to an identified person."

If an instrument is payable to bearer, an indorsement is not required for further negotiation of the instrument. Negotiation is discussed in detail in Chapter 4 of this book.

Section 3-109(b) provides that an instrument is payable to order if it is not payable to bearer and is payable "to the order of an identified person" or is payable "to an identified person or order." For example, a check issued in the following form—"pay to the order of Bill Wiltshire"—is payable to order. Another example of an instrument payable to order would be a check issued "to Bill Wiltshire or order." Section 3-109(b) also provides that "a promise or order that is payable to order is payable to the identified person." This section seems pretty obvious, but the intention is to make it clear that the only person entitled to payment of the promise or order is the identified person. Therefore, it follows (as discussed in Chapter 4 of this book), the negotiation of an order instrument requires the indorsement of the identified person. For example, a check payable to the order of Bill Wiltshire may only be negotiated with the indorsement of Bill Wiltshire. Section 3-109(c) further provides that an instrument payable to bearer may be made payable to order if specially indorsed to the order of an identified person as provided for in Section 3-205(a). Section 3-109(c) also states that an order instrument may become a bearer instrument if the item is indorsed in blank in accordance with Section 3-205(b).

Examples of the two situations under Section 3-109(c) discussed above are as follows. A check issued to the order of cash is a bearer instrument requiring only delivery of the instrument. However, if the instrument is indorsed "Pay to the order of Bill Wiltshire," the instrument becomes an order instrument payable to an identified person, Bill Wiltshire and his indorsement is required for further negotiation of the instrument. Another example is a check payable to the order of Bill Wiltshire. This check is payable to an identified person and requires an indorsement for further negotiation. However, if the check is indorsed in blank pursuant to Section 3-205(b), the instrument becomes a bearer instrument that does not require an indorsement for further negotiation.

1.3 ISSUANCE OF A NEGOTIABLE INSTRUMENT AND INCOMPLETE INSTRUMENTS

A person is not liable on an instrument unless the person signed the instrument or authorized one to sign on his or her behalf (Section 3-401). Once the person signs the instrument, he or she is bound by his or her signature and becomes liable on the instrument.

Signatures and the liability of the person signing are discussed in detail in Chapter 3 of this book. The ultimate liability of a person on an instrument may also depend upon whether or not the person issued the instrument. "Issue" is defined in Section 3-105(a) to mean "the first delivery of an instrument by the maker or drawer, whether to a holder or nonholder, for the purpose of giving rights on the instrument to any person."

Several other words must be defined to fully understand the meaning and implications of the issuance of an instrument. First of all, "instrument," as defined in Section 3-104(b), means a negotiable instrument. The instrument may be either a note or a draft and Subsection (e) of Section 3-104 states that "an instrument is a 'note' if it is a promise and is a 'draft' if it is an order." "Issuer" means a maker or drawer of an instrument according to Section 3-105(c). A "drawer" is defined in Section 3-103(a)(3) as "a person who signs or is identified in a draft as a person ordering payment." A "maker" is defined in Section 3-103(a)(5) as "a person who signs or is identified in a note as a person undertaking to pay." "Delivery," with respect to instruments, is defined in Section 1-201(14) to mean "voluntary transfer of possession." "Issue" then requires that the delivery of the instrument be intentional and not done through mistake, error, or coercion. For example, if a check was completed in favor of a payee but was mailed to the payee through mistake, then the instrument is considered to be unissued. Or if a check was made out to a payee, but the check was stolen from the drawer before it was delivered to the payee, the check would be considered unissued even if the payee was the person that stole the check.

According to Section 3-105(c), however, an unissued instrument is binding on the maker or drawer but the maker or drawer may raise the nonissuance as a defense to payment of the instrument. The defense is a personal defense and not a real defense and is, therefore, not good against a holder in due course. For example, Drawer draws a check payable to the order of Payee but does not deliver the check to Payee. Payee steals the check from Drawer and presents the check for payment to Drawer's bank. Drawer's bank refuses to pay the check because Drawer has issued a stop payment on the check. Payee then sues Drawer to collect the amount of the check. Drawer may raise the defense that the check was not issued to Payee because it was stolen. On the other hand, if the check ends up in the hands of a holder in due course, the defense of nondelivery will not be good.

For example, assume the same facts as the example above except that Payee negotiates the check to Bank who meets the requirements of a holder in due course. In this example, Bank would take the check free of Drawer's personal defense of nondelivery. Holder in due course is discussed in detail in Chapter 6 of this book.

Section 3-105(b) also applies to a situation where an unissued incomplete instrument is completed. The completed instrument is binding on the maker or drawer but the nonissuance is a defense. This section also provides that an instrument that is issued for a special purpose or is conditionally issued is binding on the maker or drawer but if the instrument is not used for the specific purpose or if the condition is not met, such failure is a defense that can be raised against payment. For example, assume that Drawer draws a check payable to Payee for which Payee is suppose to wash Drawer's house. Payee's failure to wash the house is a valid defense against Payee's demand on Drawer for payment. Here again, the defense is a personal defense and is not valid against a holder in due course.

(a) INCOMPLETE INSTRUMENTS

In certain situations, a person may sign a writing and for various reasons may not complete it but may intend for the writing to be completed by the addition of words or numbers. Section 3-115 refers to such an instrument as an "incomplete instrument" and sets out the rules that apply. If the instrument is incomplete but is sufficiently complete enough to meet the requirements of a negotiable instrument under Section 3-104, then it can be enforced according to the terms contained in the instrument.

For example, if a drawer issues a check but does not put a date on the check, under this section, the check is incomplete but may be paid according to its other terms. Or if the instrument is incomplete but meets the requirements of a negotiable instrument and is completed, then it may be enforced according to its terms as completed. In the previous example, if the check is completed by the addition of the date, then the check can be enforced even though it was completed after it was issued. If an incomplete instrument does not meet the requirements of a negotiable instrument at the time that it is issued but does meet the requirements after completion, then the instrument can be enforced according to the terms of the instrument as completed. Official Comment #3 to Section 3-115 explains this provision by using an example of a check that is issued without an amount. Section 3-104 requires that an instrument must contain a fixed amount and unless completed, the item would not be a negotiable instrument. Therefore, if the check is completed by the addition of the amount, then the check is enforceable as completed.

The completion of the instruments as described in the previous paragraph are valid only if the instruments are completed in accordance with the authority of the signer of the instrument. According to Section 3-115(c), if the words or numbers used to complete the instrument are not authorized by the signer, then the completion of the instrument is considered to be an alteration under Section 3-407. For example, if D issues a check to P and instructs P to complete the instrument by providing an amount of $10.00 but P completes the check in the amount of $100.00, this unauthorized completion is an alteration. Section 3-115(d) provides that the burden of proof that the completion was unauthorized is on the person claiming that the completion was unauthorized. In the example above, the drawer of the check would have the burden of proving that the authorized amount was $10.00 and not $100.00.

(b) CONTRADICTORY TERMS OF INSTRUMENT

Section 3-114 governs circumstances where an instrument contains contradictory terms. This section is short and to the point and states, "If an instrument contains contradictory terms, typewritten terms prevail over printed terms, handwritten terms prevail over both, and words prevail over numbers." Unfortunately, checks are encoded according to the numbers and the words are almost never referred to in the encoding process. If a check is written in numbers as $50.00 and in words as "five dollars," the check is payable in the amount of five dollars.

1.4 IDENTIFICATION OF THE PAYEE OF AN INSTRUMENT

The determination of who the payee is on an instrument is very important and is sometimes very difficult to determine. The identification of the person to whom an instrument is payable determines who has rights to the instrument, how the instrument must be indorsed, and the standard of care that must be used when dealing with instruments payable to fiduciaries. Section 3-110 provides the answers to these questions.

(a) THE INTENTION OF THE SIGNER

The primary thrust of Section 3-110 is that the identity of the payee is determined by the intent of the person issuing the instrument. Section 3-110(a) provides that "the person to whom an instrument is initially payable is determined by the intent of the person, whether or not authorized, signing as, or in the name or behalf of, the issuer of the instrument." The "issuer" of the instrument is the maker or drawer (Section 3-105). Subsection (a) further provides that if there are multiple signers that issue an instrument on behalf of the issuer, and all of the signers do not intend the same person as payee, then the instrument is payable to any person intended by one or more of the signers.

An example of the application of Subsection (a) is as follows. Bill Wiltshire issues a check payable to Cindy Faulkner and intends for Cindy Faulkner to be the payee. In this case the answer is easy and obvious; Cindy Faulkner is the person to whom the check is payable and her indorsement is required for further negotiation of the instrument. Suppose further that Joel Converse issues a check to Cindy Faulkner and forges Bill Wiltshire's signature. In this situation, Cindy Faulkner is still the person to whom the check is payable even though Joel forged Bill's signature. Since Bill's signature was forged, however, he is not liable on the instrument.

Another example of the application of this Subsection is as follows. Bill Wiltshire and Joel Converse sign a check on behalf of Flashback Music, Inc. and the named payee is Harold Wilson. Bill intended for the check to be payable to Harold Wilson but Joel intended for the check to be payable to Harold Watson. In this situation, the check is payable to either Harold Wilson or Harold Watson because Subsection (a) of Section 3-110 provides that "the instrument is payable to any person intended by one or more of the signers."

Subsection (a) also addresses the situation of where one payee is named but the signer intended for the instrument to be payable to another payee. Here again, the intent of the signer determines to whom the instrument is payable. As in the case above, the named payee of the check was Harold Wilson; but one of the signers, Joel Converse, intended for the check to be payable to Harold Watson. In this case, the person to whom the check is payable could be either Harold Wilson or Harold Watson even though the person actually named as the payee is Harold Wilson. As long as the intended payee receives the check it does not matter that the wrong payee is actually named on the check. In this example, since Harold Watson was an intended payee, he could indorse the check either as Harold Watson, Harold Wilson, or in both names (Section 3-204(d)).

Another example used in the Official Comments to this section is a check payable to "John Smith." Since there are many "John Smiths" any one of them could negotiate the check unless there was some other means to identify which "John Smith" was the intended payee or unless the intention of the signer could be determined.

Many companies use some form of automation to issue and sign checks. Many checks are issued and signed through the use of computers or check-writing machines or the check may be issued manually but the signature is made through the use of a check-signing machine. Section 3-110(b) addresses this situation and states that the person to whom the check is payable is determined by the intent of the person who supplied the name or identification of the payee. The intent of the person supplying the name of the payee controls even if the person acted without authority. For example, Bill Wiltshire works for Flashback Music, Inc. and he supplies the data processing department with the name of Cindy Faulkner as the payee of a check. The check is computer generated and signed. The check is payable to Cindy Faulkner and requires her indorsement for further negotiation even if Bill Wiltshire acted without authority.

A detailed discussion regarding employee fraud, fictitious payees, and negligence contributing to forgeries is contained in Chapter 5 of this book.

(b) METHOD OF IDENTIFICATION OF THE PAYEE

Some instruments are issued in a manner such that is difficult to determine the rightful holder of the instrument. Instruments are issued to accounts, agents, trustees, and in many other forms, and it is often difficult to determine to whom the instrument is payable. Section 3-110(c) gives specific directions on who is the proper holder of the instrument. "Holder" is defined in Section 1-201(20), with respect to a negotiable instrument, to mean, "the person in possession if the instrument is payable to bearer or, in the case of an instrument payable to an identified person, if the identified person is in possession." Subsection (c) provides that "a person to whom an instrument is payable may be identified in any way, including by name, identifying number, office, or account number." This gives the issuer total discretion as to how the instrument is issued. For the purpose of determining the holder of an instrument, the Subsection gives specific rules to be applied to when instruments are issued in certain ways. Subsection (c)(1) addresses the situation where the payee is identified by account number. If the instrument is payable to an account and the account is identified by only the account number, the instrument is payable to the person to whom the account is payable. This Subsection is easy to apply if the account is owned by only one person but may be more difficult if the account is owned by multiple account holders.

For example, if a check is payable to account number 12345 and Bill Wiltshire is the sole owner of the account, then there is no question that Bill Wiltshire is the person to whom the instrument is payable and would require his indorsement for further negotiation. On the other hand, if the instrument is payable to account number 12345, and the account is owned by Bill Wiltshire or Cindy Faulkner, the answer is not as clear.

This specific situation is not addressed in the text or the Official Comments; however, it would appear that the check would be payable to Bill Wiltshire or Cindy Faulkner alternatively and could be negotiated by either one of them. This appears to be the correct answer since the language of Subsection (c) states that "the instrument is payable to the person to whom the account is payable," and the account is a joint account payable to either.

If the instrument is payable to to an account identified by account number and is also payable to a person by name, Subsection (c)(1) states that "the instrument is payable to the named person." The section also states that the instrument is payable to the named person even if the named person is not the owner of the account identified by number. For example, if a check is issued payable to "Bill Wiltshire account number 12345" and account number 12345 does not belong to Bill Wiltshire, the check is payable to Bill Wiltshire and requires his indorsement for further negotiation. If a check such as the one just described is presented for deposit at a bank, the bank must make certain that it identifies the owner of the account before it relies on the account number. In this situation, if the check is deposited to the identified account number and the account does not belong to the person named in the instrument, the bank could be liable to the rightful holder of the instrument which, according to this section, is the named person. This rule is the exact opposite of the rule relative to funds transfers under Article 4A of the UCC. Under Article 4A, the beneficiary's bank may apply the proceeds to the account number contained in the payment order even if the account number and the name describe different people.

(c) INSTRUMENT PAYABLE TO A TRUST, AN ESTATE, AN AGENT, OR AN ORGANIZATION THAT IS NOT A LEGAL ENTITY

Section 3-110(c)(2)(i) governs instruments payable to a trust, an estate, or the trustee or representative of the estate. In this situation, the instrument is payable to the trustee, the representative, or the successor of either. This rule applies whether or not the estate or the beneficiary of the trust are also named. For example, a check issued to "Bill Wiltshire, Executor" is payable to Bill Wiltshire and he is the holder of the instrument. A check payable to "Bill Wiltshire, Executor of the Estate of Joel Converse," is payable to Bill Wiltshire and may be indorsed by him in his own name without the need of also adding the capacity in which he is indorsing. In *Bates v. City of New York, 10 UCC Rep Serv 151, (1971)*, the court held that a check made payable to the order of X "as administrator of the estate of Y" was properly indorsed by X without showing the fiduciary capacity in which he was indorsing. In this case, the court also held that the bank that took the check for deposit to the personal account of X was not liable to the estate of Y for the amount of the check even though X converted the proceeds for his personal use. The court concluded that the bank did not know that X was using the proceeds for his own benefit and had no reason to suspect his fraudulent intent.

Official Comment #2 to Section 3-110 points out that this section "merely determines who can deal with an instrument as a holder. It does not determine ownership of the instrument or its proceeds."

A situation similar to the trust and estate situation above is when an instrument is payable to an agent or representative of a named or identified person. According to Section 3-110(c)(2)(ii), the instrument is payable to the person represented or the representative or agent and may be negotiated by him or her. If a successor is named, the instrument is also payable to the successor. Under this section, a check made payable to Bill Wiltshire, President of Flashback Music, Inc., is payable to either Bill Wiltshire or Flashback Music, Inc. The instrument may be personally indorsed by Bill Wiltshire or it may be indorsed by Bill Wiltshire, President of Flashback Music, Inc. As stated above, this section does not address ownership of the instrument or the proceeds. It merely points out who is the holder of the instrument and has the authority to indorse the instrument.

Funds or organizations that are not a legal entity are always very difficult to deal with. Since the organization is not a legal entity, it is not at all clear who has the authority to transact business on behalf of the organization. As for negotiable instruments payable to one of these organizations, Section 3-110(c)(2)(iii) provides that "a fund or organization that is not a legal entity, the instrument is payable to a representative of the members of the fund or organization." The Official Comments say very little about about this section; however, they do state that "any representative of the members of the organization can act as a holder." While this section does give some guidance when dealing with unincorporated organizations, some problems will still remain. For example, if there is a split in the membership over who should and should not be a representative, the bank or any other person dealing with the disputed representative could find itself in the middle of a dispute. The point is that any person dealing with an organization that is not a legal entity should use caution.

The final rule for determining the holder of an instrument under Section 3-110 is Subsection (c)(2)(iv) which applies to an instrument payable to an office or to a person described as holding an office. In this situation, the instrument is payable to the named person, the incumbent of the office, or a successor to the incumbent. The Official Comments point out that this Subsection applies principally to instruments payable to public offices. An example of this type of payee would be a check payable to the "State Treasurer's Office" or a check payable to "Bob Jones, State Treasurer." In both of these examples, the check is payable to and may be indorsed by Bob Jones, an incumbent, or a successor to the incumbent.

(d) INSTRUMENT PAYABLE TO TWO OR MORE PERSONS

Much litigation has arisen over the payment of instruments payable to joint payees. The old version of Article 3 made it clear that if an instrument was payable to joint payees in the alternative, then either of them could indorse the instrument. If the instrument was payable to joint payees not in the alternative, then the instrument was payable to all of them and must be indorsed by all of them to negotiate the instrument. The new version of Article 3 retains this provision but clears up one area that was not addressed by the old version. Under the new version, Section 3-110(d), if an instrument is payable to two or more persons alternatively, the instrument is payable to and may be indorsed and negotiated by any of them in possession of the instrument. If the instrument is not payable in the alternative, it is payable to all of them and must be indorsed and negotiated by all of them. The following is an example of the application of this section. A check payable to "Bill Wiltshire or Cindy Faulkner" is payable alternatively and may be indorsed and negotiated by either of them. A check payable to "Bill Wiltshire and Cindy Faulkner" is not payable alternatively and must be indorsed by both of them. If either indorsement is missing or forged, the person whose indorsement is missing or forged is entitled to object to the payment of the item. Missing and forged indorsements will be discussed in detail in Chapter 5 of this book.

Sometimes it is difficult to determine whether an instrument is payable alternatively or not. The court held in *Miron Rapid Mix Concrete Corp. v. Bank Hapoalim, B.M., 30 UCC Rep Serv 1017*, that a Virgule (/) between two names indicates that the instrument is payable alternatively and that either person named may indorse the instrument. In some cases it is not clear what the intentions of the issuer was. For example a check payable as follows "Bill Wiltshire, Cindy Faulkner" is not clear as to whether it is issued alternatively or not. The new version of Article 3, in Subsection 3-110(d), includes an additional provision that states if the instrument is payable to two or more persons but the instrument is ambiguous as to whether it is payable to them alternatively, then the instrument is payable to them alternatively. This Subsection reverses court decisions such as *C.H. Sanders Construction Co., Inc. v. Bankers Trust Co., 1 UCC Rep Serv 2d 1563*. In this case, a check was issued to two payees with a Virgule (/) between the two names in addition to the word "and." The court held that if a check, ambiguous on its face regarding whether it is to be paid in the alternative or jointly, is paid on the indorsement of one payee, the other payee will be deprived of his or her interest in the instrument. For that reason, the court held, policy dictated that the subject instrument be deemed jointly payable despite the ambiguity. Applying Section 3-110(d), this case would have been decided differently. Because of the ambiguity, the court would have held that the instrument was payable alternatively and that either payee could indorse the instrument.

Another case that would have had a different result if Section 3-110(d) was applied is *General Microcomputer, Inc. v. Crow-Williams, 13 UCC Rep Serv 2d 162 (1989)*. In this case, a certificate of deposit was issued to two payees with a comma between the names. The court held that this was ambiguous and that since a comma is not a Virgule (/), the CD was issued jointly and not in the alternative and both indorsements were required. In *Boyce v. Chase Manhattan Bank, 5 UCC Rep Serv 2d 1016*, a check was made payable with a hyphen (-) between the two names. The check was made payable to "Landau-Boyce." The check was accepted by a bank for deposit with only the indorsement of Landau and the bank contends that the hyphen (-) was a Virgule and was therefore payable in the alternative. The lower court granted summary judgement to the bank. On appeal, the court held that the "-" was not a Virgule and therefore it was a question of fact as to whether it was payable in the alternative or jointly and should have been decided by the jury. This case may very well have been decided differently under the new section.

The court may have even reached a different conclusion in *Feldman Construction Co. v. Union Bank, 11 UCC Rep Serv 828*. In that case a check was issued with two payees with an "and" or "or" between the names. One name was placed above the other. The court held that it was payable jointly and required the indorsement of both parties and not just one as contended by the bank. The court could conclude that an instrument such as the one in this case is ambiguous and that since it is not clear, then it is payable alternatively.

CHAPTER 2

PARTIES TO CHECKS AND DRAFTS AND THEIR GENERAL LIABILITY

2.1 DRAFTS, CHECKS, AND THE DRAWER'S LIABILITY

The Uniform Commercial Code contains numerous definitions and, in many cases, terms must be defined in succession. The definitions of the terms in Articles 3 and 4 are a prime example of this as evidenced in the following definitions of a draft, a check, and the various parties to those instruments. A "draft" is defined in Section 3-104(e) as an instrument that is an "order." "Instrument" means a "negotiable instrument" as defined in Section 3-104(b). "Order" is defined in Section 3-103(a)(6) to mean "a written instruction to pay money signed by the person giving the instruction. The instruction may be addressed to any person, including the person giving the instruction, or to one or more persons jointly or in the alternative but not in succession." Putting all of those definitions together, a draft is a negotiable instrument that is a written instruction to pay money signed by the person giving the instruction. In other words, a draft is an order given by the drawer to the drawee to pay money to the holder presenting the item for payment. The drawer and the drawee can be the same person as is the case of some drafts issued by insurance companies. A cashier's check is another example of a draft where the drawer and the drawee are the same. A "check" is a draft and is defined in Section 3-104(f) as a draft payable on demand

and drawn on a bank. The definition specifically excludes documentary drafts even if it is drawn on a bank. The definition of a check also includes a cashier's check, a teller's check, or an instrument that is described by another term on its face such as "money order." Unless specifically excluded, the following discussion applies to checks even though the term "draft" is used.

The "drawer" is defined in Section 3-103(a)(3) as "a person who signs or is identified in a draft as a person ordering payment." The drawer is the issuer of the draft. Many times the issuer of a draft is erroneously referred to as the "maker" of the draft. A "maker" is defined in Section 3-103(a)(5) as "a person who signs or is identified in a note as a person undertaking to pay." The issuer of a draft is a drawer and the issuer of a note is the maker; the liabilities of the two are different. The obligations of a drawer are provided for in Section 3-414. Section 3-414(a) states that this section does not apply to cashier's checks or other drafts drawn on the drawer. The obligations of the issuer of a note or a cashier's check are provided for in Section 3-412.

According to Section 3-414(b), the drawer of a draft that has not been accepted by the drawee is obliged to pay a draft that has been dishonored according to the terms of the draft at the time it was issued or at the time it first comes into the possession of a holder if the draft is not issued. A discussion of when a draft is or is not issued is contained in Chapter 1 of this book. The obligation of the drawer to pay is owed to a person entitled to enforce the instrument or to an indorser who paid the draft. The person entitled to enforce the draft is governed by Section 3-301 and is discussed in Chapter 6 of this book. If the drawer signed an incomplete draft, then he or she is obligated to pay the draft according to the terms of the draft as completed. The obligation of the drawer to pay, however, is based on the draft being completed as authorized by the drawer. If the draft is completed with terms that were not authorized by the drawer, then completion of the draft with the unauthorized terms is considered to be an alteration of the draft. For example, assume that Bill Wiltshire issued a check to Cindy Faulkner but left the amount blank. Cindy was instructed to complete the check in the amount of $10.00, but instead she completed it for $100.00. Bill's obligation is to pay $10.00 and not $100.00 subject to the provisions of Section 3-407 dealing with alterations and other provisions dealing with the negligence of the drawer. Alteration is governed by Sections 3-115 and 3-407 which are discussed in Chapter 1.

The obligation of the drawer to pay is based on the draft being dishonored by the drawee. This means that the draft must first be presented for payment and dishonored. For example, Bill Wiltshire issued a check to Cindy Faulkner. Cindy calls the bank to verify sufficiency of funds and is informed by the bank that the account balance is not sufficient to pay the check. Based on this information, Cindy brings an action against Bill for the amount of the check. In this example, Bill could defend the action on the grounds that the check was never presented for payment and dishonored. Bill would rely on Section 3-414(b) which bases the obligation of the drawer on dishonor of the draft. The court in *Kirby v. Bergfield, 8 UCC Rep Serv 710*, held that inquiry by telephone of the sufficiency of funds is not presentment. The court stated that payment of a check by a drawee bank required exhibition of the item under current banking practice.

Another example of the application of this section would be as follows. Assume that Bill issues a check to Cindy and she immediately takes the check to Bill's bank and presents the check for immediate payment over the counter. The teller inquires on the balance on the account and determines that the balance is not sufficient to pay the check and refuses to pay Cindy the amount of the check. In this situation, the check was dishonored and Bill is then obligated to pay the amount of the check to Cindy, absent any other defense to payment that Bill may have. Cindy is entitled to some proof that she did in fact present the check and that it was dishonored. The teller could provide this proof by stamping, typing or writing "insufficient" on the check and also supplying the date of presentment. Tellers are, for some reason, reluctant to provide such notice. Presentment is discussed at length in Chapter 7 of this book and dishonor is discussed in Chapter 8.

Unlike the obligation of an indorser, no notice of dishonor to the drawer is required. The rationale of the no notice requirement is that the drawer issued the draft and knows in advance whether or not the drawee will pay the draft. In the example above, Cindy would not be required to notify Bill that the check had been dishonored. Bill's obligation to pay is based on the dishonor and not on any type of notice of dishonor. Notice may be required to the drawer under Section 3-414(d) discussed below where a draft has been accepted by a nonbank payor. The notice requirement to the indorser is discussed in Chapter 8 of this book.

The drawer remains liable on the draft until the obligation to pay is discharged. Discharge on an instrument can occur in several different forms which are discussed in Chapter 9 of this book. One method of discharge, however, is provided for in Section 3-414(c). According to this section, the obligation of the drawer is totally discharged if the draft is accepted by a bank. The section also states that the discharge is effective regardless of when the acceptance is obtained or by whom. A certified check is an example of a draft that has been accepted by a bank. The obligation of the drawer is discharged upon certification and is replaced by the bank's obligation to pay. Certification and acceptance are discussed in detail in section 2.4 of this chapter.

Not all drafts are drawn on banks; therefore, Section 3-414(d) provides that if a draft is accepted by a drawee that is not a bank, the obligation of the drawer is not discharged but is changed. If the accepted draft is dishonored by the acceptor, the drawer's obligation is the same as the obligation of an indorser's under Section 3-415(a) and (c). As discussed in section 2.3, the indorser's contractual obligation is that upon dishonor and timely notice of dishonor; the indorser will take the item back and will pay the party to whom the indorser is liable. If the notice of dishonor is not given timely, then the indorser's obligation to pay is discharged. An example of how this applies to a drawer is as follows. Assume that Joel Converse issues a draft and the drawee, Flashback Music, Inc., accepts the draft. Assume further that the draft is dishonored upon presentment to the drawee and the person presenting the draft gives timely notice to Joel that the draft was dishonored by Flashback Music, Inc. According to Section 3-414(d), Joel remains liable on the draft and is obligated to pay it. On the other hand, if timely notice is not given, Joel's obligation to pay is discharged. This is the exception to the rule referred to above that the drawer is not entitled to notice of dishonor.

The drawer of a draft, other than a check, can limit or completely disclaim any liability on the instrument. Section 3-414(e) provides that "if the draft is drawn 'without recourse' or otherwise disclaims liability of the drawer to pay the draft, the drawer is not liable" to pay the draft under Section 3-414(b) if the draft is not a check. The drawer of a check cannot disclaim liability on the check. As Official Comment #5 to Section 3-414 points out, "There is no legitimate purpose served by issuing a check on which nobody is liable."

Section 3-414(f) contains special circumstances under which the drawer of a check is discharged from its obligation to pay a check. That section provides that if a check is not presented for payment within 30 days from the date of the check, the drawee suspends payment after the expiration of the 30 days and the drawer is deprived of the funds maintained with the drawee to cover payment of the check, and the drawer may discharge its obligation to pay the check. The obligation of the drawer is only discharged to the extent that the drawer is deprived of the funds because of the suspension of payment.

For example, Bill Wiltshire issues a check to Cindy Faulkner dated January 15 and Cindy does not attempt to present the check to the Drawee Bank until March 5. In the meantime, the Drawee Bank suspends payment on February 28 and has already paid checks on Bill's account totalling the $100,000 amount covered by FDIC insurance. Bill is discharged from his liability to Cindy on the check since it was not presented within the 30 day period and Bill is deprived of the funds in excess of the $100,000 amount covered by insurance. As can be seen from this example, the scope of the coverage of this Subsection (f) is limited and would be applicable in very few situations.

2.2 LIABILITY OF THE DRAWEE

The "drawee" is defined in Section 3-103(a)(2) as "a person ordered in a draft to make payment." According to Section 3-408, the drawee is not liable on the instrument until it accepts the draft. This section provides further that the check or draft does not of itself operate as an assignment of the funds in the hands of the drawee available for its payment. This section applies only to the obligation of the drawee on the instrument itself and does not address the obligations of the drawee to the drawer or the obligations of the drawee under other sections of the UCC or other laws. As pointed out in Official Comment #2 to this section, Section 4-302 imposes liability on the payor bank for late return of an item. Liability is also placed on the payor bank by Federal Reserve Regulation CC. The scope of Section 3-408 is to make it clear that the drawee is not liable to any person entitled to enforce payment of the instrument as it relates to the instrument.

For example, Bill Wiltshire issues a check to Joel Converse in the amount of $200. Joel presents the check to the Drawee Bank and demands payment. The balance in Bill's account is sufficient to pay the check, but the Drawee Bank refuses to pay the amount of the check to Joel. This section makes it clear that Joel has no cause of action against the Drawee Bank for failure to pay the check. The check is not an assignment of the funds in the hands of the Drawee Bank. However, the Drawee Bank may be liable to its customer, Bill Wiltshire, for wrongful dishonor as provided for in Section 4-402 which is discussed in Chapter 8 of this book. In *First American National Bank of Nashville v. Commerce*

Union Bank of White County, 41 UCC Rep Serv 1339, the court held that "while a bank is liable to its customer for wrongful dishonor of a check drawn by the customer, the payee of the check or the depositary bank which is the holder of the check has no right to sue the drawee bank for dishonoring the check."

2.3 THE INDORSER'S LIABILITY

An "indorser" is defined in Section 3-204(b) as "a person who makes an indorsement." An "indorsement" has a lengthy definition in Section 3-204(a) and is discussed in detail in Chapter 5 of this book. For the purposes of this section of the book, an "indorsement" is a signature—other than that of a signer as maker, drawer, or acceptor—that is made on an instrument for the purpose of negotiating the instrument, restricting payment of the instrument, or incurring indorser's liability on the instrument. An indorser incurs the liablility of an indorser regardless of the reason for which the indorsement is given.

For example, a check payable to the order of Arnold Richardson must be indorsed by Arnold before the instrument can be negotiated. An exception to this requirement is found in Section 4-205 where a depositary bank is a holder even if the item is not indorsed by the payee. Arnold may indorse the instrument in a number of ways. Regardless of the manner in which he indorses, unless he indorses without recourse, he becomes liable as an indorser. On the other hand, if the check were payable to "cash," Arnold would not be required to indorse the instrument to negotiate it and, therefore, would not incur the liability of an indorser. For this reason, many banks require an indorsement on a bearer instrument even though the indorsement is not required to negotiate the instrument.

Please refer to Chapter 5 for a detailed discussion of indorsements and indorsers.

The liability of an indorser is similar to that of a drawer in that the instrument must first be dishonored before the indorser is obliged to pay the amount the instrument. Section 3-415(a) provides that if an instrument is dishonored, an indorser is obligated to pay the amount due on the instrument according to the terms on the instrument at the time it was indorsed. If the instrument was incomplete at the time of the indorsement, then the indorser is obligated to pay the amount of the instrument as completed subject to the provisions of Sections 3-115 and 3-407 dealing with incomplete instruments and alterations. The obligation of the indorser is owed to a person entitled to enforce the instrument under Section 3-301 or to a subsequent indorser who paid the instrument under this same section.

For example, assume Bill Wiltshire issues a check to D.A. Carr. D.A. indorses the check to Chip Sanders and Chip presents the check to the Drawee Bank. The Drawee Bank dishonors the check because of insufficient funds. In this example, both D.A. and Chip are indorsers and are obligated to the Drawee Bank for the amount of the check and must take it back if the notice requirements discussed below are met. Since Chip is a subsequent indorser of the instrument, D.A. would be obligated to pay the amount of the check to Chip upon dishonor and timely notice. The indorsement requirements under Section 3-415 apply to all types of instruments. The discussion of indorser liability in this section of the book, however, will only address indorser liability as it relates to drafts and checks.

As in the case of a drawer discussed above, the liability of an indorser may be limited or disclaimed. Section 3-415(b) states that "if an indorsement states that it is made 'without recourse' or otherwise disclaims liability of the indorser, the indorser is not liable under Subsection (a) to pay the instrument." Unlike the liability of a drawer, this disclaimer may also apply to checks. If in the example above, D.A. Carr indorses the check to Chip Sanders "without recourse," then upon dishonor, D.A. is not obligated to pay the amount of the instrument to either the Drawee Bank or Chip Sanders. An exception to this rule is found in Section 4-207(b) if the item is collected through the banking system.

An example of why an indorser would want to indorse without recourse may be a situation where an indorser is only indorsing for the convenience of another party. For example, if an individual obtains financing of an automobile through a bank, the title to the automobile will indicate that the bank is the first lien holder. The insurance carrier will also indicate in its records that the automobile has been pledged as collateral for the loan. In the event of an accident or some other claim, the insurance company will typically issue the claim check to both the insured and the financial institution. Suppose in this example that the insured paid off the loan to the financial institution but failed to notify the insurance company that the loan had been paid off and that the insured now holds clear title to the automobile. In the event of a claim, the insurance company will issue the check jointly to the insured and the financial institution. The insured must then either show proof of the pay off of the loan and the clear title to the insurance company and have another check issued only to the insured or the insured could ask the financial institution to indorse the check. Since the financial institution has no interest in the proceeds of the check and will not receive any of the benefit of the check, the financial institution will be reluctant to indorse the check and assume the responsibility of an indorser. However, the financial institution may be willing to indorse the check "without recourse" indicating that it is indorsing only to give title of the check to the insured and that the bank will not pay the amount of the check to any party if the check is not honored.

(a) TIMELY NOTICE OF DISHONOR AND PRESENTMENT

Notice of dishonor may be required under Section 3-503 which is discussed in Chapter 8 of this book. If such notice is required and the notice is not given, then the liability of the indorser to pay the amount of the instrument is discharged. For example, assume that Bill Wiltshire issues a check to Cindy Faulkner. Cindy indorses the check and deposits it in the First Deposit Bank. The check is presented to the Drawee Bank through the banking channels and is dishonored. The check is returned to the First Deposit Bank but for some reason notice of dishonor is not given to Cindy until one week after the item was received by the First Deposit Bank. As discussed in Chapter 8, the First Deposit Bank has an obligation to notify Cindy of dishonor by its midnight deadline. In this example, notice was a week late. Under Section 3-415(c), Cindy's liability as an indorser is discharged.

The indorser's liability may also be discharged, according to Section 3-415(d), if a draft is accepted by a bank after an indorsement is made. For example, if Arnold Richardson indorses a check and gets the check certified by the drawee bank, Arnold's liability to pay the amount of the check under Subsection (a) of Section 3-415 is discharged. Any person indorsing subsequent to the certification of the check is liable on the instrument as an indorser.

The liability of an indorser to pay the amount of a check may be discharged upon the lapse of time. Section 3-415 (e) provides that the indorser is discharged form its liability as an indorser under Subsection (a) if the check is not presented for payment or given to a depositary bank for collection within 30 days after the day the indorsement was made.

For example, assume that a check is issued to Arnold Richardson and Arnold indorses the check in blank and delivers it to Robert Hales on March 1. Robert puts the check in his desk and forgets about it until

May 15 at which time he presents the check over the counter to the payor bank. The payor bank dishonors the check for insufficient funds and marks the check accordingly. Robert then attempts to collect the amount of the check from Arnold claiming that, as an indorser, Arnold is liable to him for the amount of the check. In this example, since Robert did not present the check for payment or give it to a depositary bank for collection within 30 days from the date that Arnold indorsed the check, Arnold is discharged from his obligation to pay upon dishonor of the check. The discharge of the indorser is absolute and is not dependent upon the suspension of payment of the drawee bank as is required under Section 3-414(f) for the discharge of a drawer. Section 3-415((e) applies only to indorsers of checks.

2.4 LIABILITY OF ACCEPTOR

Section 3-408 states that a drawee is not liable on an instrument until the drawee accepts it. Section 3-409 addresses what acceptance is and how it is accomplished. Section 3-409(a) defines "acceptance" as "the drawee's signed agreement to pay a draft as presented." The acceptance must be written on the draft and may consist of the drawee's signature alone. This section is clear that the acceptance must be written on the draft and, therefore, eliminates any question as to whether or not acceptance can be oral or if acceptance can be accomplished on a separate document. Words of acceptance are not required on the draft; the signature of the drawee alone is sufficient. As the Official Comments point out, the signature is not required to be in any particular location on the check and words such as "Accepted," "Certified," or "Good," are not required. The signature of the drawee alone is sufficient because there is no other reason for the drawee to sign the draft. Subsection (a) further states, "the acceptance may be made at any time and becomes effective when notification pursuant to instructions is given or the accepted draft is delivered for the purpose of giving rights on the acceptance to any person."

The rules governing acceptance are fairly flexible as evidenced by the provisions of Section 3-409(b). According to that section, "a draft may be accepted although it has not been signed by the drawer, is otherwise incomplete, is overdue, or has been dishonored." For whatever reason, a drawee could accept a blank draft that was to be completed at some point after acceptance. As discussed below, the drawee assumes a substantial amount of risk by accepting a draft that is incomplete, especially if the amount is not specified. This Subsection makes it clear that a bank may certify a check that has been previously dishonored. For example, a drawee bank could certify a check that had been previously dishonored for insufficient funds even though the word "insufficient" was stamped on the check.

If a draft is payable at a fixed period after sight and the acceptor fails to date the acceptance, the holder may complete the acceptance by supplying the date in good faith as provided for in Section 3-409(c). If no date appears on a draft that is payable at some point after sight, the draft is incomplete. This section allows the holder to complete the instrument by supplying the date as long as it is done in good faith. As pointed out in the Official Comments to this section, unless the acceptor writes in a different date, the holder may complete the draft.

A certified check is a prime example of a draft that has been accepted by the drawee. A "certified check" is a check that has been accepted by the bank on which it is drawn as stated in Section 3-409(d). The acceptance may be in the form of a signature of an officer of the drawee bank or the check may contain a writing on the check that states that it contains words to the effect that acceptance of the check is certified and a signature of an officer is made on the face of the check. To insure that the check is paid when presented, most banks will debit the customer's account and credit the bank's certified check account at the time of certification. The customer's account number on the check is normally replaced with a sticker that contains the bank's certified check account number. Some banks simply punch holes through the MICR account number encoded on the bottom of the check.

Certification of checks seems to be somewhat of a thing of the past. In most banks and according to Subsection (d), certification is purely voluntary on the part of the drawee bank. That Subsection states that the drawee of a check has no obligation to certify a check, and refusal to certify is not dishonor of the check. As pointed out in the Official Comment to this section, a bank is under no obligation to certify a check in the absence of an agreement with the drawer. The court in *Gallinaro v. Fitzpatrick, 8 UCC Rep Serv 1054*, also held that a bank is under no obligation to certify a check.

A check is a demand instrument calling for payment and not acceptance. This section makes it clear that certification of a check is a form of acceptance; therefore, a bank that refuses to pay a check cannot avoid a wrongful dishonor claim of its customer by certifying the check. For example, assume that a check is issued by a customer of the bank and the check is presented for payment over the counter to the drawee bank. Assume further that the bank refuses to either pay the item in cash or to refuse to issue a cashier's check or some other type of bank check but does offer to certify the check. Since certification is acceptance and not payment, the bank has dishonored the check.

Section 3-410 contains several provisions for acceptance that varies the terms of a draft that may effect the obligation of the acceptor. Basically what this section states is that the holder may reject an acceptance and consider the draft dishonored if the drawee varies the terms of acceptance from the terms of the draft as presented. If this occurs, the drawee may cancel the acceptance. If a holder agrees to an acceptance that varies the terms of draft that has joint drawers or multiple indorsers, all of the drawers and indorsers must agree to the new terms. If they do not expressly assent to the acceptance, then their respective obligations on the draft are discharged. This section also provides that "the terms of a draft are not varied by an acceptance to pay at a particular bank or place in the United States, unless the acceptance stated that the draft is to be paid only at that bank or place."

The obligation of an acceptor of a draft is governed by Section 3-413 which addresses the scenarios of payment. The obligation to pay is owed to a person entitled to enforce the draft, to the drawer, or an indorser who paid the draft under Section 3-414 or 3-415. The basic obligation of an acceptor is to pay the draft upon presentment. Subsection (a) states that the acceptor is obliged to pay the draft according to its terms at the time of acceptance, even if the acceptance states that the draft is payable "as originally drawn" or other terms that mean the same thing. This obligation to pay at the time of acceptance is reasonable. It would be unreasonable to require the acceptor to be obligated to pay a draft with terms that could be substantially different at the time of presentment then they were when the draft was accepted. In other words, the acceptor is agreeing to pay the draft that it accepted and not some other draft on which the terms had been changed.

As discussed above, Section 3-410 addresses the issue of when acceptance varies the terms of the draft. If acceptance varies the terms of the draft, Section 3-413(a)(ii) provides that the acceptor is obliged to pay the draft "according to the terms of the draft as varied." As stated above, Section 3-409(b) states that a draft may be accepted although it is incomplete. If an incomplete draft is accepted, Section 3-413(a)(iii) states that the acceptor is obliged to pay the draft according to the terms of the draft as completed. This Subsection is subject to the provisions of Sections 3-115 dealing with incomplete instruments and 3-407 dealing with alterations.

Section 3-413(b) specifically addresses the amount of the obligation to pay on certified checks and other accepted drafts. That section provides that the amount that the acceptor is obligated to pay is the amount of the certified check or other accepted draft stated on the check or draft at the time of acceptance. For example, if the amount of the check or draft is left blank, the draft may be accepted by the bank but only for a specified amount agreed to by the bank. If the certification or acceptance does not state an amount, the amount of the instrument is raised, and the instrument is negotiated to a holder in due course, Section 3-413(b) provides that "the obligation of the acceptor is the amount of the instrument at the time it was taken by the holder in due course." As pointed out in the Official Comments to this section, the purpose of Subsection (b) is to protect a holder in due course that takes a certified check that has been altered after it has been accepted. Under this section, the certifying bank would be required to pay the altered certified check as altered. For example, if a check in the amount of $10.00 is certified, the bank does not state the amount that it agrees to pay, the check is skillfully raised to $10,000.00 and is negotiated to a holder in due course, the bank is obligated to pay the raised amount of $10,000.00. The bank can avoid this risk by stating on the check the amount the bank agrees to pay. Holder in due course is discussed in Chapter 6 of this book.

2.5 OBLIGATION OF ISSUER OF A NOTE, CASHIER'S CHECK, OR SIMILAR CHECK

The obligation of the issuer of a note, cashier's check, or other draft drawn on the drawer is governed by Section 3-412. According to that section, the issuer of one of those instruments is obligated to pay the instrument according to it terms at the time it was issued. If the instrument is not issued, the issuer is obligated to pay the instrument according to the terms of the instrument at the time it first came into possession of a holder. Issuance or nonissuance of an instrument is discussed in section 1.3 of Chapter 1 of this book. If an issuer signed an incomplete instrument, Section 3-412 states that the issuer is obligated to pay the instrument according to its terms when completed. Payment of the incomplete instrument is subject to Section 3-115 dealing with incomplete instruments and Section 3-407 dealing with alterations.

The obligation of the issuer to pay is owed to a person entitled to enforce the instrument under Section 3-301 or to an indorser who paid the instrument under Section 3-415.

(a) BANK'S REFUSAL TO PAY A CASHIER'S, TELLER'S, OR CERTIFIED CHECK

Cashier's, teller's, and certified checks are looked upon as substitutes for cash in our society. Whenever someone wants to ensure payment of an obligation or a debt and payment is to be made by check, they request the debtor or purchaser to pay by cashier's, teller's, or certified check. Article 3 recognizes these instruments as money substitutes, as is evidenced in Section 3-310. That section provides that if a certified check, cashier's check, or teller's check is taken for an obligation, the obligation is discharged to the same extent discharge would result if an equal amount of money were taken in payment of the obligation. The intent of the drafters of Article 3 relative to these types of checks also manifests itself in Section 3-411. This section provides for damages imposed upon a bank for refusal to pay this type of check.

"Cashier's check" is defined in Section 3-104(g) as "a draft with respect to which the drawer and drawee are the same bank or branches of the same bank." A "teller's check" is defined in Section 3-104(h) to mean "a draft drawn by a bank (i) on another bank, or (ii) payable through a bank." A "certified check" is defined in Section 3-409(d) as "a check accepted by the bank on which it is drawn." Cashier's checks are discussed above. Banks, for the most part, have stopped issuing cashier's checks. When a customer asks for a cashier's check, the bank typically issues them a teller's check. The primary reason for issuing a teller's check is that the costs associated with the teller's check are less than a cashier's check. The obligation of the bank to pay the items is the same.

On occasion, bank customers request the bank to stop payment on one of these items or to otherwise not pay the item. In most situations, the remitter has changed his or her mind about making payment and wants the bank to not honor the check. In most situations, the bank honors the customer's request and asks the customer to sign a stop payment form and in some circumstances the bank even asks for the customer to sign some form of indemnification agreement indemnifying the bank against any loss in the event that the bank check ends up in the hands of a holder in due course. The revised Article 3 may change this practice for many banks that have honored their customer's request not to pay these checks. As stated above, Section 3-411 addresses a bank's refusal to pay one of these items. Section 3-411(b) states that if the bank wrongfully refuses to pay a cashier's check or a certified check or stops payment on a teller's check or refuses to pay a teller's check that has been dishonored, the person entitled to payment may recover damages from the bank for its refusal to pay. The damages under this section are compensation for expenses and loss of interest resulting from the nonpayment. The bank may also be required to pay consequential damages if the bank refuses to pay after receiving notice of particular circumstances giving rise to the damages.

The damages under Section 3-411(b) are based on the bank's refusal to pay being wrongful. The problem for most banks is that it will be difficult to prove that the bank has a defense against payment. In most cases, the remitter of the check is the person that actually has the defense and, as pointed out in the Official Comments to this section, unless the bank is successful in asserting the defense of the customer under Section 3-305(c), the bank will be liable for the damages.

Section 3-411(c) lists several situations where the bank will not be held liable for the payment of expenses or for consequential damages. Under that Subsection, expenses or consequential damages are not recoverable if the bank suspends payment. "Suspends payment" is defined in Section 4-104(a)(12) to mean that the bank "has been closed by order of the supervisory authorities, that a public officer has been appointed to take it over, or that it ceases or refuses to make payments in the ordinary course of business." The bank may also escape liability under Subsection (b) if the bank asserts a claim or defense of the bank that it has reasonable grounds to believe it is available against the person entitled to enforce the instrument. As stated in the Official Comments to this section, very few defenses will be available to the bank; therefore, this section is of little use to the bank. The bank may also avoid the damages under Subsection (b) if the bank has reasonable doubt whether the person demanding payment is the person entitled to enforce the instrument. Here again, this defense has limited application to situations where the item is presented for payment over the counter. For example, if a cashier's check payable to Flashback Music, Inc. is presented for payment over the counter by a person claiming to be the president and having authority to act on behalf of the corporation, the bank may decline to pay the check if it is not satisfied that the person in fact does have the proper authority to act. In many situations, however, the check will not be presented over the counter but will be presented through the normal check clearing channels. One final defense available to the bank is that payment is prohibited by law.

(b) LOST, DESTROYED, OR STOLEN CASHIER'S, TELLER'S, OR CERTIFIED CHECKS

Section 3-411, discussed earlier, makes it clear that the drafters of the UCC intended for banks to pay cashier's, teller's, and certified check. This section should help banks make a decision if asked not to pay one of these checks. In a situation where the remitter of a cashier's check requests that the bank refuse to pay the amount of the check to the holder, Section 3-411 makes it clear to the bank that it may be held liable for refusal to pay the check. In this situation, the decision is easy; the bank is obligated to pay the check and should refuse a request not to pay the item. However, what should the bank do if the remitter claims that he or she lost an unindorsed cashier's check? Should the bank comply with the customer's request and risk the loss of damages imposed by Section 3-411? Or should the bank refuse to honor the customer's request and risk paying a check with a forged indorsement and being held liable for paying the proceeds to one not entitled to receive them? Because of this dilemma, Revised Article 3 was amended by the addition of Section 3-312.

Section 3-312 addresses the situation where a cashier's, teller's, or certified check is lost, destroyed, or stolen. According to this section, the person claiming to have the right to receive the amount of the check (the "claimant") must sign a written statement called a "declaration of loss" that is made under penalty of perjury and delivery of which is a warranty of the truth of the statements made in the declaration. The "declaration of loss" must state that the claimant lost possession of the check that the claimant was either the drawer or payee of in the case of a certified check or the remitter or payee of in the case of a cashier's or teller's check. The section further provides that the declaration must also state that "the loss of possession was not the result of a transfer by the declarer or a lawful seizure, and the declarer cannot reasonably obtain possession of the check because it was destroyed, its whereabouts cannot be determined, or it is in the wrongful possession of an unknown person or a person that cannot be found or is not amenable to service of process."

In other words, the claimant has rights under this section only if the check is lost, stolen, or destroyed, and the check was not transferred by the claimant. The claimant has no right to request payment from the bank for any other reason and the bank has no right to refuse to pay the check when presented by a person entitled to enforce the check even if the claimant has other reasons for not wanting the check paid. For example, if the remitter of a cashier's check sends a cashier's check to the payee in payment of car repairs and determines that the repairs were not performed, the remitter has no rights under Section 3-312 and the bank that issued the cashier's check could be subject to damages under Section 3-411 for refusal to pay the item.

Section 3-312(b) provides that the claimant may assert a claim to the amount of the check by sending a communication requesting payment to the bank that issued or certified the check. The communication to the bank must describe the check "with reasonable certainty." Reasonable certainty is not defined; however, it would appear that an accurate description of the check would be required. The claimant should be required to at least provide the bank with the amount of the check, the date of issuance, and the payee. The check number may be more difficult for the claimant to obtain unless the claimant has a copy of the check. The point here is that the claimant should give the bank such an accurate description of the check that will allow the bank to properly identify the check on its system or, in the case of a teller's check, to provide the bank on which the check is drawn sufficient information to stop payment on the check. While this section does not refer to this process as a stop payment, that is in fact what it is.

The communication must also state that the claimant is the drawer or payee of a certified check or the remitter or payee of a cashier's check or teller's check and must contain the "declaration of loss" described above. As in the case of a stop payment, the communication must be received by the bank at a time and in a manner affording the bank a reasonable time to act on it before the check is paid. It would appear that in determining whether the communication was received by the bank at a time and in a manner to act, a court would look to cases involving stop payments when the time of receipt was an issue. It would also appear that a bank could refer to Section 4-303 dealing with when items are subject to notice and stop-payment as a guide. At any rate, the bank must receive the communication before the check is paid. For example, if the payee of the check presents the check at a teller window in one branch at the same time that the remitter delivers the communication to another branch, the communication came too late. This issue of timely receipt may be of no consequences since, as discussed below, the claim must become enforceable before it has any legal effect.

The claim becomes enforceable according to Section 3-212 (b)(1) either at the time the claim is asserted or the 90th day following the date of the check or certification of the certified check, whichever is later. In other words, the check must be outstanding at least 90 days before a claim has any legal effect on the bank. For example, assume the First Deposit Bank issues its cashier's check on March 1 and on March 15, the remitter delivers a communication to the bank claiming that the cashier's check was lost or stolen and all of the other requirements above are met. In this example, the claim has no effect on the bank until May 30th, which is the 90th day after the date of the cashier's check. Another example of the application of this section is as follows. Assume the same facts as above except that the claim is made by the remitter on June 1. In this example, the claim becomes enforceable on June 1 because the claim was made after the expiration of 90 days from the date of the check.

As mentioned above, in the case of a certified check, the claim becomes enforceable at the latter of the day of the claim or the 90th day following the acceptance of the check. An example of the application of this section on a certified check is as follows. Assume the drawer issues a check on February 15. On March 1, the check is certified by the drawee bank and the claim is asserted by the payee on March 15. In this example, the claim becomes enforceable on May 30 or on the 90th day following the date on which the check was certified.

This 90 day waiting period could cause some operational problems for banks. Because of the fact that the claim is not effective until the later of the date of the claim or 90 days, banks will be required to put procedures in place to effective date stop payments. In the example above, the cashier's check was issued on March 1 and the claim was communicated to the bank on March 15, but it did not become effective until May 30. Section 3-312(b)(2) provides that "until the claim becomes enforceable, it has no legal effect and the obligated bank may pay the check or, in the case of a teller's check, may permit the drawee to pay the check. Payment to a person entitled to enforce the check discharges all liability of the obligated bank with respect to the check." This Subsection provides the bank with protection if the check is paid to a person entitled to enforce the check and this is a very important point. This takes the bank out of the middle of a dispute between the remitter and the payee or other holder of the check.

Until the claim becomes effective, the bank remains liable under Section 3-411 for damages for refusal to pay the check. When read together, Sections 3-411 and 3-312 give banks specific guidelines on what course of action to take when a claim is made but has not yet become effective on the bank. The problem, however, is that the check may be presented for payment during the period of time before the claim becomes effective by a person that is not entitled to enforce the check. For example, assume that a bank issues a cashier's check March 1, the remitter asserts a claim on March 15, and the check is presented for payment on March 20. Since the claim is not effective until May 30, the bank must pay the check to a person entitled to enforce the check. However, assume that the check is presented on March 20 by a person that is not entitled to enforce the check. In other words, the check is presented by a person that either forged the name of the payee or received the check from someone who forged the payee's name. In this situation, the bank is not discharged from its liability on the instrument if it pays the item. The problem is that during this period of time until the claim becomes enforceable, the bank is in a very vulnerable position. If a claim is made but is not yet enforceable, the bank must have some means of determining the rights of the person making presentment. If the item is presented by the payee over the counter, the bank may ask for proper identification to determine the identity of the person making presentment. However, if the check is presented through banking channels in an incoming cash letter, the bank will not have the opportunity to determine the rights of the person making presentment.

If the claim becomes enforceable before the check is presented for payment, then Section 3-312(b)(3) provides that the bank is not obligated to pay the check. For example, assume that a bank issues a cashier's check on March 1, the remitter makes a claim to the bank on June 15, and the payee presents the check on June 20. In this situation, the claim became enforceable on June 15 and the bank would not be required to pay the check when presented on June 20.

When the claim becomes enforceable, Section 3-312(b)(4) provides that the bank becomes obliged to pay the claimant the amount of the check if the bank has not already made payment to a person entitled to enforce the check. In the previous example, the bank became obligated to pay the claimant on June 15 when the claim became enforceable. This section also provides that payment to the claimant discharges all liability of the bank with respect to the check. The bank's liability is subject to Section 4-302(a)(1) which requires that the bank must settle for the item or return the item in accordance with that section or the bank remains liable on the instrument. If the bank pays the amount of the item to the claimant, however, then this section should have no application. The thrust of Section 3-312(b)(4) is that the bank is discharged of its obligations on the instrument when paid to the claimant and the bank is not liable under Section 3-411 for refusal to pay the check. For example, if the bank pays the remitter the amount of a cashier's check after the claim becomes enforceable and the bank later refuses to pay the payee upon presentment, the bank is discharged from its liability on the cashier's check and has no obligation to the payee for refusal to pay.

A major concern of any issuer of a negotiable instrument that stops payment on an instrument and issues a replacement is that the original item will end up in the hands of a holder in due course. Section 3-312(c) provides protection to the bank if this situation' occurs after payment of the amount of the check to the claimant. That section provides that if the bank pays the claimant the amount of the check and the check is later presented for payment by a holder in due course, the claimant is obliged to either refund the amount of the check to the bank or to pay the holder in due course if the check is dishonored. This section indicates that the bank may elect to pay the holder in due course and collect from the claimant or dishonor the check and require the claimant to pay the holder. Since Section 3-312(b)(4) provides that payment to the claimant discharges the bank's obligation on the check, it would appear that the bank's best option would be to dishonor the check and require the holder to seek payment from the claimant.

If the claimant is a person that is entitled to enforce a cashier's check, teller's check, or certified check which is lost, destroyed, or stolen, Section 3-312(d) provides that the claimant may assert a claim under this section or under Section 3-309 that deals with the enforcement of lost, destroyed, or stolen instruments in general. Section 3-309 is discussed in Chapter 6 of this book.

2.6 JOINT AND SEVERAL LIABILITY

The liability of a party to an instrument is based on the capacity in which he or she signs. If two or more persons sign an instrument jointly as makers, drawers, acceptors, indorsers who indorse as joint payees, or anomalous indorsers, Section 3-116(a) provides that the joint signers are jointly and severally liable on the instrument in the capacity in which they sign. Joint and several liability means that the party entitled to enforce the instrument may enforce payment jointly against all of them together or any one of them separately. For example, if a check is payable jointly to Bill Wiltshire and Cindy Faulkner, both Bill and Cindy must indorse the check. Assume that both of them indorse the check in blank to Joel Converse and the check is dishonored upon presentment. Joel may then seek recovery from either Bill or Cindy, or he may seek recovery from them jointly. The option to enforce the instrument jointly or individually is left up to the person entitled to enforce the instrument unless the parties agree otherwise. The instrument may, for example, contain a provision that states that the instrument may only be enforced jointly and not individually.

Another example of the application of this section is as follows. Assume Bill and Cindy issue a note to Joel and sign the note as co-makers. Upon maturity of the note, Joel may enforce the instrument against Bill and Cindy jointly or against Bill or Cindy individually.

Unless the parties agree otherwise, a party having joint and several liability who pays the instrument is entitled to receive contribution from any other party having the same joint and several liability on the instrument. This right to contribution is provided for in Section 3-116(b). In the example above where the check was payable jointly to Bill and Cindy and the check was dishonored, if Joel enforces the check against Bill individually, Bill is entitled to contribution from Cindy in accordance with applicable law. Another exception to the right to contribution is found in Section 3-419(e) dealing with accommodation parties. That section provides in part, "An accommodation party who pays the instrument is entitled to reimbursement from the accommodated party and is entitled to enforce the instrument against the accommodated party." For example, a person that signs a note as an indorser in the capacity of an accommodation party may recover from the maker of the note any amount that the accommodation party is required to pay. If the maker defaults on payment of the note or an installment and the accommodation party is required to pay, the accommodation party is entitled to reimbursement from the maker.

Section 3-116(c) provides that "discharge of one party having joint and several liability by a person entitled to enforce the instrument does not affect the right under Subsection (b) of a party having the same joint and several liability to receive contribution from the party discharged." In the example above where the check was payable jointly to and indorsed by Bill and Cindy, if Joel discharges Bill's liability on the instrument, the discharge does not affect Cindy's right of contribution from Bill.

2.7 EFFECT OF ISSUANCE OF AN INSTRUMENT ON THE OBLIGATION FOR WHICH IT IS GIVEN

The effect of the issuance of an instrument on the underlying obligation for which the instrument is given is dependent upon the type of instrument that is given. The reason for this dependency is because of the differences in the obligations of the various parties to the instruments as discussed in the previous sections. The following is a discussion of the issuance of those various instruments on the underlying obligation which is governed by Section 3-310.

(a) OBLIGATION DISCHARGED IF CASHIER'S, TELLER'S, OR CERTIFIED CHECK IS GIVEN

Section 3-310(a) provides, "Unless otherwise agreed, if a certified check, cashier's check, or teller's check is taken for an obligation, the obligation is discharged to the same extent discharge would result if an amount of money equal to the amount of the instrument were taken in payment of the obligation. Discharge of the obligation does not affect any liability that the obligor may have as an indorser of the instrument." The intentions of the drafters of Article 3 that a cashier's check, a teller's check, or certified check are to be considered as substitute for money comes through loud and clear in this section. While there may be some type of liability that survives payment of the obligation, the effect of the issuance of a cashier's check, teller's check, or certified check discharges the underlying obligation for which the instrument was given.

For example, if Bill Wiltshire agrees to paint Cindy Faulkner's house for an amount of $5,000 and he does in fact paint the house, Cindy is obligated to pay Bill $5,000. If Cindy remits a cashier's check to Bill, the underlying obligation to pay Bill for painting the house is discharged upon delivery of the check to Bill to the same extent as if Cindy had paid Bill in cash. The reason for discharge of the obligation upon delivery of the check is because the bank on which the check is drawn, and not Cindy, is liable on the instrument. Bill is willing to accept the cashier's check as a substitute for cash because the bank is obligated to pay the check upon presentment and is subject to damages under Section 3-411 for refusal to pay the check. The parties could, however, agree that the issuance of one of these items does not discharge the obligation.

(b) NOTE OR UNACCEPTED CHECK SUSPENDS THE OBLIGATION

If a note or an uncertified check is taken for an obligation, Section 3-310(b) provides that the underlying obligation is suspended until the note or check is paid or dishonored and different rules apply depending upon whether the instrument that is given is a note or a check and whether a third party is involved.

If a check is given for the underlying obligation drawn on the account of and by the person obligated, the obligation is suspended to the same extent as if money were given. The suspension continues in effect until the check is dishonored or paid by the drawee. If the check is paid or certified, the underlying obligation is discharged. If the check is dishonored, then the obligation is not discharged and the person obligated remains liable for the underlying obligation and the person entitled to enforce the check can either enforce the check or the obligation. An example of the application of this section is as follows. Bill Wiltshire agrees to paint Cindy Faulkner's house for $5,000 and he does in fact paint the house. Bill has performed his part of the agreement and Cindy is obligated to pay him the agreed upon amount. If Cindy issues her personal check in the full amount of $5,000, her obligation to pay Bill is suspended as though she paid him in cash until the check is paid or dishonored. During the period of time the obligation is suspended, Bill does not have a cause of action against Cindy for the underlying obligation. If the check is paid, the obligation is discharged. If the check is dishonored, the underlying obligation is no longer held in suspension and Bill may then either enforce the check or the obligation.

If the instrument of a third party is given in payment for the obligation, the obligation is likewise suspended until the instrument is paid or dishonored. However, in this situation, Section 3-310(b)(3) provides that discharge of the liability of the obligor on the instrument discharges the underlying obligation. For instance, assume in the previous example that Cindy pays Bill by indorsing a check over to Bill that was payable to Cindy. In other words, a third party had issued a check to Cindy in the amount of $5,000 and Cindy indorsed the check and delivered it to Bill in payment of the underlying obligation. The underlying obligation is suspended until the check is paid or dishonored. However, in this situation, Subsection (b)(3) provides that the discharge of Cindy's obligation on the check also discharges Cindy's obligation on the underlying obligation. As pointed out in the Official Comments to this section, Section 3-415(e) provides that the liability of an indorser is discharged if the check is not presented for payment or is not deposited for collection within 30 days from the date of the indorsement. In the example above, if Bill does not present the check for payment within 30 days from the date on which Cindy delivered the check to him, Cindy's obligation on the check as an indorser and her obligation to pay Bill for painting the house are both discharged even if the check is dishonored when it is finally presented. If the check is dishonored, Bill's recourse would be against the drawer of the check.

If a note is given for the obligation, the obligation is suspended until the note is paid or dishonored. If the note is paid, the obligation is discharged. If the note is dishonored, the obligee may either enforce the note or the underlying obligation. The effect of giving a note is basically the same as giving an uncertified check.

Apparently, the instrument that is given for the underlying obligation does not have to be payable to or otherwise be enforceable by the person entitled to payment under the obligation for which the instrument is given. The first sentence of Subsection (b)(4) states, "If the person entitled to enforce the instrument taken for an obligation is a person other than the obligee, the obligee may not enforce the obligation to the extent the obligation is suspended." The Official Comments do not give any guidance on this sentence. It is not clear why the obligee would be willing to accept an instrument as payment for the underlying obligation when the obligee is not the person that may enforce the instrument. Apparently what this sentence is intended to do is to allow the delivery of an instrument as payment for an underlying obligation, even though the obligee is not entitled to enforce the instrument.

For example, if the obligor issues a check to a payee other than the obligor and delivers the check to the obligee as payment on the underlying obligation with the understanding that the payee will indorse the check, the underlying obligation is suspended until the check is indorsed, presented, and paid, or until the check is dishonored. In this case if dishonored, the obligee could only enforce the underlying obligation and not the check since the obligee is not entitled to enforce the check.

The intent of the drafters is much more clear in the last sentence of Subsection (b)(4). That sentence reads as follows: "If the obligee is the person entitled to enforce the instrument but no longer has possession of it because it was lost, stolen, or destroyed, the obligation may not be enforced to the extent of the amount payable on the instrument, and to the extent the obligee's rights against the obligor are limited to enforcement of the instrument."

Official Comment #4 to this section clarifies this sentence by stating that the intent of it is to address the situation where the obligee is the payee and the instrument is paid over a forged indorsement. In this situation, the remedy of the obligee is on the instrument and not the underlying obligation because the underlying obligation is suspended since the instrument was not paid to a holder. The drawer could make a claim against the drawee for paying the instrument over a forged indorsement and issue a replacement check. Or the payee could make a claim against the depositary bank for conversion of the instrument. At any rate, the remedy of the obligee in this situation is on the instrument and not the underlying obligation.

Section 3-310(c) is summarized in Official Comment #5 very succinctly as follows: "Subsection (c) deals with rare cases in which other instruments are taken for obligations. If a bank is the obligor on the instrument, Subsection (a) applies and the obligation is discharged. In any other case Subsection (b) applies."

2.8 ACCORD AND SATISFACTION BY USE OF AN INSTRUMENT

Many disputes have arisen over a statement or legend placed on a check that payment is made in full satisfaction of all claims or similar words. The courts have handled this situation differently. Under the common law, a statement to that affect on an instrument was considered to be an offer to settle and if the payee accepted the check with the legend, then it operated as full satisfaction and accord. The confusion and disputes really arose out of Section 1-207 which some courts held changed the common law. Section 1-207 basically stated that one could reserve rights by using words like "without prejudice," or "under protest" and then perform in a manner demanded or offered by the other party. Some courts applied this section to cases where a check contained a statement to the affect that the check was issued in full satisfaction and held that if the payee reserved his or her rights that he or she could accept the check, reserve his rights and that the payment would not be considered as full satisfaction for the claim. Section 1-207 has been amended by the addition of Subsection (2) that states that Section 1-207 does not apply to an accord and satisfaction. This revision makes it clear that accord and satisfaction is governed solely by Section 3-311.

Section 3-311 basically provides that accord and satisfaction may be obtained by placing a communication on the instrument or on an accompanying document that payment is being made in full satisfaction. There are, however, several requirements. Subsections 3-311(a) and (b) when read together provide that a claim may be discharged if the person against whom the claim is asserted proves that the instrument or an accompanying document contained a conspicuous statement to the effect that the instrument was tendered as full satisfaction of the claim if the following requirements are met. The requirements are that the person tendered the instrument in good faith as full satisfaction, the amount of the claim was unliquidated or subject to a bona fide dispute, and the claimant obtained payment of the instrument. The discharge under these Subsections is subject to provisions of Subsection (c) and (d) discussed later.

The first requirement stated above is that the instrument must be tendered in good faith. The definition of "good faith" has been expanded to include honesty in fact and the observance of reasonable commercial standards. Official Comment #4 to this section uses the example of an insurance claim for which the insurance company offers an amount clearly well below the amount called for in the policy. In this situation, the insurance company would not be considered to have acted in good faith by offering the smaller amount knowing that the insured was in disparate need of the proceeds and would take a lesser amount. If the court found that the insurance company took unfair advantage of the insured, then an accord and satisfaction would not result by placing a statement that payment is in full satisfaction.

The second requirement is that the claim must be unliquidated or there must be a dispute over the amount. For example, if a customer received the monthly bill from the local power company in the amount of $150 and there was no dispute over the amount of the bill, the customer could not write a check for $100 and put a statement on the check that it is in full satisfaction of all claims and expect the payment to result in full accord and satisfaction. The customer would be liable for the balance of $50. On the other hand, if the bill was for $350 and the customer had had several conversations with the power company disputing the claim, then subject to Subsection (c) discussed below, accord and satisfaction could be obtained.

The third requirement is that the claimant must have obtained payment of the instrument. If the person to whom the instrument containing the statement was sent to refuses to accept the instrument, then accord and satisfaction does not occur. Refusal to accept the payment is obviously a refusal to accept the conditions under which the payment is made. On the other hand, if the claimant accepts the instrument that contains the statement that it is in full satisfaction and does in fact obtain payment, the accord and satisfaction can and will occur. The statement on the instrument or on the accompanying written communication must be a conspicuous statement. "Conspicuous" is defined in Section 1-201(10) to mean that "it is so written that a reasonable person against whom it is to operate ought to have noticed it." It would appear the location of the statement on the instrument, the size of the letters, whether it is written, typewritten, or printed and the person to whom the instrument is payable would be factors to be considered. For example, if the check is written to a consumer on a form that contains a considerable amount of printed verbiage and the statement is printed in small print in the same color as the other print, then it would appear that the statement would not meet the requirement of "conspicuous." If on the other hand, the statement were in plan view and was stamped in big red letters, then the statement would most likely meet the test of "conspicuous."

Even if all of the requirements stated above are present and the statement is very conspicuous, the claim is not discharged if the situations provided for in Subsection (c) apply. According to that Subsection, the claim is not discharged if the claimant that is an organization can prove that it sent a conspicuous statement to the person against whom the claim is asserted containing instructions on how to handle disputed claims and the instructions were not followed. The specific wording of Section 3-311(c)(1) is as follows: "Subject to Subsection (d), a claim is not discharged under Subsection (b) if either of the following applies:

(1) The claimant, if an organization, proves that (i) within a reasonable time before the tender, the claimant sent a conspicuous statement to the person against whom the claim is asserted that communications concerning disputed debts, including an instrument tendered as full satisfaction of a debt, are to be sent to a designated person, office, or place, and (ii) the instrument or accompanying communication was not received by the designated person, office, or place."

The purpose of this section is obviously to give an organization the opportunity to identify any attempts by a debtor to obtain accord and full satisfaction for a disputed claim. Large organizations processing large volumes of payments each day are not likely to notice an attempt at accord and satisfaction if the payment is sent through the normal channels or is sent directly to a lock box at a bank. Most clerks performing a specific function will not notice and should not be expected to notice such statements on checks or other payments. The claim, however, is discharged if the claimant or its agent knew that the instrument was tendered in full satisfaction as provided for in Subsection (d).

The burden of proof is clearly on the organization to prove that the statement was conspicuous, it was sent within a reasonable time before the tender and that the communication concerning the dispute was not received in the location specified by the claimant. It would appear that proving that the communication concerning the dispute was not received at the location specified may be difficult to prove unless the payment were sent by overnight, registered or certified mail. An organization that requires that this type of communication must be sent to a certain location should have procedures in place to meet the burden of proof. Otherwise, the person making the payment and claiming accord and satisfaction need only assert that the communication was sent in accordance with the instructions.

As an alternative to the provisions of Subsection (c)(1), the claimant could rely on Subsection (c)(2) to avoid discharge. Subsection (c)(2) provides that the claim is not discharged if "the claimant, whether or not an organization, proves that within 90 days after payment of the instrument, the claimant tendered repayment of the amount of the instrument to the person against whom the claim is asserted. This paragraph does not apply if the claimant is an organization that sent a statement complying with paragraph (1)(i)." This Subsection allows anyone whether an organization or not to avoid a claim being discharged. Basically what this paragraph is saying is that the person that accepted the payment has up to 90 days to reverse the payment that it has received. However, the claim is discharged if the claimant or its agent knew the instrument was tendered in full satisfaction as provided for in Subsection (d) which is discussed below.

If an organization chooses to send a statement as provided for in Subsection (c)(1)(i), then this 90 day option is not available to the organization. The organization must make a decision as to which option is best suited for its own situation. As pointed out in the Official Comments to this section, sending such a statement under Subsection (c)(1)(i) may confuse customers and a large majority of payments may be sent to the person or location designated in the statement. This could result in much more manual intervention then anticipated by the organization. For this reason, the organization may select the option under Subsection (c)(2) and put procedures in place that will help it discover the attempted discharge within the 90 day period.

As stated earlier, Subsection (c) is subject to Subsection (d) which provides, "A claim is discharged if the person against whom the claim is asserted proves that within a reasonable time before collection of the instrument was initiated, the claimant, or an agent of the claimant having direct responsibility with respect to the disputed obligation, knew that the instrument was tendered in full satisfaction of the claim." Whether or not the claimant or the claimant's agent knew is a question of fact to be determined by the trier of the fact. Section 1-201(27) states when an organization has received notice. Under that section, notice is received by an organization and is "effective for a particular transaction from the time when it is brought to the attention of the individual conducting that transaction, and in any event from the time when it would have been brought to his attention if the organization had exercised due diligence." This section also provides that the organization exercises due diligence if it maintains reasonable routines for communicating information and those routines are complied with. However, due diligence does not require every employee of the organization to communicate information. According to Section 1-201(27), an individual would be required to communicate information to the organization only "if such communication is part of his regular duties or unless he has reason to know of the transaction and that the transaction would be materially affected by the information." Official Comment # 7 to Section 3-311 contains several examples of when the claimant or its agent would or would not have received sufficient notice that would discharge the claim.

2.9 TRANSFER AND PRESENTMENT WARRANTY

In addition to the liabilities discussed above, every person that transfers or presents an item for payment makes certain warranties. These warranties are made by each transferor to each transferee and ultimately to the payor that pays the item. Unlike the contractual liability of an indorser, the liability created by the warranties survives passage of the midnight deadline. The warrantor is not discharged from his or her liabilities by payment of the item. Unless a warrantor has some type of defense, the warrantor remains liable on the item until the expiration of the statute of limitations. The transfer warranties are found in Sections

3-416 and 4-207 and the presentment warranties are found in Section 3-417 and 4-208.

(a) TRANSFER WARRANTIES

A person who transfers an instrument makes the following five warranties found in Section 3-416(a) to his or her transferee and if the transfer is by indorsement, to any subsequent transferee:

(1) The person making the transfer is the person entitled to enforce the instrument;

(2) All signatures on the instrument are authentic and authorized;

(3) The instrument has not been altered;

(4) No other party has any claim to the instrument and it is not subject to any defense; and

(5) The person making the transfer has no knowledge of any insolvency proceedings against the maker, acceptor, or drawer.

These same five warranties are contained in Section 4-207 and are made by a customer or collecting bank to the transferee and any subsequent collecting bank. A person to whom the warranty is made may enforce a breach of the warranty against the immediate transferor or against any other previous transferor. For example, consider an instrument that is transferred to the following people in the order they are listed: Bill transfers to Cindy, Cindy transfers to Joel, and Joel transfers to Chip. Chip is the last person in the chain, but he may enforce a breach of warranty against any transferor up the chain of title if the instrument is transferred by indorsement. Assume that the instrument contained a forged indorsement at the point that Bill transferred the instrument to Cindy. Chip could seek damages under Sections 3-416 or 4-207 directly from Bill since he will ultimately be liable on the instrument.

The warrantor, under Subsection (a)(1) warrants that he or she is the holder of the instrument or is authorized to transfer the instrument on behalf of a holder. The warrantor, therefore, makes a warranty that all necessary indorsements have been made on the instrument and that the indorsements are authorized. The transferee of the instrument must be assured, upon taking the instrument, that he or she will become a holder of the instrument and be a person entitled to enforce the instrument.

Each transferor warrants, under Subsection (a)(2), to every transferee that "all signatures on the instrument are authentic and authorized." This warranty is not, however, made to the payor of the instrument. As discussed below, the person presenting the item to the payor warrants only the warrantor has no knowledge of any unauthorized signatures. This warranty is necessary to ensure that the transferee will be entitled to enforce the instrument. If the instrument contained a forged drawer's signature for example, Subsection (a)(2) protects the transferee. If the signature is not authentic or authorized, the transferor may seek damages under this section for breach of this warranty.

The warranty under Subsection (a)(3) is self explanatory. Each warrantor warrants that the instrument has not been altered. The transferee is entitled to know that the instrument can be enforced for the amount on the face of instrument.

A person taking an instrument will also want to know that the instrument is free from all defenses or claims in recoupment against the warrantor. This warranty is provided for in Subsection (a)(4). The transferee will want to be entitled to enforce the instrument against the person liable on the instrument. If a defense does exist, the transferee will have recourse against the warrantor. As pointed out in Official Comment #3 to Section 3-416, although a holder in due course takes the instrument free of all claims and defenses, this warranty would give the holder in due course an option. If the drawer or maker has a defense, the holder in due course could pursue the warrantor rather than be put to the burden of proving holder in due course status.

The transferee takes on the credit risk that the drawer or maker might be insolvent. The warrantor does not warrant that the maker or drawer is solvent or that the transferee will have no trouble in receiving payment. However, under Subsection (a)(5), the warrantor does warrant that he or she has no knowledge of any insolvency proceedings against the maker, acceptor, or drawer. If the warrantor does have knowledge of insolvency proceedings and does not disclose this fact to his or her transferee, the warrantor is not only in breach of the transfer warranties but could also be subject to criminal prosecution for fraud. Such action could be construed as receiving money under false pretense.

(b) DAMAGES FOR BREACH OF PRESENTMENT WARRANTY

A person who makes these warranties is subject to damages for breach of warranty in an amount not to exceed the amount of the instrument plus collection expenses and interest, as provided for in Sections 3-

416(b) and 4-207(b). Attorney's fees are not specifically provided for under this section but are recoverable if allowed by other state law. Although not specifically provided for under Sections 3-416 and 4-207, it would appear that the damages could not exceed the amount of plaintiff's interest in the instrument. Section 3-420(b) provides that in a conversion action, the plaintiff's "recovery may not exceed the amount of the plaintiff's interest in the instrument." For example, a check payable to joint payees, not in the alternative, is payable to all of the payees, according to Section 3-110(g), and can only be enforced by all of the payees jointly. A check payable to two payees jointly must be indorsed by both of them. If one of the payees did not indorse the check, then the depositary bank that took the check with only one indorsement could be liable in conversion to the other joint payee that did not indorse the instrument. Under Section 3-420, which establishes the conversion right, the joint payee's recovery may not exceed the payee's interest in the check. If, instead of making a claim in conversion against the depositary bank, the payee proceeds against the drawer on the underlying obligation, the drawer would only be liable to the joint payee for the amount of the underlying obligation. To further illustrate this point, assume that the amount of the check payable to Bill and Joel is $10,000 and Joel's interest in the check is only $4,000. If Joel made a claim against the drawer for nonpayment of the underlying obligation, he could only recover $4,000. The drawer would then seek recovery from the payor bank for improper payment of the item and the payor bank would seek recovery for breach of warranty. The loss would ultimately be shifted up stream to the depositary bank who took the item from the forger. Therefore, the amount of the recovery from the depositary bank should not exceed the $4,000 that the depositary bank would have been liable for if Joel had brought a conversion action against the depositary bank.

(c) DISCLAIM OF TRANSFER WARRANTY

The transfer warranties may be disclaimed by a transferor on any instrument except a check. The warranties cannot be disclaimed with respect to checks according to Section 3-416(c). The transfer could be made without warranties by agreement between two parties; however, the disclaimer would apply only to the two immediate parties. The transferor could avoid the warranty liability as to subsequent transferees only by including the disclaimer in the indorsement itself. As pointed out in Official Comment #5 to Section 3-416, a statement such as "without warranty" or a similar statement in the indorsement would be required.

Subsection 3-416(c) provides that a claim for breach of warranty must be brought within 30 days after the claimant has reason to know of the breach and the identity of the warrantor. If notice of the claim is not given within that timeframe, the liability of the warrantor is discharged to the extent of the loss caused by the delay in giving notice of the claim. This same provision is found in Section 4-207(d). Sections 3-416(d) and 4-207(e) provide that a cause of action for breach of warranty under these sections accrues when the claimant has reason to know of the breach.

Section 4-207(b) contains a provision not in Section 3-416 that the warrantor will take the item back and pay for it if it is dishonored.

(d) PRESENTMENT WARRANTIES

Sections 3-417 and 4-208 contain the presentment warranties and conform to each other. Subsection (a) contains the following three warranties given by a prior transferor of the draft and person who presents a draft to a drawee that pays the draft in good faith:

(1) the warrantor is the person entitled to enforce the draft or is authorized by a person who is entitled to enforce the draft;

(2) the draft has not been altered; and

(3) the warrantor has no knowledge that the signature of the drawer of the draft is unauthorized.

The presenter and prior transferor warrant that the instrument contains all necessary indorsements and that all indorsements are genuine. If the instrument is payable to joint payees not in the alternative, for example, the warrantor warrants that the instrument contains all of the required indorsements. A recent case on this subject is *Manufacturers Hanover Trust Co. v. Manufacturers & Traders Trust Co.,* 15 UCC Rep Serv 2d 996. In that case, the depositary bank was held liable for breach of the warranty of presentment and transfer under Section 4-207 because the bank cashed a check containing the forged indorsement of the payee.

The second warranty listed is that there are no alterations. An alteration, which is governed by Section 3-407, is defined as any unauthorized change in an instrument or addition of numbers or words that modifies the obligation of a party. The two most obvious alterations would be an alteration in the amount of an instrument or in the name of the payee.

While the warrantor does not warrant the genuineness of the drawer's signature or that the signature is authorized, the warrantor does warrant that he or she has no knowledge of any unauthorized signature. If an instrument contains a forged drawer's signature, and the warrantor had no knowledge of the forgery and the instrument is paid by the drawee, the drawee is responsible for paying the forgery. However, if the warrantor had knowledge of the forgery at the time that the instrument was taken or transferred, then the warrantor would be responsible for that item.

Subsection (b) provides the amount of damages that may be recovered for breach of this presentment warranty. In summary, that section states that the warrantor is liable to the drawee that pays or accepts the amount paid by the drawee less any amount received by the drawee or is entitled to receive from the drawer because of payment, plus collection expenses and interest. In *First Virginia Bank-Colonial v. Provident State Bank, 38 UCC Rep Serv 561*, the court held the depositary bank liable for breach of presentment warranty for accepting a check payable to two payees that contained the forged indorsement of one of the payees. The court awarded damages in the amount of the item plus expenses including interest, prejudgement interest and attorney's fees. Attorney's fees are not always recoverable and are subject to local law. While the court recognized that attorney's fees may be considered expenses, the court in *McAdam v. Dean Witter Reynolds, Inc., 10 UCC Rep Serv 2d 1085*, refused to allow attorney's fees. The New Jersey court held that the New Jersey courts only award attorney's fees when expressly authorized by statute.

The right of the drawee to recover damages is not affected by the failure of the drawee to exercise ordinary care in making payment. If a drawee accepts a draft, breach of warranty is a defense to the drawee's obligation to pay the draft. If the acceptor pays the draft, it is entitled to recovery from the warrantor for breach of the warranty.

Subsection (c) provides that if the drawee asserts a claim for breach of warranty because of a forged indorsement or an alteration of the draft, "the warrantor may defend by proving that the indorsement is effective under Section 3-404 or 3-405 or the drawer is precluded under Section 3-406 or 4-406 from asserting against the drawee the unauthorized indorsement or alteration."

The following example is an application of Section 3-417 (a), (b), and (c). Bill Wiltshire issues a check to Cindy Faulkner but Cindy claims that she never received the check. Bill contacts his bank, the First Deposit Bank (FDB), on May 15, and he is advised that the check was paid on May 1. Bill obtains the check from FDB and shows it to Cindy who examines the indorsement and claims that it is not her signature. Bill then demands a refund from FDB for charging his account for a check that is not properly payable. The bank could make an immediate refund to Bill and then pursue collection from the presenting bank or directly from the depositary bank that took the item from the forger. Typically, the FDB would obtain an affidavit of forgery from Cindy and would send the item back upstream to the presenting bank and demand a refund. The presenting bank would then forward the item to the depositary bank and likewise demand payment.

Upon receipt of demand for payment, the depositary bank could immediately comply. Or the bank could defend, as provided for under Subsection (c), by raising the defenses listed in Sections 3-404 or 3-405 dealing with impostor's and employer's responsibility for an employee's actions or Sections 3-406 and 4-406 dealing with the negligence of the parties. If the defenses are not valid, then under Subsection (b), the depositary bank would be liable for the amount of the check plus interest and expenses. If the defenses are valid, then the depositary bank would refuse to pay and the drawee bank could likewise refuse to make a refund to its customer.

Subsection (d) contains the warranty made to the drawer or indorser of a draft that pays a dishonored draft or otherwise pays a draft that is presented for payment. Under this section, the warrantor warrants that he or she is the person entitled to enforce the instrument or authorized to obtain payment by a person entitled to enforce the instrument. The amount of damages for which the warrantor is liable for breach of this presentment warranty is the amount of the draft plus expenses and interest.

Subsection (e) states that the warranties cannot be disclaimed and notice of a breach of the presentment warranty must be given within 30 days from the date the claimant has reason to know of the breach and the identity of the warrantor. If the claim is not made within the 30 day period, the warrantor is discharged to the extent of any loss caused by the delay in giving notice. A cause of action for breach of warranty under Section 3-417 and 4-208 accrues when the claimant has reason to know of the breach as provided for in Subsection (f) of those sections.

CHAPTER 3

AUTHORIZED AND FORGED SIGNATURE

3.1 AUTHORIZED SIGNATURE

The liability of a party to an instrument is created by the signature of the person to be held liable or by the signature of his authorized representative. Section 3-401(a) states, "A person is not liable on an instrument unless (i) the person signed the instrument, or (ii) the person is represented by an agent or representative who signed the instrument and the signature is binding on the represented person under Section 3-402." Section 3-402 is discussed later in this chapter. "Signed" is defined in Section 1-201(39) to mean "includes any symbol executed or adopted by a party with present intention to authenticate a writing."

No particular form of signature is required to bind the party to the instrument. In fact, Section 3-401(b) states that "a signature may be made (i) manually or by means of a device or machine, and (ii) by the use of any name, including a trade or assumed name, or by a word, mark, or symbol executed or adopted by a person with present intention to authenticate a writing." This section is very flexible and looks to the intention of the party and not the form of the signature. The section recognizes the fact that many times a signature is made by a stamp, a check-signing machine, or is computer generated. The signature, of course, may be made manually in the own handwriting of the person or may be typewritten or printed. In fact, a statement that says "no signature required" can serve as a signature because it is a "word . . . adopted by a person with present intention to authenticate a writing." The point is that a signature may be made in any manner and in any form selected by the person to be bound as long as the signature is adopted by that person with the present intention to be bound. The court in *Witten Productions, Inc. v. Republic Bank & Trust Co., 14 UCC Rep Serv 2d 515,* held that a forged indorsement stamped on the back of a check was an indorsement. In *First National Bank In Alamosa v. Ford Motor Credit Co., 13 UCC Rep Serv 2d 810,* the court held that the drawee's printed name on a sight draft was not a signature designating acceptance of the draft. This same court, in referring to the drawer's signature, held that a party's full name need not be used for the words to be effective as a signature.

(a) SIGNATURE BY REPRESENTATIVE

As previously stated, the signature may be made by an authorized representative of the person to be bound. Section 3-402 addresses a signature by a representative. According to that section, if a signature is made by a representative, the person represented is bound by the signature. Subsection (a) provides that the signature may be made in the name of the person represented or in the name of the representative that signed the instrument. In either case, the signature acts as the authorized signature of the represented person and the represented person is liable on the instrument whether or not the represented person is identified in the instrument. For example, assume that Joel Converse is the authorized representative of Bill Wiltshire. Joel may either sign his own name to an instrument or he may sign Bill Wiltshire's name on the instrument. Whichever signature that Joel uses, Bill will be liable on the instrument even if he is not identified on the instrument.

Nothing in this section addresses how the representative capacity is established. Therefore, the representative capacity must be established in accordance with the general law of agency which varies state by state. Establishment of the agency status is beyond the scope of this book. However, signature authority on most deposit accounts with a bank is established by signature cards, partnership agreements, trust agreements, court documents, corporate resolutions, and the like.

Although a person may sign an instrument in a representative capacity, there are certain circumstances under which the representative will be personally liable on the instrument.

Section 3-402(b) provides that if the representative signs his own name to an instrument within the scope of his authority and the instrument unambiguously shows that the signature is made on behalf of the represented person who is identified in the instrument, the representative is not personally liable on the instrument. For example, if Joel Converse signs a note in his own name but as a representative of Bill Wiltshire, and Bill is identified in the note as the person actually making the note, then Bill, and not Joel, is liable as the maker of the note.

Subsection (b)(2) further provides, however, that a representative can be held personally liable on an instrument even if it was signed in a representative capacity. Subject to Subsection (c) dealing with checks, Subsection (b)(2) states that the representative can be held personally liable on an instrument to a holder in due course that took the instrument without notice that the representative was not intended to be liable on the instrument if the following situations exist:

(1) the form of the signature does not show unambiguously that the signature is made in a representative capacity or;

(2) the represented person is not identified in the instrument.

For example, Joel Converse is an agent of Bill Wiltshire and purchases automobiles for Bill. Joel issues a draft to a seller in payment for a car and signs his own name on the draft. The draft names Bill Wiltshire as the drawee, but does not indicate that Joel is an agent or in any way represents Bill. Assume further that the payee (seller) negotiates the draft to a holder in due course who presents the draft to Bill Wiltshire and Bill does not honor the draft. In this scenario, Joel would be held personally liable on the draft under the provisions of Section 3-402(b). Joel would not have been held liable on the instrument if he had signed Bill Wiltshire's name as the drawer or if he had shown the representative capacity in which he signed. The representative capacity must be shown without ambiguity. For example, if Joel signed the draft "Joel Converse, agent for Bill Wiltshire," there should be no question in anyone's mind that Joel is signing the draft as the agent of Bill. On the other hand, if Joel signed "Joel Converse, Agent," as pointed out in the Official Comments to this section, this signature shows a representative capacity but does not indicate the person on whose behalf Joel is acting.

The previous discussion addresses the liability of the representative to a holder in due course. Subsection (b)(2) also states, "With respect to any other person, the representative is liable on the instrument unless the representative proves that the original parties did not intend the representative to be liable on the instrument."

Under this section, as to a holder in due course, the representative may not prove the original intent of the parties. However, as to any other party, the representative may prove the original intent of the parties to avoid personal liability. In the previous example, as to the payee (the seller of the automobile) or to any other transferee of the draft that was not a holder in due course, Joel could produce evidence that the payee knew that Joel was acting in a representative capacity for Bill Wiltshire. To avoid personal liability on an instrument when signing in a representative capacity, the representative should always identify the person represented and show, unambiguously, the representative capacity in which the instrument is signed.

If the instrument that is signed by the representative is a check, Subsection (c) applies. That section states, "If a representative signs the name of the representative as drawer of a check without indication of the representative status and the check is payable from an account of the represented person who is identified on the check, the signer is not liable on the check if the signature is an authorized signature of the represented person." To avoid personal liability for the representative under this section, the first requirement is that the instrument involved must be a check. This Subsection therefore eliminates all other negotiable instruments including notes, drafts not drawn on a bank and payable through drafts. The representative capacity does not have to be shown on the check but the person represented must be identified on the check and the check must be payable from an account of the represented person. Therefore, the check could not be drawn on an account of the representative and merely name the person represented. For example, Joel Converse could not avoid personal liability by signing a check drawn on his own personal account that shows on the check that it is signed in a representative capacity for Bill Wiltshire.

Another requirement of this section is that the person signing in a representative capacity must have the authority to sign on behalf of the represented person. For example, if Joel Converse signed a check in a representative capacity drawn on the account of Bill Wiltshire and Joel was not authorized to sign on behalf of Bill, then Joel's signature does not bind Bill but does act as the signature for Joel. In this case, Joel is obviously personally liable on the check. A signature that is unauthorized may be ratified by the person to be held liable. Ratification will be discussed later.

(b) MULTIPLE SIGNATURE REQUIREMENTS

Some organizations require two or more signatures on checks. Section 3-403(b) states that "if the signature of more than one person is required to constitute the authorized signature of an organization, the signature of the organization is unauthorized if one of the required signatures is lacking." This section refers to the authorized signature of the organization as opposed to referring to multiple signatures by representatives. In other words, if multiple signatures are required on checks of an organization, the signature is considered to be unauthorized if one or more of the required signatures is missing, as opposed to referring to the check as having missing signatures. For example, if the account of the ABC Corporation requires the signatures of A, B, and C on all checks, a check that is signed only by A and B is not properly payable from the account because the check contains an unauthorized signature and not because a signature is missing. Without C's signature, the signature of the ABC Corporation is unauthorized. Regardless of the terminology, an organization is not liable for an instrument that is missing a required signature unless the signature is ratified or the organization is held liable on the instrument because of the application of some other provision of the UCC.

Classifying the signature as unauthorized is important, however, when applying sections of the code that refer to unauthorized signatures such as 4-406(f). As pointed out in the Official Comment #4 to Section 3-403, some courts refused to apply Section 4-406 if a signature was missing because the court did not consider a missing signature a forgery or an unauthorized signature. Section 3-403(b) clears this problem up by referring to the signature as unauthorized.

3.2 UNAUTHORIZED SIGNATURE INEFFECTIVE

It may seem redundant to refer to an unauthorized signature as ineffective. However, an unauthorized signature can be made effective against a person as will be discussed later. This section deals with unauthorized signatures that are not made effective. Section 3-403(a) states, "Unless otherwise provided in this Article or Article 4, an unauthorized signature is ineffective except as the signature of the unauthorized signer in favor of a person who in good faith pays the instrument or takes it for value. An unauthorized signature may be ratified for all purposes of this Article."

As stated earlier in the discussion of Section 3-402, a person is not liable on an instrument unless he or she signs it. If a person's name is signed without authority, the signature is unauthorized and therefore is ineffective as the signature of the person whose name is signed. However, as stated in 3-403(a) the signature does act as the signature of the person that actually signed the instrument. If Joel Converse writes a check on the account of Bill Wiltshire without Bill's authority and signs his own name to the check, obviously, this is an unauthorized signature and is ineffective as the signature of Bill Wiltshire. Bill is therefore not liable on the instrument unless he ratifies it or some other provision of the UCC assigns liability to Bill. If Joel Converse writes a check on Bill Wiltshire's account and forges Bill's signature on the check, this likewise is an unauthorized signature. Section 1-201(43) defines an "unauthorized" signature to mean "one made without actual, implied, or apparent authority and includes a forgery." Therefore, Joel's forgery of Bill's signature is unauthorized and is ineffective as Bill's signature. The forged signature does, however, operate as Joel's signature and is enforceable against him.

Another example of the application of this section is as follows. Assume that a husband and wife own an account jointly. The account is styled jointly and both have signed the bank's signature card. Assume further that, for whatever reason, the husband issues checks drawn on the joint account but signs the wife's name as drawer without the wife's authority. The checks are presented for payment and are in fact paid by the bank because the forgery of the wife's signature was very good and resembled the wife's signature. As fate would have it, the husband and wife separate several weeks later and the wife discovers the checks containing her forged signature. The wife immediately contacts the bank and demands a refund of the amount of the checks with the forged signature of the wife. Upon investigation, the bank discovers that the husband forged the wife's name. Applying Section 3-403(a) to this scenario, the forged signature of the wife is an unauthorized signature of the wife and is ineffective against her. However, the forged signature operates as the signature of the husband. Since the husband is a joint account holder and an authorized signatory on the account, it would appear that the signature is effective as his signature and the checks could remain paid on the account.

Section 3-403(a) does require that the bank must pay the item in good faith.

(a) MULTIPLE SIGNATURES

Instruments requiring more than one signature are discussed in Section 3.1 of this book and will not be repeated here. Section 3-403(b) governs this situation and provides that if the signature of more than one person is required on an instrument, the signature of the organization is unauthorized if one of the signatures is missing. The unauthorized signature is ineffective against the organization unless it is ratified or is made effective by some other provision.

(b) CIVIL OR CRIMINAL LIABILITY

Section 3-403(c) provides that the civil or criminal liability of a person who makes an unauthorized signature is not affected by any provision of Article 3, which makes the unauthorized signature effective for the purposes of Article 3. Not much can be said about this section other than the fact that it exists. If some criminal violation has been committed, the fact that a signature is made effective does not remove the criminal liability. For example, if an employer is negligent and an employee's signature is made effective against the employer, the fact that the forgery is made effective does not eliminate the fact that a signature was forged and a crime was committed.

3.3 UNAUTHORIZED SIGNATURE MADE EFFECTIVE

An unauthorized signature is ineffective against the person named in the instrument unless the person ratifies the signature or is otherwise held liable on the instrument because of the application of some other section of the UCC.

The following is a discussion of the sections that make an unauthorized signature effective.

(a) RATIFICATION OF AN UNAUTHORIZED SIGNATURE

Section 3-403(a), dealing with unauthorized signatures, contains the provision that "An unauthorized signature may be ratified for all purposes of this Article." Ratification does not have any special meaning under the UCC; therefore, the general definition applies. Ratification is defined in the revised fourth edition of *Black's Law Dictionary* as "a conformation of a previous act done either by the party himself or by another." Official Comment #3 to Section 3-403 defines ratification as "a retroactive adoption of the unauthorized signature by the person whose name is signed and may be found from conduct as well as from express statements." Ratification is therefore action or inaction of some sort that is taken by the person to be charged after the fact. For example, if a check is forged on a customer's account by a close relative, the customer may never object to payment of the forged check on the account, or the customer may object at first and later adopt the unauthorized signature. The customer may have received benefit from the forgery and retain the benefit. For example, the forged check may have been used to pay debts of the customer. Whatever the form of the ratification, the effect is that the ratification makes the unauthorized signature effective. In *Williams v. Johnson, 9 UCC Rep Serv 260*, the court held, "A person could be 'precluded from denying' an unauthorized signature if he knowingly retains the benefits of the fraud." The court in *Richards v. Arthaloney, 38 UCC Rep Serv 234*, also held that retention of the benefit of a forged signature is ratification of the signature. In another case, *Wiest v. First Citizens National Bank, 3 UCC Rep Serv 875*, an employee embezzled funds from her employer and forged the signature of the employer on a check on one account and transferred the proceeds to another account of the employer to cover up the embezzlement. The court held that by retaining the proceeds of the forgery, the employer ratified the unauthorized signature.

Once a signature is ratified, the ratification cannot be reversed. A person that ratifies a signature cannot later rescind the ratification. For example, assume that Bill Wiltshire ratifies his signature that was forged by Joel Converse. The forged signature has then been accepted by Bill and cannot be rejected at a later time. In addition, once a signature has been ratified, the person making the ratification cannot pick and choose which signatures will be ratified. Assume in the previous example that Joel Converse had signed Bill's name on ten checks on Bill's account. Six of the ten checks were for legitimate business purposes benefiting Bill, and the remaining four were for the personal benefit of Joel. The ratification of the six legitimate checks is also a ratification of the four checks used for Joel's personal benefit. Bill can, however rescind Joel's authority to issue checks by advising the bank of the removal of the authority. The bank could, therefore, be liable to Bill for any checks that it honors that were signed by Joel after the date that the bank received the notice from Bill. The court in *Eautsler v. First National Bank, Pawhuska, 32 UCC Rep Serv 1509*, held that ratification requires intent to ratify and full knowledge of all material facts. However, once a signature has been ratified, it cannot later be revoked. The court also held that the principal cannot pick and choose only what is advantageous to him. The principal must either ratify the entire transaction or repudiate it entirely.

(b) NEGLIGENCE CONTRIBUTING TO A FORGED SIGNATURE

Ratification is not the only manner in which a signature may be made effective against a person. Action or inaction of a party may substantially contribute to the making of a forgery. Section 3-406(a) addresses this situation. According to that section, if a person is so negligent that his or her failure to exercise ordinary care substantially contributes to the making of a forgery, then that person is precluded from asserting the forgery against a person who pays the instrument or takes it for value or for collection in good faith. There are several components to this section that must be examined. The person to be charged must fail to exercise ordinary care. "Ordinary care" is defined in Section 3-103(a)(7) and states, "in the case of a person engaged in business means observance of reasonable commercial standards, prevailing in the area in which the person is located, with respect to the business in which the person in engaged." Ordinary care will therefore vary depending on the type of business the person is engaged in. The burden of proving failure to exercise ordinary care is on the person asserting the preclusion.

The next requirement that must be met to make an unauthorized signature effective is that the failure to exercise ordinary care must substantially contribute to the making of the forged signature. "Substantially contribute" is not defined in the UCC and therefore is left up to the courts. The court in *Chicago Heights Currency Exchange, Inc. v. Par Steel Products and Service Co., Inc., 38 UCC Rep Serv 1680*, held that the question of negligence is an issue that is left strictly to the fact-finder on a case-by-case basis. The court must find that the failure to exercise ordinary care substantially contributed to the making of the forgery and was not merely a minor contribution. For example, if blank checks were left in an unlocked desk drawer inside of a secured building and the checks were stolen in a burglary, this failure to keep the checks locked away would probably not meet the test of "substantially contribute." On the other hand, if a mechanical check-signing machine were left unlocked with easy access to the machine, the court could easily find that the failure to secure the check signing machine substantially contributed to the making of the unauthorized signature. In *J. Gordan Neely Enterprises, Inc. v. American National Bank of Huntsville, 32 UCC Rep Serv 1525*, the court found that the term "substantially contributes" means that the negligence must proximately cause the making of an alteration. While this case dealt with an alteration, the interpretation of "substantially contributes" would apply equally to forgeries.

The question of negligence is a question for the finder of the facts on a case-by-case basis. The following are some cases where the court held that negligence substantially contributed to forgeries. In *G.F.D. Enterprises, Inc. v. NYE, 6 UCC Rep Serv 2d 460*, the court held that the employer was negligent under Section 3-406 and that the employer's negligence substantially contributed to the forgery of checks. In this case, the court held that it was negligent for the employer not to have investigated the employee who made the forgeries to determine that the employee had embezzled from a previous employer. The court also held that it was negligent for the employee to perform the bookkeeping functions without supervision. The court in *Commercial Credit Equipment Corp. v. First Alabama Bank of Montgomery, NA, 30 UCC Rep Serv 1185*, also held the employer negligent in hiring an employee who had defrauded a previous employer. In *Thompson Maple Products, Inc. v. Citizens National Bank of Curry, 4 UCC Rep Serv 624*, the court held that the mill was negligent in allowing one of the mill's haulers to keep both originals and duplicates of invoices that were used to supply the bookkeeper with the names of payees. The court held that the negligence substantially contributed to the forgery of the indorsements on the checks and therefore the drawer of the checks was precluded from asserting the forgery.

The next hurdle that must be met by a person asserting the preclusion is that the person that paid the instrument or took it for value or for collection did so in good faith.

"Good faith" is defined in Section 3-103(a)(4) to mean "honesty in fact and the observance of reasonable commercial standards of fair dealing." In addition, the person asserting the preclusion must comply with Section 3-406(b).

That section states that if the person asserting the preclusion under Subsection (a) fails to exercise ordinary care in paying or taking the instruments and that failure substantially contributes to the loss, the loss is allocated between the person precluded and the person asserting the preclusion according to the extent to which the failure of each to exercise ordinary care contributed to the loss. The burden of proving failure to exercise ordinary care is on the person precluded.

Subsection (b) is a substantial change from the earlier version of this section. Under the old version, if the person asserting the preclusion failed to exercise ordinary care, the right to assert the preclusion was lost. The drafters of the new version, however, recognized the inequities of such a provision and rightfully introduced the concept of comparative negligence.

For example, if a check-signing machine was left unlocked and was used by a person that issued unauthorized checks, the court could find that failure to secure the check-signing machine was not the exercise of ordinary care and that the failure substantially contributed to the unauthorized signature. Assume further in this example that the bank on which the checks were drawn had no system of verification of signatures at all. The court could conclude that the failure to make any type of signature verification when the bank's procedures call for signature verification is not the exercise of ordinary care. In this situation, however, failure to verify signatures did not substantially contribute to the loss. If the signature card authorized the use of the check signing machine, verification of a signature would not have discovered the unauthorized signature. Therefore, the court would be justified in allocating the loss to the account owner.

(c) CUSTOMER'S DUTY TO DISCOVER AND REPORT UNAUTHORIZED SIGNATURE

Another section dealing with the failure of a person to exercise ordinary care is found in Section 4-406 and is discussed in detail in Chapter 11 of this book. Subsection (c) of that section requires a customer to examine his or her bank statement and promptly notify the bank of his or her unauthorized signature. Subsection (d)(1) further provides that if the bank can prove that the customer failed to discover and report the unauthorized signature and the failure to examine and report the forgery caused the bank to suffer the loss, the customer is precluded from asserting the unauthorized signature against the bank. The bank is required, however, to exercise ordinary care in paying the item. If the bank failed to exercise ordinary care, then the loss is allocated to the bank and the customer based on the negligence of each.

Subsection (d)(2) provides that the bank statement must be examined by the customer within a reasonable time not to exceed 30 days from the date the bank makes the statement available to the customer. The period of time that is considered reasonable will depend on the facts in each case. In most situations the 30-day period will be applied. The 30-day period of time is an extension of the time allowed under the previous section, which was 14 days. If the customer fails to examine the statement and notify the bank within the specified time, the customer is precluded from asserting against the bank unauthorized signatures made by the same wrongdoer. This Subsection is aimed at the situation where multiple forgeries are made by the same wrongdoer over a period of time. For example, assume that the customer's bank statement is mailed to him on January 15, and the statement contains a check with an unauthorized signature. Subsequent bank statements also contained unauthorized signatures by the same wrongdoer until the June 15 bank statement when the fraud is discovered by the customer. If the customer had examined the January statement, he would have detected the forgery and could have prevented the subsequent losses. Provided the bank exercised ordinary care in paying the checks, the customer is precluded from asserting the unauthorized signatures against the bank.

Section 4-406(f) provides that without regard to the care or lack of care of the customer or the bank, the customer is precluded from asserting an unauthorized signature against the bank if the customer does not discover and report it to the bank within one year from the date that the statement is made available to the customer. Again, this entire section is discussed in detail in Chapter 11. The section, which also applies to alterations, is mentioned here only to make the reader aware of its existence and content.

CHAPTER 4

NEGOTIATION AND TRANSFER

4.1 NEGOTIATION DEFINED

The payee or other holder of an instrument can obtain payment for the instrument either through presentment to the person who is to pay it or by transferring possession and title to the instrument. Transfer of the instrument is accomplished by negotiation. "Negotiation" is defined in Section 3-201(a) to mean "a transfer of possession, whether voluntary or involuntary, of an instrument by a person other than the issuer to a person who thereby becomes its holder."

This definition is straightforward and does not require much explanation. However, there are several parts of the definition that are worthy of discussion. First of all, issuance of the instrument is not negotiation. Negotiation requires transfer of the instrument by the payee or another holder that is entitled to enforce the instrument. For example if Bill Wiltshire issues a check to Cindy Faulkner, it is incorrect to say that the instrument has been negotiated to Cindy. The instrument has been "issued" to Cindy. On the other hand, if Cindy wanted to transfer the instrument, she could do so by indorsing and transferring possession of the instrument to the transferee. Section 3-203(a) provides that "an instrument is transferred when it is delivered by a person other than its issuer for the purpose of giving to the person receiving delivery the right to enforce the instrument."

A second point under this section is that negotiation of the instrument requires that the person to whom the instrument is transferred must become a "holder." "Holder" is defined in Section 1-201(20) to mean "the person in possession if the instrument is payable to bearer or, in the case of an instrument payable to an identified person, if the identified person is in possession." If the instrument is not payable to bearer or is not in the possession of the person to whom the instrument is payable, then the person in possession is not a holder. For example, if Bill Wiltshire has possession of an unindorsed check payable to Cindy Faulkner, Bill is not the holder of the instrument. Bill can become the holder of the instrument if, as discussed later, the check is indorsed by Cindy.

As stated in the definition, negotiation may be either voluntary or involuntary. It is voluntary if the instrument is payable to bearer or the person to whom it is payable indorses it and voluntarily transfers possession. It is involuntary if it is payable to bearer or the person to whom it is payable indorses the check and it is transferred without the authority of the holder. In other words, a thief can become a holder. For example, assume Bill Wiltshire issues a check payable to bearer and delivers it to Cindy Faulkner. Cindy is then the holder of the check. Assume further that Joel Converse steals the check from Cindy. This is an involuntary transfer of possession of the instrument but it does qualify as negotiation because Joel became a holder. Joel can never become a holder in due course but he is a holder. Joel would not become the holder in this example, however, if the check had been drawn payable to Cindy. Only Cindy could be the holder until she indorses the check. Section 3-201(b) specifically states, "Except for negotiation by a remitter, if an instrument is payable to an identified person, negotiation requires transfer of possession of the instrument and its indorsement by the holder. If an instrument is payable to bearer, it may be negotiated by transfer of possession alone."

Subsection (b) makes it clear that negotiation requires the transfer of the instrument. Negotiation cannot take place without transfer of possession of the instrument. Subsection (b) also makes it clear that if the instrument is payable to an identified person, negotiation requires the indorsement of the person to whom it is payable. Once indorsed in blank by the person to whom the instrument is payable, the instrument no longer requires an indorsement to negotiate it unless the instrument is specially indorsed to an identified person. If the instrument is specially indorsed to an identified individual, then negotiation would require the indorsement of the person to whom the instrument has been specially indorsed to. For example, if Bill Wiltshire draws a check to the order of Cindy Faulkner and Cindy indorses the check in blank; that is, she simply indorses the back of the check by signing her name, further negotiation of the instrument requires transfer of possession only. On the other hand, if Cindy specifically indorses the check to Chip Sanders; that is, she indorses the check "pay to the order of Chip Sanders" and signs her name, then further negotiation of the check would require the indorsement of Chip Sanders.

4.2 PARTIES AGAINST WHOM NEGOTIATION IS EFFECTIVE AND WHEN NEGOTIATION IS SUBJECT TO RESCISSION

The intention of the drafters of the code to make negotiable instruments freely accepted comes through loud and clear in Section 3-202(a). That section states, "Negotiation is effective even if obtained (1) from an infant, a corporation exceeding its powers, or a person without capacity, (ii) by fraud, duress, or mistake, or (iii) in breach of duty or as part of an illegal transaction." Basically what this section is saying is that the negotiation of an instrument is effective regardless of who it was obtained from, how it was obtained, or whether the transaction was legal or not. The person to whom the instrument is negotiated becomes a holder. However, the instrument may be subject to a claim by a third party, unless the holder has attained the status of a holder in due course. Holder in due course and claims to instruments will be discussed in detail in Chapter 6 of this book.

Section 3-202(b) provides that negotiation may be rescinded in certain situations. According to that section, "to the extent permitted by other law, negotiation may be rescinded or may be subject to other remedies, but those remedies may not be asserted against a subsequent holder in due course or a person paying the instrument in good faith and without knowledge of facts that are a basis for rescission or other remedy." The negotiation may be rescinded if provided for by some other state or federal law. But even if allowed under some other law, the rescission is not valid against a holder in due course or a bank that pays the item in good faith. For example, assume that a check is payable to Bill Wiltshire and Bill indorses the check in blank and loses the check. Joel Converse finds the indorsed check and negotiates it to Chip Sanders. Any law allowing the negotiation to be rescinded would not be valid against Chip if he meets the requirements of a holder in due course. Assume further that the check is presented for payment to the drawee bank who pays it in good faith without the knowledge that there was a claim to the instrument. In this situation, even if a state law allowed rescission, it would not be effective against the drawee bank.

4.3 TRANSFER OF AN INSTRUMENT AND THE RIGHTS ACQUIRED BY TRANSFER

As previously stated and as provided for in Section 3-203, "an instrument is transferred when it is delivered by a person other than its issuer for the purpose of giving to the person receiving delivery the right to enforce the instrument." A person entitled to enforce the instrument is governed by Section 3-301 and is discussed in Chapter 6.

A transfer does not occur by delivery of the instrument by the person that issued it to the payee. For example, if Bill Wiltshire issues a check or a note to Cindy Faulkner, the instrument has not been transferred, it has been issued. If Cindy indorses the instrument and delivers it to Arnold Richardson, then the instrument has been transferred.

Another requirement of this section is that the person to whom the instrument is delivered must also acquire the right to enforce the instrument. The right to enforce the instrument is not limited to a holder of the instrument.

A person to whom an instrument is transferred may obtain the right to enforce the instrument without becoming the holder of the instrument. For example, if Cindy Faulkner, who is the payee of an instrument, delivers possession of the instrument to D.A. Carr, the instrument is "transferred" to D.A. under Section 3-203(a). However, if the transfer of the instrument from Cindy to D.A. was for value, then Section 3-203(c) provides that D.A. is entitled to the unqualified indorsement of Cindy. Negotiation does not occur, however, until the indorsement is made. As stated in that section, the transferee is entitled to the unqualified indorsement of the transferor. In other words, Cindy could not indorse the instrument "without recourse." Having transferred the instrument for value, Cindy cannot avoid the liability of an indorser by qualifying the indorsement.

Section 3-203(d) provides that negotiation does not occur if the transferor attempts to transfer less than the entire instrument and the transferee obtains no rights under Article 3 and simply has the rights of a partial assignee.

The transferee will have rights to the extent provided for under laws other than the UCC. As pointed out in Official Comment #5, an instrument indorsed "pay two-thirds to A and one-third to B" does not transfer two-thirds of the instrument to A and one-third to B." The effect of such an attempt is that negotiation does not occur. The indorsement could direct payment to A and B jointly or to A or B in the alternative. In either case, the instrument would be entirely payable to A and B or to A or B.

Subsection (b) contains a very important and powerful right of a transferee and that is that transfer of the instrument vests in the transferee the right of the transferor to enforce the instrument. The rights obtained by the transferee are vested whether the transfer was or was not a negotiation. For example, assume that Bill Wiltshire issued a check to Cindy Faulkner and Cindy transfers the check to Joel Converse without an indorsement. Joel obtains the right to enforce the instrument against Bill even though Joel is not a holder. Of course the transfer may be by negotiation in which case the transferee would become a holder and if the transferor was a holder in due course, then the transferee would also attain the rights of and status of a holder in due course. These rights of a holder in due course are vested in the transferee even if the transferee is not entitled to that status in his or her own right. In other words, the transferee may have knowledge of a fact that would prevent the transferee from being a holder in due course in his or her own right.

For example, if Bill Wiltshire indorses a check in blank and loses the check which is found by Joel Converse, Joel becomes a holder of the check. Assume that Joel negotiates the check to Cindy Faulkner for value and that Cindy meets all of the other requirements of a holder in due course. (The requirements of a holder in due course are discussed in Chapter 6 of this book.) Assume further that Cindy negotiates the check to Chip Sanders and that Chip had knowledge that Joel found the check and that Bill had a claim to it. In this example, Chip obtains Cindy's status as a holder in due course even though he took the check with knowledge of Bill's claim to the check. As a holder in due course, Chip takes the check free of Bill's claim to it.

Another example of the transferee obtaining the title of the transferor is found in *DH Cattle Holdings v. Kuntz*, 15 UCC Rep Serv 2d 178. In that case, a holder in due course transferred a note to a bank. The maker of the note refused to pay the note upon presentment claiming that the bank that took the note had knowledge of certain defenses against payment that the maker had. Additionally, the maker contended that the defendant was not a holder in due course and took the note subject to the defenses because the defendant took the note subsequent to the maturity date of the note. The court held that whether the defendant had knowledge of the defenses and the fact that the note was taken after maturity were irrelevant because the defendant took the note from a holder in due course. While the defendant was not a holder in due course in its own right, it took the note from one who was a holder in due course and thereby attained the status of the transferor.

The purpose of this section is to ensure the free flow of items. If it were not for this section allowing the transferee to obtain the status of the transferor, then in situations as described above the transferee would take the instrument subject to the claims of the true owner of the check. If it were not for this section, the holder in due course could not negotiate the check if no one would take it subject to claims and defenses. This would undermine the purpose of the holder in due course doctrine.

To avoid inequities, subsection (b) also provides that "the transferee cannot acquire rights of a holder in due course by a transfer, directly or indirectly, from a holder in due course if the transferee engaged in fraud or illegality affecting the instrument." If the transferee were a previous holder and participated in any fraud or illegality affecting the instrument, then the transferee could not improve his or her position or otherwise obtain the status of a holder in due course. In the example above where Joel Converse found the check indorsed in blank and negotiated the check to Cindy Faulkner who became a holder in due course, Joel could not become a holder in due course by reacquiring the check from Cindy. Joel could never become a holder in due course since he was involved in a fraud or illegality affecting the instrument.

4.4 REACQUISITION OF AN INSTRUMENT

A previous holder of an instrument can reacquire the instrument according to the provisions of Section 3-207 and the person who reacquires can even become the holder of the instrument. Section 3-207 provides that "Reacquisition of an instrument occurs if it is transferred to a former holder, by negotiation or otherwise." For example, if Bill Wiltshire negotiates a check to Cindy who negotiates it to Chip who negotiates it back to Bill, Bill has reacquired the check. Bill was a previous holder of the instrument to whom the instrument was transferred. This section further provides that "a former holder who reacquires the instrument may cancel indorsements made after the reacquirer first became a holder of the instrument. If the cancellation causes the instrument to be payable to the reacquirer or to bearer, the reacquirer may negotiate the instrument. An indorser whose indorsement is canceled is discharged, and the discharge is effective against any subsequent holder." In this example, Bill could cancel the indorsements of Cindy and Chip and Bill would become the holder and could negotiate the check to another party.

However, if Bill cancels Cindy's and Chip's indorsements, they are discharged from their liabilities as indorsers. If Bill negotiates the check to Joel, the cancellation of Cindy's and Chip's indorsements and subsequent discharge of their liabilities as indorsers is effective against Joel.

In the previous example, if Bill's reacquisition of the instrument was not by negotiation, Bill would still be entitled to cancel the indorsements and he could become a holder of the instrument. For example, if Bill had indorsed the check "pay to the order of Cindy" and if Cindy indorsed the check "pay to the order of Chip" but Chip did not indorse the check, Bill could cancel Cindy's indorsement and once again become a holder of the instrument. In this example, Chip would have to have been the person to transfer the check to Bill. In other words, if the check had been stolen from Chip, Bill could not cancel the indorsement. As pointed out in the Official Comments to this section, this is an exception to the rule that an instrument payable to an identified person requires an indorsement for further negotiation.

4.5 CLAIMS TO AN INSTRUMENT

In the majority of cases, instruments flow freely without any problems. Periodically, however, an instrument is lost or stolen which gives rise to a claim to the instrument. As previously stated, if the instrument is payable to an identified person, the indorsement of that person is required before the instrument can be negotiated. Any transferee that takes the instrument without the required indorsement does not become a holder and takes the instrument subject to the right to and claims of the rightful owner. No protection is given to a person who takes an instrument with a forged or missing indorsement other than the warranties of the transferor discussed below. A person taking an instrument with a forged or missing indorsement takes the instrument subject to the rightful owner's claim of conversion. Conversion of an instrument is governed by Section 3-420 and is discussed in Chapter 5 of this book. The transferee is in the best position to determine the identification of the transferor and his or her authority to transfer any rights in the instrument.

In some situations, however, an instrument payable to bearer or one that is indorsed in blank is lost. In this situation, the rights of the transferee are subject to Section 3-306. This section not only addresses the rights of the holder of the instrument but also the rights of any other person that has a property interest in the instrument. For example, a creditor may have taken the instrument as collateral for a loan or the instrument may have been taken to ensure performance of a contract. Whatever the property right, the instrument is subject to this section.

Section 3-306 states, "A person taking an instrument, other than a person having rights of a holder in due course, is subject to a claim of a property or possessor right in the instrument or its proceeds, including a claim to rescind a negotiation and to recover the instrument or its proceeds. A person having rights of a holder in due course takes free of the claim to the instrument." This section makes it clear that a holder in due course takes the instrument free of all claims to the instrument including the right to rescind the negotiation of the instrument. "Holder in due course" is discussed in Chapter 6 of this book.

Examples of the application of this section are as follows. Assume that Bill Wiltshire issues a check to Cindy Faulkner. Cindy indorses the check in blank and loses the check. Joel Converse finds the check. As discussed earlier, Joel becomes a holder of the instrument since negotiation of a "bearer instrument" requires only transfer of possession. The transfer can be voluntary or involuntary. In this case the transfer was obviously involuntary. Joel is a holder but he is not a holder in due course because he did not give value for the instrument and he obviously had notice of a claim to the instrument. Joel, therefore, takes the check subject to Cindy's rights as the owner of the instrument. Section 3-306 does not address the issue of how Cindy must go about recovering the instrument. Recovery of the instrument or its proceeds is left up to other state law.

Another example of the application of Section 3-306 is as follows. Assume that Bill Wiltshire enters into a contract with Joel Converse wherein Joel is to construct a building for Bill. Joel wants some form of guarantee of payment from Bill and asks for a performance bond. Instead of a performance bond, Bill suggests that Bill ask his local bank to issue a cashier's check payable to him and that he would deliver the unindorsed cashier's check to Joel. Joel agrees to this arrangement and in accordance with their agreement, Bill has his bank issue its cashier's check payable to Bill. Bill then delivers the unindorsed check to Joel. In this situation, the check was not negotiated to Joel, it was simply transferred to him. Upon performance of the contract, Joel will have given value and will be entitled to Bill's indorsement. Until that time, Joel has a property interest in the check and any person that takes the instrument takes it subject to Joel's claim. Therefore, in this example, if the check is lost or stolen, any person taking the instrument takes it subject to Joel's claim of a property right in the instrument.

A person may also have a claim to an instrument if the instrument is used by a fiduciary for the fiduciary's own benefit. Section 3-307 addresses the situation where a fiduciary has converted an instrument and when the person taking or paying the instrument has notice of a breach of this fiduciary duty. "Fiduciary" is defined in Subsection (a)(1) to mean "an agent, trustee, partner, corporate officer or director, or other representative owing a fiduciary duty with respect to an instrument." "Represented person" is defined in Subsection (a)(2) as "the principal, beneficiary, partnership, corporation, or other person to whom the duty stated in paragraph (1) is owed."

If a person takes an instrument from a fiduciary in payment of a debt, for collection, or for value, and the person has knowledge of the fiduciary status, Subsection (b) provides that the person taking the instrument has notice of a claim to the instrument by the fiduciary if the person taking the instrument knows that the fiduciary is in breach of the fiduciary duty. For example, if Joel issues a check on the account of Flashback Music, Inc. for a personal debt of Joel and the payee knows that Joel is in breach of his fiduciary duty, the payee takes the check with notice of a claim to the check by Flashback (the represented person).

Subsection (b)(2) addresses the situation where an instrument is payable to the represented person or to the fiduciary in his capacity as a fiduciary. Under that Subsection, the taker has notice of the breach of the fiduciary duty if the instrument is "(i) taken in payment of or security for a debt known by the taker to be the personal debt of the fiduciary, (ii) taken in a transaction known by the taker to be for the personal benefit of the fiduciary, or (iii) deposited to an account other than an account of the fiduciary, as such, or an account of the represented person." If Joel makes a payment on his personal loan with a check payable to him as Vice President of Flashback Music, Inc. the person taking the check has notice that Joel is in breach of his fiduciary duty to Flashback. If Joel deposits a check to his personal account that is payable to Flashback, the bank has notice of the breach of his fiduciary duty to Flashback.

A fiduciary normally is compensated for acting in the capacity of a fiduciary or sometimes will be reimbursed for valid expenses. Subsection (b)(3) recognizes this fact and provides, "if an instrument is issued by the represented person or the fiduciary as such, and made payable to the fiduciary personally, the taker does not have notice of the breach of fiduciary duty unless the taker knows of the breach of fiduciary duty." If Joel, as Vice President of Flashback, issues a check payable to himself and deposits the check to his personal checking account, the bank is not put on notice of a breach of fiduciary duty. The check could be in payment for his services or for expenses or for some other valid business reason. If the instrument is issued by the represented person or the fiduciary, as such, and the instrument is payable to the taker as payee, Subsection (b)(4) applies. That Subsection provides that the taker has notice of a breach of the fiduciary duty if the instrument is "(i) taken in payment of or as security for a debt known by the taker to be the personal debt of the fiduciary, (ii) taken in a transaction known by the taker to be for the personal benefit of the fiduciary, or (iii) deposited to an account other than an account of the fiduciary, as such, or an account of the represented person." If Joel, as Vice President of Flashback, issues a check drawn on the account of Flashback payable to First Deposit Bank for payment of a personal debt of Joel, the First Deposit Bank has notice of a breach of the fiduciary duty. If Joel, as Vice President of Flashback, issues a check on the account of Flashback payable to First Deposit Bank and deposits the check to his personal account, First Deposit Bank has notice of a breach of Joel's fiduciary duty. The difference in paragraphs (2) and (4) is that paragraph (2) applies to instruments payable to the fiduciary and paragraph (4) applies to instruments payable to the taker of the instrument.

4.6 TRANSFER WARRANTIES

Every person who transfers an instrument for value makes certain warranties to the transferee and if the transfer is by indorsement, to any subsequent transferee. These warranties are provided for in Section 3-416 and are discussed in detail in Chapter 2 of this book. The warranties are briefly discussed here to make the reader aware of their existence and content.

The warranties made by the transferor are as follows:

(1) the warrantor is a person entitled to enforce the instrument;

(2) all signatures on the instrument are authentic and authorized;

(3) the instrument has not been altered;

(4) the instrument is not subject to a defense or claim in recoupment or any party which can be asserted against the warrantor; and

(5) the warrantor has no knowledge of any insolvency proceeding commenced with respect to the maker or acceptor or, in the case of an unaccepted draft, the drawer.

The basic warranties established by this section are that the transferee can take the instrument without fear that there is anything wrong with it. The warranties create a guarantee for the transferee that there are no claims to the instrument, that there is nothing defective about the instrument, and if the transferee suffers a loss, the warrantor will pay for it. Subsection (b) provides that if there is a breach of these warranties, the warrantor will pay the transferee damages in an amount equal to the loss suffered, but not to exceed the amount of the instrument plus expenses and loss of interest. These warranties are only as good as the person giving them. Therefore, the transferee must know the transferor and feel confident that in the event of a breach, that the transferor will be around to collect the damages from.

A notice of breach of these warranties must be given within 30 days from the date that the claimant has reason to know of the breach and the identity of the warrantor. If the claim is not made within this 30-day period, the liability of the warrantor is discharged to the extent of any loss caused by the delay in giving notice of the claim as provided for in Subsection (c). This Subsection also states that the warranties cannot be disclaimed with respect to checks.

Subsection (d) states, "A cause of action for breach of warranty under this section accrues when the claimant has reason to know of the breach."

Transfer warranties are also given by a customer or collecting bank that transfers an item and these warranties are contained in Section 4-207. The warranties under Section 4-207 are the same as the warranties given under Section 3-416 except that Section 4-207 contains an additional provision. Subsection (b) states that the transferor warrants that if the item is dishonored, the customer or collecting bank will pay the transferee the amount of the item. This obligation may not be disclaimed by an indorsement stating that it is made "without recourse" or any other statement that attempts to disclaim liability.

The transfer warranties are discussed in detail in Chapter 2 of this book.

CHAPTER 5

INDORSEMENTS

5.1 INDORSEMENTS IN GENERAL

Indorsements are governed by numerous sections throughout Articles 3 and 4. Section 3-204, however, contains the definition, the purposes for which an indorsement is made, and how an indorsement may be made. Other sections dealing with indorsers are: 3-205 dealing with the types of indorsements, 3-206 addresses restrictive indorsements, 3-415 establishes the liability of an indorser, 3-403 deals with unauthorized indorsements, 3-404 addresses forged indorsements that are made effective, 3-405 deals with employer's responsibility for fraudulent indorsements by employees, 4-205 provides that a depositary bank becomes a holder of an unindorsed item, and 3-605 establishes discharge of an indorser. All of these sections and several more are discussed below.

An indorsement is any signature other than a signature made as drawer, maker, or acceptor, unless it is clear from the instrument that the signature was made for a different purpose. The definition of "indorsement," which is very lengthy, is contained in Section 3-204(a) and is as follows:

A signature, other than that of a signer as maker, drawer, or acceptor, that alone or accompanied by other words is made on an instrument for the purpose of (i) negotiating the instrument, (ii) restricting payment of the instrument, or (iii) incurring indorser's liability on the instrument, but regardless of the intent of the signer, a signature and its accompanying words is an indorsement unless the accompanying words, terms of the instrument, place of the signature, or other circumstances unambiguously indicate that the signature was made for a purpose other than indorsement. For the purpose of determining whether a signature is made on an instrument, a paper affixed to the instrument is a part of the instrument.

Unless the instrument specifically indicates that the signature is made in some other capacity than an indorsement, Subsection (a) provides that the signature is an indorsement. For example, the signature of the drawer is typically made on the bottom of the draft and most often is on the bottom right. A signature in that location would not be an indorsement unless a signature was made in another location on the draft that it was the signature of the drawer. If a signature was placed on the top left of a draft and indicated that the signature was that of the drawer, and if a signature was placed on the bottom right of the draft, then the signature would be an indorsement. The point here is that an indorsement does not have to be placed on the back of the instrument, and if a signature is made on the back of an instrument, that fact does not make the signature an indorsement. As pointed out in the Official Comments to this section, if the signature of the drawee is made on the back of an instrument, the signature is an acceptance since there is no other reason for the drawee to sign an instrument.

An indorsement could be placed across the face of an instrument. If, for example, a signature is made across the face of an instrument, the signature is not that of the drawee, and there is no indication as to the capacity in which the signature was made, the signature is an indorsement. The fact that an acceptance is typically made across the face of an instrument does not prohibit an indorsement from being placed in that location. In *United States v. Tufi, 19 UCC Rep Serv 543*, the court held that the signature across the face of a United States Treasury check was an indorsement.

According to Section 3-204(a), the intent of the signer is not the controlling factor. If the intention of the signer is to sign in a capacity other than an indorsement, the intention must be reflected in the instrument. As stated in this section, the accompanying words, terms of the instrument, place of the signature, or other circumstances must indicate that the signature was made for a purpose other than indorsement. The court in *Security Pacific National Bank v. Chess, 19 UCC Rep Serv 544*, held that a note containing the heading, ASSIGNMENT, followed by the language stating that the undersigned "hereby assigns . . . all right, title, and interest in and to the within note," along with a statement that the person making the assignment guaranteed payment and collection of the note, was an indorsement.

If a person places his or her signature on a check simply as a receipt to prove that cash was given to them, then the signature is an indorsement unless there is an indication that the signature is only a receipt. For example, assume that Bill Wiltshire and Joel Converse work for the same employer. On payday, Bill indorses his check in blank and asks Joel to cash the check for him. Most banks would require Joel to indorse the check primarily as a receipt to indicate that the cash was given to Joel. To avoid becoming an indorser, Joel could indicate on the instrument that he is signing the instrument only as a receipt and not as an indorsement.

The indorsement is not required to actually be on the instrument. The last sentence of Subsection (a) states, "For the purpose of determining whether a signature is made on an instrument, a paper affixed to the instrument is a part of the instrument." Nothing in this section defines what "affixed to the instrument" means. It would appear that any method of affixing the paper to the instrument would be sufficient such as staples, glue, tape, etc. In *Henderson v. Hanson*, 34 UCC Rep Serv 371, the court held that an assignment firmly attached to a note was an indorsement under the UCC. The court in *Lamson v. Commercial Credit Corp.*, 16 UCC Rep Serv 756, also held that an indorsement stapled to a note was an indorsement and the transferee became a holder of the note. However, the court in *Estrada v. River Oaks Bank & Trust Co.*, 22 UCC Rep Serv 83, held that an indorsement stapled to four notes was not an indorsement because it was not clear if the indorsement was intended for all four notes or just one. In *All American Finance Co. v. Pugh Shows, Inc.*, 3 UCC Rep Serv 2d 1421, the court mentioned that several jurisdictions have held that an indorsement on an allonge is permitted only if there is no longer room on the instrument itself due to previous indorsements. In *Controlled Atmosphere, Inc. v. Branom Instrument Co.*, 6 UCC Rep Serv 732, the court held that an indorsement on loose leafs of paper included with a note were not indorsements under the UCC because the sheets of paper were not affixed to the note.

Subsection (a) also makes reference to the purpose for which the indorsement is made. According to that section, the indorsement could be for the purpose of "(i) negotiating the instrument, (ii) restricting payment of the instrument, or (iii) incurring indorser's liability." As to negotiation of the instrument, if the person that is identified as the payee signs the instrument, there is no other reason the payee would sign other than as an indorsement that is required to negotiate the instrument. The indorsement can also be made to restrict the payment of the item for a specific purpose such as "for deposit only." An indorsement can be made solely for the purpose of incurring the liability of an indorser. For example, if a note is payable to Bill Wiltshire, is issued individually by Cindy Faulkner, and is also signed by Joel Converse, Joel is obviously signing as an indorser. Since the instrument is not payable to him and since he is not the maker, he is signing as an indorser. Since his signature is not necessary to negotiate the instrument, his indorsement is made for the sole purpose of incurring the liability of an indorser.

Joel could likewise sign a check to create the indorser liability. For example, assume that Bill issued a check to Cindy and Cindy wanted to cash the check. Joel accompanies Cindy to Joel's bank and asks the teller to cash the check for Cindy. The teller does not know Cindy and the check is not drawn on the teller's bank; therefore, the teller asks Joel to sign the check. Joel is signing as an indorser for the purpose of incurring the liability of an indorser. His signature is not required to negotiate the check and he is not the drawer or the drawee.

The capacity in which a person signs an instrument is important to determine the liability of the person. This is the reason that Section 3-204(a) is so lengthy and goes through so much detail to define an indorsement. The definition of "indorser," however, is quite brief. "Indorser" is defined in Section 3-204(b) as "a person who makes an indorsement."

Subsection (c) deals with instruments that are used for the purpose of establishing collateral for a debt. According to that section, an indorsement that transfers a security interest in the instrument is effective as an unqualified indorsement of the instrument. Such an indorsement is sufficient to transfer title to the instrument. In other words, the transferee becomes the holder of the instrument even though the indorsement may contain accompanying words that state that the indorsement is made for the purpose of creating a security interest in the instrument. For example, if Bill Wiltshire indorses a note to Chip Sanders as security for a debt, Chip becomes the holder of the note and may enforce it.

(a) INDORSEMENT WHERE NAME IS WRONG OR MISSPELLED

Occasionally, an instrument is issued to a payee and the name of the payee is misspelled or the name may be completely different than the person intended as payee. Section 3-204(d) addresses this situation and states, "if an instrument is payable to a holder under a name that is not the name of the holder, indorsement may be by the holder in the name stated in the instrument or in the holder's name or both, but signature in both names may be required by a person paying or taking the instrument for value or collection." As pointed out in the Official Comment #3 to this, Section 3-110(a) states that an instrument is payable to the person intended by the person signing as or in the name or behalf of the issuer even if that person signing is identified by a name that is not the true name of the person. In this situation, the holder may sign either in the true name of the holder, in the name as shown on the instrument, or both. Subsection (d) also gives the person paying or taking the instrument for value or collection the right to require both indorsements. In *Guaranty Federal Savings & Loan Assoc. v. Horseshoe Operating Co.*, 6 *UCC Rep Serv 774*, an official check was issued in the name of "Binnon & Co.," and was indorsed "Binnon & Co. Jack B. Binion." The actual name of the company was Binion's Horseshoe Hotel and Casino. The court held that the indorsement was proper and that the person that indorsed the check was the holder.

It would appear that in most situations, the differences between the holder that is named and true name of the holder would be small. For example, if a check were issued to Jarod Caruba and the true name of the payee is Jared Carrubba, the intentions of the drawer of the check would be obvious and the indorsement could be made in either name. However, if the check were payable to Bill Wiltshire but the drawer intended to issue the check to Joel Converse, it would appear that the best course of action would be to have the drawer cancel the first check and issue one in the proper name. On the other hand, Subsection (d) specifically addresses this situation and it would be completely within the scope of this section for Joel Converse to indorse the check in either or both names.

(b) INSTRUMENT PAYABLE TO TWO OR MORE PAYEES

If an instrument is payable to two or more payees jointly and not in the alternative, Section 3-110 provides that the instrument must be indorsed by all of the payees. If any of the joint payees' indorsement is missing, then the transferee is not a holder of the instrument. On the other hand, if the instrument is payable in the alternative, then any of the payees may indorse and negotiate the instrument so that the transferee will become a holder of the instrument. Section 3-110 is discussed in detail in Section 1.4 of Chapter 1 of this book and also in Section 5.5 of this book.

5.2 THE OBLIGATION OF AN INDORSER

The obligation of an indorser is set out in Section 3-415. According to Subsection (a), if an instrument is dishonored, an indorser is obliged to pay the amount of the instrument according to the terms of the instrument at the time it was indorsed, or according to the terms when completed if the instrument was incomplete. The obligation of the indorser of an incomplete instrument is subject to the provisions of Section 3-115 dealing with incomplete instruments and Section 3-407 dealing with alterations. The obligation of the indorser is owed to a person entitled to enforce the instrument or to a subsequent indorser who paid the instrument. The obligation to pay is subject to several other provisions of Section 3-415 and to Section 3-314(d) that are discussed later.

The obligation of the indorser to pay an instrument is conditioned upon the item being dishonored. The primary obligation to pay an item is on the maker or the drawer. The person entitled to enforce the item should first look to the maker or, in the case of a drawer, present the item to the payor. If presentment is required, as in the case of a draft or check, presentment must first be made and the item dishonored before the indorser is required to pay. For example, assume that Chip Sanders issues a check to Arnold Richardson and Arnold indorses the check to Joel Converse. Joel calls the bank on which the check is drawn to verify the sufficiency of funds and is told that the balance in the account is not sufficient to pay the check. Calling to check the sufficiency of funds is not presentment. The check has therefore not been dishonored and Arnold is not obliged to pay the amount of the instrument until it is dishonored. Presentment is discussed in Chapter 7 and dishonor is discussed in Chapter 8 of this book.

Presentment by notice of an item not payable by, through , or at a bank is allowed under Section 4-212. That section also provides that if presentment is made by notice and the item is not paid, accepted, or request for compliance with the requirements under Section 3-501 is not received within certain time periods, the item is considered dishonored and the presenting bank may charge the drawer or indorser by sending it notice of the facts. Presentment by notice has very limited application and is therefore only briefly mentioned here. Section 4-212 is also discussed in Chapter 7 of this book.

If the item being indorsed is a check, presentment must be made within a specified period of time. Section 3-415(e) provides that if the check is not presented for payment or given to a depositary bank for collection within 30 days after the indorsement is made, the liability of the indorser is discharged. In the example, if after verifying the balance, Joel did not present the check to the drawee bank before the expiration of 30 days from the date that Arnold indorsed the check, Arnold's liability of an indorser is discharged. This is a change from the previous provisions of Article 3. The prior version discharged the indorser if presentment was not made within seven days of the indorsement.

The reason for discharging the indorser after the expiration of the 30-day period is to encourage presentment of the item in a timely manner. An indorser should not be expected to remain liable on an instrument indefinitely. The person to whom the instrument is given should take action on the instrument within this period of time or assume the risk that the item will not be paid.

The indorser's liability is likewise discharged under Section 3-415(c) if notice of dishonor is required and the proper notice is not given within the prescribed period of time. Notice of dishonor is governed by Section 3-503 and is discussed in detail in Chapter 8. Basically, Section 3-503 requires that notice of dishonor must be given to the indorser within prescribed periods of time. With respect to an instrument taken for collection, notice of dishonor must be given by the bank before the expiration of the bank's midnight deadline. That is, notice must be given by the bank before midnight of the banking day following receipt of the item. For example, if notice of dishonor is received by a depositary bank on Monday, May 2, notice of dishonor must be given to the depositor who indorsed the item before midnight on Tuesday, May 3. If notice is not given within that time frame, the indorser is discharged of its liability on the instrument. Notice of dishonor is also required by Regulation CC which is discussed in Chapter 8 of this book.

As to any other person, notice of dishonor of an instrument taken for collection by a collecting bank must be given within 30 days following the day on which the person receives notice of dishonor. (Former Article 3 required notice of dishonor within three days.) For example, assume that Chip Sanders issues a check to Arnold Richardson and Arnold indorses the check to Joel Converse. Joel deposits the check in his checking account at the First Deposit Bank. Upon presentment, the check is dishonored and notice of dishonor is received by the First Deposit Bank on May 2. The bank gives the required notice of dishonor to Joel before midnight May 3. Joel must give notice of dishonor to Arnold before the expiration of 30 days from this date. In other words, Joel must give Arnold notice of dishonor by June 2. If Joel does not give notice of dishonor within this 30-day period, Arnold is discharged of his obligation to pay the item.

The liability of an indorser on a draft is discharged according to Section 3-415(d) if the draft is accepted by a bank after the indorsement is made. For example, Chip Sanders issues a check to Arnold Richardson and Arnold indorses the check to Joel Converse. Joel then has the drawee bank certify the check which is acceptance by the drawee bank. Upon certification, Arnold's liability as an indorser is discharged. Acceptance prior to the indorsement does not discharge the indorser.

An indorser can avoid the liability of an indorser imposed by Section 3-415(a). Subsection (b) states, "If an indorsement states that it is made 'without recourse' or otherwise disclaims liability of the indorser, the indorser is not liable under Subsection (a) to pay the instrument." When indorsed in this manner with words disclaiming liability, the transferee is accepting the item with the understanding that the indorser will not pay the amount of the item upon dishonor. There are any number of reasons why and indorser would indorse an instrument "without recourse." The primary reason would be a situation where an indorsement is required to negotiate the instrument. Section 3-201(b), which is discussed in detail in Chapter 3 of this book, provides that "if an instrument is payable to an identified person, negotiation requires possession of the instrument and its indorsement by the holder." In certain situations, the indorsement of a person may be required on an instrument for negotiation and that person may have no interest in the instrument or its proceeds. For example, assume that D.A. Carr financed an automobile through the First Deposit Bank and the bank was shown as the lien holder on the insurance policy. The loan was paid off, but the insurance company was not notified of this fact. Assume further that the automobile was involved in an accident and the insurance company issued its check payable to D.A. Carr and the First Deposit Bank. The indorsement of both D.A. Carr and the First Deposit Bank are required to negotiate the check as required by Section 3-110. Since the bank has no interest in the proceeds of the check, the bank has no incentive to incur the liability of an indorser. The bank may, however, be willing to indorse the check "without recourse" to avoid the obligation imposed on an indorser by Section 3-415(a).

Another example of a situation where a person might indorse an item without recourse is where a note is discounted and transferred to another person. For example, a note payable to Bill Wiltshire must be indorsed by Bill to negotiate the note to another person. Assume that Cindy Faulkner was willing to buy the note from Bill at a discount. In consideration for discounting the note, Bill did not want to incur the liability of an indorser on the note. Bill could indorse the note "without recourse" and avoid this liability.

Indorsing an instrument "without recourse" will not relieve an indorser of the transfer warranties under Section 4-207(b). Under that section, a customer or collecting bank that transfers an item and receives settlement warrants to the transferee and to any subsequent collecting bank that if an item is dishonored, the indorser will pay the transferee the amount of the instrument. This section further provides that "a transferor cannot disclaim its obligation under this Subsection by an indorsement stating that it is made 'without recourse' or otherwise disclaiming liability." Therefore, if a customer of a bank indorses a check "without recourse" and deposits the check in an account, the customer cannot disclaim the warranty that he will pay for the item if it is dishonored. Transfer and presentment warranties are discussed in Chapter 2 of this book.

The obligation of an indorser is also subject to Section 3-419(d). That section provides that if a person signs an instrument and unambiguously indicates that the person is only guaranteeing collection rather than payment of the instrument, then the signer is only obligated to pay the amount of the instrument if one of the following situations listed in Section 3-419(d) exists:

(i) execution of judgement against the other party has been returned unsatisfied,

(ii) the other party is insolvent or in an insolvency proceeding,

(iii) the other party cannot be served with process, or

(iv) it is otherwise apparent that payment cannot be obtained from the other party.

Indorsements of this nature are primarily made in the capacity of an "accommodation party." Accommodation parties are discussed in Section 5.3 below. If the indorser only guarantees payment as described above, the liability of the indorser is not merely based on dishonor of the item. The person entitled to enforce the item must make an attempt to collect the item and the indorser is only liable if one or more of the four situations listed above exists.

5.3 TYPES OF INDORSEMENTS

As stated in Section 5.2, indorsements are made for various reasons. The indorser may wish to restrict payment of the instrument, or may wish to negotiate the instrument, or may indorse only to incur the liability of an indorser.

Depending on the purpose of the indorsement, the indorsement can be made in one of several different ways provided for in Sections 3-205 and 3-206 or the indorsement can be made as an accommodation party as provided for in Section 3-419.

(a) SPECIAL INDORSEMENTS

The holder of an instrument may want to indorse an instrument in such a manner that the indorsement identifies the person to whom it makes the instrument payable. The holder may do so simply by identifying the person in the indorsement. For example, if the holder of an instrument wanted to indorse the instrument to identify Robert Hales as the person to whom the instrument is payable, the instrument could be indorsed "pay to the order of Robert Hales" followed by the signature of the holder. Such an indorsement is identified in Section 3-205(a) as a "special indorsement." Once an item has been specially indorsed, the instrument becomes payable to the identified person and further negotiation of the item requires the indorsement of that person. In the example above, negotiation of the instrument would require the indorsement of Robert Hales.

A holder of an instrument may want to specially indorse an instrument for any number of reasons. For example, assume that Bill Wiltshire owns a home in which his mother lives and damage is caused to the house by a storm. Unaware of the insurance coverage, Bill's mom has repairs made to the house and pays for the repairs. When Bill is made aware of the damage and repairs, he files a claim with his insurance company. Since Bill is named as the insured, the insurance company issues its check for the repairs payable to Bill Wiltshire. Bill could indorse the check, deposit it to his account and write a check to mom or he could indorse the insurance check and send it to her. If he indorses the check in blank, that is, indorses the check by signing his name with no other words or instruction, the instrument becomes payable to bearer and can be negotiated by transfer of possession. If indorsed in blank, anyone that gets possession of the check could negotiate it. To prevent this from occurring, Bill could specially indorse the check identifying his mother as the person to whom the check is payable. Further negotiation of the check will then require the indorsement of Mrs. Wiltshire.

The last sentence of Subsection (a) states, "The principles stated in Section 3-110 apply to special indorsement." Section 3-110 deals with the identification of the person to whom an instrument is payable and is discussed in detail in Section 1.4 of this book.

(b) BLANK INDORSEMENTS

Section 3-205(b) addresses "blank indorsements" and states, "if an indorsement is made by the holder of an instrument and it is not a special indorsement, it is a 'blank indorsement.' When indorsed in blank, an instrument becomes payable to bearer and may be negotiated by transfer of possession alone until specially indorsed." The typical blank indorsement is one where the holder of the instrument simply puts his or her signature on the back of the instrument with no other words. For example, if a check is payable to Bill Wiltshire and he signs his name on the back of the instrument with no other words or instructions, the indorsement is a blank indorsement. The check then becomes payable to bearer and may be negotiated by transfer of possession. Bill could deliver the check to Joel Converse and Joel would become the holder of the instrument. Joel may negotiate the instrument by transfer alone. Joel's indorsement is not required for further negotiation. For example, Joel could present the check over the counter to the drawee bank and his indorsement is not necessary. Many banks, however, will require Joel's indorsement primarily for identification purposes and as a receipt that the cash was paid to Joel.

As stated above, once an instrument has been indorsed in blank, negotiation requires transfer of possession only. The transfer can be either voluntary or involuntary. In other words, a thief could steal the blank indorsed check and become a holder or a person could find a lost blank indorsed check and become a holder. As to a thief or a person that finds a lost instrument, the rightful owner or other person entitled to enforce the instrument would have a claim to the instrument. However, if the instrument ends up in the hands of a holder in due course, the holder takes free of all claims to the instrument.

An instrument that contains a blank indorsement that is payable to bearer can be specially indorsed and be made payable to an identified person. A blank indorsed instrument that is further negotiated by a special indorsement will require the indorsement of the person identified. Section 3-205(c) states, "The holder may convert a blank indorsement that consists only of a signature into a special indorsement by writing, above the signature of the indorser, words identifying the person to whom the instrument is made payable." For example, if Joel Converse indorses a check in blank and negotiates it to Chip Sanders, Chip can specially indorse the check to Melonie Lee by writing above his signature, "pay to the order of Melonie Lee." Further negotiation of the check will require the indorsement of Melonie.

(c) ANOMALOUS INDORSEMENT

Another type of indorsement defined in Section 3-205(d) is an "anomalous indorsement" which is defined as "an indorsement made by a person who is not the holder of the instrument. An anomalous indorsement does not affect the manner in which the instrument may be negotiated." As pointed out in Official Comment #3 to this section, an anomalous indorsement is normally made by an accommodation party. For example, assume that a check is payable to Joel Converse and Joel does not have a banking relationship in the city in which he is located, but his friend Arnold Richardson does have an account at a local bank. Arnold accompanies Joel to his bank, which is not the drawee bank, and asks the teller to extend him the courtesy of cashing the check for his friend Joel. The teller responds that she will gladly cash the check if Arnold will indorse the check along with his good friend Joel. Arnold agrees and indorses the check. Arnold's indorsement is an "anomalous indorsement."

As stated in Subsection (d), the anomalous indorsement does not affect the manner in which the instrument may be negotiated. The anomalous indorsement in no way affects the title to the instrument nor restricts the payment of the instrument. An anomalous indorsement serves only to create the liability of an indorser for the person that indorses in that capacity.

(d) RESTRICTIVE INDORSEMENTS

The holder of an instrument is given a fair amount of latitude as to how an indorsement is made on the instrument. As previously stated, the instrument may be specially indorsed, or indorsed in blank and Section 3-206 contains provisions for restrictive indorsements. The restrictions, however, cannot restrict further negotiation or transfer of the instrument or establish conditions to payment of the instrument. Section 3-206(a) states, "an indorsement limiting payment to a particular person or otherwise prohibiting further transfer or negotiation of the instrument is not effective to prevent further transfer or negotiation of the instrument." The indorsement may not contain a statement, for example, that the instrument may only be negotiated a certain number of times or that further negotiation is prohibited. An indorsement that contains a statement that the instrument is payable only to a specific person and that person may not negotiate the instrument is invalid. The instrument may contain a special indorsement to a particular person, but the indorsement could not restrict that person's ability to negotiate the instrument.

The indorsement may not state a condition to the right of the indorsee to receive payment. One of the requirements of a negotiable instrument is that payment may not be conditional and an indorsement on a negotiable instrument cannot take away that instrument's negotiability. Subsection (b) states, "An indorsement stating a condition to the right of the indorsee to receive payment does not affect the right of the indorsee to enforce the instrument. A person paying the instrument or taking it for value or collection may disregard the condition, and the rights and liabilities of that person are not affected by whether the condition has been fulfilled." For example, an indorsement that states that the indorsee is entitled to payment only if he performs in accordance with a certain contract is not valid. Payment of the instrument cannot be conditioned upon the performance of the contract. A person taking an instrument with such an indorsement may ignore the condition to payment. Additionally, if payment is made, the fact that the condition was not met does not affect the rights of the person that took the item or paid it.

Section 3-206(c) contains some restrictions that may be placed on instruments that are enforceable. That section applies several rules to instruments that contain indorsements that are made in blank or are specially indorsed to a bank and contain words such as "for deposit only," "for collection," or other words indicating the purpose for which the instrument is being collected by a bank. The rules also apply to an instrument, described in Section 4-201(b), that has entered the bank collection process and contains an indorsement that states "pay any bank" or other indorsement that indicates that the item has entered the collection process and may only be transferred to a bank.

Subsection (c)(1) is the first rule which states, "A person, other than a bank, who purchases the instrument when so indorsed converts the instrument unless the amount paid for the instrument is received by the indorser or applied consistently with the indorsement." In other words, the instrument may only be negotiated in accordance with the indorsement or for the benefit of the indorser. If a check is indorsed "for deposit only," the check may only be taken by a bank for deposit to the account of the indorser. No other person has rights to the instrument or can enforce it with such an indorsement. If a person other than a bank takes the item so restrictively indorsed, that person is said to have converted the instrument and is liable to the rightful owner. For example, if Joel Converse accepts a check from Chip Sanders and the check contains an indorsement that states, "for deposit only to the account of Bill Wiltshire," Joel has converted the instrument and is subject to a claim to the instrument by Bill. Joel has not converted the instrument, however, if he pays the amount of the check to Bill. If the amount of the instrument is paid to Bill, then Joel has met the requirement in Subsection (c)(1) stating that the instrument is not converted if the amount paid for the instrument is received by the indorser. The effect of taking the instrument with the restrictive indorsement is the same as taking an instrument that has been specially indorsed to a person.

Subsection (c)(2) contains the rules that apply to a depositary bank that takes an instrument that has been restrictively indorsed. That Subsection states, "A depositary bank that purchases the instrument or takes it for collection when so indorsed converts the instrument unless the amount paid by the bank with respect to the instrument is received by the indorser or applied consistently with the indorsement." This Subsection is saying that a depositary bank may only apply the proceeds of the instrument only as indorsed or pay the amount of the instrument to the holder.

For example, if a check is indorsed "for deposit only to the account of Chip Sanders," the depositary bank can either pay the proceeds to Chip Sanders or deposit the proceeds to the account in compliance with the indorsement. The wording of Subsection (c)(2) indicates that proceeds of the instrument could otherwise be applied if the indorser receives the amount paid. For example, it would appear that in the example above, the bank would not be considered to have converted the instrument if the proceeds were applied to a loan of Chip Sanders, or if a cashier's check were issued payable to Chip Sanders or were issued to another person if Chip Sanders were the remitter. In each of those situations, the amount paid by the bank with respect to the instrument would have been received by the indorser.

The depositary bank converts the restrictively indorsed instrument if the indorser does not receive the proceeds or if the instrument is not applied consistently with the indorsement. For example, if a check is indorsed "for deposit only to the account of Flashback Music, Inc." and the depositary bank pays the item in cash to an employee of Flashback that keeps the money for his own benefit, the bank has converted the instrument and is liable to Flashback. The bank would likewise be liable if it took the deposit "less cash" and gave the cash to the employee that kept it for his own benefit. Other examples of where the bank could be held liable for conversion would be if the bank accepted a check indorsed "for deposit only to the account of Flashback Music, Inc." and applied the proceeds of the check to a personal loan of an employee, if an employee deposits the entire amount or a partial amount of the check to his or her own account. Each of the above examples would be subject to any defenses that the bank may have against the employer.

The courts have had varying opinions as to what is a restrictive indorsement and what is not a restrictive indorsement. In *AmSouth Bank, N.A. v. Reliable Janitorial Service Inc.*, 10 UCC Rep Serv 2d 903, the court held that a check indorsed "For Deposit Only, Reliable Janitorial Service, Inc.," was a restrictive indorsement and held the bank liable to Reliable for allowing an employee of Reliable to deposit checks to employee's personal account. However, in *Stewart Office Supplies, Inc. v. First Union National Bank*, 13 UCC Rep Serv 2d 797, the court held that an indorsement that read "Stewart Office Supplies For Deposit Only" was not a restrictive indorsement. In that case, someone added the name of another account after the indorsement into which the checks were deposited. The court reasoned that the check was in fact handled for deposit but to the account named after the words "for deposit only." A completely different finding was held in *Travis v. La Junita State Bank*, 38 UCC Rep Serv 1677. In that case, the client of an attorney indorsed a check in blank by signing her name only on the back of the check. The attorney put the words "for deposit" on the check underneath the signature of the client and deposited the check into his own account. The court held that the attorney became a holder of the instrument but by placing the words "for deposit" on the check made the indorsement a restrictive indorsement. The court further held that since only the indorsement of the client was on the back of the check, the depositary bank was required to apply the proceeds to the client's account. What can be learned from these cases is that the intentions of the indorsement should be clearly reflected in the indorsement.

Subsection (c)(3) applies to the situation where the payor bank is also the depositary bank. That section states, "A payor bank that is also the depositary bank or that takes the instrument for immediate payment over the counter from a person other than a collecting bank converts the instrument unless the proceeds of the instrument are received by the indorser or applied consistently with the indorsement." This Subsection is similar to Subsection (c)(2), except it addresses the liability of the payor bank for paying the item over the counter to a person other than a collecting bank or for the benefit of the indorser. For example, the payor bank could be liable to the indorser if it pays cash to a person other than the holder that presented the check over the counter that was restrictively indorsed "for deposit only."

A restrictive indorsement has no application to and is not binding on an intermediary bank or a payor bank that is not also the depositary. Section 3-206(c)(4) states, "except as otherwise provided in paragraph (3), a payor bank or intermediary bank may disregard the indorsement and is not liable if the proceeds of the instrument are not received by the indorser or applied consistently with the indorsement."

The payor bank is not required to examine the indorsement on every check that is presented for payment, other than over the counter, to determine if the check contains a restrictive indorsement and if it does contain a restrictive indorsement to determine how the proceeds were applied. If the proceeds of a check are not paid to the indorser or are not applied in accordance with a restrictive indorsement, neither the payor bank nor an intermediary bank are liable for conversion of the instrument. It is the responsibility of the depositary bank to ensure that the proceeds are properly applied. For example, assume that a check indorsed "for deposit only to the account of Flashback Music, Inc." is stolen and is deposited to the account of the thief. The check is sent through banking channels to the payor bank who pays the item in good faith. Neither the collecting banks nor the payor bank are liable to Flashback for conversion of the check. The depositary bank, on the other hand, is liable to Flashback for conversion unless the depositary bank has a valid defense.

Section 3-206(d) addresses instruments that bear an indorsement using words to the effect that payment is made to the indorsee as agent, trustee, or other fiduciary for the benefit of the indorser or another person. In such situations, Subsection (d)(1) provides that a person who takes the instrument for collection or payment may take the instrument without regard to whether the indorsee violates a fiduciary duty to the indorser. This Subsection is subject to the provisions of Section 3-307 dealing with notice of a fiduciary duty. An example of the application of this section is as follows. A check is indorsed "pay to the order of Bill Fisher, executor of the estate of Stan Fisher." A depositary bank could take the check from Bill Fisher and pay the proceeds to him without regard to whether he is violating his fiduciary duty. The depositary bank could be liable to the estate of Stan Fisher if the bank had received notice of the breach of the fiduciary duty as provided for in Section 3-307. Section 3-307 is discussed in Chapter 4 of this book.

Subsection (d)(2) addresses the liability of a payor bank or other transferee that deals with an instrument with this type of indorsement. This section states, "a subsequent transferee of the instrument or person who pays the instrument is neither given notice nor otherwise affected by the restriction in the indorsement unless the transferee or payor knows that the fiduciary dealt with the instrument or its proceeds in breach of fiduciary duty." This section is similar to (c)(4) in that the payor bank or other transferee cannot be expected to inspect every indorsement on every check that it handles and make an inquiry as to whether or not the proceeds were handled properly.

Section 3-206(e) provides that the fact that an instrument contains a restrictive indorsement does not preclude a purchaser of the instrument from becoming a holder in due course unless he or she has converted the instrument, in which case he or she would not meet the requirements of a holder in due course. The transferee also could not become a holder in due course if he or she had notice of a breach of fiduciary duty discussed above.

Section 3-206(f) states, "in an action to enforce the obligation of a party to pay the instrument, the obligor has a defense if payment would violate an indorsement to which this section applies and the payment is not permitted by this section." For example, Bill Wiltshire issues a check that is indorsed, "For deposit only to the account of Flashback Music, Inc." and the check is dishonored upon presentment. The depositary bank determines that it had taken the check for deposit to the account of Joel Converse and not to the account of Flashback. In this situation, the depositary bank could not enforce the obligation of Bill to pay the instrument. The check was not taken in accordance with the restrictive indorsement; therefore, Bill Wiltshire, the drawer, cannot be held liable on his obligation to pay the instrument upon dishonor of the item by the drawee.

5.4 DEPOSITARY BANK BECOMES HOLDER OF UNINDORSED ITEM

The general rule governing negotiable instruments as stated above and in Chapters 1 and 4, is that negotiation of an instrument payable to an

identified person requires the indorsement of that person. An exception
to that general rule is when a depositary bank takes a check from its
customer for collection. Section 4-205 provides the following:

If a customer delivers an item to a depositary bank for collection:
(1) the depositary bank becomes a holder of the item at the time it receives the item for collection if the customer at the time of delivery was
a holder of the item, whether or not the customer indorses the item,
and, if the bank satisfies the other requirements of Section 3-302, it is a
holder in due course; and (2) the depositary bank warrants to collecting
banks, the payor bank or other payor, and the drawer that the amount
of the item was paid to the customer or deposited to the customer's
account.

The previous version of Article 4 allowed a bank to supply a missing indorsement. The problem with that section, from the standpoint of
a depositary bank, was that the bank only became a holder of the item
if it did in fact supply the indorsement prior to entering the item into
the bank collection process. Since the bank was not a holder of the item
in this situation, the bank could not be a holder in due course and took
the item subject to all claims and defenses. For example, assume that
Flashback Music, Inc. deposited a check but neglected to indorse the
check. The check is presented for payment and payment is refused because the drawer had stopped payment on the check. The depositary
bank unsuccessfully attempts to collect the check from Flashback. The
depositary bank then attempts to enforce payment against the drawer
of the check. The drawer defends on the grounds that Flashback did not
make an appearance. The depositary bank claims holder in due course
status and the drawer argues that the bank was not a holder and therefore could not be a holder in due course (see *Barber v. United States
National Bank of Oregon, 5 UCC Rep Serv 2d 1399*). This problem is resolved for the depositary bank under the revised Section 4-205. The depository bank becomes a holder of the instrument even though the
customer fails to indorse the instrument. By virtue of the fact that the
bank took the item for collection, the bank becomes a holder of the item
even without the indorsement of the customer.

Under this section, the depositary bank warrants that the proceeds
of the instrument were paid to the customer or deposited to the customer's account. The section does not address the outcome for breach of
the warranty. It would appear that if the amount of the item was not
paid to the customer or deposited to the account, that the depositary
bank would not be a holder of the item, could not enforce the item

against and would be subject to an action of conversion of the instrument on the part of the customer.

This section will also provide much needed relief to banks with manual lockbox and mail in teller operations. These banks currently must manually supply the indorsement on checks sent in for deposit.

5.5 ITEMS INDORSED "PAY ANY BANK"

Typically, most depositary banks indorse checks with the words "pay any bank." The purpose of this indorsement is to prevent the item from being transferred outside of bank collection channels. Section 4-201(b) states, "After an item has been indorsed with the words "pay any bank" or like, only a bank may acquire the rights of a holder until the item has been:

(1) returned to the customer initiating collection; or

(2) specially indorsed by a bank to a person who is not a bank."

This section is an exception to Section 3-206 that an indorsement cannot restrict negotiation of an instrument. The affect of this section is to restrict negotiation of an instrument to banks only. The item may be negotiated by a holder other than a bank if the item is returned to the customer initiating collection. The item would obviously only be returned after it had been presented and dishonored. The customer initiating collection could then negotiate the item to a person other than a bank. The person to whom the item is negotiated becomes a holder of the item.

A person other than a bank can also become a holder of the item if the item is specially indorsed by a bank. For whatever reason, a bank could indorse a check to an identified person to take the item out of the banking channels. The bank could, for example, indorse the check to a person that is not a bank for collection of the item.

5.6 FORGED AND MISSING INDORSEMENTS

One of the major causes of loss for banks and one of the major sources of litigation arise out of forged or missing indorsements. Since numerous claims arise out of employee theft, hopefully, many of the disputes will be resolved by Section 3-405 dealing with employer's responsibility for fraudulent indorsements by an employee. Unfortunately the disputes will continue as long as dishonest people are allowed to obtain possession of instruments to which they have no rights.

The issuer of a negotiable instrument is entitled to an indorsement if the instrument is payable to an identified person. Of course, if the instrument is payable to bearer, no indorsement is required. Section 3-201 states that negotiation of an instrument payable to an identified person requires the indorsement of that person to negotiate the instrument. The transferee of the instrument does not become the holder if a required indorsement is forged or missing. The rightful owner of the instrument or the person entitled to enforce the instrument has a claim to the instrument if the indorsement is forged or the instrument is transferred without the proper indorsement. This section will address the rights, liabilities, and obligations of the parties to an instrument containing forged or missing indorsements.

(a) UNAUTHORIZED INDORSEMENT

An unauthorized signature is defined in Section 1-201(41) as a signature "made without actual, implied, or apparent authority and includes a forgery." If an instrument is payable to an identified person, that person's indorsement is required for negotiation of the instrument. If the holder loses possession of the instrument and his signature is made on the instrument without authority, then the indorsement is unauthorized. Section 3-403(a) states that an unauthorized signature is ineffective as the signature of the person's name that is signed. For example, if a check is payable to Bill Wiltshire and Joel Converse steals the check and indorses the check by signing Bill's name, the indorsement is ineffective except as the signature of Joel.

An instrument that contains an unauthorized indorsement, therefore, cannot be enforced against the person whose name is forged on the instrument or against the drawer. The check payable to Bill Wiltshire in the example above cannot be enforced against the drawer since it contains an unauthorized indorsement. Any person dealing with the instrument containing the unauthorized indorsement is subject to the claims of the rightful owner of the instrument or the person entitled to enforce the instrument.

The unauthorized indorsement can, however, be made effective against the person to be charged. The methods of making the indorsement effective are discussed in Section 5.7.

(b) CONVERSION OF INSTRUMENT

"Conversion" is defined in the Revised Fourth Edition of Black's Law Dictionary as "any unauthorized act which deprives an owner of his property permanently or for an indefinite time." A thief that steals an instrument or a person that finds a lost instrument and signs the name of the holder or transfers the instrument without the required indorsement has converted the instrument. Section 3-420 addresses conversion of an instrument and states, in part, in Subsection (a), "The law applicable to conversion of personal property applies to instruments. An instrument is also converted if it is taken by transfer, other than negotiation, from a person not entitled to enforce the instrument or a bank makes or obtains payment with respect to the instrument for a person not entitled to enforce the instrument or receive payment." In addition to state law applicable to conversion, this Subsection states that an instrument is converted if it is taken by transfer from a person not entitled to enforce the instrument and the transfer was not by negotiation. What this means is that a person converts an instrument if he or she takes an unindorsed instrument that requires an indorsement. For example, assume that a check payable to Bill Wiltshire is stolen and his name is forged by the thief. The thief then transfers the check to Joel Converse who had no knowledge of the theft. Joel has converted the check and is subject to an action for conversion of the property of Bill.

As stated above, a bank that makes payment to or obtains payment for a person not entitled to enforce the instrument also converts the instrument. In the example above, if Joel Converse deposits the check in a bank, and the bank obtains payment for Joel, the bank has converted the instrument and is subject to an action for conversion by Bill.

Subsection (a) also specifically designates the persons that may not bring an action for conversion. A person must own or be entitled to property before it can be converted. This is also true of instruments. A person that does not own or that is not entitled to an instrument cannot bring an action for conversion for an instrument. Section 3-420(a) also provides, "An action for conversion of an instrument may not be brought by (i) the issuer or acceptor of the instrument or (ii) a payee or indorsee who did not receive delivery of the instrument either directly or through delivery to an agent or a co-payee." Finally, this section will straighten out the problems caused by courts that have allowed issuers, payees, and indorsers to successfully bring conversion actions. This section recognizes that the issuer of a check or other instrument is not the owner of the instrument. Other than the value of the paper on which the instrument is written, the issuer has no property interest in and has no right to enforce the instrument. The drawer of a check for example, issues an order to the drawee to pay the instrument to a holder. If the drawee pays the amount of the check to one that is not a holder, the drawer's remedies are against the drawee bank and not against the depositary bank that took the item. This section should once and for all settle this issue and make it clear that the issuer of an instrument does not have a cause of action and may not bring an action for conversion on an instrument he or she issues.

The other problem cleared up by this section is the question of whether a payee or an indorser can bring an action for conversion of an instrument that has not been delivered to the payee or the indorsee. As stated above, the answer is that an action for conversion of an instrument may not be brought by the payee or indorser that has not received delivery of the instrument. An example of the application of this section is as follows. Chip Sanders writes a check to Cindy Faulkner and leaves the check on his desk. That night a thief steals the check, forges Cindy's indorsement and obtains payment for the check by depositing the check in the First Deposit Bank. Section 3-420(a) makes it clear that Cindy may not bring an action for conversion for the check against the First Deposit Bank. Cindy did not receive delivery of the check so the check was therefore not issued to her, she had no property interest in the check and she certainly could not enforce the check against Chip Sanders. Issuance of an instrument is discussed in Section 1.3 of Chapter 1 of this book.

Cindy is not without remedies, however. The underlying obligation for which the check was issued has not been satisfied or suspended. Since the check was not issued, the underlying obligation for which Chip issued the check still exists. Chip is still obligated to Cindy for the obligation and Cindy's remedy is against Chip for nonpayment of the obligation. As discussed above, Chip also has remedies. Chip has a cause of action against the payor bank for paying the item with a forged indorsement. The payor bank then has a cause of action against the First Deposit Bank for breach of the presentment warranties under Sections 3-417 and 4-208. Both of these sections are discussed in Chapter 2 of this book.

An issue that must be addressed under Subsection (a) is the issue of whether the instrument has or has not been delivered to the payee or indorser. Subsection (a)(ii) does state that delivery may be either directly or indirectly through an agent or a co-payee. If a check is delivered to the payee and is stolen from the payee's mailbox, then the check was delivered and the payee may bring an action for conversion. If a check was delivered to an employee, a partner or other agent acting for and on behalf of the payee, then delivery has been made. An instrument payable to joint payees, whether in the alternative or not, is delivered upon receipt of the instrument by one of the co-payees. A check payable to Bill and Joel is delivered upon receipt of the check by Bill. If Bill transfers the check without Joel's indorsement, then Joel may bring an action for conversion of the check.

The measure of damages for conversion of an instrument under Subsection (a) is provided for in Section 3-420(b). That section states, "In an action under Subsection (a), the measure of liability is presumed to be the amount payable on the instrument, but recovery may not exceed the amount of the plaintiff's interest in the instrument." This section also clears up the controversy over the amount the plaintiff is entitled to. Some courts have awarded the plaintiff the entire amount of the instrument when the plaintiff only had a partial interest in the instrument. Equity requires that the plaintiff be paid no more than the plaintiff's interest in the instrument. For example, if a check was issued payable jointly to Chip Sanders and Mike Harris and Mike Harris had only one-fourth interest in the check, then the amount of recovery that Mike is entitled to, if the check is converted by Chip, is only one-fourth of the amount of the check.

A significant change, to the detriment of depositary banks, is that under the previous version of Article 3, a depositary bank was liable in conversion only for the amount of the proceeds remaining in the hands of the bank. This limitation of liability applied only if the depositary bank exercised reasonable commercial standards in accepting the item for deposit. The revised version completely excludes the depositary bank from this limitation. Subsection (c) states, "A representative, other than a depositary bank, who has in good faith dealt with an instrument or its proceed on behalf of one who was not the person entitled to enforce the instrument is not liable in conversion to that person beyond the amount of any proceeds that it has not paid out." The depositary bank was excluded from this limitation, according to Official Comment #3 to Section 3-420, because the depositary bank will ultimately be liable. If the owner of the instrument or a person entitled to enforce it may not recover from the depositary bank, then multiple actions will be required to recover the proceeds. The rightful owner would have to obtain payment from the issuer of the item, who in turn would bring an action against the payor bank, who would bring an action for breach of presentment warranty against the depositary bank.

Subsection (c) does apply to any intermediary collecting banks between the payor bank and the depositary bank. For example, a check payable to Bill is stolen from Bill and his indorsement is forged. The check is deposited in an account in the depositary bank and is sent to the payor bank through collecting banks A and B. Shortly after the check is deposited in the account at the depositary bank, all of the funds are withdrawn from the account. All three banks are liable for conversion under Subsection (a); however, collecting banks A and B are only liable for the amount of money that they have not paid out. Since A and B have paid out all of the proceeds, neither one of the banks is liable for conversion. On the other hand, the depositary bank remains liable in conversion to the person entitled to enforce the instrument. All three banks remain liable for breach of presentment warranty under Sections 3-417 and 4-207.

(c) CLAIMS TO AN INSTRUMENT

Section 3-420 deals only with instruments that were not transferred by negotiation. In other words, the transferee did not become a holder of the instrument because a required indorsement was missing or unauthorized. Section 3-306 deals with all situations wherein a person takes an instrument that is subject to the rights of another person. That section provides, "A person taking an instrument, other than a person having rights of a holder in due course, is subject to a claim of a property or possessory right in the instrument or its proceeds, including a claim to rescind a negotiation and to recover the instrument or its proceeds. A person having rights of a holder in due course takes free of the claim to the instrument." This section makes it clear that a holder in due course takes the instrument free of all claims to the instrument on the part of all parties.

For example, if Bill Wiltshire indorses a check in blank and loses the check and the check is found by Joel Converse, Joel is a holder of the instrument. Bill, of course, has a claim to the instrument and he may recover the instrument or its proceeds from Joel.

Assume further in this example that Joel negotiates the check to Leonard Wink and Leonard meets all of the requirements of a holder in due course. Although Bill is the rightful owner of the check, Leonard takes the check free of Bill's claim to it. Holder in due course is discussed in detail in Chapter 6 of this book.

This section also applies to the rights of a party that is not the owner of the instrument. It applies to any person that has a property or possessory right in the instrument. For example, assume that Mike Harris and Leonard Wink enter into a contract wherein Mike is to perform a service for Leonard and Mike is concerned as to whether Leonard is capable of paying for the service. At the same time, Leonard is not willing to pay in advance for the services. Leonard does agree, however, to have his bank issue a cashier's check payable to Leonard and he delivers the unindorsed check to Mike. Leonard agrees that upon completion of the work he will indorse the check. During the course of performing the service, a thief steals the unindorsed cashier's check. Mike is not the holder of the check, but he does have a possessory right in the instrument and he, therefore, has a claim to the instrument under Section 3-306.

5.7 FORGED INDORSEMENTS MADE EFFECTIVE

Section 5.6 of this chapter dealt with forged or missing indorsements wherein the holder or other person entitled to enforce the instrument was entitled to recovery from the person that dealt with the forger. This section will address the situations wherein the unauthorized or missing indorsement is made effective against the holder or other person entitled to enforce the instrument.

(a) NEGLIGENCE CONTRIBUTING TO A FORGED SIGNATURE

The fact that a person's signature is forged does not automatically relieve that person from all obligation and liability on an instrument. The facts and circumstances surrounding the forgery are very important and play an important part in determining the liability of the parties. If a bank handles an item that has a forged or unauthorized indorsement, the first impression is that the bank is liable and should pay the proceeds of the item to the claimant. On the contrary, the bank may have no liability at all because of the failure of the claimant to exercise the proper care to prevent the loss in the first place. Section 3-406 is one such section that looks at the conduct of the party making a claim. Subsection (a) states, "A person whose failure to exercise ordinary care substantially contributes to an alteration of an instrument or to the making of a forged signature on an instrument is precluded from asserting the alteration or the forgery against a person who, in good faith, pays the instrument or takes it for value or for collection."

The standard of care to be used is not defined but is left up to the courts to make this determination. The person must, however, exercise "ordinary care" which is defined in Section 3-103(a)(7) as "in the case of a person engaged in business means observance of reasonable commercial standards, prevailing in the area in which the person is located, with respect to the business in which the person is engaged." The definition also includes the care for a bank which is not stated here. The facts of each case will be different and will have to be examined to determine the impact of the action on the outcome.

The failure to exercise ordinary care must "substantially contribute" to the making of the forgery. Once the care or lack of care is determined, the next question to be answered is, did it substantially contribute to the forgery?

"Substantially contributes" is not defined anywhere in the Uniform Commercial Code. Official Comment #2 to Section 3-406 does attempt to define "substantially contributes" as follows: "Conduct substantially contributes to a material alteration or forged signature if it is a contributing cause of the alteration or signature and a substantial factor in bringing it about." Here again, the court will have to make the determination as to whether or not the conduct "substantially contributed" to the making of the forged signature.

The court in *Chicago Heights Currency Exchange, Inc. v. Par Steel Products And Services Co., Inc., 38 UCC Rep Serv 1680*, held that the question of negligence that "substantially contributes" to a forgery is a question best left up to local law and should be determined on a case-by-case basis. The court found that a stockbroker's negligence substantially contributed to the making of a forged indorsement in *Bagby v. Merrill Lynch, Pierce, Fenner & Smith, Inc. v. Commerce Bank Of Kansas City v. Traders National Bank, 11 UCC Rep Serv 766*. In that case, the stockbroker allowed an attorney to open up several accounts for the attorney's client without the proper authority of the client. The attorney then sold securities and forged the client's signature on checks issued by the stockbroker in settlement of the securities that were sold. The actions of the broker were in violation of internal procedures and the Rules of the New York Stock Exchange.

An example of where the conduct of a party substantially contributed to the making of a forged indorsement is contained in Official Comment #3 to Section 3-406. In that example, an insurance company sends a check to the wrong policy holder with the same name as that of the person to whom the insurance intended to send the check to. The wrong policy holder signs the name of the intended payee to the check and cashes the check. In this case, the failure to exercise ordinary care could be found by the court to have substantially contributed to the making of the forgery. The indorsement would then be made effective against the drawer of the check and the drawer would be precluded from asserting the forged indorsement against the payor bank.

As provided for in Section 3-406(b) if the person asserting the preclusion under Subsection (a) fails to exercise ordinary care that substantially contributes to the loss, the loss is apportioned among the parties based on their respective contributions to the loss. This section applies the comparative negligence approach. Section 3-406 is also discussed in Chapter 3 of this book. Please refer to that Chapter for additional information on this section.

(b) RATIFICATION OF AN UNAUTHORIZED INDORSEMENT

An unauthorized signature is ineffective as the signature of the person whose name is signed. But the signature is effective as the signature of the unauthorized signer as provided for in Section 3-403. That section also states, "An unauthorized signature may be ratified for all purposes of this Article." If a person's indorsement is forged on an instrument, the indorsement is ineffective as that of the person and any transferee that takes the instrument does not become a holder. However, the person whose indorsement is forged, can ratify the indorsement as provided for in Section 3-403(a). Ratification is discussed in Chapter 3 and will only be briefly addressed here.

An example of ratification of an indorsement is as follows. A check made payable to Bill Wiltshire is stolen and his indorsement is forged. Upon investigation, Bill determines that the check was stolen by his good friend Joel Converse. Bill forgives his friend and a month later Joel steals another check and forges Bill's name. Bill is upset with his friend but once again forgives his friend and ratifies the indorsement. A third check is stolen by Joel and Bill, who is not at all forgiving this time, advises the drawer of the check that this time he wants to claim that his indorsement has been forged. Upon investigation, the drawer determines that on two previous occasions on checks issued by the same drawer that Joel had forged Bill's signature but that Bill had ratified Joel's signature. The drawer would be justified in refusing to issue a replacement check to Bill since he had ratified the signature on two other occasions.

Another example of the application of this section dealing with a check payable to joint payees is as follows. Henry and Melonie jointly own stock in a corporation. The quarterly dividend checks are issued to them jointly and not in the alternative. Section 3-110 provides that the indorsement of all payees is required to negotiate a check that is payable to two or more people jointly. Most of the time, Henry indorses the checks for both he and Melonie and deposits the checks to their joint account. This arrangement went on for two years until the marriage of Henry and Melonie started having difficulties. While trying to reach a property settlement, Melonie realizes that she did not indorse as many as three-fourths of the dividend checks. She obtains copies of the checks from the corporation and claims that she did not indorse the checks and that she is entitled to at least half of the proceeds of the checks on which her indorsement is forged. The corporation could claim that Melonie had ratified her husband's actions because he had indorsed the checks for two years, she was aware of this fact, and she never objected to his signing her name. Additionally, the checks were deposited to a joint account to which she had access and she also received the benefit of the proceeds of the check.

(c) IMPOSTORS AND FICTITIOUS PAYEES

Section 3-404 offers one of the most powerful tools available to a person attempting to make an indorsement effective. This section addresses situations involving fictitious payees, impostors, and persons supplying names to the issuer of the instrument. The section is based on the principle that the issuer of the instrument is in the best position to prevent a loss of this nature.

DRAWER INDUCED TO ISSUE CHECK

Subsection (a) provides that an indorsement is effective as the indorsement of a payee if an impostor induces the issuer to issue the instrument to the impostor or to a person acting in concert with the impostor. The inducement to issue the instrument can be made by use of the mails or any other method such as by phone, fax, telegram, or even in person. The method of the inducement is not material.

The impostor must, however, impersonate the payee of the instrument or a person authorized to act for the payee. The impostor could impersonate an agent of the payee that the issuer knew had the authority to act on behalf of the payee. This is a change from the previous version of this section. Under the old version, the impostor had to impersonate the payee. The indorsement was not effective if the impostor impersonated a person acting on behalf of the payee, so held some courts.

The indorsement can be made by any person in the name of the payee. When so indorsed, the instrument is effective as the indorsement of the payee in favor of a person who pays the instrument or takes it for value or for collection. The instrument must, however, be taken in good faith. For example, Joel Converse writes a letter to the Flashback Insurance Co. representing himself as Bill Wiltshire and requests the insurance company to send the cash value of his life insurance policy to him at his new address. The insurance company writes a check payable to Bill Wiltshire and mails the check to the address provided in the letter. The address, of course, is that of Joel Converse. Joel forges Bill's name on the check and deposits the check in his, Joel's, account at the First Deposit Bank. The check is presented to the payor bank and is paid. Section 3-404 makes the forged indorsement effective against the drawer, Flashback Insurance Co. The insurance company was induced by Joel, who impersonated Bill, to issue the check.

PAYEE NOT INTENDED TO RECEIVE PAYMENT

Subsection (b) contains additional provisions that make an indorsement effective. This Subsection addresses the situation where a person whose intent determines to whom an instrument is payable does not intend the person identified as payee to have any interest in the instrument or the person identified as payee is a fictitious person. This situation typically involves someone that is signing in a representative capacity on behalf of the issuer, such as the treasurer or some other officer or employee. However, it may also be a situation where the signature of the issuer is forged. In this situation, the indorsement is made effective and any person that has possession of the instrument is its holder.

Identification of the person to whom an instrument is payable and the intention of the person signing the instrument is governed by Section 3-110, which is discussed in section 1.4 of Chapter 1 of this book. Briefly stated, that section provides the person to whom an instrument is payable is determined by the person signing, with or without authority, as or on behalf of the issuer of the instrument. If more than one person signs, the instrument is payable to any person intended by one or more of the signers. If the signature of the issuer is made by automated means, the payee is determined by the intent of the person who supplied the name of the payee, whether or not authorized.

The following is an example of the application of this subsection. Cindy Faulkner is the treasurer of Flashback Music, Inc. and is an authorized signatory on Flashback's checking account. Cindy draws a check and makes the instrument payable to Melonie Lee and she does not intend for Melonie to have any interest in the check. She then forges Melonie's indorsement and deposits the check in her personal account with the First Deposit Bank. The check is presented to the drawee bank and is paid. The indorsement is effective against Flashback. Flashback would not have a claim against the drawee bank because the indorsement is made effective. Since the indorsement is made effective, there is no forged indorsement and the First Deposit Bank has not breached its transfer or presentment warranties.

Another example of the application of Subsection (b) is as follows. In the example above, assume that Cindy names Amy Carr as the payee and Amy Carr is a fictitious person. The indorsement is effective even though Amy Carr does not exist.

As stated above, this Subsection also applies to situations involving the forged signature of the issuer. For example, a thief steals blank checks from Flashback Music, Inc., writes several checks to various payees, and forges the name of Cindy Faulkner as the authorized signer on the account. The checks are deposited to various accounts in several different depositary banks. The checks are then presented for payment to the drawee bank and are paid on the account of Flashback. Unless the drawee bank has a defense, the drawee bank is liable to Flashback for paying the checks with the forged signature of Cindy Faulkner. The drawee bank must absorb the loss. The indorsements on the checks are made effective and the drawee bank would not have a claim against the depositary banks for breach of presentment warranty. Official Comment #2 to Section 3-404 contains several excellent examples of the application of Subsection (b).

Subsection (b) also contains a statement of the impact and effect of the issuance of an instrument under this section. Subsection (b) provides that, unless the instrument is negotiated by special indorsement, any person in possession of the instrument is its holder. This section is an exception to the rule that an instrument that identifies a person to whom the instrument is payable requires the indorsement of the identified person to negotiate the instrument. In other words, if an instrument is payable to the order of an identified person, that person must indorse the instrument before any subsequent transferee can become a holder. Subsection (b) states an exception to that general rule and provides that if an instrument is issued as described under the section, any person is the holder. For example, if Cindy Faulkner, treasurer of Flashback, Inc., names Melonie Lee as payee of an instrument but does not intend for Melonie to have any interest in the instrument, any person that has possession of the instrument is a holder even without the indorsement of Melonie. In this example, if the check is delivered to Chip Sanders, Chip becomes the holder of the check even without Melonie's indorsement.

Section 3-404(b)(2) further provides that "an indorsement by any person in the name of the payee stated in the instrument is effective as the indorsement of the payee in favor of a person who, in good faith, pays the instrument or takes it for value or for collection." In the preceding example, if Chip Sanders indorses the check by signing Melonie Lee's name, the indorsement is effective, the same as if Melonie had indorsed the instrument.

Under previous Article 3, some courts held that an indorsement was effective only if it were made exactly in the name of the named payee. Any variation in the indorsement from the name of the payee would make the indorsement ineffective. Section 3-404(c) corrects this defect. Subsection (c) states, "Under Subsection (a) or (b), an indorsement is made in the name of a payee if (i) it is made in a name substantially similar to that of the payee or (ii) the instrument, whether or not indorsed, is deposited in a depositary bank to an account in a name substantially similar to that of the payee." Under the old version, if a check were payable to Flashback Music, Inc. and was indorsed "Flashback," the indorsement would not be effective. Under the revised version quoted above, it would appear that the indorsement is "substantially similar" and would therefore be effective.

Section 4-205(a) provides that instruments may be deposited without indorsements and the depositary bank becomes a holder of the instrument provided the instrument is deposited to the account of the person entitled to enforce the instrument. Subsection (c) recognizes that items may be taken by depositary banks without indorsements. In this case, the instrument must be deposited to an account styled "substantially similar" to the name of the person entitled to enforce the instrument.

Subsection (d) provides that "with respect to an instrument to which Subsection (a) or (b) applies, if a person paying the instrument or taking it for value or for collection fails to exercise ordinary care in paying or taking the instrument and that failure substantially contributes to loss resulting from payment of the instrument, the person bearing the loss may recover from the person failing to exercise ordinary care to the extent the failure to exercise ordinary care contributed to the loss." As in many other revised sections of Article 3, comparative negligence has been introduced to this section. The loss is allocated among the parties based on their care or lack of care. For example, if a check were payable to Flashback Music, Inc. and the depositary bank allowed a person to open an account without the proper corporate board of directors resolution, the court could find that such a failure on the part of the depositary bank was a failure to exercise ordinary care that substantially contributed to the loss. The loss would then be allocated between the bank and the other party based on the extent to which the failure contributed to the loss.

(d) EMPLOYER'S RESPONSIBILITY FOR FRAUDULENT INDORSEMENT BY EMPLOYEE

Section 3-405 is a new section that specifically addresses and recognizes the responsibility of an employer relative to the fraudulent activities of an employee. Many cases of forged indorsements are the result of a fraudulent employee and an employer that had very little or no procedures in place to detect or prevent the fraudulent activities of a dishonest employee. This section basically holds the employer liable for the fraudulent activities of an employee that is given certain responsibilities relative to instruments that are issued to the employer as payee or by the employer to other persons. Subsection (b) provides the following:

For the purpose of determining the rights and liabilities of a person who, in good faith, pays an instrument or takes it for value or for collection, if an employer entrusted an employee with responsibility with respect to the instrument and the employee or a person acting in concert with the employee makes a fraudulent indorsement of the instrument, the indorsement is effective as the indorsement of the person to whom the instrument is payable if it is made in the name of that person.

The indorsement is made in the name of the person to whom an instrument is payable if the indorsement is made in a name substantially similar to the name of that person as provided for in Subsection (c). That Subsection also provides that the indorsement is made in the name of the payee if the instrument is deposited in a depositary bank to an account in a name substantially similar to the name of that person. Subsection (c) is identical to Section 3-404(c) discussed earlier.

Subsection (a) contains three definitions that are vitally important in determining the application of Subsection (b).

The terms defined are: "employee," "fraudulent indorsement," and "responsibility." The definition of "employee" in Subsection (a)(1) is intended to include the normal definition of employee but also "includes an independent contractor and employee of an independent contractor retained by the employer." "Independent Contractor" is defined the Revised Fourth Edition of Black's Law Dictionary as "One who, exercising an independent employment, contracts to do a piece of work according to his own methods and without being subject to the control of his employer except as to the result of the work."

"Fraudulent indorsement" is defined in Subsection (a)(2) to mean "(i) in the case of an instrument payable to the employer, a forged indorsement purporting to be that of the employer, or (ii) in the case of an instrument with respect to which the employer is the issuer, a forged indorsement purporting to be that of the person identified as payee." "Fraudulent indorsement" therefore applies to both a situation where an instrument is payable to the employer and the situation where the employer issues a check to a payee.

The definition of "responsibility" is contained in Subsection (a)(3). According to that section, "responsibility" includes any activity involving instruments other than authority that merely allows an employee to have access to instruments or blank or incomplete instrument forms that are being stored or transported. Activities specifically included are authority:

(1) To sign or indorse instruments on behalf of the employer,

(2) To process instruments received by the employer for bookkeeping purposes, for deposit to an account, or for other disposition,

(3) To prepare or process instruments for issue in the name of the employer,

(4) To supply information determining the names or addresses of payees of instruments to be issued in the name of the employer,

(5) To control the disposition of instrument to be issued in the name of the employer, and

(6) To act otherwise with respect to instrument in a responsible capacity.

The determination as to whether or not an activity is included in the definition of "responsibility" will be a key determinant in establishing liability. In some cases, the activity will be specifically excluded as those stated in the Subsection where the employee merely has access to the instruments. However, in other situations, the distinction will not be as clear. For that reason, each of the six items listed above will be discussed. The first is the authority of the employee "to sign or indorse instruments on behalf of the employer." Establishing this authority may or may not be a simple matter. If the authority is actual authority established by a writing such as a corporate resolution, the authority to sign is clear. However, if the authority to act in this capacity is not clearly established, it may be difficult to establish the authority. For example, if Melonie Lee's responsibilities did not normally include processing items or fall within any of the other listed items, but on occasion she signed checks for her boss, the fact that she did sign checks in the past would have to be established to show her authority. This type of authority may be very difficult to establish. Once the authority is established, then the activities of the employee fall squarely within this Subsection.

The next item listed is the authority "to process instruments received by the employer for bookkeeping purposes, for deposit to an account, or for other disposition." This authority is fairly broad but is tempered by the last sentence in Subsection (a) that states that responsibility does not include authority that merely allows an employee to have access to instruments. It appears there is a fine line between authority that only allows an employee to have access to an instrument and authority to process instruments. For example, an employee that simply picks items up at the post office and delivers them to the proper department for processing only has access to the instrument. What about the employee that opens up envelopes and extracts the checks for further processing? It would appear that this activity would still only fit into the "has access" category and would not establish the required authority to constitute "responsibility." Having said that, however, the best interpretation of this section might simply be that if the employee has any authority whatsoever over the instrument, other than pick-up or delivery, that such activity establishes the required authority to constitute "responsibility."

The authority "to prepare or process instruments for issue in the name of the employer" deals with instruments issued by the employer as opposed to those above where the employer was named as payee. In some situations, employees fill in the blanks on the instrument issued by the employer and the employer signs the completed instrument. For example, assume that the employee types the information in the blanks on a check and the employer signs the check. Instead of mailing the check to the payee, the employee forges the indorsement of the payee. In this example, the employee had the authority to prepare or process the instrument for issue. This duty meets the requirements to designate that employee as having "responsibility" with respect to the instrument. The indorsement in this example is therefore effective against the employer. Another example of duties that would fit into this category is an employee that prepares checks that are computer generated. Many employers issue payroll and accounts payable checks by computer and employees are responsible for the preparation of these items.

Two more duties are listed in Subsection (a)(3) that deal with the issuance of instruments. One involves the authority of an employee to supply information determining the names or addresses of payees and the other deals with the authority to control the disposition of instruments to be issued in the name of the employer. An example of the first of these two is what is referred to as the "padded payroll." This situation involves a supervisor or other person in position of authority that supplies the employer with the names of payees that either do not exist or payees that do exist but for which the employee does not intend for them to have an interest in the check. If an employee with this authority forges the indorsement of the payee, the indorsement is made effective against the employer. Another example of this duty is an employee that supplies the employer with the address of the payee and supplies the employee's own address. If the employee then forges the indorsement of the payee, the indorsement is effective against the employer. In the second situation describing the duty of the employee, the employee is responsible for the disposition of instruments issued by the employer. An example of this duty is where the employer simply signs checks and it is the duty of the employee to get the checks to the payee. Unless controls are put in place by the employer, a dishonest employee could steal the check and forge the indorsement of the payee. If such a forgery occurs, the indorsement is effective against the employer.

The final item listed in paragraph 3 is somewhat of a general statement relative to an employee's duties that applies to both instruments that are issued to the employer and those issued by the employer. It is a "catch all" phrase that states that an employee has "responsibility" with respect to an instrument if the employee has the authority "to act otherwise with respect to instruments in a responsible capacity." Again, responsibility does not include authority that merely allows an employee to have access to instruments, but if the employee has any other duties of a responsible nature, then a court could find that the employee had responsibility with respect to the instrument. Any indorsement made by the employee or other person working in concert with the employee could be made effective against the employer.

The employer is not automatically assigned strict liability if an employee with responsibility with respect to an instrument forges the indorsement of the payee. The last sentence of Section 3-405(b) states, "If the person paying the instrument or taking it for value or for collection fails to exercise ordinary care in paying or taking the instrument and that failure substantially contributes to loss resulting from the fraud, the person bearing the loss may recover from the person failing to exercise ordinary care to the extent the failure to exercise ordinary care contributed to the loss."

For example, Melonie Lee is an employee of Flashback Music, Inc. and part of her duties are to prepare checks for payment of accounts payable invoices. Melonie receives an invoice from Sanders Musical Equipment, Inc. She prepares a check payable to Sanders Musical Equipment, Inc. and has the president of Flashback Music, Inc. sign the check. Instead of mailing the check to the payee, Melonie forges the indorsement of Sanders Musical Equipment, Inc. on the check and deposits it in her personal account at the First Deposit Bank and withdraws the proceeds. The court could find that the First Deposit Bank did not exercise ordinary care by allowing Melonie to deposit a check payable to a corporate payee to her personal account. The court could further determine that the failure of the Bank to exercise ordinary care substantially contributed to the Loss and could assign part or all of the loss to the Bank.

5.8 DISCHARGE OF INDORSER

The discharge of an indorser is governed by Section 3-605 which is discussed in Chapter 10 of this book. Please refer to Chapter 10 for a detailed discussion of the indorser's discharge.

CHAPTER 6

HOLDER, NONHOLDER, AND HOLDER IN DUE COURSE

The concept of holders was discussed in a fair amount of detail in previous chapters. The reader should be familiar with the concept of negotiation and how a person becomes a holder before reading this chapter. One must first be a holder before one can become a holder in due course. For this reason, the reader must understand fully how a person becomes a holder. This chapter discusses the rights of a holder, a transferee that is not a holder, and a holder that has attained the coveted status of holder in due course.

6.1 HOLDER DEFINED

The transferee of an instrument that obtained the instrument through negotiation is said to be a holder. Negotiation and transfer are governed by Section 3-201 and are discussed in detail in Chapter 4. A "holder" is defined in Section 1-201(20) as "with respect to a negotiable instrument, the person in possession if the instrument is payable to bearer or, in the case of an instrument payable to an identified person, if the identified person is in possession." The determination as to whether an instrument is payable to bearer is governed by Section 3-109, which is discussed in Chapter 1. According to that section, an instrument payable "to order or bearer" is payable to bearer and any person in possession is a holder. An instrument payable to cash or indicates that it is not

115

payable to an identified person, is payable to bearer. An instrument that does not state a payee is payable to bearer. Likewise, an instrument that is payable to an identified person but is indorsed in blank, is payable to bearer. In each of these situations, any person in possession of the instrument is a holder.

The person in possession of an instrument that is payable to the order of an identified person is only a holder if the person in possession is the person identified. For example, if Bill Wiltshire is in the possession of a check payable to "Bill Wiltshire," he is the holder of the instrument. If Bill Wiltshire is in possession of an instrument that is payable to any other identified person, he is not a holder, but he may be a transferee with rights to enforce the instrument. The fact that a person is not a holder does not mean that that person does not have an interest in the instrument or rights to enforce it. Rights acquired by transfer are governed by Section 3-203 and are discussed in Chapter 4 of this book.

6.2 PERSON ENTITLED TO ENFORCE AN INSTRUMENT

Many of the sections throughout Article 3 make reference to the "person entitled to enforce" an instrument. "Person entitled to enforce" an instrument is defined in Section 3-301 as the following:

(i) the holder of the instrument,

(ii) a nonholder in possession of the instrument who has the rights of a holder, or

(iii) a person not in possession of the instrument who is entitled to enforce the instrument pursuant to Section 3-309 or 3-418(d). A person may be a person entitled to enforce the instrument even though the person is not the owner of the instrument or is in wrongful possession of the instrument.

(a) HOLDER OF THE INSTRUMENT

The first person listed under Section 3-301 who is entitled to enforce an instrument is the holder of the instrument. This should be obvious and should go without saying. In most situations, the holder of the instrument is the owner of the instrument and there should be no question as to the rights of the holder to enforce the instrument. However, the holder is not always the owner of the instrument. This section only addresses the person entitled to enforce the instrument and does not consider any potential claims that may be made by the rightful owner or defenses that may be raised. As stated above and in earlier chapters, any person in possession of an instrument payable to bearer is the holder of the instrument regardless of how that person became the holder. This holder, whether obtaining that status through voluntary or involuntary negotiation, is the person entitled to enforce the instrument. The holder's right to enforce the instrument may be subject to a superior claim to the instrument or to some defense on the part of some party. Claims and defenses to an instrument will be discussed later. The point here that must be made clear is that the holder of the instrument is the "person entitled to enforce" an instrument.

An example of the application of this section is as follows. A check was issued to Bill Wiltshire by Flashback Music, Inc. in the amount of $1,000. Bill is the holder of the check because the check is payable to him and he is in possession of it. However, assume that Bill indorsed the check in blank without any restrictions and placed the check in his wallet. Assume further that Bill lost his wallet, Joel Converse found it and took the check. Joel became the holder and is the person entitled to enforce the instrument. Upon indorsement of the check, the check became payable to bearer and Joel became the holder of the check by possession. The check is still subject to a claim by Bill.

(b) NONHOLDER OF THE INSTRUMENT

A nonholder of the instrument in possession of the instrument who has the rights of a holder is also a person entitled to enforce the instrument. Section 3-203(a), which is discussed in Chapter 4 of this book, provides that "an instrument is transferred when it is delivered by a person other than its issuer for the purpose of giving to the person receiving delivery the right to enforce the instrument." For example, Robert Hales agrees to perform certain services for Flashback Music, Inc. Robert wants payment in advance but Flashback is not willing to pay until the work is performed. Flashback suggests, and Robert agrees, that Flashback will have its bank issue a cashier's check payable to Flashback and Flashback will deliver the check to Robert. Upon completion, Flashback will indorse the check to Robert. Upon delivery of the check to Robert, he became the person entitled to enforce the instrument even though he is not the holder.

(c) PERSON NOT IN POSSESSION

A person not in possession of an instrument may have the right to enforce an instrument if that person meets the requirements of Section 3-309 dealing with enforcement of lost, destroyed, or stolen instruments. Section 3-309 is discussed below in the following section. A person not in possession may also enforce the instrument if he or she meets the requirements of Section 3-418(d), which is discussed in Chapter 9 of this book. If an instrument is paid by mistake, the payor or acceptor may recover payment from the person to whom payment was made. The person from whom the payment is recovered from then has the right to enforce the instrument even if that person does not have possession of the instrument. Under Section 3-418(d), the instrument is considered dishonored and deemed not to have been paid.

6.3 ENFORCEMENT OF LOST, DESTROYED, OR STOLEN INSTRUMENTS

Many people are under the mistaken impression that the only solution available to receive payment for a missing instrument is to stop payment on the missing instrument and to issue a new instrument. All too often, payment is stopped on the original that has been reported lost or stolen and the instrument ends up in the hands of a holder in due course and the issuer ends up paying twice. Section 3-309 addresses this situation and offers a solution to both the person obligated on the instrument and the person entitled to enforce the instrument. Section 3-309 (a) provides as follows:

A person not in possession of an instrument is entitled to enforce the instrument if (i) the person was in possession of the instrument and entitled to enforce it when loss of possession occurred, (ii) the loss of possession was not the result of a transfer by the person or a lawful seizure, and (iii) the person cannot reasonably obtain possession of the instrument because the instrument was destroyed, its whereabouts cannot be determined, or it is in the wrongful possession of an unknown person or a person that cannot be found or is not amenable to service of process.

The person attempting to enforce the instrument must have been in possession of the instrument and must have been entitled to enforce the instrument. For example, if Bill Wiltshire wrote a check to Cindy Faulkner but never delivered the check to her, she would not be entitled to enforce the instrument. For this reason, Section 3-420 dealing with the conversion of an instrument provides that an action for conversion may not be brought by a payee or indorsee who did not receive delivery of the instrument. Delivery must have been made before a person has a right to enforce an instrument. In the previous example, the fact that Bill may be liable to Cindy for a debt and the fact that Bill may have actually drawn a check payable to her does not give her the right to enforce the instrument. Therefore, Section 3-309 does not apply to this situation and Cindy would have to pursue collection of the underlying obligation.

The fact that a person had possession of an instrument at one time is not sufficient to give that person the right to enforce a missing instrument. The person must have also had the right to enforce the instrument along with the possession of the instrument. In the example above where Bill had drawn the check to Cindy, assume that Bill did not deliver the check to Cindy, but she got possession of the instrument by some other means and that the check was destroyed. Since Bill did not deliver the check to Cindy, the check was not "issued" to her and Bill would have a defense against payment of the instrument to her. Cindy did not have the right to enforce the instrument; therefore, despite the fact that she had possession, she does not have the right to enforce the destroyed instrument.

The second hurdle that a person attempting to enforce a missing instrument must meet is that the loss of possession was not the result of a transfer by the person or a lawful seizure of the instrument. If Bill issues a check to Cindy and Cindy transfers the check to Joel, Cindy could not enforce the missing instrument. Cindy could not enforce the instrument even if the transfer were not by negotiation. In other words, if Cindy transferred the check to Joel without indorsement, Joel becomes the person entitled to enforce the instrument. If Joel gave value for the check, he is entitled to the unqualified indorsement of Cindy. Upon transfer of the instrument, Cindy lost the right to enforce the instrument unless the instrument was dishonored upon presentment or unless Cindy took the item back from Joel. The point here is that in order to enforce the instrument, the instrument must have been lost, destroyed, or stolen, and not transferred.

The third requirement of Section 3-309 is that the possession of the instrument cannot be reasonably obtained. The instrument must have been destroyed, or its whereabouts cannot be determined, or it is in the possession of some unknown person. Or, if the person that has possession is known, that person cannot be found or is not amenable to service of process. The point of this third requirement is that not only is the instrument missing, but it cannot be found or retrieved. Retrieval of the instrument cannot merely be a hindrance or inconvenience, it must practically be an impossibility to locate and retrieve the instrument. If the instrument can be found or retrieved, then the person entitled to enforce the instrument must pursue retrieving the instrument and then enforce the original instrument.

In addition to Subsection (a), a person attempting to enforce a lost, destroyed, or stolen instrument must also meet the requirements of Subsection (b). Subsection (b) requires that the person seeking to enforce the missing instrument must prove the terms of the instrument and the person's right to enforce the instrument. This burden of proof may be very difficult to meet. It may be easier to pursue collection of the underlying obligation then to attempt to meet the burden of proof required of Subsections (a) and (b). If the person obligated on the instrument denies the existence of the instrument, then it would be very difficult for that person to claim discharge or suspension of the underlying obligation under Section 3-310. On the other hand, if the instrument has been copied in some form or fashion, then the terms of the instrument and the right to enforce the instrument can be determined from the copy. If an instrument has entered the bank collection process, then the item will most likely be filmed on several occasions and production of a copy would be a relatively easy and inexpensive process.

Subsection (b) also provides protection for the person obligated to pay the instrument. A major concern of a person obligated on a missing instrument is that the instrument may end up in the hands of a holder in due course and the obligated person may end up paying twice for the same instrument. For example, Bill issues a check to Joel and Joel claims that the instrument was lost. Joel also states that the instrument was not indorsed before it was lost; however, Joel did in fact indorse the instrument in blank with no restrictions. Bill then issues a replacement check to Joel. In the mean time, Chip finds the lost check and cashes it at the Check Cashing Service, Inc. (CCSI). CCSI presents the check to Bill's bank and is informed that Bill has placed a stop payment on the check. CCSI then brings an action against Bill to collect the amount of the check claiming holder in due course status. CCSI would prevail, because a holder in due course takes the instrument free of all claims and defenses, and Bill would be required to pay. If Joel had already cashed the second check or if the second check ends up in the hands of a holder in due course, Bill would end up paying for both checks.

In order to protect the person required to pay the instrument, Subsection (b) provides, "The court may not enter judgment in favor of the person seeking enforcement unless it finds that the person required to pay the instrument is adequately protected against loss that might occur by reason of a claim by another person to enforce the instrument. Adequate protection may be provided by any reasonable means." This section does not attempt to establish what is meant by "adequate protection." Each case will be different and as stated in the Official Comments to Section 3-309, "the type of adequate protection that is reasonable in the circumstances may depend on the degree of certainty about the facts in the case." If the court finds that the risk of loss is minimal, then the amount of protection required should match the risk. On the other hand, if the risk of loss is substantial, because of the credibility of the person seeking payment for example, then the court may require substantial protection. The protection may be that the person seeking enforcement of the instrument may be required to post a bond.

6.4 HOLDER IN DUE COURSE

The holder in due course doctrine recognizes the fact that a person who takes an instrument for value, wants to take the instrument free of all claims to and defenses against the instrument. If it were not for the protection provided by the status of a holder in due course, few people would be willing to give value for an instrument. The holder in due course doctrine is easy to understand but is fairly complex because of the many requirements contained in Section 3-302 which govern holder in due course. The definition of "holder in due course" is quite lengthy and is quoted below in its entirety. A discussion of each of the components follows the definition to give the reader a thorough understanding of the subject matter.

"Holder in due course" is defined in Section 3-302(a) as "the holder of an instrument" if the following are true:

(1) the instrument when issued or negotiated to the holder does not bear such apparent evidence of forgery or alteration or is

not otherwise so irregular or incomplete as to call into question its authenticity; and

(2) the holder took the instrument (i) for value, (ii) in good faith, (iii) without notice that the instrument is overdue or has been dishonored or that there is an uncured default with respect to payment of another instrument issued as part of the same series, (iv) without notice that the instrument contains an unauthorized signature or has been altered, (v) without notice of any claim to the instrument described in Section 3-306, and (vi) without notice that any party has a defense or claim in recoupment described in Section 3-305(a).

A holder in due course must first be a holder. "Holder" is defined in Section 1-201(20) and is discussed in Chapters 1, 4, and 5 of this book and will not be repeated here. The reader should refer to the appropriate sections of those chapters to gain a full understanding of how one becomes a holder. The holder must be a holder of a negotiable instrument. If the instrument is not a negotiable instrument because it does not meet the requirements of a negotiable instrument as required under Section 3-104, then the holder cannot be a holder in due course. For example, if an instrument that is supposed to be a note is not payable "to order" or "to bearer," the instrument is not negotiable and the holder cannot be a holder in due course. Early in the history of negotiable instruments, attempts were made to enforce ordinary agreements as negotiable instruments to take advantage of the benefits given to a holder in due course.

As provided in Subsection (a)(1) the instrument, when issued or negotiated, cannot bear "such apparent evidence of forgery or alteration or is not otherwise so irregular as to call into question its authenticity." If anything on the face of the instrument indicates that the instrument is a forgery, or has been altered, or is not authentic, then the holder cannot be a holder in due course. The holder has notice of a claim or defense if any of the above-mentioned items are obvious on the face of the instrument even if the holder did not notice the forgery, alteration, or irregularity. Some examples of items mentioned in Subsection (a)(1) could be as follows: a check that contains an indorsement that is spelled differently than the name of the payee; an instrument that contains erasures or other obvious changes in the terms of an instrument; a check that is an obvious copy of an original check. Any of these items should put a holder on notice that something is wrong with the instrument and that an inquiry before accepting the would be the prudent thing to do.

(a) VALUE

The instrument must be accepted for value. Section 3-303 lists several items constituting when an item has been transferred for value. Subsection (a)(1) states that an instrument is issued or transferred for value if "the instrument is issued or transferred for a promise of performance, to the extent the promise has been performed." For example, If Bill Wiltshire agrees to pay Joel Converse $5,000 upon Joel's promise to paint Bill's house and Joel paints the house, Joel has given value. If Bill issues a check to Joel, if Joel meets all of the other requirements, he is a holder in due course of the instrument. Joel gave value when he performed the agreed-upon promise.

If a promise of performance is the consideration and the performance is only partially performed, Section 3-302(d) provides "that the holder may assert rights as a holder in due course of the instrument only to the fraction of the amount payable under the instrument equal to the value of the partial performance divided by the value of the promised performance." In the example above, if Joel performs one half of his promise, he is a holder in due course to the extent of one half of the $5,000 check, or $2,500.

(b) VALUE—SECURITY INTEREST

Subsection (a)(2) states that an instrument is issued or transferred for value if "the transferee acquires a security interest or other lien in the instrument other than a lien obtained by judicial proceeding." This section applies where an instrument has been taken as collateral or where a security interest has been created when a bank has taken an item for collection. The instrument must have been given as collateral and cannot have been obtained as the result of a judicial proceeding such as an attaching creditor. For example, the First Deposit Bank makes a loan to Bill Wiltshire and Bill secures the debt by giving the bank a security interest in a note issued to Bill by Cindy Faulkner. If the bank meets all of the other requirements of a holder in due course, The First Deposit Bank has given value for the instrument and in the event of default on the loan by Bill, the bank can enforce the note against Cindy as a holder in due course. If Bill had not given the note as collateral to secure the debt but the bank obtained a lien on the note as the result of a judicial proceeding against Bill, then the bank has not given value. The bank may end up with a lien on the note and in fact get possession of it, but the bank will not be a holder in due course and will take the instrument subject to any defenses that the issuer, Cindy, has.

According to Section 3-302(e), the First Deposit Bank in the example above can assert its right as a holder in due course only to the amount payable under the instrument which does not exceed the amount of the unpaid obligation secured. If Cindy had a defense to payment of the note she issued to Bill and the First Deposit Bank did not have notice of the defense at the time that it took the note as collateral, the First Deposit Bank could only enforce the note to the extent of the outstanding balance on Bill's loan. Assume that the loan balance was $3,000 and the note issued by Cindy was $5,000. The First Deposit Bank could only require Cindy to pay them $3,000. The First Deposit Bank's status as a holder in due course is not extended to Bill and he would not be entitled to the remaining $2,000 free of Cindy's defense.

A collecting bank gives value for an instrument to the extent that the bank has obtained a security interest in the item. Section 4-211 states, "for purposes of determining its status as a holder in due course, a bank has given value to the extent it has a security interest in an item if the bank otherwise complies with the requirements of Section 3-302 on what constitutes a holder in due course." Section 4-210 establishes when a bank obtains a security interest in a item. According to that section, a collecting bank obtains a security interest in an item in several situations. The bank has a security interest in an item and any accompanying documents or the proceeds of either to the extent to which credit has been withdrawn or applied in the case of an item deposited in an account. For example, Chip Sanders deposits a check into his checking account at the First Deposit Bank and the bank allows Chip to withdraw the proceeds immediately. The bank obtained a security interest in the item deposited upon withdrawal of the proceeds. If the bank exercised its right of setoff against the account and applied the proceeds to a loan, then the bank also would have a security interest in the item deposited.

If a customer has the right to withdraw funds from an account, the bank also has a security interest in the item even if the funds have not been withdrawn or the bank does not have the right of charge-back on the item. For example, Chip Sanders deposits an item into his checking account at the First Deposit Bank. According to the bank's availability policy, the funds are available for withdrawal on the day following deposit of the item. The bank obtains a security interest in the item the day following deposit of the item when the funds become available for withdrawal. The bank also has a security interest in an item if it makes an advance on or against the item. For example, if the bank cashes a check for a person, the bank has a security interest in the check when the bank gives cash for the item.

If a bank takes several items from a customer at one time and only a portion of the credit given is withdrawn or applied, Section 4-210(b) provides that "the security interest remains upon all the items, any accompanying documents or the proceeds of either." If it were not for this section, the bank would be put to the impossible task of keeping up with which items it has given credit for or which items it has made advances on or allowed withdrawals. This Subsection gives the bank a security interest in all of the items and the bank has given value for all of them for purposes of determining the bank's rights as a holder in due course. This Subsection also addresses credit given for items handled by the bank in multiple transactions. As is usually the case when a customer makes deposits to an account, the funds are commingled and are represented by one balance in the account. For purposes of determining which items the bank has a security interest in, credits first given are first withdrawn. Consider the following example. A customer makes deposits to an account in the following order: $200 on May 1, $100 on May 3, and $400 on May 4. The total balance in the account is $700. Assume that the customer then withdraws $300 from the account leaving a balance of $400. For purposes of determining which items the bank has a security interest in, the customer is considered to have withdrawn the $200 deposited on May 1 and the $100 deposited on May 3. If the item in question was included in either of these deposits, the bank has given value for purposes as a holder in due course. If the item in question was included in the $400 deposit made on May 4, the bank has not given value.

The security interest in the items handled by a bank for collection exists only during the collection process and is self-liquidating. Section 4-210(c) states, "Receipt by a collecting bank of final settlement for an item is a realization on its security interest in the item, accompanying documents, and proceeds." The intent of giving a bank a security interest in an item is to protect the bank during the collection process. After the collection process is complete, the need for the security interest no longer exists. Once the bank has received final settlement for the item and there is no chance that the item can be dishonored and returned, there is no reason to give the bank a secured position. One point of potential conflict under this Subsection is that settlement for checks is final when received under Section 229.36 of Federal Reserve Regulation CC. As stated above, the intention of giving the bank a security interest in the item is to protect the bank during the collection process. If the final settlement provision of Regulation CC were applied to checks under Section 4-210(c), a bank could never become a holder in due course of an item because it would not have given value. Certainly this will not be the case and the courts will interpret the reference to final settlement in this section to mean that the item has been finally paid by the drawee bank and cannot be dishonored and returned.

During the collection process, the collecting bank has the status of a perfected secured creditor without the need of a security agreement and without the need of filing a financing statement. The second part of Section 4-210(c) states the following:

So long as the bank does not receive final settlement for the item or give up possession of the item or accompanying documents for purposes other than collection, the security interest continues to the extent and is subject to Article 9, but:

(1) no security agreement is necessary to make the security interest enforceable (Section 9-203(1)(a));

(2) no filing is required to perfect the security interest; and

(3) the security interest has priority over conflicting perfected security interest in the item, accompanying documents, or proceeds.

Article 9 contains specific requirements for perfecting a security interest and establishing priorities of those security interests. Subsection (c) makes it clear that the collecting bank is not required to comply with the perfecting requirements of Article 9 and that the collecting bank has priority over a conflicting security interest. For example, assume that Mike Harris deposits a check in the amount of $100,000 into his checking account with the First Deposit Bank (FDB). The check is presented to the drawee bank, dishonored and returned to FDB. A secured Creditor of Mike Harris discovers the existence of the check and claims that the check represents proceeds from the sale of accounts receivable over which the creditor has a perfected security interest. The secured creditor attempts to get possession of the check from FDB. Section 4-210(c) gives FDB priority over the perfected security interest of the creditor and FDB may enforce the item as a holder in due course against the drawer of the check.

(c) VALUE—ANTECEDENT CLAIM

Section 3-303(a)(3) states that an instrument is issued or transferred for value if "the instrument is issued or transferred as payment of, or as security for, an antecedent claim against any person, whether or not the claim is due." This section establishes that value is given for an instrument if the instrument is given in payment of an existing debt or claim. The point here is that the requirement that the holder give value does not mean that the creation of the value and the issuance or transfer of the instrument must be simultaneous. For example, Bill Wiltshire lends Joel Converse $5,000 on May 1 and evidences the debt by issuance of a note due on September 1. On June 15, Joel delivers a cashier's check, payable to Joel, to Bill as collateral for the debt. Bill has given value for the cashier's check and may become a holder in due course. Another example; Bill Wiltshire's account at the First Deposit Bank is overdrawn $3,000. Bill deposits a check to cover the overdraft. The First Deposit Bank has given value for the check that is deposited because the overdraft represents an antecedent claim.

(d) VALUE—EXCHANGE FOR NEGOTIABLE INSTRUMENT

An instrument is issued or transferred for value, according to Section 3-303(a)(4), if "the instrument is issued or transferred in exchange for a negotiable instrument." This section is self-explanatory and needs little discussion. A classic example of this section would be where a bank issues its cashier's check in exchange for a check issued by the remitter. The bank gave value when it issued the cashier's check. Another example would be where Bill Wiltshire issues a check to Cindy Faulkner in exchange for a negotiable note. Bill gave value when he issued his check.

(e) VALUE—IRREVOCABLE OBLIGATION

Section 3-303(a)(5) states that an instrument is issued or transferred for value if "the instrument is issued or transferred in exchange for the in-

curring of an irrevocable obligation to a third party by the person taking the instrument." An example of this section, as pointed out in the
Official Comments, is where a bank has issued an irrevocable letter of
credit in exchange for a negotiable instrument. A specific example is as
follows. Bill Wiltshire requests his bank, the First Deposit Bank, to issue
an irrevocable letter of credit in favor of a third party. In exchange for
issuance of the letter of credit, Bill issues the bank a negotiable note.
The bank gave value for the note when it issued the letter of credit. The
bank has incurred an irrevocable obligation to pay the third party the
amount of the letter of credit. On the other hand, if the letter of credit is
revocable, then the bank has not given value and cannot become a
holder in due course.

(f) CONSIDERATION

Section 3-303(b) defines "consideration" and basically states that if an
instrument is issued for consideration and the consideration is not performed, the person that issued the instrument has a defense against the
person to whom the instrument was issued that failed to perform the
consideration. Subsection (b) defines "consideration" as "any consideration sufficient to support a simple contract." Subsection (b) goes on to
say, "The drawer or maker on an instrument has a defense if the instrument is issued without consideration." If an instrument is issued for a
promise of performance, the issuer has a defense to the extent performance of the promise is due and the promise has not been performed. If
an instrument is issued for value as stated in Subsection (a), the instrument is also issued for consideration. The defenses stated above are not
valid against a holder in due course. For example, assume that Bill issues a check to Cindy as a gift. Cindy has not given value or consideration for the check and Bill could use that as a defense to paying the
check to Cindy. If Cindy presents the check for payment to the drawee
and the drawee dishonors the check, Bill has a defense of lack of consideration. On the other hand, if Cindy transfers the check to Joel for
value and Joel otherwise meets the requirements of a holder in due
course, Bill's defense of lack of consideration is not valid against Joel.

(g) GOOD FAITH

The second requirement under Section 3-302(a)(2) is that the instrument
must be taken in good faith. "Good faith" is defined in Section 3-
103(a)(4) to mean "honesty in fact and the observance of reasonable

commercial standards of fair dealing." The definition of "good faith" has been expanded to require the observance of reasonable commercial standards of fair dealing. The prior version of Article 3 required only "honesty in fact." If a holder takes an instrument with knowledge of a claim to the instrument, then the holder is obviously not taking the instrument in good faith. This expanded definition of "good faith" would require more than the absence of knowledge. For example, a person may not have specific knowledge of a fact, but if the "observance of reasonable commercial standards" requires that the holder make certain inquiries, then the holder will be required to investigate further. A specific example of this requirement is as follows. Mike cashes a check at the Check Cashing Service, Inc. (CCSI). The check, in the amount of $5,000, is drawn on the account of Flashback Music, Inc. and made payable to its president Bill. Mike has no connection with Flashback Music, Inc. and offered no explanation as to how he acquired the check. It would appear that "good faith" would require CCSI to at least inquire as the rights of Mike to have possession of the instrument.

(h) OVERDUE AND DISHONORED INSTRUMENT

The holder of the instrument must take the instrument without notice that the instrument is overdue or has been dishonored as provided for in Section 3-302(a)(2)(iii). Section 3-304 establishes when an instrument becomes overdue and distinguishes between an instrument payable on demand and an instrument payable at a definite time. Subsection (a) governs instruments payable on demand and it states the following:

An instrument payable on demand becomes overdue at the earliest of the following times:

(1) on the day after the day demand for payment is duly made;

(2) if the instrument is a check, 90 days after its date; or

(3) if the instrument is not a check, when the instrument has been outstanding for a period of time after its date which is unreasonably long under the circumstances of the particular case in light of the nature of the instrument and usage of the trade.

Regardless of whether the demand instrument is a check or not, the instrument is overdue on the day after demand for payment is made if the demand is made before the expiration of time stated in (a)

(1) or (2). For example, consider a check dated May 1, that is presented for payment on May 3 and dishonored. The check is considered overdue on May 4. A holder taking the check after May 4, could not be a holder in due course because the check is overdue. Additionally, the holder could not be a holder in due course because the instrument had been dishonored. Consider another example. A check is issued on May 1 to Bill. Bill puts the check in his wallet and on August 15, he negotiates the check to Joel. Joel cannot become a holder in due course because the check was overdue. The previous version of this article established a period of 30 days before a check became overdue. As stated above, a check is overdue 90 days after the date it was issued.

If the instrument is not a check and has not been presented for payment, the period of time that the instrument is outstanding before it is considered overdue is left up to the court. The court will consider the type of instrument, the circumstances surrounding the reason the item remains outstanding, the nature of the transaction, the usage of the trade, and any other factors that the court deems necessary to consider.

If the item is payable at a definite time, Subsection (b) establishes when the instrument is overdue and the determination is dependent upon whether the instrument is payable in installments or not and whether the due date has been accelerated. If the principal is payable in installments and the due date has not been accelerated, Subsection (b)(1) states, "The instrument becomes overdue upon default under the instrument for nonpayment of the installment, and the instrument remains overdue until the default is cured." If the instrument is negotiated during the period of time that it is in default, the holder cannot become a holder in due course. If the default is cured (a payment is made and the note is made current) the instrument is no longer overdue. If the principal is not payable in installments and the due date has not been accelerated, Subsection (b)(2) states, "The instrument becomes overdue on the day after the due date." An instrument with a due date of May 1 that is not payable in installments becomes overdue on May 2. A holder taking the instrument after the due date cannot be a holder in due course.

If the due date with respect to principal has been accelerated, Subsection (b)(3) states, "The instrument becomes overdue on the day after the accelerated due date." A note with a due date of September 1, for example, that is accelerated to May 1, becomes overdue on May 2. Unless it were obvious on the face of the instrument that the due date had been accelerated, it would appear that any potential holder that expects holder in due course status would be required to determine the status of the due date on the instrument before taking it.

Section 3-304(c) addresses overdue interest and that Subsection states, "Unless the due date of principal has been accelerated, an instrument does not become overdue if there is default in payment of interest but no default in payment of principal." A one-year note, for example, with monthly interest payments will not be overdue upon default of payment of one or more of the interest payments. However, if the note provides that failure to timely make an interest payment is a default and that the due date may be accelerated, the note becomes overdue the day after acceleration of the due date if it is in fact accelerated.

(i) NOTICE OF UNAUTHORIZED SIGNATURE OR ALTERATION

Subsection (a)(2)(iv) requires that the instrument must be taken "without notice that the instrument contains an unauthorized signature or has been altered." If the holder takes the instrument with notice of the forgery or alteration, the instrument is taken subject to those deficiencies. In the case of an alteration, Section 3-407(b) states that an alteration fraudulently made discharges a party whose obligation is affected by the alteration. If the holder takes an instrument with notice that the instrument has been altered, the holder is not entitled to enforce the instrument. On the other hand, if the instrument is taken without notice of the alteration and the holder meets all of the other requirements of a holder in due course, the holder may enforce the instrument as originally drawn. Even a holder in due course cannot enforce an instrument as altered unless the person obligated on the instrument assented to the alteration or is precluded from denying the alteration for some other reason.

6.5 CLAIMS TO AND DEFENSES AGAINST AN INSTRUMENT

A holder in due course takes an instrument free of the claim to an instrument contained in Section 3-306, which is discussed in Chapters 4 and 5 of this book. Basically, that section states that a person taking an instrument, other than a holder in due course, takes the instrument subject to the property or possessory right in an instrument. The holder in due course, therefore, takes the instrument free of a claim to an instrument on the part of any person. For example, assume that Bill issues a check to Cindy, she indorses the check in blank and loses the check. Joel finds the check and cashes it at the Check Cashing Service, Inc. (CCSI). Cindy contacts Bill and advises him that she lost the check and asks him to issue her a replacement. Bill contacts his bank to stop payment on the check and is told that the check has already been paid. Bill tells Cindy that the check has been paid by his bank and that according to the indorsement, the check was cashed by CCSI. Cindy then contacts CCSI and demands payment from them, claiming that they converted her check. CCSI advises Cindy that CCSI is a holder in due course and they took the instrument free from her claim. Unless Cindy can prove that CCSI had notice of her claim to the instrument, they are correct in their assertion that they took the instrument free of her claim.

A holder in due course also takes an instrument free of most defenses. For example, Bill issues a check to Joel to paint Bill's house. Joel does not paint the house but he does indorse the check and cashes it at the Check Cashing Service, Inc. (CCSI). Upon realizing that the house has not been painted, Bill issues a stop payment order on the check. The check is dishonored and returned to CCSI. CCSI demands payment from Bill as the drawer. Bill raises the defense of lack of consideration because Joel did not paint the house. CCSI then claims its status of a holder in due course and maintains that as a holder in due course they took the check free from Bill's defense of lack of consideration. CCSI is correct in its assertions and will be able to enforce the instrument against Bill. Section 3-305, which is discussed in Chapter 2 of this book, lists the defenses against payment to which an instrument is subject to.

Subsection (b) of that section states that a holder in due course is not subject to those defenses with the exception of the ones listed in Subsection (a)(1). A holder in due course takes an instrument subject to the following defenses of the obligor listed in that Subsection:

(i) infancy of the obligor to the extent it is a defense to a simple contact,

(ii) duress, lack of legal capacity, or illegality of the transaction which, under other law, nullifies the obligation of the obligor,

(iii) fraud that induced the obligor to sign the instrument with neither knowledge nor reasonable opportunity to learn of its character or its essential terms, or

(iv) discharge of the obligor in insolvency.

The validity of the defense is subject to the application of local law. If local law merely makes the transaction voidable, the defense is cut off. If the local law renders a transaction void, then the defense applies and the holder in due course may not enforce the instrument. An example of the application of one of these defenses is as follows. Bill is forced by gunpoint to issue a check to Joel. Joel indorses the check and cashes it at the Check Cashing Service, Inc. In the mean time, Bill stops payment on the check and when the check is presented for payment, the check is returned "payment stopped." Upon receipt of the dishonored check, CCSI contacts Bill and demands payment claiming their holder in due course status. Bill's defense of duress is valid against CCSI. As pointed out in Official Comment #1 to Section 3-305, "An instrument signed at the point of a gun is void, even in the hands of a holder in due course." The reader should refer to Section 2.9 of Chapter 2 of this book for a detailed discussion of the defenses of an obligor.

Section 3-302(b) provides that "notice of discharge of a party, other than discharge in an insolvency proceeding, is not notice of a defense under Subsection (a), but discharge is effective against a person who became a holder in due course with notice of the discharge. Public filing or recording of a document does not of itself constitute notice of a defense, claim in recoupment, or claim to the instrument."

Section 3-308 also reinforces the right of a holder in due course to enforce payment. This section deals with the authenticity of a signature and states that if the validity of a signature is admitted or proved, the plaintiff producing the instrument is entitled to payment, but the payment is subject to any defense or claim in recoupment unless the plaintiff is a holder in due course. If the plaintiff is a holder in due course, the instrument may be enforced against the person obligated on the instrument even if a defense exists.

6.6 PERSON DOES NOT ACQUIRE RIGHTS AS HOLDER IN DUE COURSE

A person that meets all of the requirements of a holder in due course does not always acquire the rights of a holder in due course. Section 3-302(c) states the following:

Except to the extent a transferor or predecessor in interest has rights as a holder in due course, a person does not acquire rights of a holder in due course of an instrument taken (i) by legal process or by purchase in an execution, bankruptcy, or creditor's sale or similar proceeding, (ii) by purchase as part of a bulk transaction not in ordinary course of business of the transferor, or (iii) as the successor in interest to an estate or other organization.

Subsection (c) deals with transfers of instruments in conjunction with the sale of a business or the transfer of an instrument as the result of a sale of a debtor's assets. The transferee of the instrument does not become a holder in due course unless the person from whom the instrument is transferred was a holder in due course or unless the person whose assets are being sold was a holder in due course. For example, assume that the assets of Flashback Music, Inc. are being sold in a bulk transfer to ABC Music Co. Part of the assets being sold to ABC are checks that have been taken from customers for goods and services sold by Flashback. ABC does not acquire the rights of a holder in due course in the checks unless Flashback was already a holder in due course. If ABC were given the rights of a holder in due course, ABC would take the checks free of any claim or defenses. If Flashback had received payment for goods but had not delivered the goods to the customer that issued the check, it would not be equitable to allow ABC to enforce payment of the check as a holder in due course. In all likelihood, ABC would have possession of the goods and the checks and would be unjustly enriched if allowed to enforce payment of the checks without allowing the customer to raise the defense of failure of consideration.

6.7 HOLDER IN DUE COURSE RIGHTS ACQUIRED BY TRANSFER

A holder of an instrument may become a holder in due course even if that person does not meet all of the requirements of a holder in due course. Section 3-203(b) states, "Transfer of an instrument, whether or not the transfer is a negotiation, vests in the transferee any right of the transferor to enforce the instrument, including any right as a holder in due course, but the transferee cannot acquire rights of a holder in due course by a transfer, directly or indirectly, from a holder in due course if the transferee engaged in fraud or illegality affecting the instrument."

An example of the application of this section is as follows. Assume that a check was issued to Bill and Bill indorsed the check and put it in the top pocket of his shirt. Later that night, Cindy took the check from Bill's shirt pocket and convinced Joel to cash the check for her. Joel was not aware of the fact that Cindy had stolen the check from Bill. Assume further that Joel met all of the other requirements of a holder in due course. Joel needed some cash, so he asked his friend Chip to cash the check for him and Chip did in fact cash the check. Chip was, however, aware that the check had been stolen. Therefore, Chip could not be a holder in due course in his own right since he had knowledge of Bill's claim to the check. However, Chip does become a holder in due course and takes the check free of Bill's claim to it because Joel was a holder in due course. As stated above and in Section 3-203(b), transfer of an instrument vests in the transferee any right of the transferor, including any right as a holder in due course. The purpose of this section is to further protect a holder in due course. If a person that could not become a holder in due course in his own right were not granted the rights of a holder in due course from his transferee, that person would be reluctant to take the instrument. This reluctance to take an instrument would limit the ability of the holder in due course to transfer the instrument.

Section 3-203(b) prevents Cindy from reacquiring the check from Joel or Chip and becoming a holder in due course. In fact, no person that is involved in fraud or illegality affecting an instrument can acquire the rights of a holder in due course. In the example above, if Chip had been involved in any way with the theft of the check from Bill, Chip could not acquire the rights of a holder in due course.

CHAPTER 7

PRESENTMENT, COLLECTION, AND SETTLEMENT

PART I: PRESENTMENT

7.1 PRESENTMENT

The liability of a drawer and an indorser is based on presentment and dishonor of the instrument. "Presentment" is defined in Section 3-501(a) as "a demand made by or on behalf of a person entitled to enforce an instrument (i) to pay the instrument made to the drawee or a party obliged to pay the instrument or, in the case of a note or accepted draft payable at a bank, to the bank, or (ii) to accept a draft made to the drawee." The presentment does not have to be made by the person entitled to enforce the instrument but, as stated above, may be made by a person on behalf of a person entitled to enforce the instrument. Most checks and drafts are presented by a collecting bank on behalf of the person entitled to enforce the instrument. Over the counter presentment for cash or acceptance may also be made by the person entitled to enforce the instrument.

(a) PLACE OF PRESENTMENT

There is no shortage of directions as to where presentment of an item may be made. Directions are contained in Article 3, Article 4, in the ABA routing number policy, and in Regulation CC. Section 3-501(b)(1) contains rules for presentment of items but the rules are subject to the provisions of Article 4, agreement of the parties, and clearinghouse rules and other similar rules or agreements. In other words, the place of presentment and the rules surrounding presentment may, and most likely will, change based on the type of item and rules to which the item is subject to. According to Section 3-501(b)1, presentment may be made at the place of payment of the instrument. If the instrument is payable at a bank in the United States, presentment must be made at the place of payment. The place of payment is provided for in Section 3-111 but is subject to Article 4, clearinghouse rules, regulations, and all other agreements. That section states the following:

> Except as otherwise provided for items in Article 4, an instrument is payable at the place of payment stated in the instrument. If no place of payment is stated, an instrument is payable at the address of the drawee or maker stated in the instrument. If no address is stated, the place of payment is the place of business of the drawee or maker. If a drawee or maker has more than one place of business, the place of payment is any place of business of the drawee or maker chosen by the person entitled to enforce the instrument. If the drawee or maker has no place of business, the place of payment is the residence of the drawee or maker.

Section 4-204(c) allows the payor or other payor to designate the place of presentment. That section states, "Presentment may be made by a presenting bank at a place where the payor bank or other payor has requested that presentment be made." Typically, the payor bank will designate the place of presentment by use of the routing number of the bank. However, in some cases, the payor bank will request the Federal Reserve Banks and other presenting banks to make presentment at a processing center or some other centralized location that is not related to the routing number on the check. The payor bank may have centralized its operations or may have contracted with a third party to perform its processing. Whatever the reason, this section would give the

payor bank the right to designate such a place as the place of presentment of cash letters.

(b) PLACE OF PRESENTMENT UNDER REGULATION CC

Although Section 4-204(c) gives the payor bank flexibility in designating
the place of presentment, Article 4 is subject to the provisions of Federal
Reserve Regulation CC (Regulation CC). The place of payment of
checks or drafts payable through or payable at a bank is governed by
Section 229.36 of Federal Reserve Regulation CC. Section 229.36 states
the following:

A check is considered received by the paying bank when it is received:

(1) at a location to which delivery is requested by the paying
bank;

(2) at an address of the bank associated with the routing number
on the check, whether in magnetic ink or in fractional form;

(3) at any branch or head office, if the bank is identified on the
check by name without address; or

(4) at a branch, head office, or other location consistent with the
name and address of the bank on the check if the bank is identified on the check by name and address.

Regulation CC does not specifically direct where presentment is to
be made but rather states the places at which the payor bank must receive the checks. This section somewhat shifts the selection of the place
of presentment from the paying bank to the person presenting the item.
The person presenting the item may select any one of the four locations
listed as the place of presentment. The stated purpose of this section in
the commentary is to facilitate efficient presentment of checks to pro-
mote early return or notice of nonpayment to the depositary bank and
to clarify the law as to the effect of presentment by routing number.

Section 229.36(b)(1) follows Section 4-204(c) and allows for presentment at a location to which delivery is requested by the payor bank.
The payor bank can request presentment at a certain location simply by
advising the presenter of the location. In the case of direct presentment

by a collecting bank, the location is typically designated by agreement. For items presented by a Federal Reserve Bank, the payor bank can give instructions, following Federal Reserve procedures, and the Federal Reserve Bank is normally very accommodating. The Federal Reserve Bank will even route checks to a processing center or location not associated with the routing number on the check.

Presentment may also be made, according to Section 229.36(b)(2), at an address of the bank associated with the routing number on the check. The address of the office associated with the routing number can be found in a Rand McNally publication entitled "Key to Routing Number." The routing numbers for all banks are administered by the Routing Number Administrative Board of the American Bankers Association. The Routing Number Administrative Board adopted a new routing number policy in 1988 and the ABA published a statement of this policy. The stated purpose of the routing number in that statement "is to identify in numeric form the location selected by the drawee or payor at which checks, drafts, and other items must be presented." The policy statement goes on to say that the "Routing Number Policy is designed to benefit collecting depository financial institutions by ensuring that the items can be presented in as expeditious and direct manner as possible with minimal float accruing in the payments system." The payor bank may select the location to which items must be presented, but the location selected must also benefit the collecting bank by reducing float.

A routing number will only be issued to federal or state chartered banks. The word "bank" includes savings and loan associations, savings banks, credit unions, and other entities that meet the definition of a bank. The policy specifically prohibits the issuance of a routing number to a nonbank. Routing numbers may not be issued to bank holding companies, third party processors, or processing centers established by depositor financial institutions. While the routing number may not be issued to a nonbank, as provided by Regulation CC and Article 4, the payor bank may designate the location to which presentment must be made. The payor bank could, therefore, request that presentment be made to a processing center or to a third party processor. However, the presenter may present the item to any four of the places stated in Section 229.36(b) and the payor bank would be required to receive the item.

The policy further provides that each bank may have only one routing number. Exceptions to this rule are provided in certain circumstances. The bank may make a request for additional routing numbers to the Routing Number Administrative Board. The policy allows more than one routing number for a bank for branches if the branch is a "place where data on paper items are captured for transmission or posting." Additional routing numbers may be assigned "in special circumstances" or if the additional routing number will expedite the collection of the item if the bank has branches located in different Federal Reserve territories. There are some conflicts concerning additional routing numbers within the routing policy. These conflicts are beyond the scope of this book and will not be addressed. The point here is that a bank and its branches may currently have numerous routing numbers on checks, but the bank may request that all or a portion of the items be presented at a centralized location.

(c) PLACE OF PRESENTMENT—SEPARATE OFFICE OF BANK

While the other sections of Article 3 and 4 and Regulation CC actually determine the place of presentment, Section 4-107 must also be considered. That section states, "A branch or separate office of a bank is a separate bank for the purpose of computing the time within which and determining the place at or to which action may be taken or notice or orders must be given under this article and under Article 3." While this section deals with many more issues than presentment, the discussion here will only address presentment.

Many banks acquired branches through mergers and acquisitions of banks that obviously had their own routing numbers. Some of these banks retained the routing numbers of the branches and continue to use the routing number of the individual banks on checks and other items. In some instances, the branches maintain their own operations and perform the proof, capture, and payment functions at the individual branches. Under these circumstances, the bank would want the checks to be presented to the specific bank on which the check is drawn. If an item drawn on one branch is received at another branch, the branch at which it is received is considered a collecting bank. For example, assume that a check drawn on Branch A is deposited to an account in Branch B on Monday. The check must be sent by Branch A to Branch B just like any other item requiring collection. Branch A would be required to send the item to Branch B no later than midnight Tuesday, and Branch B would be required to pay or return the check by midnight Wednesday. The point here is that Branch A is not the place of payment; therefore, the midnight deadline for dishonor of the item is Wednesday and not Tuesday.

Some banks maintain separate routing numbers for each branch location but the operations of the bank are consolidated or centralized in regional locations or one site. All of the operations process is performed in the consolidated site including proof, capture, and the payment function. In this situation, the bank would request that the items be presented to the centralized site. As stated previously, under Section 4-204 (c) the centralized site would be the proper place for presentment unless superseded by Regulation CC. The fact that the branch is a separate bank under Section 4-107 would have no effect on the proper place of presentment. Having said that, Section 4-107 makes no reference to the method of operations of the banks. The section simply states that a branch "is a separate bank." The previous version of Section 4-107 was contained in Section 4-106 in the previous version of Article 4. The revised section deletes a reference to the location of the deposit ledger. That version stated, "A branch or separate office of a bank [maintaining it own deposit ledger] is a separate bank. . . ." The fact that the bracketed language was deleted is an indication that the intentions of the drafters of the revised sections was that the location of the bank's deposit records is of no significance in establishing the fact that a branch is a separate bank for certain purposes.

Section 4-107 does not and should not attempt to identify every situation that could arise under the section. It simply states that a branch is a separate office for certain purposes and leaves it to the courts to determine its application on a case by case bases. It would appear, however, that if all of the bank's operations were consolidated and the branches were not at all involved in the processing of items that the proper place of presentment is the consolidated site. However, items drawn on one branch that are presented over the counter at another branch should be received by that branch and presentment should be considered made to the payor bank.

Regulation CC takes a different view of a separate branch when considering the availability of funds. According to Section 229.10(c)(vi) a check deposited in a branch of the depositary bank and drawn on the same or another branch of the bank located in the same state or same check-processing region, must be made available to the customer on the next banking day after receipt of the deposit. This section applies regardless of the fact that the items may be processed at each branch and presentment must be made by one branch to the other branch.

(d) HOW PRESENTMENT MAY BE MADE

Section 3-501(b)(1) states that presentment "may be made by any commercially reasonable means, including an oral, written, or electronic communication." When read by itself, this Subsection could be interpreted to mean that presentment, which is demand for payment, may be made by notice alone. However, Section 4-212 provides that a collecting bank may present an item not payable by, through, or at a bank by sending notice that the bank holds the item for payment. Since a check is payable by a bank, it would be excluded from presentment by notice under Section 3-501(b)(1). Likewise, drafts payable through or by a bank would be excluded and presentment must include presentment of the item or electronic presentment as discussed later.

In addition to the restriction of presentment by notice under Section 4-212, the communication by itself may not be sufficient. Section 3-501(b)(2) states, "Upon demand of the person to whom presentment is made, the person making presentment must (i) exhibit the instrument, (ii) give reasonable identification and, if presentment is made on behalf of another person, reasonable evidence of authority to do so, and (iii) sign a receipt on the instrument for any payment made or surrender the instrument if full payment is made." These requirements, of course, apply to all types of negotiable instruments but are more applicable to items presented over the counter or notes, certificates of deposits, and other similar types of negotiable instruments. While a paying bank could technically require a person to jump through the hoops in Subsection (b)(2), the paying bank would not require this information of a collecting bank presenting a cash letter to the payor bank. On the other hand, if a person made demand for a check over the counter at a teller's window, the teller would have the right to ask the person presenting the check for proper identification. If the person refuses to produce the required information, the bank would be within its rights to refuse the presentment.

While Section 3-501(b)(1) states that presentment may be made by any reasonable means including an oral communication, several courts have held that a telephone inquiry as to the sufficiency of funds of the balance of a customer's account was not presentment of the item. One case in point is *Kirby v. Bergfield, 8 UCC Rep Serv 710*. It would also appear that sending the paying bank a letter without presenting the item would not be sufficient. The courts have held that physical presentment of the item was required to hold the drawer liable on the instrument. Physical presentment would not be required under an electronic presentment of the item subject to an agreement as discussed later.

The bank may refuse the presentment and return the instrument without dishonoring it, according to Section 3-501(b)(3), if the instrument is missing a necessary indorsement or if the presentment does not comply with the terms of the instrument, an agreement of the parties, or other applicable law or rule. For example, if the payor bank required items to be bundled in a certain way and the presenter had agreed to the presentment requirement, the payor bank could refuse the items when presented if they did not conform to the presentment requirements. In this example, the payor bank's refusal to pay or accept the item would not be dishonor. The presenting bank could not look to an indorser to enforce the item because proper presentment had not been made. Another example of the return of an item without dishonor would be an item that is missing an indorsement. If a collecting bank presents an item to the payor bank that is missing an indorsement, the paying bank may refuse to pay the item and the return is not considered to be dishonor of the item. The presenting bank could then look to the person that presented the item to it for breach of the transfer warranty.

(e) PRESENTMENT BY A COLLECTING BANK

A collecting bank may present items to the payor bank in several different ways. Section 4-204(a) states, "A collecting bank shall send items by a reasonably prompt method, taking into consideration relevant instructions, the nature of the item, the number of those items on hand, the cost of collection involved, and the method generally used by it or others to present those items." A collecting bank has a responsibility to its customer for which it is collecting an item to present the item in a reasonably prompt period of time. The bank is not required, however, to send the item in the most expeditious manner but may take into consideration other factors. Collecting banks have numerous clearing alternatives and will select the most expeditious manner in presenting the item taking into consideration the dollar amount of the item, availability, deadlines, processing cost and capabilities, clearing agent fees, transportation cost, and many other factors.

It is to the collecting bank's advantage to collect the item as soon as possible. In addition to the float cost to the bank, the bank must make the funds available to the customer within the time periods specified in Federal Reserve Regulation CC. Therefore, the collecting bank will, in most cases, collect the item as quickly as possible. The problem arises when a customer is of the opinion that the collecting bank should have or could have presented the item in a shorter period of time. For example, consider a check that is presented for payment and is dishonored for insufficient funds. Assume that if the check had been presented for payment one day earlier by the collecting bank, the balance in the account on which the check was drawn would have been sufficient to pay the check. Also assume that if the item had been presented directly to the payor bank, presentment would have in fact been made one day earlier. Section 4-204 does not and should not require the collecting bank to send an item for collection in the most direct and expeditious manner. The collecting bank must, however, exercise good faith and ordinary care in collecting the item. If the bank is negligent in collecting the item it could be held liable for failure to send the item in a reasonably prompt method as provided for in Section 4-204(a). The court in *Rapp v. Dime Savings Bank of New York 24 UCC Rep Serv 1220*, held that a bank must use ordinary care during the collection process. According to the court, ordinary care can be measured by the general standards of banking usage. The collection process is discussed below in more detail.

A collecting bank may delay presentment of an item drawn on a payor other than a bank for a period not exceeding two days according to Section 4-109(a). The time period may be extended only in a good faith effort to collect an item other than a check. The collecting bank may extend the time period without the authority of any person unless the bank has instructions not to extend the time.

The bank may also delay collection of an item (including checks) or other actions beyond time limits prescribed by the UCC or by instructions, according to Subsection (b), if "(i) the delay is caused by interruption of communication or computer facilities, suspension of payments by another bank, war, emergency conditions, failure of equipment, or other circumstances beyond the control of the bank, and (ii) the bank exercises such diligence as the circumstances require."

If availability and speed of collection were the only consideration, the most expeditious method of collection of an item would be by direct presentment to the payor bank. Direct presentment is specifically allowed under Section 4-204. That section states the following:

A collecting bank may send:

(1) an item directly to the payor bank;

(2) an item to a nonbank payor if authorized by its transferor; and

(3) an item other than documentary drafts to a nonbank payor, if authorized by Federal Reserve regulation or operating circular, clearinghouse rule, or the like.

As stated in Official Comment #2 to this section, "Subsection (b)(1) codifies the practice of direct mail, express, messenger or like presentment to payor banks." Direct presentment may be made in many different ways. This section does not specify the manner in which the direct presentment must be made. The collecting bank could present the item itself, use the services of a courier company, or use the mail or other messenger type service. Regardless of the method or presentment, the collecting bank should retain some form of proof that the item was sent to the payor bank.

This Subsection also allows the collecting bank to send an item directly to a nonbank payor if the transferor authorizes direct presentment. The reason authorization from the transferor is required, especially in the case of documentary drafts, is because of the unknown nature and character of the nonbank payor. With authorization, the transferor assumes the risk of loss of the item by direct presentment. For example, if the item is sent by mail to the nonbank payor, the nonbank payor may simply keep the item and not remit payment. If documents of title are attached, the nonbank payor will have possession of and title to the product or goods and will not have paid the transferor. The collecting bank may send items other than documentary drafts directly to a nonbank payor without authorization from the transferor if allowed under Subsection (b)(3). This Subsection envisions such items as insurance claim drafts issued by reputable insurance companies and the like. If no documents are attached and the payor is reputable, the risk of loss is small.

7.2 TIME OF RECEIPT OF ITEM

According to Section 501(b)(1), presentment is effective "when demand for payment or acceptance is received by the person to whom presentment is made." The determination as to the time that an item is received by the person to make payment is a factual determination. There is no requirement under Articles 3 or 4 that the item be time stamped or that a record of the time be kept that a bank or other payor received the item. If a dispute arises as to the time of receipt, the trier of the fact would examine the available facts and make the determination. The time of receipt should not be a problem for items received by a bank through the Federal Reserve or other clearing agent. Many banks keep time logs for the receipt of cash letters. If the bank does not keep records, many times the courier company that delivered the items will have the records. The date that the item was presented should not be a problem to prove because the date is included in the indorsement by most collecting banks and the Federal Reserve. It would appear that if a problem were to arise, it would be over items presented directly to the bank, especially items presented over the counter.

A payor bank and other payor to whom an instrument is presented may establish a time within a day in which items must be presented. Section 3-501(b)(4) states, "The party to whom presentment is made may treat presentment as occurring on the next business day after the day of presentment if the party to whom presentment is made has established a cut-off hour not earlier than 2 p.m. for the receipt and processing of instruments presented for payment or acceptance and presentment is made after the cut-off hour."

Article 4 contains a similar provision providing for a cut-off hour. Section 4-108 states the following:

(a) For the purpose of allowing time to process items, prove balances, and make the necessary entries on its books to determine its position for the day, a bank may fix an afternoon hour of 2 p.m. or later as a cutoff hour for the handling of money and items and the making of entries on its books.

(b) An item or deposit of money received on any day after a cut-off hour so fixed or after the close of the banking day may be treated as being received at the opening of the next banking day.

The cut-off hour established under Section 3-502 applies only to the presentment of an instrument to the payor. Section 4-108 applies to both the presentment of an item, which would include presentment through the bank collection system and over-the-counter deposit of items, and the deposit of money. The cut-off under Section 4-108 not only applies to the receipt of an instrument for payment but also to the acceptance, processing, and posting of a deposit to a customer's account. Whether an item was received for payment before or after the cut-off hour is important in determining the time within which the payor bank must act on the item. That is, the time of receipt will determine when the clock starts to tick on the bank's midnight deadline.

For example, if a bank has established a cut-off hour of 2 p.m. and a check is presented to the bank for payment at 3 p.m. on Monday, the bank's midnight deadline expires on Wednesday. If the item had been presented before the cut-off hour of 2 p.m., the midnight deadline would have expired on Tuesday. For this reason, the determination of the time of receipt of an item by a payor is important. In *Third Century Recycling, Inc. v. Bank of Baroda, 8 UCC Rep Serv 2d 105*, the court held that the burden of proof of the time of receipt of an item is on the payor bank. In that case, the payor bank claimed that the checks that were the subject of the litigation were presented after the bank's cut-off hour. The payee claimed that they were presented before the cut-off hour and were not returned timely by the bank. The court agreed with the payee stating that the payor bank failed to demonstrate by a preponderance of the evidence that the checks were received after the cut-off time and the bank was, therefore, liable to the payee for the amount of the checks.

The time of receipt of a deposit is also important. If a bank establishes a cut-off and a deposit is received after that cut-off hour, the deposit is considered to have been received on the next banking day. If the customer makes the deposit before the cut-off, but the bank does not process the deposit until the next day, the bank could be liable to the customer for wrongful dishonor. If the customer is not given proper credit for a deposit, the bank could also be liable for violation of the provisions of Regulation CC. Regulation CC, in Section 229.19(a)(5)(ii), also establishes a cut-off hour of 2 p.m. or later for the receipt of a deposit.

The cut-off hour applies to a time within the day that the payor is open for business. Nothing in Article 3, Article 4, or Regulation CC dictates the days on which a payor must remain open or the hours of operation. A bank, for example, could end its "banking day" at 12:00 noon. "Banking day" is defined in Section 4-104 (a)(3) of Article 4 and Section 229.2(f) of Regulation CC as "the part of a day on which a bank is open to the public for carrying on substantially all of its bank functions." Even if a bank provides a night depository or a place for delivery of cash letters by a presenting bank, if the items are delivered after the close of the banking day, the items are considered to have been received on the next banking day.

7.3 PAYABLE THROUGH OR PAYABLE AT DRAFTS

A payable through or payable at draft is a draft that is drawn on a nonbank, but as the name implies, it is payable through or at the bank named in the instrument. The bank identified on the draft is designated as the bank to which presentment must be made. Payable through or payable at drafts may be handled as any other cash item and typically flow through the banking collection system as a check. Because of the wording on many of these types of items, some banks do not feel comfortable handling them as cash items and enter them for collection.

Section 4-106 addresses drafts that are payable through or payable at a bank. Section 4-106(a) addresses a draft payable through a bank and states, "If an item states it is "payable through" a bank identified in the item, (i) the item designates the bank as a collecting bank and does not by itself authorize the bank to pay the item, and (ii) the item may be presented for payment only by or through the bank." This section does two things; it designates the payable through bank as a collecting bank and it establishes the fact that the item must be presented for payment to the named bank.

Regulation CC has some specific rules regarding payable through drafts discussed later. The designation of the bank as a collecting bank means that the standard of care applicable to the payable through bank will be that of a collecting bank and not a payor bank. For example, Section 4-302 dealing with the payor bank's responsibility for late return of an item would not apply to the payable through bank. Under that section, the payor bank becomes accountable for the amount of an item that the bank holds past its midnight deadline. A collecting bank is not held to this standard but is only liable for the damage caused by its failure to exercise ordinary care. The point here is that there are specific differences between a payor bank and a collecting bank and the bank designated as the payable through bank is a collecting bank. As a collecting bank, the payable through bank is not authorized, without specific authority of the drawee, to pay the payable through draft. Likewise, the payable through bank could not be held liable for wrongful dishonor under Section 4-402 for returning an item that is properly payable. The court in *Messeroff v. Kantor, 10 UCC Rep Serv 826,* held that the bank through which a draft was payable was a collecting bank and not was liable as a drawee bank.

A bank is typically designated as a payable through bank by placing the words "payable through" followed by the name of the bank on the draft. The drafts also contain the routing number of the payable through bank encoded in magnetic ink. The drafts are typically presented to the payable through bank in the same manner as a check. Upon receipt, the bank captures the MICR line and presents the items and the data to the payor. After examining the item, the payor makes the decision to pay or return the items and settle with the bank that same day. The items that will be dishonored will be netted out of the settlement total and returned. Under this scenario, there is no question that the items are truly payable through items. However, if the procedures make the payable through look too much like a check and there is a dispute over this issue, the court may find that the item is a check and not a payable through draft.

For example, if the drafts are presented to the payable through bank, are processed in the same manner as a check, and each individual draft is debited to an account designated by account number on the draft, a court might find that the item is a check and not a payable through draft. In fact, the court held that a bank was the drawee bank and not a collecting bank in *Berman v. United States National Bank, 21 UCC Rep Serv 209.* In that case it was not clear from the face of the instrument that it was payable through the bank. The face of the instrument stated "through" the bank. The court also found that the bank was performing the functions of a payor bank for the customer and, therefore, was the payor bank.

Section 4-106(b) deals with items that are "payable at" a bank and this Subsection lists two alternatives. Alternative A states, "If an item states that it is 'payable at' a bank identified in the item, the item is equivalent to a draft drawn on the bank." Under this alternative, the item is considered a check, the payable at bank is the drawee, and the midnight deadline applicable to a payor bank under Sections 4-301 and 4-302 would apply. Alternative B treats an item payable at a bank the same as a payable through draft under Section 4-106(a) discussed above. A note payable at a bank would be considered the same as a draft drawn on that bank.

The capacity of a bank identified on an item is not always immediately clear or apparent on the item. Section 4-106(c) addresses this issue and states, "If a draft names a nonbank drawee and it is unclear whether a bank named in the draft is a co-drawee or a collecting bank, the bank is a collecting bank." As pointed out in Official Comment #3 to this section, "Subsection (c) rejects the view of some cases that a bank named below the name of a drawee is itself a drawee."

7.4 PAYABLE THROUGH OR PAYABLE AT DRAFTS UNDER REGULATION CC

Regulation CC considers a draft payable through or at a bank as a check. The definition of "check" under Section 229.2(k) states that a check means "a negotiable demand draft drawn on or payable through or at an office of a bank." Section 229.36(a), entitled "Payable-through and payable-at checks," states, "a check payable at or through a paying bank is considered to be drawn on that bank for purposes of the expeditious-return and notice-of-payment requirements of this subpart." The bank through which or at which the draft is payable is still considered a collecting bank for other purposes. That is, this section does not give the payable through bank the authority to pay the draft and the bank cannot be held liable as a paying bank. The bank is not held accountable for the amount of the item for failure to meet the deadlines under Section 4-301 and 4-302. The bank is liable, however, as a payor bank for failure to meet the requirements under Section 229.30 dealing with a paying bank's responsibility for return of checks and the notice requirements under Section 229.33.

Because of the liability under Regulation CC, a payable through bank should enter into an agreement with any customer that issues a draft payable through. The agreement should contain provisions that establish the obligations of the bank and the customer and it should establish the timeframes in which items must be presented to the customer and the cut-off time for return of dishonored items. The agreement should also contain provisions protecting the bank in the event of a delayed return or notice of dishonor. The protection could be in the form of an indemnification by the customer to the bank.

7.5 ELECTRONIC PRESENTMENT

Section 4-212 allows a collecting bank to make presentment of an item not payable by, through, or at a bank by sending notice to the party to pay the item that the bank holds the item. Therefore, if the item is payable by, through, or at a bank, the item itself must be presented. An exception to this rule has been established under the revised versions of Article 3 and 4 for items to be presented by electronic notice. Section 3-501(b)(1) clears the way for electronic presentment. That section states that presentment may be made by "any commercially reasonable means," including "electronic communication." "Electronic communication" is not defined and is left to agreements and court decisions. Section 4-110 specifically provides for electronic presentment that is made subject to an "agreement for electronic presentment." This section is apparently based on the provision for electronic presentment contained in Regulation CC. Section 229.36(c) provides that a bank may present a check to a paying bank by transmission of information describing the check in accordance with an agreement with the paying bank. Section 4-110 provides the following:

(a) 'Agreement for electronic presentment' means an agreement, clearing-house rule, or Federal Reserve regulation or operating circular, providing that presentment of an item may be made by transmission of an image of an item or information describing the item ('presentment notice') rather than delivery of the item itself. The agreement may provide for procedures governing retention, presentment, payment, dishonor, and other matters concerning items subject to the agreement.

(b) Presentment of an item pursuant to an agreement for presentment is made when the presentment notice is received.

(c) If presentment is made by presentment notice, a reference to 'item' or 'check' in this Article means the presentment notice unless the context otherwise indicates.

This section does not specifically state that checks may be presented electronically. It defines an "agreement for electronic presentment" but it does not specifically state that items may be presented electronically. The inference is that if banks enter into such an agreement then they will do so for the purpose of making electronic presentment. It is interesting to note, however, that the drafters did not state that items may be presented electronically in accordance with an agreement.

The "agreement for electronic presentment" may be made bilaterally between two banks and may be made multilaterally between numerous banks on a local, regional, or nationwide basis. The multilateral agreements will most likely be in the form of clearinghouse rules as opposed to specific agreements between the individual banks. The agreement can affect all aspects of the check collection process including presentment, payment, and dishonor. In addition to the authority given here allowing for agreements for electronic presentment, Section 4-103 allows for the effects of Article 4 to be varied by agreement. The agreement would be binding and enforceable to the parties to the agreement as long as the agreement did not attempt to disclaim a bank's responsibility for its lack of good faith or failure to exercise ordinary care. The agreement, according to Official Comment # 2 to Section 4-103, would not affect the owners or other interested parties "unless they are parties to the agreement or are bound by adoption, ratification, estoppel, or the like." However, Subsection (b) of Section 4-103 states that, "Federal Reserve regulations and operating circulars, clearing-house rules, and the like, have the effect of agreements under Subsection (a), whether or not specifically assented to by all parties interested in items handled." The court in *David Graubart, Inc. v. Bank Leumi Trust Co. of New York, 27 UCC Rep Serv 1184*, held that only parties to the agreement are bound by its terms but that by presenting the check to the depositary bank for collection, an agency relationship was established and the customer was subject to agreements entered into by the agent-bank. The court also held that not every act performed by the agent will be considered to have been consented to by the payee; the act must also be reasonable. The court stated that not only must the bank act in good faith, the agreement must be reasonable. In that case, the court held that it was reasonable to extend the midnight deadline and that the extension was binding on the payee of the check.

Section 4-110(b) provides that presentment is made when the presentment notice is received, indicating that the timeframe for action and all of the other implications of presentment are activated by receipt of the presentment notice. Official Comment # 1 to this section states, "The electronic presentment agreement may provide that the item may be retained by a depositary bank, other collecting bank, or even a customer of the depositary bank, or it may provide that the item will follow presentment notice. The identifying characteristic of an electronic presentment is that presentment occurs when the presentment notice is received."

(a) AGREEMENT FOR ELECTRONIC PRESENTMENT

The agreement for electronic presentment will be the document that governs the obligation and liabilities of the parties to the agreement. The content of the agreement will vary with the type of presentment, whether the checks will follow, the technology utilized, and many other factors. The following is a brief discussion of some of the items that might be considered for inclusion in an agreement. The agreement should establish the manner in which presentment will be made. That is, will the presentment be made by data transmission or by tape or other storage media? The agreement should also establish the content of the information, how the information should be formatted and whether an image of the item is acceptable or required. Because of the varying levels of a bank's technical ability, the parties to the agreement must agree on all of these technical details. Presentment times may vary with the different forms of presentment. The agreement should clearly establish the presentment times and provide for the availability of funds based on meeting the various deadlines. Other items that must be considered in the agreement are the disposition of rejects and how adjustments will be handled. The banks may also want to include a warranty provision in the agreement that warrants the accuracy of the information including the amount of the item, the customer's account number, and that the item being presented is in fact an item drawn on the bank receiving the electronic presentment.

If the checks are to be retained by the depositary or collecting bank, the agreement must establish the responsibilities of the parties to the agreement. Section 4-406 requires a bank that does not return the checks to the customer to retain a copy of the item for a period of seven years and to provide the customer with a legible copy of the item within a reasonable time of a request for a copy of the item by the customer. The agreement should specifically require the bank retaining the item to maintain the ability to produce a legible copy of the front and back of the items for the seven-year period. The bank should also consider requiring the retaining bank to maintain a duplicate copy for back up purposes. A provision should also be included detailing the information required of the bank requesting the copy of the item and how the request is to be made.

The agreement should also consider all of the issues associated with the dishonor and return of items. As stated above, Subsection (b) states, "Presentment of an item pursuant to an agreement for presentment is made when the presentment notice is received." This presentment starts the running of the midnight deadline clock for return of the item. The payor bank will be required to return the item, which in this case will be a return notice since the item itself will not yet have arrived, by midnight of the day following presentment of the item. The payor bank will be able to determine from the presentment notice the sufficiency of funds in an account, and in most cases it will be able to identify items on which stop payments have been placed. However, unless the presentment notice is in the form of an image of the item, the bank will not be able to verify the signature of the drawer. Under current bulk file systems, banks set a dollar limit and examine checks over that dollar limit. The bank will not have the items to examine to determine the authenticity of the signature if the items are presented electronically. The bank will likewise not have the item to provide the necessary information required for large dollar return item notifications. For this reason, the banks may want to establish a dollar limit for electronic presentment. That is unless an image of the check is sent that can be examined. Again, the effects of Article 4 may be varied by agreement. The agreement for electronic presentment may include a variation of the method of presentment, dishonor, returns and the timeframes, as long as the agreement is reasonable.

If the item is retained by the depositary or a collecting bank, and the drawee bank dishonors the item, the item must be returned timely to the last indorser by the bank retaining the item. Another point to consider is that Section 229.30(d) of Regulation CC requires a paying bank that returns a check to "clearly indicate on the face of the check that it is a returned check and the reason for return." The agreement should address this issue. It would appear that the bank retaining the item will have to be given the responsibility of returning the physical item and supplying the required notification on the face of the check. A provision should also address the failure of the retaining bank to perform the required duties.

The agreement must also address when and how settlement will be made for the items presented. Settlement could be based on the receipt of the electronic presentment notice or upon receipt of the item if the item follows the electronic presentment. Settlement for return items must also be addressed. The agreement should also clearly define areas of Article 3 & 4 that will be varied by agreement. For example, if the method of presentment is electronic presentment with the checks to follow, the agreement must clearly state that presentment does not occur until the paper is presented if that is the intention of the parties. Otherwise, the provisions of Article 4 will apply and the electronic notice will be considered the presentment and not the paper that follows.

7.6 EXCUSED PRESENTMENT

Presentment is not always required to charge a party liable on an instrument. Section 3-504(a) lists five specific situations where presentment is excused:

> Presentment for payment or acceptance of an instrument is excused if (i) the person entitled to present the instrument cannot with reasonable diligence make presentment, (ii) the maker or acceptor has repudiated an obligation to pay the instrument or is dead or in insolvency, (iii) by the terms of the instrument presentment is not necessary to enforce the obligation of indorsers or the drawer, (iv) the drawer or indorser

whose obligation is being enforced has waived presentment or otherwise has no reason to expect or right to require that the instrument be paid or accepted, or (v) the drawer instructed the drawee not to pay or accept the draft or the drawee was not obligated to the drawer to pay the draft.

If the drawee bank has suspended payment, and payment will not be made by the FDIC or the amount of the item exceeds the coverage, presentment would not be required to enforce the item against the drawer. If the drawer has issued a stop payment order on a check and advised the payee of the stop payment order, presentment would not be required. In this instance, the payee already knows that the item will not be paid by the drawee, therefore, presentment is not necessary. The purpose of presentment is obviously to receive payment for an item. If the person entitled to enforce the instrument has already received knowledge that the drawee will not pay the item because of one of the reasons listed above, presentment is not necessary. Presentment of a check was excused in *Smith v. Gentilotti*, 20 *UCC Rep Serv* 1222. In that case, the plaintiff's father issued a check to the plaintiff in 1969 and postdated the check for 1984. The father indorsed the check "For Edward Joseph Smith Gentilotte My Son If I Should Pass Away the Amount of $20,000.00 Dollars Shall Be Taken from My Estate at Death." The father died in 1973 and the son made demand on the estate for payment. The court held that presentment was excused since the payor bank could not pay the check after 10 days after the death of the drawer if it had notice of the death. Obviously, since the father died in 1973 and the check was postdated 1984, the check would not be honored by the drawee bank even if presented.

Presentment is not excused if the person entitled to enforce the item merely has knowledge of the fact that the balance in a drawer's account is not sufficient to pay a check. In other words, if the payee of a check calls a bank to verify a check and is informed that the balance is not sufficient, presentment is still required to enforce the check against the drawer. In *McLaughlin v. Sports & Recreation Club, Inc.*, 39 *UCC Rep Serv* 1373, the court held that funds do not have to be deposited into an account before a check is presented for payment. In this case, the payee of the check claimed that it would not have done any good to have presented the check because the balance in the account was not sufficient. The court held that this was not an excuse for presentment especially since that payee was not aware of the insufficient balance until several years later.

PART II: COLLECTION

7.7 STATUS OF COLLECTING BANK

There has been a fair amount of litigation over the question of who owns an item after a bank has taken the item for collection. The issue normally arises when a creditor of the depositing customer attempts to get to the deposit represented by the items. The creditor's contention is that a debtor creditor relationship exists from the point the items are deposited with the bank. The customer's position is that the bank is only an agent for the customer and that the bank does not possess a property right that is subject to a creditor's claim. Another question that comes up concerning ownership of the item is who assumes the risk of loss? Section 4-201 answers these questions. That section states that a collecting bank is the agent or subagent of the owner of the item unless a contrary intent clearly appears. The debtor creditor relationship does not begin until final settlement for the item is made. Likewise, the risk of loss of the item remains with the customer who is the owner of the item. The collecting bank retains a security interest in the item and has a preferred position against creditors for items on which the bank has made advances. The collecting bank may also exercise its right of setoff during this period that the agency status exists.

Any settlement given by the collecting bank is provisional and the agency status remains until settlement for the item is or becomes final. If the person settling for the item pays with a draft or check, the agency status remains until payment of the draft or check becomes final. As to checks, settlement is final when given according to Section 229.36(d) of Regulation CC. The fact that settlement is final does not change the collecting bank's obligation as an agent for the owner of the item. As the commentary to this section of Regulation CC points out, the collecting bank remains liable to the customer for its negligence. According to one court, the bank's agency status ends when the account is closed. In *General Apparel Sales Corp. v. Chase Manhattan Bank, N.A., 8 UCC Rep Serv 1071,* the court held that the bank had no right to accept for deposit and handle an item for collection after the customer had closed the account. In this case, the bank accepted a deposit some six months after the account was closed and the funds were withdrawn without proper authority.

The agency status applies regardless of the form of the indorsement or the lack of an indorsement. The fact that the owner of the instrument may have indorsed the instrument in blank, or made a restrictive indorsement, or failed to indorse the instrument at all does not affect the agency status. Section 4-201 also applies if the customer has the right to immediately withdraw the amount of the credit given or in fact does withdraw the funds. The ownership of the item remains in the customer. However, the bank retains the rights that it has, such as the right of setoff or rights of recoupment, and the rights resulting from outstanding advances on the item.

The last sentence of Section 4-201(a) states, "If an item is handled by banks for purposes of presentment, payment, collection, or return, the relevant provisions of this Article apply even though action of the parties clearly establishes that a particular bank has purchased the item and is the owner of it." The purpose of this sentence is to clearly establish the fact that the provisions of Article 4 apply to every item that flows through the banking system regardless of the status of the ownership of the item. The Official Comments to this section contain a lengthy discussion about the impact of this section.

In addition to being an agent or a subagent of the customer that owns the item, a collecting bank also obtains a security interest in the item and any accompanying documents or proceeds of either. The security interest is created by Section 4-201 which is discussed in Section 6.4 of Chapter 6 of this book. Briefly, the security interest is created in an item that has been deposited in an account when the credit given for the deposit is withdrawn or applied, or when the customer has the right to withdraw the funds even if the funds are not withdrawn. The bank also has a security interest in an item if it makes an advance on or against the item. If credit is given for several items and a portion of the credit is withdrawn, the bank continues to have a security interest in all of the items. This prevents having to try to perform the impossible task of determining which of the several items deposited has been withdrawn. As to multiple deposits reflected in a customer's balance, the security interest is created in the items on a first in first out bases.

As in the case of the agency status, receipt of final settlement for the item by the collecting bank is a realization of the security interest in the items collected by the bank. Once the items are paid by the drawee bank, there is no longer a need for the security interest. Before the items are finally settled for, the collecting bank continues to have a security interest in the items and has a preferred position over other creditors.

The security interest is created and is considered perfected under Article 9 without the need of the formal requirements of Article 9 of a security agreement or filing to perfect.

Taken together, Section 4-201 creates an agency relationship between the customer and the bank, and Section 4-210 gives the bank a perfected security interest in the item during the collection process. The customer continues to own the items, but because of the security interest in the items, the bank has certain claims that it may exert against the items. Although the bank is only an agent during the collection process, by virtue of the security interest, the bank has given value for the items for the purpose of obtaining holder in due course status of the items. Holder in due course is discussed in detail in Chapter 6 of this book.

7.8 COLLECTING BANK'S RESPONSIBILITY DURING COLLECTION

As discussed previously, a collecting bank is the agent for its customer for the purpose of collecting the item delivered to the bank. As an agent, the bank has certain duties of care and responsibilities to the customer. Section 4-202 contains the responsibility that the bank has during the forward collection and return process. Section 4-202 states the following:

(a) A collecting bank must exercise ordinary care in:

    (1) presenting an item or sending it for presentment;

    (2) sending notice of dishonor or nonpayment or returning an item other than a documentary draft to the bank's transferor after learning that the item has not been paid or accepted, as the case may be;

    (3) settling for an item when the bank receives final settlement; and

    (4) notifying its transferor of any loss or delay in transit within a reasonable time after discovery thereof.

(b) A collecting bank exercises ordinary care under Subsection (a) by taking proper action before its midnight deadline following receipt of an item, notice, or settlement. Taking proper action within a reasonably longer time may constitute the exercise of ordinary care, but the bank has the burden of establishing timeliness.

(c) Subject to Subsection (a)(1), a bank is not liable for the insolvency, neglect, misconduct, mistake, or default of another bank or person or for loss or destruction of an item in the possession of others or in transit.

Subsection (a) establishes that a collecting bank must exercise ordinary care during the normal collection process of presentment, selection of a clearing agent, and settlement for an item. The bank must also exercise ordinary care in the return process of a dishonored item and in sending any required notices. In *Norstar Bank of Upstate New York v. Southeast Bank, N.A., 10 UCC Rep Serv 2d 433*, a collecting bank was held liable for the amount of loss caused by its failure to give timely notice of return. The collecting bank was an intermediary collecting bank that failed to notify the depositary bank. The court held that although the notice of return erroneously identified the collecting bank as the depositary bank, the bank failed to exercise ordinary care in identifying the proper depositary bank. "Ordinary care" is defined in Section 3-103(a)(7) as the following:

. . . in the case of a person engaged in business means observance of reasonable commercial standards, prevailing in the area in which the person is located, with respect to the business in which the person is engaged. In the case of a bank that takes an instrument for processing for collection or payment by automated means, reasonable commercial standards do not require the bank to examine the instrument if the failure to examine does not violate the bank's prescribed procedures and the bank's procedures do not vary unreasonably from general banking usage not disapproved by this Article or Article 4.

Based on this definition of "ordinary care," the bank's standard of care will not be measured in a vacuum but will be measured in relation to other banks in the area and generally acceptable banking practices. If a bank makes an error, for example, and as a result of the error the presentment of a check is delayed causing a loss to the depositing customer, the bank will not automatically be held liable for the loss. If the bank exercised good faith, and the manner in which it processed the item was not negligent in comparison to other banks in the area, then the bank will have met the requirements of Section 4-202(a). In *Pan American World Airways v. Bankers Trust Co. v. Royal Bank of Canada, 37*

UCC Rep Serv 1636, a collecting bank was held liable to its customer for its failure to exercise ordinary care in collecting checks that were deposited with the bank. In this case, the customer deposited several checks that were held for some unexplained reason by a bank clerk for several weeks. When the checks were finally presented, they were dishonored. The court held the bank liable for failure to exercise ordinary care. The amount of damages awarded was the face amount of the checks because the facts showed that the checks would have been paid if not for the delay.

Regardless of the manner in which a bank processes items or how it presents the items, Subsection (b) provides that the bank exercises ordinary care if it takes proper action before its midnight deadline. The midnight deadline for a bank is defined in Section 4-104(a)(10) as midnight of the next banking day following the banking day on which a bank receives an item or notice. For example, if a bank receives an item on Monday, the bank exercises ordinary care relative to the item if it forwards the item for collection or takes any other required action before midnight on Tuesday. If Tuesday is not a banking day for the bank, then the bank's midnight deadline expires on Wednesday. The bank may take a reasonably longer period of time than the midnight deadline to take proper action on the item, but the bank has the burden of establishing the timeliness of the action as held by the court in *Pandol Brothers, Inc. v. NCNB National Bank of Florida, 38 UCC Rep Serv, 944.* Official Comment #3 to this section states, "In the case of time items, action after the midnight deadline, but sufficiently in advance of maturity for proper presentation, is a clear example of a 'reasonably longer time' that is timely." The bank that takes action after its midnight deadline exercises ordinary care if the delay was caused by one of the items listed in Section 4-109 which is discussed above.

A collecting bank may present an item directly to a payor or to the payor through an intermediary bank as stated in Section 4-204. The selection of the clearing agent is left entirely up to the collecting bank. However, the collecting bank must exercise good faith and ordinary care in the selection of the clearing bank. According to Section 4-202(c), as long as the collecting bank exercises ordinary care, the bank is not liable for the insolvency, neglect, misconduct, mistake, or default of any other person. The bank is likewise not liable for the loss or destruction of the item in the possession of another or while the item is in transit. For example, if an item is stolen from a courier during the collection process, the bank, as an agent of the owner of the item, is not responsible for the loss of the item. If an intermediary collecting bank does not settle for an item, the collecting bank is not liable to the customer unless the collecting bank did not exercise good faith or ordinary care in the selection of the clearing agent. If the collecting bank had reason to know of the insolvency of the clearing bank, for example, then the collecting bank may not have exercised ordinary care by continuing to send checks to the insolvent clearing bank. If the collecting bank is negligent, the collecting bank is liable to the bank that sent the item to it and not to the depositary bank's customer. In *Childs v. Federal Reserve Bank, 37 UCC Rep Serv 515*, the court held that a collecting bank, that is not the depositary bank, is not the agent of the owner of the check and owes no duty to a party for whom it is not an agent. Additionally in that case, the court pointed out that according to Regulation J, a Federal Reserve Bank is not liable to the owner of a check for negligence in collecting a check.

7.9 EFFECT OF INSTRUCTIONS ON A COLLECTING BANK

A collecting bank may take instructions from its transferor and follow those instructions without fear of liability to any other party. Section 4-203 states, "Subject to Article 3 concerning conversion of instruments (Section 3-420) and restrictive indorsements (Section 3-206), only a collecting bank's transferor can give instructions that affect the bank or constitute notice to it, and a collecting bank is not liable to prior parties for any action taken pursuant to the instructions or in accordance with any agreement with its transferor." This section allows a collecting bank to only take instructions from its transferor and not be placed in the situation of not knowing whose instructions it is to follow if it receives conflicting instructions from another party.

For example, assume that Bill issues a check to Joel and Joel indorses the check in blank and loses the check. D. A. finds the check and deposits it to his account with the First Deposit Bank (FDB). That same day, Joel determines that D. A. had deposited the item at the FDB. Joel then informs the bank of the facts and directs the bank not to send the check for collection but to give it to him. According to Section 4-203, the bank is not liable to Joel. The problem that may arise, however, is that the person from whom the bank receives the item may have forged the indorsement of the true owner. If the indorsement on the item is forged or a necessary indorsement is missing, then the bank is subject to a claim of conversion of the item by the true owner.

The collecting bank is required to follow the instructions of its transferor and is not liable to any party for following those instructions. In *Engine Parts, Inc. v. Citizens Bank of Clovis, 23 UCC Rep Serv 120,* the court held that the bank through which drafts were payable was not liable to the payee of the drafts or the forwarding bank for following the instruction of the forwarding bank.

Likewise, a depositary bank must adhere to a restrictive indorsement and is liable to the owner of the item if the proceeds of the item are not applied in accordance with the restrictive indorsement. For example, if a check is indorsed "for deposit only," the bank must adhere to the restrictive indorsement and only take the item for deposit. If the payee of a check informs the bank that its employee has received cash back on an item that was indorsed "for deposit only," this section does not protect the bank. The bank could not rely on this section and continue to accept checks from the employee.

7.10 IDENTIFICATION OF TRANSFEROR DURING COLLECTION

Negotiation of an item that is payable to an identified person requires the indorsement of that person according to Section 3-201. This rule does not apply to items transferred between banks. Section 4-206 states, "Any agreed method that identifies the transferor bank is sufficient for the item's further transfer to another bank." The purpose of this section is to ensure the speedy collection of items through the banking system. A depositary bank or any collecting bank may use any type of indorsement on a check that identifies the fact that the item was handled by that bank. An indorsement containing the routing number only of the bank is sufficient. In the event that the item is dishonored and it is necessary to identify a bank that handled the item, the routing number would serve that purpose.

Any bank handling an item must adhere to the requirements of Section 229.35 and Appendix D of part C of Regulation CC. According to Appendix D, the depositary bank must indorse an item using "the bank's nine-digit routing number, set off by arrows at each end of the number pointing toward the number." The indorsement must also contain the bank's name/location, and the indorsement date and may contain certain optional information. The indorsement must be written in dark purple or black ink and must "be placed on the back of the check so that the routing number is wholly contained in the area 3.0 inches from the leading edge of the check to 1.5 inches from the trailing edge of the check." Each subsequent collecting bank must protect the indorsement of the depositary bank to ensure that the indorsement remains legible so that the depositary bank can be easily identified by the paying bank. The indorsement of the subsequent collecting bank must include only its nine-digit routing number, the indorsement date and may include an optional trace or sequence number. The indorsement may be in any color except purple and must be placed on the back of the check from 0.0 inches to 3.0 inches from the leading edge of the check. Section 5.5 of Chapter 5 in this book contains a detailed discussion of other indorsement requirements of Section 229.35.

7.11 TRANSFER AND OTHER WARRANTIES MADE BY COLLECTING BANK

Each collecting bank that handles an item, with or without an indorsement, makes the transfer warranties provided for under Sections 3-416 and 4-207. These sections are discussed in Section 2.9 of Chapter 2 of this book. In addition to those warranties, a depositary bank that takes an item for collection from a customer, whether the item is or is not indorsed by the customer, makes the following warranty under Section 4-205(2), "The depositary bank warrants to collecting banks, the payor bank or other payor, and the drawer that the amount of the item was paid to the customer or deposited to the customer's account."

Section 4-205(1), which is discussed in Section 5.4 of Chapter 5 of this book, establishes the depositary bank as a holder of an item even if that item is not indorsed. This section replaces the previous version which allowed the depositary bank to supply a missing indorsement. The rationale behind this section is that since the depositary bank is not required to obtain an indorsement, it should at least warrant that the proceeds did get to the proper person. This warranty is in addition to the transfer and presentment warranties.

(a) ENCODING WARRANTIES

The longstanding question of who is liable for an item that is misencoded and what grounds is the liability based on, is finally answered by Section 4-209. A misencoded item is not an alteration of the item as some courts have held. It is simply an error made by the person who encodes the item in MICR. Section 4-209(a) addresses this issue and states, "A person who encodes information on or with respect to an item after issue warrants to any subsequent collecting bank and to the payor bank or other payor that the information is correctly encoded. If the customer of a depositary bank encodes, the bank also makes the warranty." The warranty refers to any information encoded on the check, not just the amount. Therefore, the person who encodes the check could be liable under Subsection (c) for loss caused by any field on the check that is misencoded. Most depositary banks only encode the amount field of a check and the potential liability here is obvious. If a drawer wrote a check for $1,000 but the depositary bank encoded the item for $10,000, the depositary bank would be liable to the payor bank for the $9,000 for which the check was over encoded plus other damages under Subsection (c) discussed below. The payor of the item is allowed, under this section, to look immediately and directly to the depositary bank without first attempting to collect the proceeds from the payee of the check. If the check was written by the drawer for $10,000 but was encoded as $1,000, the payor could first attempt to charge the customer's account for the $9,000 underencoded amount. If the customer's account balance was not sufficient, the payor bank could look directly to the depositary bank without first pursuing collection from the drawer. Some banks have reciprocal agreements to encode other information on the check such as the customer's account number and the check number. The depositary bank would be liable to the payor bank for any loss caused by an error in this encoded information. Any loss caused by an error in the bank routing number encoded by the depositary bank would likewise be absorbed by the depositary bank.

The depositary bank also warrants that the information is correct even if the depositary bank's customer encoded the information on the check. Many corporate customers encode the amount of the check as part of their own process and to pay a lower fee to the depositary bank. If the customer makes an error, the depositary bank could be liable to the payor bank. While the customer who encoded the amount makes the warranty to the payor bank, the payor bank could look to the depositary bank to recover any loss. The depositary bank could then look to the customer who made the error because the warranty is also made by the customer to the depositary bank as a collecting bank. As an added precaution, the depositary bank should consider including a warranty provision in the customer agreement that protects the bank in this regard.

The damages for breach of warranty under this section are addressed in Subsection (c). Subsection (c) states, "A person to whom warranties are made under this section and who took the item in good faith may recover from the warrantor as damages for breach of warranty an amount equal to the loss suffered as a result of the breach, plus expenses of interest incurred as a result of the breach." The "loss suffered" may certainly exceed the error made in the encoded amount. The amount of damages under this section is not limited to actual damages and could include consequential damages plus any collection expenses and interest. Attorney's fees could also be included depending on local law. The wording of the amount of damages under this section is very broad because it states that the person who pays the item may recover "an amount equal to the loss suffered as a result of the loss." Assume that a check in the amount of $100 is encoded by the depositary bank as $1,000 and is paid by the payor bank in the amount of $1,000 causing other checks that the customer had written to be dishonored. The payor bank could be liable to the customer for wrongful dishonor for the check that was erroneously returned. Since the loss was the result of the encoding error, the depositary bank could be liable to the paying bank for any loss that the paying bank incurs as a result of the wrongful dishonor.

Other examples of the application of this section are as follows. Assume that the depositary bank erroneously encodes an account number on a check and the check is paid on the wrong account causing other checks on the account to be returned. The paying bank could be liable for wrongful dishonor to the customer whose account was erroneously charged. The depositary bank could be liable to the paying bank for any loss suffered by the paying bank as a result of the wrongful dishonor. Assume that the depositary encodes the wrong check number or the wrong amount on a check which causes the paying bank to miss a valid stop payment order and other checks are returned as a result of the check paying over the valid stop payment order. In this example, the depositary bank could be liable to the paying bank for the loss caused by paying the check over the stop payment order plus any damages caused by wrongful dishonor of the other checks.

The warranty under this section would also apply to information that is transmitted to the payor bank in accordance with an electronic check presentment agreement. The warranty is not limited to information actually encoded on the check. The first sentence of Subsection (a) states that, "A person who encodes information on or with respect to an item. . ." The "with respect" language would extend the warranty to items that are presented electronically. In addition to that wording, Section 4-110(c) states, "If presentment is made by presentment notice, a reference to 'item' or 'check' in this article means the presentment notice unless the context otherwise indicates." Therefore, the provisions of the section would apply equally to electronic presentment.

(b) RETENTION WARRANTIES

Electronic presentment may be made in accordance with an "agreement for electronic presentment" as defined in Section 4-110(a), which is discussed above in Section 7.5 of this chapter. In order for electronic presentment to be successful, the presentment must be made in accordance with the agreement. Section 4-209(b) acknowledges and addresses this issue. That Subsection states, "A person who undertakes to retain an item pursuant to an agreement for electronic presentment warrants to any subsequent collecting bank and to the payor bank or other payor that retention and presentment of the item comply with the agreement. If a customer of a depositary bank undertakes to retain an item, that bank also makes this warranty." If the agreement requires that the items be compiled in a certain format, for example, and the presenting bank makes an error in the sequence of the information that causes a loss, the bank retaining the checks could be liable under this section for the loss.

The warranty under this section not only applies to the presentment of the item but to all other terms of the agreement. For example, assume that the agreement requires the bank retaining the items to maintain the capability to produce a copy of the item for a period of seven years. If the retaining bank is unable to produce a copy during the seven year period, the bank would not only be liable for breach under the agreement, but would also be subject to any damages provided for under Subsection (c) caused by the breach. The depositary bank gives this warranty even if a customer keeps the items. The depositary bank would not be liable and does not give this warranty if the items are truncated by a subsequent collecting bank.

(c) APPLICABILITY OF THE ENCODING
AND RETENTION WARRANTIES

The warranties under Section 4-209 are given by any person who encodes information on or with respect to an item. The warranty is given to any subsequent collecting bank and to the payor bank or any other payor of the item. Unlike the presentment and transfer warranties, the encoding and retention warranty is not given by a collecting bank that did not encode the item. For example, if Bank A erroneously encodes a check which causes a loss to the payor bank and sends the check to Bank B who presents the item to the payor bank, Bank B is not liable to the payor bank for the damages caused by the encoding error. The warranty is given by Bank A in this example to Bank B and to the payor bank. The payor bank would have to look to Bank A to satisfy its claim for any loss. The warranty is not extended to the customer that deposited the item. For example, if the depositary bank erroneously encodes the wrong bank routing number on the check which causes a delay in presentment, the depositary bank would not be liable to the customer for breach of warranty under this section. The depositary bank may, however, be liable to the customer for failure to exercise the required degree of ordinary care under Section 4-202. The customer may be able to raise the issue that Section 4-209 creates a duty on the part of the depositary bank to ensure the accuracy of the information encoded on a check and that failure to do so is not the exercise of ordinary care.

While Section 4-209 appears to be directed towards the forward collection process only, a court could interpret the language to apply this section to the return process. Or the court, by analogy, may apply this section to the return process. Under Regulation CC, the payor bank may qualify a return item by encoding the routing number of the depositary bank, the amount of the check, and a "2" in position 44 of the MICR line of the check. A loss could be incurred by the depositary bank as a result of the erroneous encoding of the information. The return process under Regulation CC is discussed in Chapter 8 of this book. By really stretching the wording in Section 4-209, a court could conclude that the warranty is given by a payor bank who encodes the information. Again, the first sentence of Subsection (a) states, "A person who encodes information on or with respect to an item after issue warrants to any subsequent collecting bank and to the payor bank or other payor that the information is correctly encoded." The payor bank is "a person who encodes information on a check" even though the information is for the return of the item. The depositary bank is a collecting bank and the warranty is given by the person who encodes the information to any subsequent collecting bank. While the depositary bank is a collecting bank in the forward collection process, it appears that it could be considered a collecting bank in the return process. The intention of Regulation CC is to expedite the return process by allowing return items to be processed as forward collection items; therefore, it seems reasonable to apply this section to the return process.

PART III: SETTLEMENT

7.12 SETTLEMENT DEFINED

"Settlement" is a term used throughout the UCC and Regulation CC and comes in many different forms depending on the item and whether it is used in conjunction with other words such as "provisional," "conditional," "final," or other terms. The term "settlement" is defined in Section 4-104(a)(11) and means "to pay in cash, by clearinghouse settlement, in a charge or credit or by remittance, or otherwise as agreed. A settlement may be either provisional or final." Payment of cash over-the-counter is settlement for an item and in the case of an "on-us" item is final settlement. In the check collection process, the form or medium of settlement will be determined by the method of collection and the agreement of the parties. If checks are cleared through a clearinghouse, settlement will made in accordance with the rules of the clearinghouse and may take many different forms. If presentment is made directly to the payor bank or through a correspondent bank, the settlement may take the form of debits or credits to accounts, remittance of payment by draft, teller's check, cashier's check, through bilateral or multilateral netting, or any other agreed method.

7.13 MEDIUM AND TIME OF SETTLEMENT

The medium of settlement may come in many different forms and typically will be determined by Federal Reserve Regulation or operating circular, clearinghouse rule, or other agreement. The medium of settlement was provided for in Section 4-211 in the previous version of Article 4. The medium and time for settlement are now stated in Section 4-213 which has been completely revised. Section 4-213(a) and (b) provide the following:

(a) With respect to settlement by a bank, the medium and time of settlement may be prescribed by Federal Reserve regulations or circulars, clearinghouse rules, and the like, or agreement. In the absence of such prescription:

(1) the medium of settlement is cash or credit to an account in a Federal Reserve bank of or specified by the person to receive settlement; and

(2) the time of settlement is:

(i)   with respect to tender of settlement by cash, a cashier's check, or teller's check, when the cash or check is sent or delivered;

(ii)   with respect to tender of settlement by credit in an account in a Federal Reserve Bank, when the credit is made;

(iii)   with respect to tender of settlement by a credit or debit to an account in a bank, when the credit or debit is made or, in the case of tender of settlement by authority to charge an account, when the authority is sent or delivered; or

(iv)   with respect to tender of settlement by a funds transfer, when payment is made pursuant to Section 4A-406(a) to the person receiving settlement.

(b) If the tender of settlement is not by a medium authorized by Subsection (a) or the time of settlement is not fixed by Subsection (a), no settlement occurs until the tender of settlement is accepted by the person receiving settlement.

In most situations, the medium of settlement for checks will be prescribed by one of the items listed in Subsection (a)(1). If the checks are not cleared through the Federal Reserve, a clearinghouse, or are not subject to an agreement that prescribes the manner of settlement, the person making presentment can demand settlement in cash or through credit to an account in a Federal Reserve bank. The presentment of the item is, of course, subject to Section 3-501(b) wherein the payor bank can require production of proper identification to ensure that payment is made to the proper person.

The time when settlement occurs is governed by Subsection (a)(2), as stated above, and is important under other sections of Article 4. For example, Section 4-301, which is discussed in Chapter 8 of this book, creates the payor bank's right of deferred posting. Under that section, the bank must settle for an item by midnight of the day on which the item is presented. Settlement is also a key factor under Section 4-215 in determining when an item is finally paid by the payor bank. Subsection (a)(2) is essential in determining whether or not settlement has occurred. As stated in Subsection (a)(2), the fact that tender of settlement is made does not constitute settlement. In the case of cash or bank check, settlement does not occur until the cash is delivered to the person making presentment. The bank's acknowledgement of its obligation or its agreement to settle is not sufficient. Actual delivery of the cash or bank check is required.

In the case of settlement through the Federal Reserve or debit or credit to an account, settlement does not occur until the entry is made. Unless the entries are made on-line, the exact time that the debit or credit is made will be virtually impossible to determine. Although not addressed, the section does not require that the entries be made on line. It would appear that preparation of paper entries and entry into the capture process would be sufficient. The point here is that initiation of the process of settlement in the case of credit or debit entries would be sufficient to satisfy this section. For example, assume that Bank A presents checks to Bank B and Bank B settles for the items by making a credit to Bank A's account maintained with Bank B. Assume further that the items are presented by Bank A to Bank B at 11:00 a.m. and Bank B prepares the credit entry to Bank A's account at 2:00 p.m. that same day. The paper credit entry must be encoded in MICR and captured by the bank's capture system. The actual credit to Bank A's account may not actually happen until some time later that night or early the next morning when the bank runs its posting programs. It would appear that in this example, settlement for the items presented by Bank A occurred at the point that Bank B made the decision to settle for the items and made the paper entries not when the bank actually performed its posting run.

Subsection (b) provides that if the tender of settlement is not by a medium authorized by Subsection (a), settlement does not occur until the settlement is accepted by the person making presentment. For example, if a payor bank tenders settlement by offering the person making presentment a note issued by the payor bank, settlement does not occur until the presenter accepts the note as settlement. Subsection (b) also states that settlement does not occur until accepted if the time for settlement is not fixed by Subsection (a).

(a) PROVISIONAL SETTLEMENT

Unless a contrary intent clearly appears, settlement made by a collecting or payor bank is provisional according to Section 4-201(a). While provisional settlement is not defined, the concept is that during the collection process, each bank gives credit to the presenter with the understanding that the credit that is given is subject to final payment of the item by the payor bank. This process envisions that the item will flow through the collection process and if dishonored, will be returned to the first indorser through the same chain. Therefore, the credit that is given is subject to reversal if the item is not finally paid. The last sentence of Section 4-104(a)(11), which defines "settlement," states that settlement may be provisional or final. The concept of final and provisional settlement is present in a number of sections in Articles 3 and 4.

Section 4-201(a) considers settlement for checks as provisional. Regulation CC, which supersedes Article 4, states in Section 229.36(d) that settlement for checks is final when made. One of the intended purposes of Regulation CC is to expedite the forward and return collection process. By making settlement between banks final when made, Regulation CC allows the payor bank to return an item directly back to the depository bank thereby eliminating the requirement and time that it would need to return the check by the same route that it was presented. The commentary to Section 229.36(d) states that final settlement does not affect the liability scheme under Section 4-201 that is created because of the agency status of a collecting bank. The commentary also states that final settlement under this section is not intended to render an item finally paid under Section 4-215(a). Even though settlement is final when made under Regulation CC, any collecting bank remains liable on the item until it is finally paid by the payor bank.

(b) FINAL SETTLEMENT

The point at which provisional settlement becomes final is dependent on the medium of the settlement and the action or inaction of the person to whom settlement is made. Sections 4-213 and 4-215 both contain provisions that address when settlement becomes final. Section 4-213(c) states, "If settlement for an item is made by cashier's check or teller's check and the person receiving settlement, before its midnight deadline: (1) presents or forwards the check for collection, settlement is final when the check is finally paid; or (2) fails to present or forward the check for collection, settlement is final at the midnight deadline of the person receiving settlement." Under this section, settlement becomes final when the check that is given as settlement is finally paid if the person receiving settlement presents the cashier's or teller's check for payment before the expiration of the midnight deadline. If the person receiving settlement holds on to the check and does not send it for collection by its midnight deadline, final settlement occurs by the midnight deadline. The person receiving settlement assumes the risk that the check will not be paid if it does not act by its midnight deadline. For example, if Bank A presents a check to Bank B and Bank B settles with Bank A by issuing a cashier's check to Bank A, settlement becomes final when the cashier's check is finally paid. If Bank A does not initiate collection of the cashier's check by its midnight deadline (midnight of the day following receipt of the cashier's check), the settlement becomes final at the midnight deadline of Bank A.

If settlement for an item is made by giving authority to charge the account of the bank giving settlement in the bank receiving settlement, Subsection (d) states, "Settlement is final when the charge is made by the bank receiving settlement if there are funds available in the account for the amount of the item." For example, assume that Bank A presents an item to Bank B and the settlement agreement provides that Bank A is to receive settlement from Bank B by charging Bank B's account with Bank A. Settlement becomes final when Bank A charges Bank B's account for the amount of the items Bank A presented to Bank B.

Section 4-215 also governs when settlement becomes final and addresses the relationship between final settlement and final payment. Final payment is discussed in Chapter 9 of this book. As to settlement, Subsection (c) states, "If provisional settlement for an item between the presenting and payor banks is made through a clearinghouse or by debits or credits in an account between them, then to the extent that provisional debits or credits for the item are entered in accounts between the presenting and payor banks or between the presenting and successive prior collecting banks seriatim, they become final upon final payment of the items by the payor bank." This section states that provisional credit becomes final when the payor bank pays the items that are presented. The settlement becomes final only if the settlement was made through a clearinghouse or through debits or credits to accounts. The settlement by the payor bank could not have been made by a cashier's or teller's check. If it were, payment is not final until final payment of the cashier's or teller's check. As pointed out in Official Comment #9 to this section, "The 'firming up' continues only to the extent that provisional debits and credits are entered seriatim in accounts between banks which are successive to the presenting bank." If any of the collecting banks in the chain of presentment settled in a manner other than through debit or credits to accounts, then this section would not apply.

The effect of a collecting bank receiving final settlement for an item is that the bank becomes accountable to its customer for the amount of the item. Section 4-215(c) states, "If a collecting bank receives a settlement for an item which is or becomes final, the bank is accountable to its customer for the amount of the item and any provisional credit given for the item in an account with its customer becomes final." While the bank is accountable to the customer for the amount of the item, this Subsection does not require that the bank make the funds available to the customer. Subsection (e) discussed below establishes when funds become available as of right. If the item that is deposited is a check, Regulation CC establishes when the funds must be made available to the customer. The point here is that when the collecting bank receives final payment, any provisional credit that the bank has given to the customer becomes final.

(c) WHEN FUNDS BECOME AVAILABLE TO CUSTOMERS

While Regulation CC has specific guidelines for when banks must make funds available to customers for checks that have been deposited, Section 4-215(e) also contains provisions for when funds become available for withdrawal. That section states the following:

Subject to (i) applicable law stating a time for availability of funds and (ii) any right of the bank to apply the credit to an obligation of the customer, credit given by a bank for an item in a customer's account becomes available for withdrawal as of right: (1) if the bank has received a provisional settlement for the item, when the settlement becomes final and the bank has had a reasonable time to receive return of the item and the item has not been received within that time; (2) if the bank is both the depositary bank and the payor bank, and the item is finally paid, at the opening of the bank's second banking day following receipt of the item.

This Subsection is applicable to all items taken by a bank but is subject to Regulation CC as to checks and certain other items. Regulation CC contains specific guidelines as to when funds are to be made available to customers and those guidelines supersede Article 4. One major problem with attempting to apply this section along with Regulation CC is that settlement between banks is final when given under Regulation CC. Section (e)(1) quoted above states that the funds become available to the customer when settlement becomes final. Since settlement between banks is final when given under Regulation CC, the bank would be required to make the funds available under Subsection (e)(1) immediately upon settlement. Because of this problem, the availability of checks should be left to Regulation CC.

Subsection (e)(2) deals with "on-us" checks that are deposited. According to that Subsection quoted above, the bank must make funds available to the customer "at the opening of the bank's second banking day following receipt of the item." If the bank receives an "on-us" item on Monday, the bank must make the funds available to the customer at the opening of business on Wednesday. This time period allows the bank time to determine if it is going to pay the item. One requirement under Subsection (e) is that the "on-us" item must be finally paid before the bank is required to make the funds available to the customer. If the customer deposits money, Subsection (f) applies. That section states, "Subject to applicable law stating a time for availability of funds and any right of a bank to apply a deposit to an obligation of the depositor, a deposit of money becomes available for withdrawal as of right at the opening of the bank's next banking day after receipt of the deposit." This Subsection is likewise subject to the availability requirements of Regulation CC. Under both Subsection (e) and (f) the right of the customer to withdraw the funds in an account are subject to the bank's right of setoff.

7.14 SETTLEMENT AND SUSPENSION OF PAYMENT

The presentment, collection, and settlement functions normally flow rather smoothly. As long as banks in the collection chain make timely presentment and settlement for items, there should be few problems. However, if a collecting bank or a payor bank suspends payment, then many issues arise. Section 4-216 addresses the situation of a collecting bank's rights if another collecting or payor bank suspends payment. "Suspends payment" is defined in Section 4-104(12) as "with respect to a bank means that it has been closed by order of the supervisory authorities, that a public officer has been appointed to take it over, or that it ceases or refuses to make payments in the ordinary course of business." Many different scenarios can arise if a bank suspends payment depending on which bank suspends payment and what action has taken place. A payor bank could suspend payment after receipt of an item but before settling for the item or making final payment. The payor bank could make final payment but not settle before suspending payment or the payor or collecting bank could give provisional settlement and suspend payment before settlement becomes final. Finally, a collecting bank could receive final settlement for an item but suspend payment without making settlement with a customer. Each of these situations are addressed under Section 4-216.

Section 4-216(a) addresses the situation of a payor bank or a collecting bank that obtains possession of an item but suspends payment before the item is paid. In this situation, Subsection (a) requires the receiver, trustee or agent in charge to return the check to the presenting bank or to the customer of the closed bank. The presenting bank is entitled to the item since it made some type of settlement for the item and has not received payment. If the item is returned to the presenting bank, the presenting bank could revoke any provisional payment that it has given and return the item to the person who presented the item. If the depositary bank suspends payment after receipt of the item from the customer and still has possession of the item at the time that it suspends payment, the customer of the closed bank is entitled to the item.

Subsection (b) addresses the situation of a payor bank suspending payment after it finally paid an item but before it settled for the item. In this situation, the owner of the item is given a preferred claim against the payor bank. A collecting bank, under Section 4-201, is an agent of the owner of the item. The owner of the item assumes the risk of this situation occurring and is obviously the person who should be given the preferred status. The collecting bank will reverse the provisional credit that it gave to its customer and it, therefore, does not have a claim against the payor bank.

Subsection (c) states, "If a payor bank gives or a collecting bank gives or receives a provisional settlement for an item and thereafter suspends payments, the suspension does not prevent or interfere with the settlement's becoming final if the finality occurs automatically upon the lapse of certain time or the happening of certain events." The fact that a bank has suspended payment does not affect the provisional payment from becoming final. For example, if a collecting bank gives a presenting bank provisional settlement and forwards the item on to the payor bank before the collecting bank suspends payment, the settlement becomes final when the payor bank finally pays the item. In this situation, the provisional settlement given to the presenting bank by the collecting bank that suspended payment becomes final.

The final situation addressed under Section 4-216 is covered by Subsection (d). Subsection (d) addresses the situation where a collecting bank has received final settlement for an item but suspended payment before settlement was made to its customer. Under these circumstances, the owner of the item is given a preferred claim against the collecting bank that suspended payment. The preferred claim may or may not be worth much value to the owner of the item. The bank will not likely have the ability to pay the face amount of the item, but the owner is given a preferred claim over other general creditors of the bank.

CHAPTER 8

DISHONOR, NOTICE OF DISHONOR, RETURN ITEMS, AND WRONGFUL DISHONOR

8.1 DISHONOR OF A NOTE

The liability of an indorser and a drawer to pay an instrument is contingent upon dishonor of the instrument. If the instrument is paid by the maker or the drawee, the obligation of an indorser is discharged. The drawer's liability on the instrument is likewise based on dishonor of the instrument. Dishonor may or may not first require presentment of the item depending on the nature of the instrument and the instructions contained in the instrument. Typically, the indorser's and drawer's liability requires presentment and dishonor while presentment is not required to charge the maker of a note.

(a) DISHONOR OF A NOTE PAYABLE ON DEMAND

A note payable on demand is an exception to the rule that presentment is not necessary to charge the maker. Since the note is payable on demand, the liability of the maker to pay the note requires that demand must first be made. "Presentment," which is discussed in Chapter 7, is defined in Section 3-501(a) as demand. Therefore, presentment is required of a note payable on demand. Section 3-502(a)(1) governs dishonor of a note payable on demand. That section states, "If the note is payable on demand, the note is dishonored if presentment is duly made to the maker and the note is not paid on the day of presentment."

(b) DISHONOR OF A NOTE NOT PAYABLE ON DEMAND

If the note is not payable on demand but is payable through a bank and the terms of the note requires presentment, Section 3-502(a)(2) governs. That section states that "the note is dishonored if presentment is duly made and the note is not paid on the day it becomes payable or the day of presentment, whichever is later." If the note is payable through a bank, the proper place of presentment is the bank through which the note is payable. The note is not dishonored until it is presented to the bank and payment is refused. If the terms of the note require presentment, dishonor does not occur until the note is presented in accordance with the terms and payment is refused. If presentment is made before the date that the note becomes payable, dishonor does not occur until the date that payment is due and payment is refused.

If a note is not payable on demand, is not payable through a bank and the terms of the note do not require presentment, Subsection (a)(3) states that "the note is dishonored if it is not paid on the day it becomes payable." Presentment is not required in this instance. The maker of the note issued the note and is fully aware of the payment date and the amount of payment that is due. The person entitled to enforce the instrument is not required to make demand for payment. The note is dishonored if payment is not made on the due date of the note. For example, assume that Bill issues a note to D.A. that is due on June 15. On the payment date, June 15, D.A. is not required to take any action at all. If Bill does not pay the note on or before June 15, then the note is dishonored.

As a practical matter, the person entitled to enforce the instrument will make some sort of demand for payment before initiating an action to collect on the instrument. If any penalties or other types of damages are hinged on dishonor, then the penalties or damages would become payable as a result of the dishonor.

8.2 DISHONOR OF A DRAFT

As in the case of a note, dishonor of a draft has several different scenarios depending on the wording of the draft and whether the draft is a check. Unlike a note, however, a draft must first be presented before it can be dishonored, unless presentment is excused under Section 3-504. Different rules of dishonor apply to drafts depending on whether the draft has been accepted or not and whether the draft is a documentary draft. Subsection (b) of Section 3-502 addresses an unaccepted draft that is not a documentary draft, Subsection (c) addresses an unaccepted documentary draft, and Subsection (d) addresses an accepted draft.

(a) DISHONOR OF A CHECK

There is no question that a check must be presented to the drawee bank before the check can be dishonored. The physical check must be presented or a presentment notice may be made in accordance with an electronic presentment agreement. The drawer of the check is not liable for dishonor of the check until it is presented and payment is refused by the payor bank. The payor bank may refuse to make payment without dishonor of the check if the person making presentment does not make proper presentment, does not show reasonable identification, the instrument is not properly indorsed or for any of the other reasons described in Section 3-501 which is discussed in Chapter 7. If a check is properly presented, Section 3-502(B)(1) states, "If a check is duly presented for payment to the payor bank otherwise than for immediate payment over the counter, the check is dishonored if the payor bank makes timely return of the check or sends timely notice of dishonor or nonpayment under Section 4-301 or 4-302, or becomes accountable for the amount of the check under Section 4-302."

This Subsection applies to checks that are presented to the payor bank as part of the check collection system. It does not apply to checks that are presented for immediate payment in cash or some other form. Those items are addressed by Subsection (b)(2) discussed below. Sections 4-301 and 4-302, also discussed below, basically require that a bank return an item or give notice of return by its midnight deadline. Section 4-301 deals with deferred posting, which basically means that the payor bank may return a check by its midnight deadline if it settles for an item on the date of receipt. The bank becomes accountable for the amount of an item under 4-302 if it does not pay or return the item by its midnight deadline.

(b) DISHONOR OF DRAFTS PAYABLE ON DEMAND

Subsection (b)(2) governs drafts payable on demand that are not subject to Subsection (b)(1), and states, "If a draft is payable on demand and paragraph (1) does not apply, the draft is dishonored if presentment for payment is duly made to the drawee and the draft is not paid on the day of presentment." The deferred posting provision of Section 4-301 allows the payor bank to give provisional credit for an item on the day of presentment and to dishonor the item and revoke the provisional settlement if the bank takes the appropriate action by midnight of the banking day following receipt of the item (the midnight deadline). However, if the item is presented for immediate payment over the counter or paragraph (1) does not otherwise apply, the bank must dishonor the item by midnight of the day of presentment. Therefore, dishonor under paragraph (2) occurs if the draft is not paid by the drawee on the day of presentment.

The following example contrasts dishonor under Subsections (b)(1) and (b)(2). Assume that a check is presented to the payor bank in a cash letter from a collecting bank on Monday, June 15 and the payor bank settles for the cash letter before midnight on Monday. The bank processes the check along with other checks in the cash letter on Monday night and during the posting process it is determined that the check is insufficient. Because of the deferred posting provision, the payor bank may dishonor the check and return it or send notice of dishonor by midnight Tuesday. The check was dishonored by the bank on Tuesday when the check was returned. This is an example of the application of Subsection (b)(1). Under Subsection (b)(2), if the check was presented over the counter for immediate payment, the bank would be required to pay or return the check by midnight Monday. If the bank refused to pay the check, dishonor occurred on Monday as compared to Tuesday in the previous example.

(c) DISHONOR OF A DRAFT PAYABLE
ON A STATED DATE

Subsection (b)(3) governs the dishonor of a draft that is payable on a stated date. That paragraph states, "If a draft is payable on a date stated in the draft, the draft is dishonored if (i) presentment for payment is duly made to the drawee and payment is not made on the day the draft becomes payable or the day of presentment, whichever is later, or (ii) presentment for acceptance is duly made before the day the draft becomes payable and the draft is not accepted on the day of presentment." Presentment of a draft for payment cannot be made prior to the date on the draft. If presentment is made prior to the date on which payment is due, refusal to pay the draft is not dishonor. If presentment is made after the date of payment or if presentment is made before the date of payment and the drawee refuses to pay the draft on the payment date, then dishonor occurs on the date the refusal is made. If a draft is payable on or after June 15, and if the draft is presented before that date, refusal to pay before that date is not dishonor. If the draft is presented prior to June 15, refusal by the drawee to pay the draft on June 15 is dishonor.

If the draft is presented for acceptance prior to the date of payment, refusal to accept the draft is dishonor. Acceptance is an acknowledgement on the part of the payor that the draft will be paid on the payment date upon proper presentment of the draft. If a draft, payable on June 15, is presented for acceptance prior to that date, refusal to accept the draft is dishonor.

Drafts are sometimes issued with a payment date after sight or acceptance. Subsection (b)(4) governs this type of draft and states, "If a draft is payable on elapse of a period of time after sight or acceptance, the draft is dishonored if presentment for acceptance is duly made and the draft is not accepted on the day of presentment." In the case of a draft that is payable after the elapse of a certain period of time, the draft is not properly payable until the elapse of the prescribed period of time. Refusal to pay the draft before the elapse of time is not dishonor. However, refusal to accept the draft when presented so that the period of time may start to run is dishonor. For example, if a draft is payable 10 days after sight, and the draft is presented for acceptance, refusal to accept the draft is dishonor under Subsection (b)(4).

In all of the Subsections that refer to acceptance, refusal of a bank to certify a check is not dishonor. While certification of a check is a form of acceptance, Section 3-409(d) provides that a bank is not required to certify a check; therefore, refusal to do so has been held by several courts not to be dishonor. The court in *Gallinaro v. Fitzpatrick, 8 UCC Rep Serv 1054*, held that a bank is under no obligation to certify a check.

(d) DISHONOR OF AN UNACCEPTED DOCUMENTARY DRAFT

The same rules that govern dishonor of drafts in Subsections (b)(2), (b)(3), and (b)(4) also apply to an unaccepted documentary draft according to Subsection (c). However, the time period for action is different for a documentary draft. Subsection (c) states that payment or acceptance of a documentary draft "may be delayed without dishonor until no later than the close of the third business day of the drawee following the day on which payment or acceptance is required by those paragraphs." More time is allowed for a documentary draft to examine the documents that are attached to the draft. By their nature, documentary drafts are more complicated and require more time and deliberation to determine whether the draft should be paid.

(e) DISHONOR OF AN ACCEPTED DRAFT

Subsection (d) governs dishonor of accepted drafts and the rules stated there are the same as in Subsections (a)(1) and (b)(2). If a draft is payable on demand, the draft is dishonored when the draft is properly presented and payment is refused by the acceptor of the draft. If the draft is not payable on demand, as discussed earlier, it is not properly payable until the payment date. Refusal to pay prior to that date is not dishonor. Refusal, by the acceptor, to pay the accepted draft upon presentment on the payment date is dishonor. If presentment is not made until after the payment date, then dishonor does not occur until the draft is presented. If the payment date is June 15, but presentment for payment is not until July 1, dishonor does not occur until July 1.

8.3 DISHONOR AND EXCUSED PRESENTMENT

Dishonor of an item can occur on an item that requires presentment according to Subsection (e). That subsection states, "In any case in which presentment is otherwise required for dishonor under this section and presentment is excused under Section 3-504, dishonor occurs without presentment if the instrument is not duly accepted or paid." Section 3-504 lists several situations under which presentment is excused and the person to be charged is required to pay the instrument even though presentment has not been made. In other words, in those situations described in 3-504, payment is required without presentment of the instruments. Subsection (e) simply states that dishonor occurs in those situations if the instrument is not accepted or paid.

8.4 DISHONOR AND LATE ACCEPTANCE

In certain circumstances, refusal to accept a draft is dishonor. A draft payable on a certain date is not properly payable until that date. However, according to Subsection (b)(3)(ii) refusal to accept the draft before the draft becomes payable is dishonor. Likewise, a draft that is not payable until the elapse of a specified period of time after sight or acceptance, is not properly payable until after the time has elapsed. However, refusal to accept the item is dishonor under Subsection (b)(4). Subsection (f) states, "If a draft is dishonored because timely acceptance of the draft was not made and the person entitled to demand acceptance consents to a late acceptance, from the time of acceptance the draft is treated as never having been dishonored." Under Subsections (b)(3)(ii) and (b)(4), if after refusing to accept a draft when first presented, the acceptor later accepts the draft, Subsection (f) treats the dishonor as never having happened. For example, a draft with a payment date of July 15 is presented for acceptance on June 20 and is dishonored by the acceptor. On June 25, the acceptor has a change of heart and accepts the draft. Under Subsection (f), the dishonor of June 20 is treated as never having happened.

If the acceptor refuses to pay the draft on the payment date, then the draft if considered dishonored at that time. In the example above, if the acceptor does not pay the draft on July 15, the draft is dishonored.

8.5 NOTICE OF DISHONOR

The obligation of an indorser under Section 3-415 is that if the instrument is dishonored, the indorser will pay the amount of the instrument to the person entitled to enforce the instrument or to a subsequent indorser that pays the instrument. Under Section 3-414(d), if a draft is accepted and the acceptor is not a bank, the obligation of the acceptor, if the draft is dishonored, is the same as an indorser. The liability of both an indorser under 3-415 and a drawer under 3-414(d) is contingent upon the indorser or drawer receiving proper notice of dishonor. The requirements of notice of dishonor are contained in Section 3-503. Subsection (a) contains the requirement of notice of dishonor. That section states, "The obligation of an indorser stated in Section 3-415(a) and the obligation of a drawer stated in Section 3-414(d) may not be enforced unless (i) the indorser or drawer is given notice of dishonor of the instrument complying with this section, or (ii) notice of dishonor is excused under Section 3-504(b)." In *Samples v. Trust Co., of Georgia, 5 UCC Rep Serv 998*, the court held the bank had not given timely notice of dishonor and was not entitled to recover from the indorser. The bank is required to give timely notice of dishonor even if the bank had previously dishonored the check, so held the court in *Sun River Cattle Co., Inc. v. Miners Bank Of Montana, N.A., 14 UCC Rep Serv 1004*. The court in *Leaderbrand v. Central State Bank Wichita, 6 UCC Rep Serv 172*, came to a different conclusion about multiple notices. In that case, a check had been orally dishonored twice when presented for cash over the counter. The court found that failure of the bank to give notice of dishonor before its midnight deadline when the check was presented a third time through a collecting bank was excused.

The notice requirement applies to all indorsers. The notice requirement for a drawer is limited to the drawer of a draft that is accepted by a nonbank payor. In the case of an indorser, it makes sense that notice should be required. The indorser is fully expecting the maker or the drawee to pay the instrument and if the instrument is not paid, the indorser is entitled to the notification. In the case of a drawer, the drawer is in a position to know if the draft is going to be paid. For example, the drawer of a check knows, or should know, if the balance in the account on which the check is drawn is sufficient to pay the check. If the account is closed or if payment is stopped on a check, the drawer certainly knows that the item will not be paid. It makes sense that the indorser should be given notice and, except in the one case noted, that notice to the drawer is not necessary.

(a) MANNER OF COMMUNICATING NOTICE

No particular form or manner of notice of dishonor is required. Section 3-503(b) addresses this issue and states, "Notice of dishonor may be given by any person; may be given by any commercially reasonable means, including oral, written, or electronic communication; and is sufficient if it reasonably identifies the instrument and indicates that the instrument has been dishonored or has not been paid or accepted. Return of an instrument given to a bank for collection is sufficient notice of dishonor." The notice of dishonor is sufficient regardless of who gave it or how it was received. As long as the person to be charged has notice of the dishonor, it is immaterial as to who gave the notice or how it was sent. The notice could be given by telephone, wire, fax, electronically through a terminal, by letter, messenger, or any other commercially reasonable means. Oral notice of dishonor has been held sufficient in numerous cases: *Financial Universal Corp. Mercantile National Bank at Dallas, 40 UCC Rep Serv 1334, Laurel Bank and Trust Co. v. Sahadi, 17 UCC Rep Serv 1259, Yoder v. Cromwell State Bank, 41 UCC Rep Serv 173.* This last court also held that oral notice is sufficient even though Section 4-212 states that the payor bank must return the item or "send" notice of dishonor. The argument that oral notice is not sufficient stems from the definition of "send" in Section 1-201(38). This court flatly refused to require written notice and declared that oral notice is sufficient even for Section 4-212. The court in *Clements v. Central Bank of Georgia, 29 UCC Rep Serv 1536,* also held that oral notice was sufficient in spite of the language in Article 4 and the definition of "send." The main theme of these cases is that notification is sufficient regardless of the manner in which it is given as long as the indorser is given notice sufficient to identify the instrument being returned. A California court, however, held to a strict interpretation of Section 4-302 that states that the payor bank must return the item or send notice of return. That court in *Los Angeles National Bank v. Bank of Canton of California, 14 UCC Rep Serv 2d 848,* held that Section 4-302 requires written notice and that oral notice is not sufficient.

The typical form of notice of dishonor of checks, other than large dollar notification discussed below, is return of the check itself with the reason for return stamped on the check. Return items under the UCC and Regulation CC are discussed in Sections 8.6 and 8.7, respectively.

(b) TIME OF NOTICE OF DISHONOR

Section 503(c) provides for the time within which notice of dishonor must be given unless notice of dishonor is excused by Section 3-504. As to checks and other instruments taken for collection by a collecting bank, notice of dishonor must be given by a bank by its midnight deadline. In other words, before midnight of the next banking day following the banking day on which the bank receives notice of dishonor of the item. If a bank receives notice of dishonor on Monday, the bank must give notice before midnight on Tuesday, even if the bank does not actually receive the item until after that time unless the notice received by the bank does not give enough information about the item to identify the bank's customer.

The court in *Lufthansa German Airlines v. Bank of America N.T.S.A.,* *27 UCC Rep Serv 1067*, held that the information in the notice of dishonor may be sufficient to meet the notice requirement but may not be sufficient to identify the bank's customer. In this case, the notice of dishonor did not identify the branch of the Bank on which the check was drawn; therefore, the bank could not identify the customer. In this case, the court held that the bank's midnight deadline did not start to run when the bank received the notice of dishonor but when the bank received the item. It was not until the bank received the item that it could identify its customer.

As to any person other than a bank, notice of dishonor must be given within 30 days following the day on which the person receives notice of dishonor. The time for giving notice under the previous version of Article 3 was three days. The revised version has expanded the time to 30 days. As to any instrument other than an instrument taken for collection by a bank, notice of dishonor must be given within 30 days following the day on which dishonor occurs.

(c) EXCUSED NOTICE OF DISHONOR

Notice of dishonor may be excused and is not necessary to charge a person obligated on the instrument in certain instances. Section 3-504(b) states that notice of dishonor is excused if the terms of the instrument state that notice is not required to enforce the obligation of the party to pay the instrument. That section also states that notice of dishonor is excused if the person to be charged waives the notice of dishonor. The manner in which the waiver is communicated is not addressed in this section. Therefore, it would appear that the waiver could be given in any manner that clearly indicates that the party to be charged has waived the requirement of notice. The person to be charged could excuse the requirement of notice after the fact by paying the instrument even though the proper notice was not given.

The last sentence of Subsection (b) states, "A waiver of presentment is also a waiver of notice of dishonor." Waiver of presentment is provided for in Section 3-504(a) and is discussed in Chapter 7 of this book. If any of the five situations occur in that section, notice of dishonor is also waived.

In some circumstances, timely notice cannot be given and the delay of notice may be excused. Section 3-504(c) states, "Delay in giving notice of dishonor is excused if the delay was caused by circumstances beyond the control of the person giving the notice and the person giving the notice exercised reasonable diligence after the cause of the delay ceased to operate." This section is similar to Section 4-109 which excuses delay in time limits prescribed by the UCC or by instructions as they relate to actions by a collecting bank or a payor bank. That section specifically lists several circumstances which could cause a delay beyond the control of the bank. Some of the items listed are interruption of communication or computer facilities, war, emergency conditions, and failure of equipment. The court in *Sun River Cattle Co., Inc. v. Miners Bank of Montana, N.A., 14 UCC Rep Serv 1004*, applying the previous version of Section 4-108, held that a payor bank was excused from strict liability for failure to return an item or send notice of dishonor by the midnight deadline if the bank showed that the circumstances causing the delay were beyond the control of the bank. The court held that the burden of proof was on the bank to prove that it exercised the "diligence as the circumstances required." In this case, a computer malfunction and a breakdown in the courier service caused the delay.

While not addressed in this section, it would appear that the burden of proof that the delay is excusable would be on the person claiming the delay and that reasonable diligence was exercised after the cause for the delay ceased to operate. For example, if a bank experienced computer failure that delayed processing by one day, the bank could not delay the notice of dishonor for five days and use the computer failure as an excuse unless the computer failure actually caused a five-day delay.

(d) EVIDENCE OF DISHONOR

Section 3-505 sets forth specific items that are admissible as evidence and create a presumption of dishonor and of any notice of dishonor stated. Dishonor may be evidenced by a document that is a formal protest under Subsection (b). That Subsection lists the requirements of a formal protest which is no longer mandatory. As pointed out in the Official Comments to this section, protest is not a condition to liability of an indorser or a drawer. Dishonor may be proven by the use of a stamp or a writing on the instrument or accompanying the instrument made by the drawee, payor bank or presenting bank that states that acceptance or payment has been refused. If the reasons stated are not consistent with dishonor, then the stamp or writing is not evidence of dishonor. Banks typically return items and do not send a separate notice of dishonor unless the item is considered a large dollar return item under Regulation CC. As required by Regulation CC, the fact that the item was returned and the reason for return are stamped on the face of the item. Most banks also include a return notice along with the item that states the reason for dishonor. The stamped item is sufficient evidence of the return of the item.

Evidence of dishonor may also be established by the books or records of the drawee, payor bank, or collecting bank that are kept in the usual course of business and which show that the instrument was dishonored. Evidence of who made the entry on the books or records is not necessary. The payor bank will typically have records indicating the date that an item was presented for payment, the balance in the customer's account on the day of presentment, the opened or closed status of the account, whether a stop payment order was placed on the account and other evidence that shows that the item was presented for payment, that the item was dishonored, and the reason for dishonor. In *Serve v. First National Bank of Atlanta, 22 UCC Rep Serv 1001*, the court held that a stamp on the check that stated "account closed" was sufficient evidence of dishonor even though the stamp was not placed on the check by the plaintiff bank.

8.6 RETURN ITEMS UNDER ARTICLE 4

Many of the items discussed in the previous sections apply to items that are presented and returned through the banking system. However, because of the fact that Article 4 and Regulation CC also apply to so many of the sections, return items handled through the banking system are discussed separately in this section.

(a) BANK'S RESPONSIBILITY WHEN RETURNING ITEM

Section 4-202 establishes a collecting bank's responsibility for presenting and returning items and sending notice of dishonor. Section 4-202(a)(2) states that the bank must exercise ordinary care in sending notice of dishonor, or nonpayment or in returning an item to the bank's transferor after learning that the item has not been paid or accepted. Return of the original item is not required according to *Sun Bank/Miami, N.A. v. First National Bank of Maryland, 7 UCC Rep Serv 2d 1576*. The court held in that case that return of a photocopy in lieu of the original is common practice among banks and that the UCC does not require that the original item be used. Subsection (b) states that a collecting bank exercises ordinary care by taking proper action before its midnight deadline following receipt of an item or notice of dishonor. The bank may take a longer period of time to act in certain circumstances, but the bank has the burden of establishing the timeliness of its actions.

An example of the application of this section follows. Assume that a collecting bank receives an item on Monday that has been returned by the payor bank. The collecting bank must send the item to its transferor by its midnight deadline, which is midnight Tuesday. If the bank did not receive the actual item but received a notice of dishonor that adequately described the item, the bank would be required to send notice of dishonor by its midnight deadline. As long as the bank takes the appropriate action by its midnight deadline, Subsection (b) states that the bank has exercised ordinary care. The court applied this section in *Citizens Bank, Bentonville v. Chitty, 40 UCC Rep Serv 989*, and held that the burden of establishing the reasonableness of a delay in notice is on the bank. Failure of the collecting bank to use ordinary care in returning an item could result in liability to the collecting bank according to the court in *Suburban National Bank of Palatine v. Federal Reserve Bank of Chicago, 10 UCC Rep Serv 2d, 932.*

Regulation CC also contains requirements that must be met by a returning bank and are discussed below.

(b) RIGHT OF CHARGE BACK AND RETURN OF ITEMS

Section 4-214 establishes a collecting bank's right to revoke any provisional credit given for an item and to charge the item back to the customer's account. Subsection (a) states that if a collecting bank has made provisional settlement with its customer for an item and the collecting bank does not receive final settlement for the item because it is dishonored or returned for any reason, the collecting bank may revoke the provisional settlement and charge the amount of the item back to the customer's account or obtain a refund from the customer. The bank may charge the amount of the item back to the customer's account or obtain a refund even if it is not able to return the item, if it returns the item, or sends notification of the facts to the customer by its midnight deadline. The bank may take longer period of time but the bank must prove that taking longer is reasonable under the circumstances.

The bank may revoke the settlement and charge back the amount of the item or obtain a refund from the customer even if the return or notice is delayed beyond the bank's midnight deadline. If the bank does delay beyond the midnight deadline, it is liable for any loss resulting from the delay. In *Bank of New York v. Asati, Inc., 15 UCC Rep Serv 2d*

555, the court held that the depositary bank had the right to charge an item back to a customer's account. The court further held that the bank could charge the item back to the customer's account even though the bank failed to notify the customer by the its midnight deadline because the customer did not rely on the provisional settlement to its detriment. In this case the customer deposited the check that was dishonored and issued certified checks to officers of the customer. The court held that the purpose of notification is to notify an unsuspecting customer and to protect him from having his own checks returned unpaid.

The right of the collecting bank to revoke the credit and charge the item back or obtain a refund from the customer terminates if and when the settlement for the item received by the bank is or becomes final. Once the collecting bank has received final settlement, the reason for charging the item back no longer exists. In *Boggs v. Citizens Bank And Trust Co Of Maryland, 20 UCC Rep Serv 148*, the court held that a bank's right of charge back terminates when the bank receives final settlement for an item. In this case, the depositary bank charged an item back to an account for the reason of "forged indorsement" seven months after the item was deposited. While the customer may be liable to the bank for breach of presentment warranty, the bank did not have the right to charge back the item after final settlement. The court also held the bank liable for wrongful dishonor of other items on the account that were returned as a result of the charge back.

The mere passage of time does not make settlement final and terminate the right of charge back. In *Symonds v. Mercury Savings and Loan Assn. 13 UCC Rep Serv 2d 316*, the depositary bank delayed presenting a check for eight months. When the check was finally presented, the balance was insufficient to pay the check and the check was dishonored by the payor bank. Upon receipt of the returned item, the depositary bank charged it back to the customers account. The court held that the charge back was proper since settlement for the item was not final. The court did, however, hold the bank liable for its negligence in presenting the item. In *Smallman v. Home Federal Savings Bank of Tennessee, 11 UCC Rep Serv 2d 1202*, the court held that the bank did not have the right of charge back when it failed to charge a check back to an account by the bank's midnight deadline. In that case, the copy of a check, which had been lost while being returned by the payor bank, was charged back to the customer's account four months after the date of deposit. Upon receipt of the check, the bank failed to charge it back by its midnight deadline. The bank received the copy of the check back on August 30 which was the Friday before Labor Day, therefore the midnight deadline was on Tuesday Sept. 3. The bank charged the item back on Sept. 5. The court held the bank liable for the amount of the check regardless of the fact that no loss was caused by the delay.

Settlement for checks under Section 229.36 is final when given between banks. The settlement given by the depositary bank may be provisional in that the depositary bank remains liable on the item as an indorser until the check is paid.

Section 4-214(b) provides when a collecting bank returns an item. That section states, "A collecting bank returns an item when it is sent or delivered to the bank's customer or transferor or pursuant to its instructions." This section envisions items to be returned through the same path that the instrument took on the forward collection process. Checks, under Regulation CC, may be returned by the paying bank directly back to the depositary bank and may never be returned to a prior transferor. Therefore, as pointed out in Official Comment #4 to this section, Subsection (b) is preempted by Regulation CC.

A depositary bank that is also the payor bank also has the right of charge back. Subsection (c) provides "A depositary bank that is also the payor may charge back the amount of an item to its customer's account or obtain refund in accordance with the section governing return of an item received by a payor bank for credit on its books (Section 4-301)." Section 4-301 is discussed in detail below. An example of the application of Subsection (c) is as follows. Assume that Bill issues a check drawn on the First Deposit Bank (FDB) to Joel and Joel deposits the check in his account with the FDB on Monday. FDB gives Joel provisional credit for the check based on the account agreement that states that the settlement is provisional. FDB determines that the check is insufficient during its posting process on Monday night and early Tuesday morning. On Tuesday, FDB makes the decision to return the check. FDB may revoke the credit given to Joel and charge the item back to Joel's account as long as the bank acts by its midnight deadline which is midnight Tuesday. The court in *Sunshine v. Bankers Trust Co.*, *14 UCC Rep Serv 1416*, held that the depositary bank that is also the payor bank has the right to charge a check back if the bank acts within the provisions of Section 4-301. In this case, however, the check was charged back two or three days after it was deposited which is too late under Section 4-301.

The right of charge back, according to Subsection (d), exists even if the customer has used all or part of the credit given. If the customer has withdrawn the funds, the bank will typically charge the customer's account and create an overdraft. That is exactly what happened in *In Re*

Cohn Bros., Inc. Mushkin v. Cohn Bros., Inc., *40 UCC Rep Serv 545* and the court held that the bank had the right of charge back. The right of charge back also exists if any bank fails to exercise ordinary care with respect to the item; however, any bank failing to exercise ordinary care remains liable for any loss for its failure to exercise ordinary care. This was the case in *Symonds v. Mercury Savings And Loan Assn.* discussed earlier.

A collecting bank is not required to exercise its right of charge back or right to claim a refund. Subsection (e) states, "A failure to charge back or claim refund does not affect other rights of the bank against the customer or any other party."

(c) DEFERRED POSTING, RETURN OF ITEMS BY A PAYOR BANK AND TIME FOR RETURN

Section 4-301 governs what is referred to as deferred posting, and return of items by a payor bank and the time within which the bank must act. A payor is required to either pay or return an item by its midnight deadline. Section 4-301(a) allows a payor bank to defer posting of an item under certain circumstances. Subsection (a) provides that a payor bank may revoke settlement that it has given for an item and recover the settlement from the person to whom settlement was given if certain requirements are met. First of all, the item may not be a documentary draft and the item may not have been presented for immediate payment over the counter. Therefore, the deferred posting applies to items that have been presented by a presenting bank in the form of a cash letter either directly or through a clearinghouse, or presentment in some other form than over the counter. Secondly, the payor bank must settle for the item before midnight of the day of receipt of the item. If the bank does not settle by midnight of the day of receipt, the bank becomes accountable for the amount of the item under Section 4-302 discussed below. The third requirement is that the payor bank must take one of the following two actions before it makes final payment on the item or before its midnight deadline expires. Before final payment or before its midnight deadline it must either (1) return the item, or (2) send written notice of dishonor or nonpayment if the item is not available for return.

The following is an example of the application of Subsection (a). Assume that Bank A presents a cash letter to Bank B on Monday. Bank B must settle for the amount of the cash letter before midnight on Monday. If it does not settle, Bank B becomes accountable for the amount of the items in the cash letter. If Bank B does settle before the midnight deadline, and does not finally pay an item in the cash letter, Bank B may revoke the amount of the settlement and charge the amount of the item back to Bank A if it returns the item or, if the item is unavailable, sends written notice of dishonor by midnight Tuesday.

Deferred posting also applies to "on-us" checks that are deposited to an account maintained with the payor bank. Subsection (b) states, "If a demand item is received by a payor bank for credit on its books, it may return the item or send notice of dishonor and may revoke any credit given or recover the amount thereof withdrawn by its customer, if it acts within the time limit and in the manner specified in Subsection (a)." In other words, the payor bank may revoke any credit given if it returns the item or sends notice of dishonor by midnight of the day following receipt of the item. Under this Subsection, however, settlement before midnight of the day of receipt is not required. The bank could take the deposit from the customer and not settle that same day. In fact, if the bank does settle with the customer, the Official Comments to Section 4-213 states that the settlement could be considered final settlement and final payment of the item if the bank does not have an agreement with the customer or put a notice on the deposit ticket that settlement is provisional. Final payment will be discussed in detail in Chapter 9 of this book.

Subsection (c) establishes the time when an item is dishonored by the payor bank. That Subsection states, "Unless previous notice of dishonor has been sent, an item is dishonored at the time when for purposes of dishonor it is returned or notice sent in accordance with this section." Dishonor occurs when the item is returned only if the intention is to dishonor the item. The item is not dishonored, for example, if it is being returned for lack of a necessary indorsement. If notice has already been sent before the item is returned, then dishonor will have occurred when the notice is sent and not when the item is returned. In *Union National Bank of Little Rock v. Metropolitan National Bank, 26 UCC Rep Serv 449,* the court held that Section 4-301 is satisfied if the check to be returned is placed in the mail, and addressed to the transferor before midnight of the day following receipt of the item. In *Pulaski Bank & Trust Co. v. Texas American Bank/Fort Worth, N.A., 7 UCC Rep Serv 2d 335,* under the circumstances of that case, return of the item occurred when the check was pulled and the entries reversed.

The question of when an item is returned is answered by Subsection (d). That Subsection provides the following:

An item is returned:

(1) as to an item presented through a clearing house, when it is delivered to the presenting or last collecting bank or to the clearing house or is sent or delivered in accordance with clearing-house rules; or

(2) in all other cases, when it is sent or delivered to the bank's customer or transferor or pursuant to instructions.

This section is fairly straightforward and does not leave much room for discussion. If the item were presented through a clearing house, the item is returned when it is delivered to the bank described in paragraph (1) or when it is delivered or sent in accordance with clearing-house rules. "Send" is defined in Section 1-201(38) as the following:

In connection with any writing or notice means to deposit in the mail or deliver for transmission by any other usual means of communication with postage or cost of transmission provided for and properly addressed and in the case of an instrument to an address specified thereon or otherwise agreed, or if there be none to any address reasonable under the circumstances. The receipt of any writing or notice within the time at which it would have arrived if properly sent has the effect of a proper sending.

This Subsection envisions that the item will be returned through the same path that it was presented and, therefore, does not address the situation where the item is returned directly back to the depositary bank or if the item is sent to a returning bank as provided for under Regulation CC. It would appear that the same test under paragraphs (1) and (2) could be applied. The item could be considered returned if it were delivered or sent to the depositary bank or to a returning bank.

(d) PAYOR BANK'S RESPONSIBILITY FOR LATE RETURN OF AN ITEM

The payor bank's responsibility for late return of an item is provided for in Section 4-302. That Subsection states that the payor bank becomes accountable for the amount of a demand item in which it is not also the depositary bank if it retains the item and does not settle for the item by midnight of the banking day of receipt of the item. The bank is accountable for the item whether or not the item is properly payable. The bank is also accountable for the amount of an item, whether or not it is also the depositary bank, if it does not pay or return the item or send notice of dishonor until after its midnight deadline. For example, assume that Bank A presents a check to Bank B on Monday. If Bank B does not settle for the item with Bank A before midnight Monday, Bank B becomes accountable for the amount of the item whether the item is properly payable or not. "Accountable" was found to be synonymous with "liable" in *Sun River Cattle Co., Inc. v. Miners Bank of Montana, N.A.*, 14 *UCC Rep Serv 1004*.

The payor bank is strictly liable for failure to dishonor a check by its midnight deadline. In *Los Angeles National Bank v. Bank of Canton of California*, 14 *UCC Rep Serv 2d 848*, the court held that Section 4-302 creates liability of the payor bank if the bank holds an item past its midnight deadline. The payor bank's liability for delay in return is independent of its liability for negligence or conversion. Likewise, the court in *Citizens Fidelity Bank & Trust Co. v. Southwest Bank & Trust Co.* held that if a payor bank fails to return a check by its midnight deadline, it is strictly liable to a depositary bank for the face amount of the item and the depositary bank is not required to prove damages.

An example of the application of this section to an item wherein the payor bank is also the depositary bank is as follows. Bill issues a check drawn on the First Deposit Bank to Joel. Joel also has an account with the FDB and deposits the check to his account on Monday. FDB is not required to settle for the item on Monday but must return the item or send notification to Joel by midnight Tuesday if it plans to dishonor the item. If the bank does not return the check by its midnight deadline on Tuesday, the bank becomes accountable for the amount of the item. If the check is properly payable, the bank can pay the item on Bill's account. If the item is not properly payable, the bank has passed its deadline to return the check and since the check is not properly payable, the bank cannot charge Bill's account.

Subsection (b) provides that if a payor bank is liable for an item under Subsection (a), the bank can raise a defense based on breach of presentment warranty under Section 4-208 if there is in fact a breach of the presentment warranty. The payor bank may also raise the defense that the person seeking enforcement of the liability presented or transferred the item for the purpose of defrauding the payor bank. For example, assume that Bank A presents a check to Bank B on Monday and

Bank B fails to settle for the item before midnight on Monday or settles for the item but fails to revoke the settlement and return the item by its midnight deadline on Tuesday. Bank B becomes accountable for the amount of the item. However, assume further that the check that Bank A presented contains a forged indorsement. By presenting a check with a forged indorsement, Bank A breached its presentment warranty and Bank B may raise that defense to its liability under Section 4-302(a).

8.7 RETURN ITEMS UNDER REGULATION CC

In addition to the provisions of Article 3 and 4, return items and notice of return are subject to Federal Reserve Regulation CC. In some situations, where there are conflicts between the UCC and Regulation CC, Regulation CC supersedes the UCC. Subpart C of Regulation CC entitled "Collection of Checks" governs the return of checks and the required notification of return. Subpart C addresses the paying, returning, and depositary banks' responsibilities for return of items in separate consecutive sections discussed in that same order below.

(a) PAYING BANK'S RESPONSIBILITY FOR RETURN OF CHECKS

The paying bank's responsibility for the return of checks is governed by Section 229.30. According to that section, if a paying bank determines not to pay a check, it must return the check in an expeditious manner in addition to returning the check within the time frames established by the UCC and Regulation J. An "expeditious manner" is established in paragraphs (a)(1) and (a)(2). Under those paragraphs, a paying bank returns a check in an expeditious manner if the check is returned within the time frames established in the "two-day/four-day test" or the "forward-collection test." Under the two-day/four-day test, the paying bank returns the check in an expeditious manner if the check would normally be received by the depositary bank not later than 4:00 p.m. on the second business day following the banking day on which the check was presented to the paying bank if the check is a local check, or by the fourth business day following the banking day on which the check was presented to the paying bank if the check is a nonlocal check. A check is a local check if the paying bank is located in the same check-processing region as the depositary bank and a nonlocal check if it is located in a different check-processing region.

Under the forward-collection test described in paragraph (a)(2), "a paying bank returns a check in an expeditious manner if it sends the returned check in a manner that a similarly situated bank would normally handle a check :

(i)   of similar amount,

(ii)   drawn on the depositary bank; and

(iii)   deposited for forward collection to the similarly situated bank by noon on the banking day following the banking day on which the check was presented to the paying bank."

As long as the item is returned in an expeditious manner, the paying bank may return the check directly to the depositary bank or the returning bank. A returning bank is any bank that agrees to return the check in an expeditious manner. The paying bank may return the check as a raw return or it may convert the check to a qualified returned check. A qualified return check is a check on which the routing number of the depositary bank, the amount of the check, and a "2" in position 44 of the MICR line is encoded in magnetic ink.

UNIDENTIFIABLE DEPOSITARY BANK

The paying bank will not always be able to identify the depositary bank for some reason or another. In this case where the depositary bank cannot be identified, Subsection (b) states that the paying bank may send the check to any bank that handled the check for forward collection and the check does not have to be handled in an expeditious manner. The paying bank must advise the collecting bank to which it sends the item that it cannot identify the depositary bank.

EXTENSION OF UCC DEADLINE

The deadline for return of a check or the notice of nonpayment under the UCC or Regulation J may be extended in two situations. One is if the paying bank expedites delivery of the returned item in a manner that the check will be received by the receiving bank by the next day following the otherwise applicable deadline. For example, if the paying bank's midnight deadline expires on Tuesday, the paying bank may hold the check past the Tuesday midnight deadline if the returned check will reach the receiving bank by Wednesday. The deadline may be extended further if the paying bank uses a highly expeditious means of transportation even if the check does not reach the receiving bank by the close of the next banking day. The key here is that the check must reach the receiving bank sooner than if the midnight deadline had been met by the paying bank. The UCC deadline may also be extended if the applicable midnight deadline for a paying bank is on Saturday because that is a banking day for the paying bank and the check will still reach the receiving bank by its next processing cycle. In other words, the paying bank could hold the check until Sunday or even Monday if the check will reach the receiving bank before the cutoff hour of its next processing cycle.

IDENTIFICATION OF RETURNED CHECK

Subsection (d) requires that the paying bank must clearly indicate on the face of the returned check the fact that the check is returned and the reason for the return. Most banks typically stamp the reason for return on the front of the check such as "insufficient funds" or "payment stopped." The commentary to this section states that such a stamp is sufficient even though it does not state that the check is returned.

NOTICE IN LIEU OF RETURN

If a check is not available for return, Subsection (f) allows the paying bank to send a copy of the front and the back of the check in lieu of the original. If a copy is not available, then the bank may send a notice of nonpayment that contains the information in Section 229.33(b). The copy or the notice must clearly state that it is being returned in lieu of return. The notice in lieu of return must be returned expeditiously.

RELIANCE ON ROUTING NUMBER

Subsection (g) states, "A paying bank may return a returned check based on any routing number designating the depositary bank appearing on the returned check in the depositary bank's indorsement." The depositary bank is responsible for the indorsement on the check and is responsible for placing the routing number in the proper location. If the number is wrong, the depositary bank should assume the risk.

(b) RETURNING BANK'S RESPONSIBILITY FOR RETURN OF CHECKS

In addition to meeting the time requirements of the UCC, a returning bank must also meet the expeditious return requirements when returning an item. The two-day/four-day test and the forward collection test applies to a returning bank in determining whether a check was returned expeditiously.

UNIDENTIFIABLE DEPOSITARY BANK

If a returning bank is unable to identify the depositary bank, Subsection (b) states that the returning bank may return the item to any collecting bank that handled the check for forward collection if the returning bank was not a collecting bank with respect to the returned check. Also the returning bank may return the check to a prior collecting bank, if the returning bank was a collecting bank with respect to the returned check. The returning bank is not required to return the check in an expeditious manner if the depositary bank is not identifiable. However, "a returning bank that receives a returned check from a paying bank under section 229.30(b), or from a returning bank under this paragraph, but that is able to identify the depositary bank, must thereafter return the check expeditiously to the depositary bank." For example, Paying Bank A dishonors a check but is unable to identify the depositary bank. Paying Bank A returns the check to Returning Bank B who is able to identify the depositary bank. In this example Returning Bank B is required to meet the expeditious return requirements. If the bank had not been able to identify the depositary bank, then the check would not have been required to be returned in an expeditious manner.

SETTLEMENT

Settlement for items between banks in the forward collection process is final when made under Regulation CC. The concept behind this final settlement is the fact that check may not be returned in the same path that it took on the forward collection path. The check may be returned to a returning bank that had not previously handled the check. Therefore, returned checks can no longer be settled for by charge back. Prior to Regulation CC, a bank that was returning a check to a presenting bank would simply charge the account of the presenting bank for the amount of the return item.

Regulation CC, in Section 229.31(c), eliminates this right of charge back between banks and establishes settlement for return items in the same manner that checks are settled for in the forward collection process. Subsection (c) provides, "A returning bank shall settle with a bank sending a returned check to it for return by the same means that it settles or would have settled with the sending bank for a check received for forward collection drawn on the depositary bank. This settlement is final when made."

An example of the settlement process is as follows. Paying Bank A returns a check to Returning Bank B. Returning Bank B normally settles for forward collection items by entering a credit to the account of the presenting bank and making the funds available to the presenting bank based on an availability schedule. In this example, Returning Bank B would settle with Paying Bank A in the same manner for the returned item by entering a credit to Paying Bank A's account and making the funds available to Paying Bank A according to an availability schedule.

NOTICE IN LIEU OF RETURN AND RELIANCE ON ROUTING NUMBER

A returning bank is allowed to send a notice of return in lieu of return of the original check in the same manner as a paying bank. The returning bank may also rely on the routing number of the depositary bank identified on the check.

(c) DEPOSITARY BANK'S RESPONSIBILITY FOR RETURNED CHECKS

The responsibilities of a depositary bank are obviously different than those of a paying bank or a returning bank. The depositary bank is the bank to which the item is returned. Section 229.32 addresses the requirements of a depositary bank but only addresses the relationship between the depositary bank and the returning bank. This section does not govern the relationship between the bank and its depositing customer. That relationship is governed by the UCC discussed earlier.

ACCEPTANCE OF RETURNED CHECKS

The objective of Regulation CC is to speed up the return of a check by making the return process similar to the forward collection process. That process has been made similar up to the point of the acceptance of the item by the depositary bank. Subsection (a) requires that the depositary bank accept all returned checks and written notices of nonpayment and the items or notices must be accepted at certain locations. A returning bank must accept the items or notices at any location at which presentment of checks for forward collection is requested by the depositary bank. Return items and notices must also be accepted at a number of other locations listed below:

> (1) At a branch, head office, or other location consistent with the name and address of the bank in its indorsement on the check;

(2) At a branch or head office associated with the routing number of the bank in its indorsement on the check, if an address is not included in the indorsement;

(3) At a location consistent with the address in the indorsement and at a branch or head office associated with the routing number in the bank's indorsement if the address is not in the same check-processing region as the address associated with the routing number that is contained in the indorsement;

(4) At any branch or head office if no routing number or address appears in its indorsement on the check.

Although qualified returned items must be identified with a "2" placed in position 44 of the MICR line, the depositary bank may require that returned checks be separated from forward collection checks. The depositary bank may be required to accept returned items at the same location as forward collection items, but the bank may require that returned checks be presented in a separate "return item cash letter."

PAYMENT

As stated above, the right of charge back between banks was basically abolished by Regulation CC. Banks may, of course, allow charge back as the method of settlement by agreement. Subsection (b) addresses the acceptable methods of payment for returned items by the depositary bank. That Subsection requires that the depositary bank pay off the returned items prior to the close of business on the banking day of receipt of the returned check. This requirement is similar to the requirement of settlement of a check for forward collection except that the forward collection check must be settled for by midnight of the day of receipt. The depositary bank may settle for the returned item by one of the following methods:

(1) Debit to an account of the depositary bank on the books of the returning or paying bank;

(2) Cash;

(3) Wire transfer; or

(4) Any other form of payment acceptable to the returning or paying bank.

The payment by the depositary bank to the paying or returning bank is final when made. The funds represented by the payment must be made available to the paying or returning bank on the "payment date." The "payment date" is the day of receipt of the returned item by the depositary bank. In other words, the depositary bank must make payment to the paying or returning bank before the close of business on the banking day that the items are presented and the funds must be made available that same day. If the payment date is not a banking day for the returning or paying bank or the depositary bank is not able to make payment on the payment date, the funds must be made available on the next banking day.

MISROUTED RETURNED CHECKS AND
WRITTEN NOTICES OF NONPAYMENT

Periodically, forward collection items are misrouted. This same problem may and will occur on returned items. Subsection (c) addresses that problem and states that the depositary bank has one of three options. If the depositary bank receives a misrouted item of notice of return, the bank may expeditiously return the check directly to the right depositary bank, or expeditiously return the check to a returning bank, or send the check or notice back to the bank from which it was received. If the bank decides to return the item to the depositary bank or to a returning bank, the depositary bank is assuming the responsibilities of a returning bank. If the bank simply returns the item to the bank from which it was received, the depositary bank has not assumed the responsibility of a returning bank.

CHARGES

Subsection (d) states that, "A depositary bank may not impose a charge for accepting and paying a check being returned to it." If the returned checks are commingled with forward collection checks, it could be difficult to distinguish the returned item from the forward collection item. Unless the depositary bank is aware of this provision and makes specific programming changes to prevent charging for the returned items, the bank could be in violation of this section.

8.8 NOTICE OF NONPAYMENT

Section 229.33 contains a requirement of notice of return of items and the content of the notice. This section requires a paying bank to send notification of nonpayment of all checks in the amount of $2,500 or more to the depositary bank. The notice must be sent in a manner such that the notice is received by the depositary bank by 4:00 p.m. of the second business day following the banking day on which the check was presented to the paying bank. The 4:00 p.m. time requirement is 4:00 p.m. local time for the depositary bank. If the day on which the notice is required to be received by the depositary bank is not a banking day for the depositary bank, then notice is timely if it is received by the bank on its next banking day. The notice may be given by any reasonable manner including return of the item, written notice including a copy of the notice, telephone, Fedwire, telex, or other form of telegraph. Basically, any form of notification would be acceptable if it contains the requirement of the contents of the notice discussed below. While not specifically mentioned in the regulation, an image of the item would also be acceptable.

(a) CONTENT OF NOTICE

The content of the notice is contained is Subsection (b), which states the following:

Notice must include the:
(1) Name and routing number of the paying bank;

(2) Name of the payee(s);

(3) Amount;

(4) Date of the indorsement of the depositary bank;

(5) Account number of the customer(s) of the depositary bank;

(6) Branch name or number of the depositary bank from its indorsement;

(7) Trace number associated with the indorsement of the depositary bank; and

(8) Reason for nonpayment.

The bank is not required to supply information not contained on the item. If the paying bank is not sure of the information, it must include the information in the notice but must also indicate that it is not sure of its accuracy by placing a question mark (?) next to the information.

ACCEPTANCE OF NOTICE

The depositary bank is required to accept the notice when sent by the paying bank. It cannot refuse the notice or make it difficult for the paying bank to comply with the notice requirement. At the same time, the paying bank is required to ensure that the notice is sent or given to the proper location. Subsection (c) addresses acceptance of the notice and provides that the notice must be accepted during its banking day at several locations. If the depositary bank includes a telephone number in its indorsement, then the bank must accept the notice at the number in the indorsement. If no number is provided or the number provided is illegible, then the bank must accept the notice at the general-purpose telephone or telegraph number of its head office or the branch indicated in the indorsement. The bank must also accept the notice at any other number held out by the bank for receipt of notice of nonpayment. If written notice is given, the notice must be accepted at any of the locations at which a return item must be accepted listed in Section 229.32(a) discussed earlier.

NOTIFICATION TO CUSTOMER

Subsection (d) requires that the depositary bank must give notice of return of an item to its customer by midnight of the banking day following the banking day of receipt of the notice of nonpayment. The notice may be given within a longer reasonable time. It would appear that some reason would have to exist for the bank to take longer than its midnight deadline to give the notice. The content of the notice to the customer must contain the facts of the notice received by the bank. The purpose of this notice is to advise the customer of the return of the item and to provide the customer with sufficient information to identify the item that is being returned.

DEPOSITARY BANK WITHOUT ACCOUNTS

Subsection (e) provides that the requirements of this section do not apply to a bank that does not maintain accounts.

8.9 WARRANTY BY PAYING BANK AND RETURNING BANK

In the forward collection process, each transferor and the person presenting an item to the payor makes certain transfer and presentment warranties. This concept is also utilized in the return process and a paying bank and each returning bank makes certain warranties. These warranties are contained in Section 229.34. According to that section, the paying bank and each returning bank warrants to any transferee that settles for a returned item and to the owner of the item that the paying bank returned the item in a timely manner under the UCC and under Regulation J; the bank is authorized to return the item; the check has not been materially altered; in the case of a notice in lieu of return, the original check has not and will not be returned.

The warranties are not given with respect to checks drawn on the Treasury of the United States, U.S. Postal Service money orders, or checks drawn on a state or other local government that are not payable through or at a bank.

Each paying bank that sends notice of nonpayment or return of an item warrants to the transferee bank, any subsequent transferee banks, the depositary bank and the owner of the check that the check has been returned timely under the UCC and Regulation J, that it is authorized to sent the notice, and that the check has not been materially altered. The warranty does not apply to checks drawn on a state or governmental unit that are not payable through or at a bank.

Damages for the breach of the warranty are limited to the amount of the consideration received by the paying or returning bank plus interest and expenses.

8.10 LIABILITY FOR FAILURE TO COMPLY WITH SUBPART C

(a) STANDARD OF CARE AND MEASURE OF DAMAGES

A bank is required to exercise ordinary care and good faith in acting and performing its duties under subpart C. If the bank fails to exercise ordinary care and good faith, it may be liable to the depositary bank, the depositary bank's customer, the owner of the check, or another party to the check. The measure of damages for failure to exercise ordinary care is the amount of the loss, not to exceed the amount of the item. The amount recoverable is also reduced by the amount that would have been lost even if the bank had exercised ordinary care. If a bank fails to exercise good faith, it may also be liable for additional damages caused as a consequence of its actions. Subsection (c) also provides for comparative negligence. If a bank fails to exercise ordinary care and becomes liable to another bank or other person, if that other person or bank is also negligent, the amount of damages payable to that person or other bank is reduced by the amount of damages attributable to the negligence of that other person or bank. In other words, the amount of damages will be apportioned among the parties based on their negligence.

A bank must exercise ordinary care and good faith in selecting a returning bank. Other than this obligation to exercise ordinary care and good faith, the bank is not responsible for the actions of any third party that handles the check including that party's negligence, misconduct, mistake, insolvency, or default. The bank is likewise not responsible for the loss or destruction of the item or the notice of nonpayment while in transit or in the possession of a third party. The paying bank remains liable to its customer for any duties imposed by the UCC or other laws.

If a paying bank fails to make timely return of an item, the bank is only liable for its failure under the provisions of the UCC or the provisions of Regulation CC, but not both. For example, if a check is not returned by the paying bank's midnight deadline and it is not received by the depositary bank within the time frame established by Regulation CC, the paying bank is either liable under the UCC or Regulation CC, but not both.

8.11 WRONGFUL DISHONOR

(a) WRONGFUL DISHONOR DEFINED

A bank may only pay an item and charge a customer's account for an item that is properly payable as discussed in Chapter 10 of this book. On the other hand, the bank is required to pay a check that is properly payable and is liable to its customer for failure to pay a properly payable item. Section 4-402(a) states, "Except as otherwise provided in this Article, a payor bank wrongfully dishonors an item if it dishonors an item that is properly payable, but a bank may dishonor an item that would create an overdraft unless it has agreed to pay the overdraft." This Subsection is new. It defines what wrongful dishonor is and provides that the bank cannot be held liable for wrongful dishonor for refusing to pay a check that will create an overdraft unless the bank has agreed to pay the overdraft.

Wrongful dishonor can occur in a number of ways. Refusal by a teller to pay a check over the counter that is properly payable is wrongful dishonor if the person presenting the check has complied with all of the bank's requirements of presentment. Wrongful dishonor can occur if the bank dishonors a check that is presented through the collection system by a presenting bank or through a clearinghouse. The point here is that the item must first be presented and dishonored and the dishonor must be wrongful. In *Fidelity National Bank v. Kneller, 11 UCC Rep Serv 2d 905*, the court held a bank liable for returning checks on an account that was closed by the bank. The court held that the bank was not justified in closing the account and was therefore liable to the customer for returning checks for the reason "account closed." This case does not mean that a bank cannot close an account, but it does mean that if an account is closed the customer should be given proper notification. In this case, the bank had paid a check on which a stop payment had been placed and also paid checks that had been forged. The court found that the bank was negligent in the manner in which it had handled the account and the bank's action was the cause of the checks being wrongfully dishonored and returned.

The bank is not required to pay a check that will create an overdraft unless the bank has agreed to pay the item in the overdraft. This new provision could cause problems for banks in that the manner in which the bank acknowledges its agreement to pay checks in the overdraft is not defined. The provision simply states, "A bank may dishonor an item that would create an overdraft unless it has agreed to pay the overdraft." The agreement is not required to be in writing. Therefore, it would appear that it could be oral or a court could consider past actions by the bank of paying checks as an agreement. If a bank establishes an overdraft limit for a customer and advises the customer of the limit, the court could consider the overdraft limit as an agreement to pay checks in the overdraft. If a bank officer simply made a comment to a customer that his credit was good and checks would not be returned, that could potentially be considered an agreement to pay checks in the overdraft. The point here is that the statute is very loosely written and leaves a lot of room for interpretation.

In the absence of an express written agreement, it would appear that a court would consider all of the surrounding circumstances relative to the banks decision not to pay a check. For example, assume that a bank had paid checks for a customer in the overdraft up to $10,000 and checks had never been presented that would create an overdraft in excess of $10,000. However, on one occasion a check is presented that, if paid, would create an overdraft of $15,000. The officer decides not to pay the check and returns it insufficient. Has the bank wrongfully dishonored the check? Assume the same facts except that the check that is presented, if paid, would only create and overdraft of $5,000 but the officer that normally handles this account is on vacation and the account is referred to another officer who returns the check. Is this wrongful dishonor? Or, assume the same facts but the officer in charge of the account becomes concerned about the financial condition of the customer and returns the check. Is this wrongful dishonor? The court would have to consider all of the circumstances surrounding the return of a check and make a decision. The court held that a bank could be held liable for acting in a manner in contrast to past activities of the bank.

In *Murdaugh Volkswagen, Inc. v. First National Bank of South Carolina*, 2 *UCC Rep Serv 2d 25*, the plaintiff claimed that the bank had always paid checks on uncollected funds, allowing plaintiff to withdraw funds that were deposited that same day. The bank would also call the customer if checks were presented against the account when the balance was insufficient and allow the customer to make a deposit to cover the checks. The court held that the past actions of the bank amounted to an agreement and that the bank could not return checks contrary to that agreement without giving notice to the customer. The court therefore held that dishonor of the checks was wrongful.

The court, in *Schaller v. Maine National Bank of Neenah*, 1 *UCC Rep Serv 2d 1283*, held that the bank was not liable for wrongful dishonor for refusing to pay checks in the overdraft when the bank had done so in the past. The court held that the bank's action of paying checks in the overdraft was not a "course of dealing" that required the bank to do so in the future. The court went on to say that in the absence of an agreement to pay in the overdraft, it is within the bank's discretion as to whether it pays checks in the overdraft. The court in *Thiele v. Security State Bank of Salem*, 3 *UCC Rep Serv 2d 686*, also held that past practice of paying checks in the overdraft is not an agreement to pay checks in the overdraft. In the absence of an agreement, the bank is not liable to the customer for not paying checks that would create an overdraft. The court held that paying checks in the overdraft is an extension of credit by the bank and that it is within the discretion of the bank to extend the credit or not. In this case, the customer account agreement contained a statement that the bank was not obligated to pay checks in the overdraft. The court therefore held that the bank was not liable for wrongful dishonor.

Because of the uncertainty caused by this provision, a bank should consider addressing this issue in its customer account agreement or some other agreement that defines the bank's responsibilities and obligation. The bank may want to include a provision in the account agreement that states words to the effect that the bank will not pay checks in the overdraft or that the bank agrees to pay checks in the overdraft only if a specific written agreement is entered into with the customer outlining the responsibilities of the bank and the customer. An agreement of this nature will take out some of the uncertainty created by Section 4-402(a).

Wrongful dishonor may also include rightfully dishonoring and returning a check but returning it for the wrong reason. For example, the court in *Johnson v. Grant Square Bank & Trust Co., 31 UCC Rep Serv 1062*, held that returning a check for the reason or "insufficient funds" when the check should have been returned for the reason of "payment stopped" was wrongful dishonor. However, in *Raymer v. Bay State National Bank, 31 UCC Rep Serv 1537*, the court held that the fact that a bank erroneously returned a check as "uncollected funds" was not wrongful dishonor even though the proper reason for return was "insufficient funds."

(b) BANK'S LIABILITY—CUSTOMER DEFINED DAMAGES

The payor bank is liable to its "customer" for damages proximately caused by the wrongful dishonor according to Subsection (b). Subsection (b) further provides, "Liability is limited to actual damages proved and may include damages for an arrest or prosecution of the customer or other consequential damages. Whether any consequential damages are proximately caused by the wrongful dishonor is a question of fact to be determined in each case."

The first issue to be addressed under this section is the issue of who is a customer. The liability of the bank is owed only to the payor bank's customer. "Customer" is defined in Section 4-104(5) to mean "a person having an account with a bank or for whom a bank has agreed to collect items, including a bank that maintains an account at another bank." The bank is therefore only liable for wrongful dishonor to a person who has an account with the bank or a person for whom the bank has agreed to collect items. The payee presenting the check over the counter for immediate payment is not a customer under the definition. The bank, as drawee, is not liable on a check, according to Section 3-408 until it accepts the check. Therefore, the bank is not liable to a payee on the check for wrongful dishonor.

The court in *Bon Bon Productions, Ltd. v. Xanadu Productions, Inc., 32 UCC Rep Serv 253*, held that the only party having a cause of action for wrongful dishonor is the customer of the payor bank. The payee of the check does not have standing to claim wrongful dishonor. In *First American National Bank of Nashville v. Commerce Union Bank of White County*, 41 UCC Rep Serv 1339, the court held that neither the payee of a check nor the depositary bank was a customer of the drawee bank and therefore did not have a cause of action for wrongful dishonor. The depositary bank did not carry an account with the drawee bank and the drawee bank had not agreed to collect an item for the depositary bank.

Another issue that has been raised is who is the "customer"? In *Murdaugh Volkswagen, Inc. v. First National Bank of South Carolina*, 2 UCC Rep Serv 25, the court held that the president and the sole stockholder of a corporation was the "customer" of the drawee bank for purposes of Section 4-402. The court held that the bank treated the president and the company as one entity. The court came to the opposite conclusion in *Koger v. East First National Bank*, 37 UCC Rep Serv 531. In that case, the court held that the proper plaintiff was the corporation or the partnership and not the individual partner or stockholder. In this case, checks of the corporation were returned and the court held that the corporation was the "customer" even though the individual was a majority stockholder.

One change in the revised version of this section is that in the previous section liability for damages was limited only if the wrongful dishonor was caused through mistake. The reference to mistake has been stricken from this section. Damages are limited to actual damages but may include consequential damages if consequential damages can be proved by the customer. In *Morse v. Mutual Federal Savings & Loan Association of Whitman*, the court held that damages were not limited to actual damages because the wrongful dishonor was not caused by mistake. In this case, the bank wrongfully put a "freeze" on the customer's account without giving notice to the customer. Consequential damages may be awarded, according to *Raymer v. Bay State National Bank*, 31 UCC Rep Serv 1537, if the evidence shows the requisite causal connection between the dishonor of the checks and the damages suffered by the plaintiff. Consequential damages were awarded in *In Re Brandywine Associates Hooper v. Bank Of New Jersey v. Hooper* 30 UCC Rep Serv 1369, but the court refused to award punitive damages because the bank was acting on advice of legal counsel. In *Buckley v. Trenton Saving Fund Society*, 6 UCC Rep Serv 2dL 1040, the court held that compensation for emotional distress inflicted by a bank because of wrongful dishonor of checks would only be awarded if the action of the bank was not only intentional but also reckless or outrageous and the distress is severe or results in bodily injury. In this case, the required damages were not proved.

(c) DETERMINATION OF CUSTOMER'S BALANCE

Subsection (c) is a new provision that was added to Section 4-402. Subsection (c) allows the bank to determine the sufficiency of available funds in an account at any time after receipt of an item and to base its decision of whether to pay or return the item on this one determination. At its discretion, the payor bank may decide to make a subsequent balance determination for the purpose of reevaluating its decision to dishonor the item. If it does in fact make a subsequent determination, the issue of whether the return of the item was wrongful will be based on the subsequent   determination. Besides the obvious, this section addresses two not so obvious issues. One of those issues is that the determination as to whether or not to pay the check may be based on the "available funds" in the account. This section therefore authorizes dishonor of checks on available funds and not simply the book or ledger balance in the account. The second issue is that this section positions the bank to address daylight overdrafts by allowing the bank to base its determination of the sufficiency of funds on the available funds at any time after receipt of the item. Under the current method of batch processing, most banks make the determination as to the sufficiency of funds at some point during the posting of transactions, taking into consideration deposits that have been made that same day.

This section would specifically allow the bank to determine the sufficiency of funds at the time that the check was presented. Consider the following example. A check in the amount of $10,000 is included in a cash letter presented to the payor bank at 9:00 a.m. At that time, the available balance in the customer's account was only $2,000. Assume further that the customer makes a cash deposit of $15,000 at 1:00 p.m. that same day. The payor bank could determine the sufficiency of funds at any time after the check was presented at 9:00 a.m. and the bank could dishonor the check for insufficiency of funds if it made the determination prior to 1:00 p.m. It could dishonor the check after 1:00 if the deposit made at that time was not considered part of the available balance until the day following receipt of the deposit.

CHAPTER 9

PAYMENT AND DISCHARGE

A party to an instrument creates his or her liability on the instrument by signing in the capacity in which he or she signs. In other words, the drawer of a draft creates the liability of a drawer by signing the draft as drawer, an indorser creates the liability of an indorser by indorsing, etc. The person that signs the instrument remains liable on the instrument until discharged. Discharge can be accomplished in a number of different ways governed by Articles 3 and 4. This chapter will discuss those methods of discharge. One manner of discharge is through payment of the item. Final payment of an item discharges all of the parties on the instrument as to their contractual liability on the instrument but does not affect any warranty liabilities. For example, upon payment of an item, an indorser is discharged from its contractual obligation to pay the amount of the instrument if it is dishonored. If the indorser is a transferor of the instrument, the transfer warranties survive payment of the item.

Other examples of discharge of an obligation to pay an instrument are discharge by cancellation, accord and satisfaction, and discharge of an indorser or accommodation party. Each of these methods of discharge are discussed below.

9.1 DISCHARGE AND THE EFFECT OF DISCHARGE

The obligation of party to pay an instrument is discharged, according to Section 3-601(a), "as stated in this Article or by an act or agreement

215

with the party which would discharge an obligation to pay money under a simple contract." Discharge may be accomplished in accordance with the provisions of Article 3 or in a manner agreed upon by the parties. As stated above, there are a number of ways in which discharge may be accomplished. The effect of discharge is that the party is relieved of their contractual obligation on the instrument. In *Rood v. Tooley*, 9 *UCC Rep Serv 2d 987*, three parties signed a note as co-makers. The language of the note indicated that all three were signing in the capacity of co-makers and all three signed the note at the lower right of the note's final page, a place customarily reserved for the signature of the makers. Two of the co-makers were husband and wife and the third co-maker was a partner of the husband. The wife was involved because she was the owner of a house that was put up as collateral to secure the debt. The note was not paid at maturity and the lender began foreclosure proceedings on the house to pay the debt. To prevent foreclosure, the husband and the wife paid the note plus interest and instigated this action to collect from the third co-maker. The husband and wife claimed that they became holders of the note when they paid the note and the lender surrendered the note to them. The court held that the husband and wife were co-makers on the note and that when they paid the note all of the parties were relieved of their obligation on the instrument. The husband, the wife, and the husband's partner were all co-makers and all three were relieved of their obligation on the note when it was paid. The court did not mention any potential recovery that the husband and wife might be entitled to for contribution under the common law. The court in *Awed v. Marsico*, 9 *UCC Rep Serv 2d 1302*, also held that payment of the note discharged all of the co-makers. The court reversed the holding of the lower court that allowed recovery of one co-maker based on contribution. The court held that the UCC is silent as to whether a co-maker has a right of recourse on the instrument against his co-makers or only a right to common law contribution. The point in this case is that discharge relieves all of the co-makers on the instrument. The court did point out that the co-maker may be entitled to contribution in an action for equitable contribution toward the amount he paid on the note, but he is not entitled to contribution in an action on the note.

Subsection (b) addresses discharge and a holder in due course. That subsection states, "Discharge of the obligation of a party is not effective against a person acquiring rights of a holder in due course of the instrument without notice of the discharge. For example, if the maker of a note pays the note prior to the due date on the note but does not cancel the note or obtain possession of the note, the note could end up in the hands of a holder in due course. In this example, payment of the note by the maker does not discharge the maker from its obligation to pay the note as to the holder in due course if the holder did not have knowledge of the discharge. In *Coplan Pipe & Supply Co., v. Ben-Frieda Corp., 10 UCC Rep Serv 408*, the court held that even though the holder of a note had the status of a holder in due course, discharge would be a valid defense if the holder had actual notice of the discharge. In this case, the holder of the note had notice that the maker of the note went into bankruptcy and therefore, the discharge was effective against the holder.

9.2 DISCHARGE BY PAYMENT

(a) WHEN AN OBLIGATION IS DISCHARGED BY PAYMENT

Section 3-602(a) contains the provision for discharge by payment of the instrument. That section states that, "To the extent of the payment the obligation of the party obliged to pay the instrument is discharged even though payment is made with knowledge of a claim to the instrument under Section 3-306 by another person." Section 3-306 contains the rights of a person who has a claim to an instrument. Section 3-602(a) also establishes when an item is paid. An item is paid, to the extent of the amount of the payment, when payment is made by or on behalf of a party obliged to pay the instrument and when payment is made to a person entitled to enforce the instrument. If payment is made to a person that is not entitled to enforce the instrument or has not been authorized by that person to obtain payment, then the item has not been paid.

(b) FINAL PAYMENT

The drawer of a check and all indorsers are discharged from their obligation to pay the check when the check is finally paid by the payor bank. Section 4-215 governs when a bank finally pays an item. According to that section, the following occurs:

   An item is finally paid by a payor bank when the bank has first done any of the following:

   (1) Paid the item in cash;

(2) Settled for the item without having the right to revoke the settlement under statute, clearinghouse rule or agreement; or

(3) Made provisional settlement for the item and failed to revoke
the settlement in the time and manner permitted by statute,
clearinghouse rule, or agreement.

If an item is presented over the counter and the person presenting
the item is paid in cash, the check is paid at that point and payment is
final. At that point, the obligation of the drawer is discharged, and the
obligations of all indorsers on the item are discharged including the
person that presented the item. Unless the item is paid by mistake as
provided for under Section 3-418 which is discussed later, the payor
bank may not return the item to the indorser. The bank cannot return
the item to the indorser even if the item contains a forged drawer's
signature, funds in the account are insufficient to pay the check, there is
a stop payment on the check, or for any other reason. The person presenting the check and each indorser and transferor on the instrument
remains liable for the transfer and presentment warranties that flow
with the item. In *Kirby v. First & Merchants National Bank, 6 UCC Rep
Serv 694*, the court held that payment "in cash" is final payment and
that if the payor bank makes final payment, it cannot sue the name on
the check except for breach of warranty. In the typical case, the payee
presents the check at the teller's window and the teller gives the payee
the amount of the check in cash. In a situation where the full amount of
the check is paid in cash, there is no question that the check is paid
under Section 4-215(a)(1). In the Kirby case, the payee presented a
$2,500 "on-us" item to the teller on January 3, along with a deposit slip
in the amount of $2,300. The deposit slip listed the $2,300 as currency.
The teller accepted the deposit slip and gave the payee $200 in cash.
The next day, January 4, the bank noticed that the check was insufficient. On January 5, an officer called the customer and advised him that
the check was insufficient and requested reimbursement from the customer. The customer never came in to pick up the check as he said he
would and on January 10, the bank charged the check to the customer's
account creating an overdraft.

The bank claims that it handled the transaction as a less-cash deposit and that the customer was given $200 back in cash. The customer
contends that the bank cashed the check and deposited $2,300 in cash as
evidenced by the deposit ticket and the testimony of the bank officer.
When asked, the bank officer stated that the bank had cashed the check.

The court held that the bank paid the item in cash and that the item was finally paid at that point. The bank also contended that final payment had not been made because the deposit ticket stated that all items were accepted subject to final payment. The court addressed this by stating that the court need not consider this argument because the item was paid in cash and even if it had not, the bank did not act by its midnight deadline. The check was taken for deposit on January 3, but the customer was not notified of dishonor of the item until January 5, after the expiration of the midnight deadline on January 4.

Next the bank contended that the customer was liable as an indorser since the check contained their indorsements. To this the court stated that the liability of the indorser is contingent upon the item being dishonored. In this case, the item was not dishonored but was paid in cash at the teller's window.

Payment in cash by one branch of a check drawn on another branch of the same bank is not final payment. The court in *Lawrence v. Bank of America, 40 UCC Rep Serv 201*, held that under California law, two branch offices of the same bank were separate "banks." The court stated that the branch to which the check was presented was a collecting bank and could not make final payment of a check drawn on the payee bank. In this case, the checks were cashed at one branch and before the checks reached the branch on which they were drawn, the drawer stopped payment on the checks. Since the items were not finally paid, the drawee bank had an obligation to its customer to accept the stop payment order.

If an item is presented over the counter and the bank settles with the customer by cashier's check or teller's check, the payment is final unless the bank has an agreement with the presenter that states that settlement is provisional. The court in *First National Bank of Fort Worth v. United States* held that the rule that payment is final when payment is made in case is extended to cash-equivalent. The court stated that the bank made final payment when it issued a cashier's check for a check presented for payment over the counter and the bank could not get reimbursed from the customer even though the account on which the check was drawn was insufficient. The bank would not have the right to stop payment on the teller's check or refuse to pay the cashier's check unless there was fraud involved in the presentment of the item. The court in *Rezapolvi v. First National Bank of Maryland, 35 UCC Rep Serv 1559*, also held that the issuance of a cashier's check is final payment of a check to the payee because a cashier's check is the equivalent of cash. The bank's issuance of a stop payment order on the check does not negate the final payment of the item. Issuance of the cashier's check discharged the drawer from his obligation on the instrument and was final payment which cannot be reversed by stopping payment on the cashier's check. The court went on to say that the bank has an obligation to honor its own check. The bank is not entitled to dishonor its own cashier's check, which is a bill of exchange drawn on itself. On the other hand, the court in *Roberts Fertilizer, Inc. v. Steinmeier, 6 UCC Rep Serv 2d 797*, held that a bank disbursement check is not the equivalent of a cashier's check, nor of cash, and it did not effect final payment in cash under Article 4. Additional facts that lead the court to its decision were that the disbursement check contained a statement that stated "Disbursement Account (Not a Cashier's Check)" and also stated "Not Good for More than $50,000." The amount of the check in question was $70,500. The court held that these legends on the check should have put the customer on notice that the disbursement was not the equivalent of cash.

Another example of Section 4-215(a)(2) is pointed out in the Official Comments. Unless the bank has an agreement with customers that settlement for deposits of an "on-us" check is provisional, the item is finally paid by the bank when it accepts the deposit. Settlement for an item over the counter is excluded from the provisional settlement and deferred posting provisions of Section 4-301, according to that comment. The agreement of the provisional nature of the settlement could be included in the customer account agreement or could be stated on the customer's deposit ticket. The courts tend to lean towards provisional settlement when an "on-us" item is taken for deposit. The court in *Douglas v. Citizens Bank of Jonesboro, 5 UCC Rep Serv 189*, held that by delivering deposit slips to the customer, the bank did not accept the checks for payment and could dishonor the checks the next day and charge the amounts back to the customer's account. In this case, the deposit ticket contained language that stated that "items drawn on this bank not good at close of business day on which they have been deposited may be charged back to depositor." The customer claims that he had not read nor been notified of the statement on the deposit ticket. The judge stated that whether the customer saw the statement was irrelevant. The judge stated out right that "by stamping the endorsement upon the checks deposited by appellants, and by delivering to appellants the deposit slips," the bank did not accept the items for payment.

The court in *Pracht v. Oklahoma State Bank, 26 UCC Rep Serv 141* agreed with the court in the Douglas case cited above. The court stated, "This court agrees with the principle announced in that case; that issuance of a deposit slip does not constitute a final settlement for an item. Another conclusion would destroy the Code's provisions in Article 4 Bank Deposits and Collections, that establish procedures for deferred posting and conditional settlement." In this case, the deposit slips also contained a statement that finality of the deposit was subject to receiving final payment. It appears that depositary banks should put such language on their account agreements or on their deposit slips. According to the Douglas case, it is not necessary.

If provisional settlement is made for an item that is presented to the bank in a cash letter by a clearing bank or through a clearinghouse, the payor bank must act by its midnight deadline to revoke the settlement and return the item to avoid final payment. If settlement is not revoked by the midnight deadline, the item is finally paid and the payor bank may not return the item to the indorser even if the item is not properly payable or if the balance is insufficient. "Midnight deadline" is defined in Section 4-104(a)(10) as "with respect to a bank is midnight on its next banking day following the banking day on which it receives the relevant item or notice or from which the time for taking action commences to run, whichever is later." The effect of the passage of time after provisional settlement is that the provisional settlement becomes final.

In *Hedglin v. Community Bank, Kinde, Michigan, 28 UCC Rep Serv 1450*, the court held that the payor bank makes final payment on a check when it makes provisional settlement and fails to revoke the settlement within the time permitted by statute, rule, or agreement. In this case, the payor bank did not revoke the provisional settlement by the midnight deadline and therefore made final payment on the item. The court in *Former Distributors, Inc. v. Bankers Trust Co., 8 UCC Rep Serv 1298*, also held that the payor bank had made final payment on a check by failure to return the check by the bank's midnight deadline.

Section 4-215(b) states, "If provisional settlement for an item does not become final, the item is not finally paid." As pointed out in the Official Comments, if settlement is made by cashier's or teller's check and the settlement check is not paid, settlement does not become final and payment is not final. In this situation, payment is not final even though the payor bank does not return the item by its midnight deadline. In this situation the drawer and indorsers would not be discharged from their respective obligations on the instrument.

(c) WHEN AN OBLIGATION IS NOT DISCHARGED BY PAYMENT

An obligation is not always discharged by payment. Section 3-602(b) contains several circumstances under which an obligation is not discharged by payment. Subsection (a), discussed earlier, states that the obligation is discharged even though payment is made with knowledge of a claim to the instrument. Subsection (b) qualifies that discharge and states that the obligation is not discharged if the following exists:

(1) Aclaim to the instrument under Section 3-306 is enforceable against the party receiving payment and (i) payment is made with knowledge by the payor that payment is prohibited by injunction or similar process or a court of competent jurisdiction, or (ii) in the case of an instrument other than a cashier's check, teller's check, or certified check, the party making payment accepted, from the person having a claim to the instrument, indemnity against loss resulting from refusal to pay the person entitled to enforce the instrument; or

(2) The person making payment knows that the instrument is a stolen instrument and pays a person it knows is in wrongful possession of the instrument.

The gist of this Subsection is that payment by a person that is obligated on an instrument is not discharged if an injunction has been issued against payment, the payor has received indemnification against loss, or if the payor knows that the person receiving payment has obtained the instrument through fraud. For example, assume that Bill Wiltshire issued a note to Joel Converse and Bill paid the amount of the note upon presentment to D.A. Carr with full knowledge that D.A. had stolen the note from Joel. In this example, Bill's obligation as the maker of the note survives the payment and Bill remains liable on the note to Joel.

(d) PAYMENT BY MISTAKE

Payment of an item may not be final in spite of Section 4-215 if the payment was made by mistake. Section 3-418 address payment and acceptance by mistake. According to Subsection (a) of that section, if the drawee of a draft pays or accepts a draft by mistake without knowledge that a stop payment has been placed on the item or that the signature of the drawer on the instrument was a forgery, the drawee may recover the amount of the draft from the person to whom or for whose benefit payment was made. If the item was accepted by mistake, the acceptance may be revoked. The right of the drawee to recover any payment made is not affected by the fact that the drawee failed to exercise ordinary care in paying or accepting the draft. Subsection (a) is subject to Subsection (c). Subsection (c) states that the drawee may not recover the amount paid on the draft if the proceeds were paid to a person who took the draft in good faith and for value or from a person who changed position, in good faith, in reliance on the payment or acceptance. Subsection (c) does not affect the rights that the drawee has for breach of warranty under Section 3-417 or 4-407.

Subsection (b) is applicable to any case other than the case described in Subsection (a) is also subject to Subsection (c). According to Subsection (b), a person that has paid or accepted an instrument by mistake may recover the payment from the person to whom payment or for whose benefit payment was made, or may revoke the acceptance. Recovery under this Subsection may be made to the extent permitted by the law governing mistake and restitution.

If an item is paid or accepted by mistake and recovery is made under Subsection (a) or (b), the instrument is deemed not to have been paid or accepted and is considered dishonored in spite of final payment under Section 4-215. The person from whom payment is recovered has rights as a person entitled to enforce the dishonored instrument as provided for in Section 3-418(d).

Section 3-418 would be applied to situations where a person obtained payment of an item with knowledge that the payment is wrong. For example, if the payee of a check presented the check to the payor bank with knowledge that the drawer had stopped payment on the check, the payor bank would be entitled to recover from the payee despite final payment of the item by the payor bank. Another example of the application of Section 3-418 would be a situation where the payee of a check forged the signature of the drawer of a check and obtained payment from the payor bank. In this situation, the payor bank could recover from the payee on the checks even though the bank made final payment. In applying the previous version of Section 3-418, the court in *Bartlett v. Bank or Carroll, 22 UCC Rep Serv 458*, held that the bank would not be liable to the plaintiff for refusal to pay checks where the plaintiff acted in bad faith in depositing the checks. In this case, the depositary bank was also the payor bank which was two days late in charging checks back to the plaintiff's account. Because of the plaintiff's bad faith, the court stated that the bank was not wrong in its actions of refusing to pay the checks.

9.3 TENDER OF PAYMENT

An indorser or accommodation party of an instrument may be discharged of their respective obligations if tender of payment is made and payment is refused. Section 3-603(b) provides that if tender of payment is made by a person entitled to enforce the instrument and payment is refused, the refusal to accept the payment discharges the obligation of an indorser or accommodation party who has a right of recourse against the party making the tender of payment. The obligation to pay is discharged to the extent of the amount of the tender. For example, assume that Bill issued a note to Joel and Cindy signed the note as an accommodation party. Assume further that Bill tendered payment to Joel but Joel refused to accept the payment. Joel's refusal to accept Bill's tender of payment discharged Cindy's obligation as an accommodation party.

The obligation of the party making the tender is not discharged. However, Subsection (c) provides that the person making tender would not be liable for interest on the amount of the tender after the date of the tender. In the example above, assume that Bill made the offer to Joel on June 15. Bill's obligation to pay interest on the note is discharged after June 15. In *Guaranty Bank v. Thompson, Guaranty Bank v. O'Dowd, 33 UCC Rep Serv 629*, the court held that tender of payment of the entire amount of a debt owing to plaintiff would discharge the debtor of liability of interest, costs and attorney's fees, but not from liability for the principal outstanding debt. In *Jessee v. First National Bank Atlanta, 31 UCC Rep Serv 637*, a surety who was liable for 20% of a note made tender of payment for the amount he was liable for. The court held that the surety was not discharged from his liability on the note but that he was discharged from this liability to pay interest, costs, and attorney's fees.

9.4 DISCHARGE BY CANCELLATION OR RENUNCIATION

The obligation of a party to pay an instrument may be discharged by a person entitled to enforce the instrument by an intentional voluntary act to discharge the person obligated. Discharge by cancellation or renunciation is provided for in Section 3-604(a). Methods of cancellation listed in that section are surrender of the instrument to the party, destruction, mutilation, or cancellation of the instrument, cancellation or striking out of the party's signature, or the addition of words to the instrument indicating discharge. For example, the payee on a note or a check could intentionally destroy the instrument to cancel it. The destruction of the instrument is a discharge of the obligation of the maker or drawer to pay the instrument. A person who is entitled to enforce an instrument could cancel the obligation of a specific person on the instrument. For example, the payee of a note could intentionally strike out the name of an indorser and thereby discharge that indorser. In that event, Subsection (b) states, "Cancellation or striking out of an indorsement pursuant to Subsection (a) does not affect the status and rights of a party derived from the indorsement."

A person obligated on an instrument may also be discharged by renunciation of rights by a person entitled to enforce an instrument. Subsection (a) provides that a person entitled to enforce an instrument may discharge the obligation of a party to pay the instrument "by agreeing not to sue or otherwise renouncing rights against the party by a signed writing." The writing may apparently be a separate writing from the instrument itself. The renunciation does not have to be placed on the instrument.

In the case of cancellation or renunciation, the person entitled to enforce the instrument may cancel or renounce the right to enforce the instrument with or without consideration. This provision makes it clear that no party would have any right to complain that the cancellation or renunciation was done without consideration. The person entitled to enforce the instrument could not later come back and complain that the obligation of a party was discharged without consideration. In *J.J. Schaefer Livestock Hauling, Inc. v. Gretna State Bank, 7 UCC Rep Serv 2d 143*, the bank set-off against the debtor's accounts, marked the notes "PAID," and returned the notes to the debtor. In a later action by a third party beneficiary, it was determined that the set-off was wrongful because the proceeds did not belong to the debtor. The court held that the debt was canceled even though the debt ended up being discharged without consideration. The court further stated that this was not merely some clerical error. The officer involved was an experienced lending officer that should have known what he was doing.

According to Section 3-605(b), the discharge of a party under Section 3-604 does not affect an indorser's or an accommodation party's rights against the discharged party. If an indorser or accommodation party has the right of recourse against a party whose obligation on the instrument is discharged, the discharge of that party does not affect the indorser's or accommodation party's right of recourse.

As stated above, the cancellation must be intentional. In *Los Alamos Credit Union v. Bowling, 8 UCC Rep Serv 2d 73*, the court held that a cancellation, release, or surrender of an instrument must be intentional and is ineffective if it is unauthorized, unintentional, or done by mistake. In this case, through a clerical error, a note was marked "PAID" and sent to the customer. The court held that the cancellation was through mistake and was therefore ineffective. The court in *Rubbelke v. Strecker, 8 UCC Rep Serv 2d 765*, held that cancellation of a promissory note must be intentional. In this case, the holder canceled the note by marking the note canceled, writing a statement to that effect, and returning the note to the debtor. The cancellation was done on the condition that the debtor deliver certain assets to the holder of the note. The debtor never delivered the assets; therefore, the court held that the cancellation was unintentional.

9.5 DISCHARGE OF INDORSERS AND ACCOMMODATION PARTIES

Action by the person entitled to enforce an instrument can discharge an indorser or accommodation party even if that person does not intend to discharge them. Section 3-604(c) provides if the person entitled to enforce an instrument extends the due date of an instrument, any indorser or accommodation party is discharged to the extent of the damage caused to the indorser or accommodation party as a result of the extension. This discharge applies only if the indorser or accommodation party has a right of recourse against the party for whom the due date was extended and the indorser or accommodation party can prove that the extension caused the loss. The discharge is effective against the person who extended the due date whether the extension was with or without recourse. In *Rogers v. Merchants & Planters Bank of Newport, Ark., 11 UCC Rep Serv 2d 1198*, the court held that the accommodation party was discharged for his liability on a note where the note was extended four times. The accommodation party was discharged even though the accommodation party consented to the extension two of the four times that the note was extended.

Likewise, if a person entitled to enforce an instrument agrees to a material modification of the obligation of a party, other than an extension of the due date, the modification discharges any indorser or accommodation party having a right of recourse against the party whose obligation is modified. The discharge is only to the extent that the modification causes a loss with respect to the right of recourse. Subsection (d) establishes the amount of loss suffered by the indorser or accommodation party as an "amount equal to the amount of the right of recourse unless the person enforcing the instrument proves that no loss was caused by the modification or that the loss caused by the modification was an amount less than the amount of the right of recourse."

The indorser or accommodation party may also be discharged if collateral is given to secure the loan and the value of the collateral interest is reduced or impaired by the person entitled to enforce the instrument. The discharge of the indorser and accommodation party as a result of the impairment of the collateral is governed by Subsections (e), (f), and (g) of Section 3-605. The court in *In Re Murchison, 9 UCC Rep Serv 2d 1305*, held that release of stock to the debtor that was held as collateral was a discharge of the guarantor. The court also held that release of a co-maker, co-guarantor, or endorser from liability may also discharge the guarantor as it did in this case.

9.6 ACCORD AND SATISFACTION

In an effort to settle disputes over the payment of a debt, some debtors will offer an instrument in full payment and satisfaction of a claim. Section 3-311 settles this longstanding dispute and contains provisions addressing when an instrument containing such a statement is accord and satisfaction. According to this section, a "claim is discharged if the person against whom the claim is asserted proves that the instrument or a accompanying document contained a conspicuous statement to the effect that the instrument was tendered as full satisfaction of the claim." Several conditions must be met before the claim is discharged. Tender of the instrument must be in good faith as full satisfaction, the amount of the claim was unliquidated or subject to a bona fide dispute, and the claimant obtained payment of the instrument. If all three of these requirements are not met, then the debt is not discharged.

For example, assume that Bill owes Joel $1,000 and there is no dispute over the amount owed. In an effort to avoid paying the entire amount, Bill sends Joel a check in the amount of $800 with a statement on it the check is in full satisfaction of the debt that Bill owes Joel. Joel never notices that the statement was placed on the check and deposits the check to his account and the check is paid. In this instance, the debt would not be discharged because there was no dispute over the amount. The amount was totally liquidated. Assume, however, that there was a dispute as to the amount of money that Bill owed Joel and that they had been arguing over the amount for two weeks. Joel receives the check from Bill and deposits it to his account. In this case, a dispute did exist and by accepting the check with the statement on it, Joel discharged the obligation that Bill owed to him.

The previous version of the UCC did not contain a similar provision. This situation was left entirely up to the courts to decide the outcome. Some courts held that a claim could be discharged if the claim was unliquidated and the statement was placed on the check. However, the courts held that if the person accepting the check reserved their rights by placing a statement such as "without prejudice" on the check, the person accepting the check could reserve his rights and the claim was not discharged. The courts looked to Section 1-207 which stated, "A party with explicit reservation of rights performs or promises performance or assents to performance in a manner demanded or offered by the other party does not thereby prejudice the rights reserved. Such words as "without prejudice," "under protest," or the like are sufficient. This section has been revised with the addition of a new Subsection that states "Subsection (1) does not apply to an accord and satisfaction." Therefore, if all of the conditions of Section 3-311 are met, the claim is discharged even if the person accepting the instrument attempts to reserve his rights.

All claims are not discharged if the instrument with the statement that it is issued in full satisfaction is accepted. Section 3-311(c) contains a provision under which a claim is not discharged. That Subsection provides that an organization may issue a notice to its customers and other persons that send payments to the company that states that all disputes over a debt, including checks that are issued as full satisfaction, should be sent to a designated person, office or place. The claim is not discharged if the payment containing the statement of full satisfaction is not received by the designated person, office, or place. The statement sent by the organization must be conspicuous. It could not be printed in small print in the middle of a complicated document. If the court finds that the statement is not conspicuous, then the claim would probably be discharged.

An example of the application of Subsection (c) is as follows. Flashback Music, Inc. issued a statement to its customers that stated that all disputed claims should be sent to a specified person at a certain location. A dispute arose over a certain performance and the person owing money to Flashback sent the payment to the normal lockbox address instead of to the designated person. The payment contained a statement that payment was in full satisfaction and accord for the debt that was owed to Flashback. The payment was processed by the bank and the communication by the debtor went unnoticed. The debtor claims that it has been discharged from its obligation because Flashback accepted the check. In this case, the debt would not be discharged because the payment was not sent to the designated person. Subsection (c) was designed for the situation described in this example.

Subsection (c) also provides that a claim is not discharged if, "The claimant, whether or not an organization, proves that within 90 days after payment of the instrument, the claimant tendered repayment of the amount of the instrument to the person against whom the claim is asserted. This paragraph does not apply if the claimant is an organization complying with paragraph (1)(i)." This Subsection allows the person accepting payment 90 days within which to revoke the payment and return the proceeds to the person that sent them. This Subsection gives the claimant sufficient time to discover that payment has been received and that the issuer of the instrument is offering a settlement. If the claimant does not discover and refuse the offer within 90 days, then the offer is accepted and the claim is discharged. This Subsection does not apply if payment was sent to the location or person designated by an organization. If the payment was sent to the designated person or location and the payment was accepted, the organization could not revoke the payment within the 90-day period.

Subsection (d) contains a provision that makes it clear that a claim is discharged without regard to Subsection (c) if the claimant accepted the payment with full knowledge that the payment was offered in full settlement. That Subsection states, "A claim is discharged if the person against whom the claim is asserted proves that within a reasonable time before the collection of the instrument was initiated, the claimant, or an agent of the claimant having direct responsibility with respect to the disputed obligation, knew that the instrument was tendered in full satisfaction of the claim."

CHAPTER 10

WHEN A BANK MAY CHARGE A CUSTOMER'S ACCOUNT

10.1 PROPERLY PAYABLE ITEMS

A bank may only charge a customer's account, according to Section 4-401, for an item that is properly payable from the customer's account. The section goes on to state that "an item is properly payable if it is authorized by the customer and is in accordance with any agreement between the customer and bank." An item that contains a forged drawer's signature is not authorized and is therefore not properly payable. As discussed in Chapter 3 however, the forged signature can be made effective against the drawer in certain circumstances. A check that contains a forged indorsement is likewise not properly payable. The bank may only make payment to a holder of the instrument even if that person is not the owner of the instrument. A person presenting an item that contains a forged or missing indorsement is not a holder of the instrument.

If the bank has agreed to certain requirements, the bank may only pay the item if those requirements are met. For example, if the bank entered into an agreement to only pay checks with two signatures, a check with only one signature is not properly payable. In this situation, if one of the signatures is missing, according to Section 3-403(b), the signature of the organization is unauthorized. If the bank agreed not to pay checks presented for payment more than 30 days from the date of the check, payment of the check after the expiration of 30 days is not proper. If the bank agreed not to pay checks over a certain dollar limit, checks in excess of the dollar limit are not properly payable. The bank is not required to examine each and every check to exercise ordinary care. Therefore, it would appear that the bank would not be bound by a legend unless it agreed. The best action for the bank is to put specific language in the customer account agreement that provides that the bank is not bound by legends on checks.

(a) OVERDRAFTS

Subsection (a) also allows a bank to charge a customer's account for a check that is properly payable even if it creates an overdraft. In *Pulaski State Bank v. Kalbe, 40 UCC Rep Serv 1794*, the court held that the bank properly paid a check issued by Kalbe even though it created an overdraft and held the defendant liable for the amount of the overdraft. The court stated paying a check in the overdraft is within the discretion of the bank and the customer has no reason to object even if payment creates an overdraft. However, Section 4-401(b) states, "A customer is not liable for the amount of an overdraft if the customer neither signed the item nor benefitted from the proceeds of the item." This is a new section that will not be popular with banks that codifies the holding of the court in *Cambridge Trust Co. v. Carney, 16 UCC Rep Serv 1078*, and *United States Trust Co. of New York v Mcsweeney, 35 UCC Rep Serv 205*. In the Carney case, the court held that the wife was not liable for an overdraft created by the husband for which the wife received no benefit and in which she did not participate. The court also held an indemnification agreement invalid against the wife. The indemnification agreement was part of the customer account agreement but the court held that the agreement was an attempt by the bank to insulate itself from liability for failure to exercise ordinary care. In this case, the officer in charge of the account requested to be notified immediately if any checks were presented that would create an overdraft and that since the bank was so concerned about the overdraft, it was not the exercise of ordinary care for the bank to pay checks in the overdraft. In the McSweeney case, the court held that in the absence of an agreement, the question of a joint account holder's liability for an overdraft is based on the benefit received, the exercise of control over the account, the participation over the day-to-day operations of the account and similar activities. In this case, the husband was not held liable for overdrafts created by the wife.

This section is intended to protect the innocent person that is authorized to sign checks on an account that becomes overdrawn by another signer on the account. This section, while not limited to joint accounts, will most likely be applied to joint accounts in most cases. For example, if a husband and wife are both authorized to sign on an account that becomes overdrawn, the bank will be put to the task of proving which of the two signed the check. Even after proving who signed the check that created the overdraft, the bank could attempt to prove that the other person received some benefit from the check.

The bank can, however, avoid this problem by incorporating into the signature card or account agreement a provision that states that all parties authorized to sign checks on an account agree to be liable for any overdraft regardless of who signed the check that actually created the overdraft. An agreement to this effect will avoid a lot of litigation and a lot of work trying to prove who signed the instrument and who got the benefit of it. In this regard, if an item that was previously deposited is charged back to an account and an overdraft is created, an agreement that binds all of the authorized signatories on the account will substantially reduce the burden of proof on the bank. For example, Bill and Cindy are both authorized to sign checks on an account and a check that was previously deposited is returned and the chargeback creates an overdraft. Both Bill and Cindy have written checks on the account. If no agreement exists between the bank and Bill and Cindy, the bank will be put to the burden of proof of which one, between Bill and Cindy, issued the checks or received the benefit of the checks.

(b) POSTDATED CHECKS

A postdated check is a check that has a date that is some time in the future. If Bill issues a check on May 2 and dates the check May 25, the check is postdated. In many situations, a customer gives a payee a postdated check with the understanding that the payee will not present the check until the date on the check. Invariably, the payee presents the check to the payor bank before the ink even dries on the check. The customer, of course, becomes very upset with the bank for paying the check before the date of the check. Under the previous version of Article 3, the check was not properly payable until the date of the check. The new version of Article 3 has changed this position. Section 3-113 states, "Except as provided in Section 4-401(c), an instrument payable on demand is not payable before the date of the instrument." Section

4-401(c) provides that a check is an exception to this rule. Subsection (c) states that if a check is otherwise properly payable, a bank may charge a postdated check against a customer's account. However, the bank may not charge the customer's account for a postdated check if the customer has given the bank notice that the customer issued a postdated check. The notice, which must describe the check with "reasonable certainty," is effective against the bank for the same period of time as for stop payment orders. An oral notice would be effective for fourteen (14) days, unless confirmed in writing, in which case the notice is effective for six (6) months.

Just like a stop payment order, the notice must be received at such time and in such manner as to afford the bank a reasonable opportunity to act on it before the bank takes any action with respect to the check described in Section 4-303. That section establishes when a stop payment order, notice, or legal process comes too late. It establishes the priority between items that are presented for payment against a customer's account and stop payment orders and the like. For example, if the bank pays a postdated check over the counter at 9:15 a.m. and the customer calls the bank at 9:30 a.m. and gives a postdated notice, the notice comes too late. In this example, the bank may charge the customer's account for the check if the check is otherwise properly payable.

If the postdated notice adequately describes the check and is received timely by the bank, the bank may not charge the customer's account for the item. If the bank does charge the customer's account after notice is received, Section 4-401(c) states, "The bank is liable for damages for the loss resulting from its act. The loss may include damages for dishonor of subsequent items under Section 4-402." Section 4-402 establishes when a bank is liable to a customer for wrongful dishonor of a check. An example of the application of this part of Subsection (c) is as follows. Assume that a customer issues a check on May 2, and dates the check May 25. The customer calls the bank and gives the bank proper notice of the postdated check, but for some reason, the bank mistakenly pays the check before the date on the check. Assume further that because of paying the postdated check, the bank returns other checks that were properly payable. In this example, the bank could be liable to the customer for any damages resulting from its act of paying the postdated check and for wrongful dishonor of the other checks that were properly payable. This section does not state who has the burden of proof of the amount of damages resulting from the bank's acts. It would appear that the customer would have the burden of proof of establishing the loss as in the case of a bank paying a check over a valid

stop payment order. The bank's right to subrogation on improper payment under Section 4-407, which is discussed in Chapter 11 of this
book, would apply in this situation.

Subsection (c) does not require a bank to pay a postdated check.
This section states "a bank may charge against a customer's account."
This section recognizes the automation of the process of paying items
by banks and the fact that banks no longer examine each and every
check. However, if the bank does notice that a check is postdated, the
bank could refuse to pay the check and should not be held liable to the
customer for wrongful dishonor. For example, if the bank files checks in
bulk, as most banks do, and the bank examines the signatures on checks
over $10,000 and happens to notice that a check is postdated, the bank
would be within its rights to return the check. Or if a teller notices that
a check is postdated that has been presented over the counter, the teller
could refuse to honor the check.

(c) STALE DATED CHECKS

A check that is outstanding for more than six months is considered stale
and some banks will not pay a stale check without first consulting with
the customer. The number of banks that actually check with customers
is probably very small. Section 4-404 states "A bank is under no obligation to a customer having a checking account to pay a check, other than
a certified check, which is presented more than six months after its date,
but it may charge its customer's account for a payment made thereafter
in good faith." This section gives the bank the option to pay a stale
dated check, other than a certified check. The bank has no option on
payment of a certified check that is stale dated. The court in *M.G. Sales,
Inc. v. Chemical Bank*, 12 UCC Rep Serv 2d, 177, held that a bank is not
obligated to pay a check over six months old but the bank is not prohibited from paying a check older than six months. In this case, the payor
bank paid a check that was 15 months old on which the customer had
previously stopped payment. The court held that the payment was
proper. A written stop payment is valid for six months and it is the
customer's obligation to renew the stop payment.

The one part of this section that could cause some banks problems is
the requirement that the check must be paid in good faith. Is "good faith"
merely the absence of "bad faith" in this situation? It would appear that
unless the bank had some reason to know that the customer did not want
the bank to pay the check, the check would be properly payable. In *Granite
Equipment Leasing Corp. v. Hempstead Bank*, 9 UCC Rep Serv 1384, the

drawer of a check issued a stop payment on the check. After the expiration of the stop payment order, the check was presented and paid. The court held that the check was properly payable and that the bank had exercised "good faith" in paying the check. The court held that in the absence of dishonesty, bad faith, recklessness, or lack of ordinary care in the face of the circumstances actually known, the bank is not liable for payment of a stale check. In *New York Flameproofing Co., Inc. v. Chemical Bank, 15 UCC Rep Serv 1104,* the court held that the bank did not produce proof that it paid a check in good faith. The check in this case was ten years old, was a different color than other checks currently being written by the customer and was drawn on a closed account. Based on these facts the court held that the bank did not prove its good faith. The court in *Charles Ragusa & Son v. Community State Bank, 24 UCC Rep Serv 725,* also held that the bank must prove that it acted in good faith. In this case, the bank paid a check that was three years old and the court held for the customer because the bank failed to introduce any evidence which showed that the bank acted in good faith. The court held that it was not sufficient for the bank to claim protection under Section 4-404 allowing a bank to pay a check over six months old.

One rule of thumb that the bank may want to use is that if the bank does not notice that the check is six months old or older, then it may pay the item. But if the bank notices the stale date, the bank should at least inquire as to whether the customer wants the check paid. As stated in earlier sections, because of the automated method of processing checks, banks simply do not examine each and every check. Therefore, the likelihood of a bank noticing that a check is stale is very slim. On the other hand, when a check is presented for payment over the counter, the teller is likely to notice the date on the check. In this case, a good rule of thumb would be for the bank to contact the customer.

The Official Comments to this section states that a bank may pay the check if the bank is in a position to know that the customer wants the check paid. The comment uses dividend checks as an example and states that the bank is given the option in this situation because the customer would normally want dividend checks paid even after six months.

The wording of this section indicates that the primary purpose of the section is to make it clear that a bank is not obligated to pay a check more than six months old because the first sentence of the section states so. However, most problems arise out of banks paying checks that are older than six months rather than banks not paying checks that are stale dated.

(d) ALTERED AND INCOMPLETE CHECKS

An "alteration" is defined in Section 3-407 to mean an unauthorized change in an instrument or an unauthorized addition of words or numbers that changes the obligation of a party on the instrument. This section provides that a payor bank that pays a fraudulently altered instrument in good faith, may pay the instrument according to its original terms on an incomplete instrument as completed. Section 4-401(d) follows the terms of Section 3-407 and states the following:

A bank that in good faith makes payment to a holder may charge the indicated account of its customer according to:

(1) the original terms of the altered item; or

(2) the terms of the completed item, even though the bank knows the item has been completed unless the bank has notice that the completion was improper.

A check issued for $10 and raised to $100 may be paid by the payor bank but for only $10. The customer may, however, be liable for the amount of the check as altered. Section 3-406 provides that a person whose negligence substantially contributes to an alteration of an item is precluded from asserting the alteration against a payor bank that pays the item in good faith. This preclusion also applies to the person who takes the instrument in good faith for value or collection. In the example above, the bank could charge the customer the altered amount of $100 for the check if the customer were negligent in the manner in which the check was drawn. For example, if the customer left blanks on the check or wrote the check in a manner that would allow the check to be easily altered, a court could find that the customer's negligence substantially contributed to the alteration.

Section 3-406(b) provides that if the payor bank fails to exercise ordinary care in paying the item and that failure substantially contributes to the alteration, the loss will be allocated between the two parties according to the extent to which the failure of each to exercise ordinary care contributed to the loss. In other words, the court will analyze the care exercised by both parties and determine to what extent the negligence of each party actually contributed to the loss. If the court, for example, determines that both the customer and the bank were negligent but that the loss would have been sustained even if the bank had exercised ordinary care, the entire loss could be allocated to the customer.

As stated above, the bank may pay an item that was completed after it was signed even if the bank has knowledge of the fact that the incomplete item has been completed. For example, if the terms of a check are typed with the exception of the amount which is filled in with a red ink pen, if the bank examines checks, the bank might be put on notice that the check was completed. The bank may pay the check even with the knowledge that the check was completed unless the bank knows that the completion was improper. In the previous example, if the customer had called the bank and advised the bank that the amount, which the customer had intended to be $10, was left blank, the bank would have notice that the completion was improper if the amount of the check was completed as $100. The court in *AmSouth Bank N.A. v. Spigner, 4 UCC Rep Serv 2d 115*, held that the completion of a blank check in the amount of $25,000 was an alteration of the check. The court held that the bank had a duty to check with its customer before cashing a check that was written on a counter check that was 13 years old, did not contain an account number and was obviously completed by the drawer's ex-wife. The court held that the check was not properly payable.

The customer also has a duty under Section 4-406 to discover an alteration within a reasonable time and report the alteration to the bank within a reasonable amount of time after receiving a bank statement. The customer's duty to examine a bank statement is discussed in detail in Chapter 11 of this book. Another issue related to alterations is the presenter's warranty under Section 3-417 and 4-208, which are discussed in Chapter 7 of this book.

10.2 DEATH OR INCOMPETENCE OF CUSTOMER

The incompetence of a customer does not effect a bank's right to accept, pay, or collect an item for that customer, unless the bank has notice of the adjudication of incompetence. Section 4-405(a) states "A payor or collecting bank's authority to accept, pay, or collect an item or to account for proceeds of its collection, if otherwise effective, is not rendered ineffective by incompetence of a customer of either bank existing at the time the item is issued or its collection is undertaken if the bank does not know of an adjudication of incompetence. Neither death nor incompetence of a customer revokes the authority to accept, pay, collect, or account until the bank knows of the fact of death or of an adjudication of incompetence and has reasonable opportunity to act on it." This section allows a collecting bank to accept an item from an incompetent person, pay an item on an incompetent person's account, and settle with an incompetent person after the item is presented to and paid by the payor bank.

As long as the bank does not have knowledge of the death of or the incompetence of a person, the bank may deal with the item issued by or accepted from that person. Neither the incompetent person, the family of the incompetent person, nor the estate of a deceased person would have a cause of action against a bank that dealt with such an item. For example, Bill, an incompetent person, issues a check to Flashback Music, Inc. Flashback deposits the check to its checking account and the check is presented for payment at the First Deposit Bank and is paid. A week later, Bill's family advises the bank that Bill had been adjudicated incompetent before the time that the check was issued and that the bank was not authorized to charge Bill's account for the check. Section 4-405 protects the bank and allows the bank to pay the check as long as the bank was not aware of the adjudication of incompetence at the time that it paid the check. The difficult issue to address is whether the bank had knowledge of the adjudication. If Bill's family claims that the bank had knowledge of the adjudication, the burden of proof would be on the family that the bank did in fact have knowledge.

In the case of the death of a person, Subsection (b) provides "Even with knowledge, a bank may for 10 days after the death pay or certify checks drawn on or before that date unless ordered to stop payment by a person claiming an interest in the account." As long as the bank does not have knowledge of the death of a person, the bank may pay checks that were issued by that person prior to his or her death. In *Cirar v. Bank of Hartshore, 22 UCC Rep Serv 428*, the court held that the bank may pay checks up to ten days after the drawer's death even with knowledge of the death. In this case, the bank was advised of the drawer's death but the bank was not instructed to stop payment on the checks issued by the decedent. The court therefore held that the checks were properly payable even though the check in question was payable to the bank.

The problem that arises sometime is whether the deceased person had actually issued the check. If the check is dated after the death of the person, then quite obviously, the check was not issued by that person. The problem arises where checks that are dated prior to the death of the person are presented and paid after the date of that person's death and the authenticity of the signature of the decedent is questioned. If the signature is a forgery, the check is not properly payable and the bank does not have the authority to pay the item on the account. The problem, however, is establishing the fact that the signature is a forgery after the death of that person. Section 3-308 states that the there is a presumption of validity of a signature unless the action is to enforce the liability of the purported signer and the signer is dead or incompetent at the time of the trial.

Subsection (b) allows the bank to pay checks with knowledge of the death of the customer for ten days unless a stop-payment order is received by a person claiming an interest in the account. Any person claiming an interest in the account can issue the stop-payment order. The person does not have to be a relative or potential heir of the decedent; it could be any interested party including a creditor of the decedent. The bank is not required to determine the validity of the interest claimed by the person issuing the stop-payment order. The person need only claim that he or she has an interest in the account and the bank would be protected by Subsection (b). The bank, of course, must exercise good faith in accepting the stop-payment order. In *Holsomback v. Akins, 17 UCC Rep Serv 181*, the court held that a stop payment placed on a check by an employee of the drawer prior to the death of the drawer is not a stop payment by a person claiming an interest in the account within the meaning of Section 4-405. In this case, the decedent had issued a check to the plaintiff with instructions that the defendant should complete the blank check upon the death of the drawer. The check was presented within ten days of the drawer's death and paid. The plaintiff, an employee of the decedent and an heir had placed a stop payment on the check a year earlier claiming the she was instructed to issue the stop payment order by the drawer. The court held that the alleged instructions were hearsay and not admissible. Therefore, the stop payment was not valid.

10.3 CUSTOMER'S RIGHT TO STOP PAYMENT

A check is an order issued by the drawer to the drawee to pay the amount of money stated on the check to the holder. If the item is properly payable, the payor bank may then charge the customer's account for the amount of the check. Since the customer gives the order to the bank to pay a check, the customer also has the right to instruct the bank not to pay a check. Section 4-403 establishes the customer's right to stop payment on a check. If the customer has issued a stop payment order to the bank, the bank no longer has the authority to pay the check on the customer's account. After the stop payment order is issued, the check is no longer properly payable. The bank does, however, have certain rights discussed below if it does pay a check over a valid stop payment order.

(a) WHO MAY STOP PAYMENT

Section 4-403(a) states that a customer or any person authorized to draw on an account may stop payment on a check. The former version of this section stated only that "a customer" could stop payment on a check. "Customer" was defined as "any person having an account with a bank or for whom a bank has agreed to collect items..." The former section limited who could issue a stop payment on a check. The revised version expands the authority to stop payment to any person authorized to draw checks on the account. This would include a person signing in a representative capacity as well as a joint holder of an account. For example, if the president of a company issues a check, a vice president or any other person that is authorized to sign checks on behalf of the company could stop payment on the check issued by the president. A wife who is a joint owner of an account can stop payment on a check issued by her husband.

This section also allows the customer or any person authorized to draw on the account to close the account. Additionally, if the signature of more than one person is required to draw on an account, any one of the persons may stop payment on a check or close the account. Other than in the case of a person who has an interest in the account of a deceased person discussed above, only the customer or a person authorized to draw checks on an account may stop payment on a check. Neither the payee or any other interested party may issue a stop payment order.

In *Steenbergen v. First Federal Savings & Loan of Chickasha*, 5 UCC Rep Serv 2d 1054, and *Lo Monaco v. Belfiore*, 15 UCC Rep Serv 2d 991, the court held that a bank that issued a teller's check on another bank is a "customer" and has the right to stop payment on the teller's check.

(b) DESCRIPTION OF THE ITEM

As to the description of the item to be stopped, Section 4-403(a) only states that the item must be described "with reasonable certainty." "Reasonable certainty" is not defined in Article 4; however, the use of this terminology is significant. The previous version of this section did not contain language requiring such a description of the item. The courts in the past have had many different views on this subject as is evidenced by the many cases and different findings by the courts. Some courts recognize the automated process used by banks while some courts have ignored this fact. Evidently it was the intention of the drafters of the code to require that the stop payment order must accurately describe the item to reverse some of the decisions that did not require accurate information. The courts in *Best v. Dreyfus Liquid Assets, Inc.*, 3 *UCC Rep Serv 2d 704*, *Hughes v. Marine Midland Bank, N. A.*, 40 *UCC Rep Serv 998*, and *Elsie Rodriguez Fashions, Inc. v. Chase Manhattan Bank*, 23 *UCC Rep Serv 133*, held that a minor error in the amount does not relieve a bank from its obligation to stop payment on a check, especially if the bank does not notify the customer of the need for accuracy in all of the information.

The new revised Section 4-403 appears to follow the Florida statue that requires that the item be described with "reasonable accuracy." The court, in *Capital Bank v. Schuler*, 34 *UCC Rep Serv 1287*, held that the term "reasonable accuracy" requires the customer to accurately describe the item. The court held that since the wording of the Florida statute varied from the uniform law, it was apparently the intention of the legislature that a greater burden be placed on the depositor in describing the item. In this case, the customer did not supply the bank with a check number and gave the bank the wrong amount. With the change in the wording of Section 4-403 to require that the item be described with "reasonable certainty," perhaps the courts in the future will follow the Capital Bank decision. The court also held that the customer has a duty to accurately describe a check in *Poullier v. Naucua Motors, Inc.*, 32 *UCC Rep Serv 258*. The court held in that case that banks must rely on computers and automation to stop payment on checks and that "one digit can be a world of difference to a computer."

Most banks have systems that key on the amount of the check and the check number. If the amount is off by as little as one cent, the system will not recognize the item as the item on which the stop payment order was placed. If the amount and the check number are correct, the system will identify the item and reject it allowing manual intervention. Some systems allow the bank to load a range for both the amount and the check number. If a check within that range is presented for payment, the check will be listed on a "suspect" list and the item will have to be manually inspected to determine if the suspected item is the actual item on which the stop payment order was placed. Another problem arises if the customer makes an error in describing the payee on the check. If the amount and the check number are correct, the check should reject. However, on manual inspection if the payee is listed wrong, the bank may not stop the check.

One way to help reduce the potential for problems is to include a provision in the customer account agreement and on any written stop payment forms or confirmations that states that the item must be accurately described in every detail. Section 4-103 allows for provisions of Article 4 to be varied by agreement as long as the bank does not attempt to void its obligation to exercise ordinary care. A requirement that the customer accurately describe a check in every detail is not an attempt to avoid an obligation to exercise ordinary care. The current state of automated processing dictates that the item must be accurately described. In an electronic check presentment environment, the check on which the stop payment order is placed must be accurately described. If not, the customer can agree to sustain the loss, if any, for his or her own failure to accurately describe the item.

(c) TIME AND MANNER OF RECEIPT
OF STOP PAYMENT ORDER

The stop payment order must be received by the bank, according to Section 4-403(a), "at a time and in a manner that affords the bank a reasonable opportunity to act on it before any action by the bank with respect to the item described in Section 4-303." Section 4-303, which is discussed below in Section 10.4, deals with when items are subject to notice, stop payment, etc. Basically, the stop payment order must be received by the bank before the bank has paid the item or before the cutoff time established by the bank. The major source of problems in this area is the situation when the customer and the holder of the check race to the bank. The bank must be given a reasonable opportunity to react to the customer's stop payment order. The period of time that is reasonable is dependent upon the capabilities of the bank and therefore will vary from bank to bank, where and how the stop payment order is received, and where the check is presented for payment. In other words, there is no set period of time within which the bank is given to react such as an hour or six hours or even 24 hours.

Consider the following example. The First Deposit Bank is a community bank with six branches. At 9:00 a.m. on May 15, a customer calls the Hill Street branch and issues a stop payment on a check that is described in sufficient detail. The branch secretary completes the proper forms and calls the Account Service department and relays the stop payment information to the appropriate personnel. At 10:30 a.m., the payee of the check presents the check over the counter to the Barlow Road branch. The tellers do not have the capability of making an on-line inquiry on an account to check the account balance or to determine if a stop payment has been placed on a specific check. In this example, it would appear the that bank did not have a reasonable opportunity to act on the stop payment order before the check was paid. Assume in the example above that the bank had a very sophisticated on-line teller network and that the stop payment order was loaded immediately upon receipt by the Hill Street branch. Assume further that the stop payment order was reflected on the on-line teller system and that the teller at the Barlow Road branch did not notice the stop payment flag on the account. In this case, it would appear that the bank would have had a reasonable opportunity to act on the stop payment order before the check was paid.

In *Tusso v. Security National Bank v. Adamson Construction Corp., 13 UCC Rep Serv 1131*, the customer issued a stop payment on a check at 9:00 a.m. and the payee presented the check to the bank at 10:40 a.m. The court held that in this case one and one half hours was sufficient time for the bank to stop payment on the check. The court also held that the customer has the burden of proof that the stop payment order was received by the bank at such time as to afford the bank a reasonable opportunity to act on the order.

The question of whether a stop payment order was received by a bank in time to afford the bank a reasonable opportunity to act on the order is a question of fact for the trier of the facts, so holds the court in *Stanek v. National Bank of Detroit, 7 UCC Rep Serv 2d 282*. In that case, the customer placed a stop payment order on a check at 9:35 a.m. and the check was paid sometime later that same day. The court held that the question of whether the stop payment was timely was a question of fact even though the customer account agreement stated that the bank had "one full banking day" in which to act on the stop payment. The court held that such exculpatory language was an attempt by the bank to avoid liability for its failure to exercise ordinary care, which is contrary to Section 4-103. The court held as a matter of law that the bank had sufficient time to act on a stop payment order in *Hughes v. Marine Midland Bank, N.A., 40 UCC Rep Serv 998*. In that case, the customer issued the stop payment order at 8:55 a.m. on Friday and the check was paid sometime on Monday.

The point in all of the above discussion is that the bank must be given a reasonable opportunity to act on a stop payment and that the amount of time required will vary from bank to bank depending on a number of factors. Each case will have to be determined on its own merits. The bank does have certain rights discussed below if it improperly pays an item.

(d) HOW LONG EFFECTIVE

The length of time that a stop payment is effective is governed by Section 4-403(b). According to that section, an oral stop payment order is effective for 14 calendar days. A written stop payment order and an oral stop payment order that is confirmed in writing is effective against the bank for six months. A stop payment order may be renewed for additional six-month periods by a written request given to the bank within a period during which the stop payment order is effective. Upon the expiration of a stop payment order, whether oral or written, the bank is not liable to the customer for payment of the item if the item is otherwise properly payable. It is the responsibility of the customer to renew a stop payment order or to confirm an oral stop payment order in writing. Although not required, before releasing an oral stop payment, the bank could send a notification to the customer advising them that the oral stop payment expires at the end of the 14-day period.

In *Granite Equipment Leasing Corp. v. Hempstead Bank, 9 UCC Rep Serv 1384,* the court held that a written stop payment order is valid against the bank for six months and that the check is properly payable after the expiration of the stop payment order. It is the responsibility of the customer to renew the stop payment order to keep it in effect after the six-month period.

The bank and the customer, by agreement, could vary the length of time that the stop payment is effective. For example, if the customer wanted to make the stop payment effective for one year, the bank could vary Subsection (b) and bind itself by agreement to the one-year period.

(e) BURDEN OF ESTABLISHING LOSS

The burden of establishing the fact that the customer experienced a loss and the amount of the loss resulting from payment of an item over a valid stop payment order is on the customer, according to Section 4-403(c). The customer must prove that the loss was the result of payment of the check over the stop payment order and that the loss would not have occurred if the bank had not paid the item. For example, assume that certain services were rendered for a customer and the customer paid for the services with a check. Later the customer decides that he or she cannot afford to pay for the services and places a stop payment on the check. The payee of the check rendered the services in accordance with the agreement with the customer and was due the money. Through an error, the bank paid the check over the valid stop payment order of the customer and the customer demands a refund from the bank. The customer has the burden of proving that the actions of the bank was the cause of the loss. In this example, the customer could not meet the burden of proof because the customer had received the benefit of the services rendered by the payee. The customer, therefore, did not experience a loss.

Suppose in the example above that the payee did not perform the services and the customer placed a valid stop payment order on the check. Assume further that the payee presented the check for payment over the counter and the bank paid the check in cash over the valid stop payment order. In this example, the customer has sustained a loss because he or she has paid for services that were not rendered. In *Mitchell v. Republic Bank & Trust v. Weathers Bros. Office Equipment Co.,* 23 *UCC Rep Serv* 712, the court held that the mere fact that a bank paid a check over a valid stop payment order of the customer and debited the customer's account is not sufficient proof of loss. The court held the customer must prove that payment of the check over the stop payment order was the cause of the loss. The question of whether the customer suffered a loss is a question for the finder of the fact, according to the court in *Kunkel v. First National Bank of Devils Lake,* 2 *UCC Rep Serv* 574.

The customer would also have the burden of proof of the amount of the loss, which in this case would most likely be the amount of the check. In *Hughes v. Marine Midland Bank N.A.,* 40 *UCC Rep Serv* 998, the court held that if the bank pays out a sum of money over a valid stop payment order and the customer proves that the amount of loss is the amount paid out, the customer has meet the burden of proof. The amount of damages could, however, exceed the amount of the check. Subsection (c) also provides that "the loss from payment of an item contrary to a stop payment order may include damages for dishonor of subsequent items under Section 4-402." Section 4-402, which is discussed in Chapter 8, deals with wrongful dishonor. In the previous example, if payment of the item over the stop payment order caused other checks that were properly payable to be returned, the bank could be liable to the customer for wrongful dishonor of those items.

10.4 WHEN ITEMS ARE SUBJECT TO NOTICE, STOP PAYMENT, LEGAL PROCESS, OR SETOFF

The race for the balances in a customer's account is subject to the provisions of Section 4-303. This section establishes when any knowledge, notice, or stop payment order that is received by a bank, or when legal process is served on the bank, or setoff exercised by the bank comes too late. This section sets the priority between paying an item that is presented for payment or taking action on one of the items previously listed. For example, if a garnishment is served on a bank for the balance in a customer's account and a check is presented for payment, this section governs whether the bank must honor the garnishment or pay the check that has been presented for payment. Obviously, the payee of the check will want the check paid and the creditor garnishing the account balance will want the bank to dishonor the check and pay the garnishment.

According to Subsection (a), the notice, stop payment order, the legal process, or the setoff, which are referred to as the "four legals," comes too late if the bank has accepted or certified the item, paid the item in cash, or has settled for the item without having a right to revoke settlement under statute, clearing house rule, or agreement. The first two items listed are simple and require little discussion. The four legals come too late if the bank has certified a check or paid the item in cash. If a customer requests the bank to stop payment on a check and the bank has already certified the check or paid it in cash over the counter, the stop payment order comes too late. The check must remain paid or accepted. The third item listed is more complicated and requires some discussion. In *First Commercial Bank v. Gotham Originals, Inc., 40 UCC Rep Serv 582*, the court held that an injunction restraining an issuing bank from honoring drafts drawn under a letter of credit came too late if the bank had previously accepted the drafts. In this case, the bank notified the holder of the drafts that the drafts would be paid. The court held that the injunction came too late when it was served on the bank 36 days after the acceptance.

The four legals come too late if the bank has settled for the item without having the right to revoke settlement under statute, clearing-house rule or agreement. Section 4-301 is a statutory provision that allows for the revocation of settlement. Under that section, which is discussed in Chapters 7 and 8 of this book, settlement for an item may be revoked if the bank to which the item is presented, other than for immediate payment over the counter, settles for the item before midnight of the day on which the item is presented. This right to revoke payment is referred to as "deferred posting." If no statute, clearing-house rule, or agreement exists, the bank does not have the right to revoke the settlement and the settlement is final when made. If final settlement is made for the item, the four legals come too late. The check is considered paid and payment of the check takes priority over the four legals. As pointed out in Official Comment #3 to Section 4-303, a bank that issues a cashier's check for a check drawn on that same bank has made final settlement for the item. Unless the bank has entered into an agreement with the person presenting the check in exchange for the cashier's check, the settlement is final. Section 4-301 establishes deferred posting and does not apply to an item that is presented for immediate payment over the counter.

The four legals also come too late according to Subsection (a)(4) if "the bank becomes accountable for the amount of the item under Section 4-302 dealing with the payor bank's responsibility for late return." Section 4-302, which is discussed in Chapters 7 and 8 of this book, basically states that a payor bank must pay or return an item by its midnight deadline. If one of the four legals occurs after the passage of the midnight deadline, then the stop payment, service of process, etc., has priority over the check. A bank becomes liable for the amount of an item if it retains the item past its midnight deadline even if the bank had a valid reason to return the item. In *American National Bank & Trust Co. of Chicago, N.A. v. Central Bank of Denver, N.A., 16 UCC Rep Serv 2d 456*, the customer of the drawee bank filed bankruptcy on December 14. Thereafter on December 18 and on December 21, checks were presented for payment. Both checks were held by the drawee bank past the midnight deadline before they were returned. The court held that while the bankruptcy had priority over the payment of the checks, this fact did not relieve the payor bank of its strict liability for failure to return the checks by the midnight deadline.

Under the previous version of this section, one of the measurements as to whether the four legals came too late is if the bank had completed the process of posting. If the bank had completed the process of posting of the item, the four legals came too late. The revised version of Article 4 does not contain the process of posting and for good cause. The process of posting was an antiquated process that could not be applied to the automated processes used by banks today. Subsection (a)(5) is intended as a gauge to be used in the place of the process of posting. According to that Subsection, the four legals come too late with respect to checks if it comes after "a cutoff hour no earlier than one hour after the opening of the next banking day after the banking day on which the bank received the check and no later than the close of that next banking day or, if no cutoff hour is fixed, the close of the next banking day after the banking day on which the bank received the check."

With respect to checks, the bank will establish a cutoff time when notice, stop payment, legal process, or setoff comes too late. For example, assume that the bank establishes a cutoff hour of 11:00 a.m. and the customer calls the bank to stop payment on a check that was received by the bank on the previous day. The customer's stop payment order comes too late if it is given to the bank after the cutoff hour of 11:00 a.m. Likewise, any notice or legal process received or any setoff exercised after the 11:00 a.m. cutoff comes too late. Payment of the check takes priority over the four legals. If any of the four legals comes before the cutoff hour, the notice, stop payment, legal process, or setoff would take priority over the payment of the check.

(a) ORDER IN WHICH ITEMS MAY BE ACCEPTED OR PAID

Section 4-303(b) allows a bank to pay checks in any order. That section states, "Subject to Subsection (a), items may be accepted, paid, certified, or charged to the indicated account of its customer in any order." As pointed out in the Official Comments to this section, it would be virtually impossible to establish some order or sequence in which a bank must pay checks. The customer issued all of the checks that are presented and should have sufficient funds to cover all of the checks. The bank may pay checks in the order that they are processed through its system or in ascending or descending order. The bank may establish priorities for checks paid at the teller window, for payments to the bank, for items used to purchase cashier's checks, traveler's checks, money orders, or the like. Since a check is not an assignment of the proceeds in an account, the bank has no obligation to a payee on a check. Therefore, a payee does not have a right to demand that the bank pay its item first and the bank is not liable to that payee for paying another item ahead of its item.

The court applied this section in *Andrews v. Citizens Bank, 20 UCC Rep Serv 709*, and held that the bank may pay checks in any order convenient to the bank. In this case, the wife presented a check for cash at the teller's window but the branch officer refused to pay the proceeds to her for some reason. That same morning, a check had been received by the bank in a night depository box and was paid. The next day when the wife returned, the balance was depleted and the wife filed suit claiming that the bank should have paid her check. The court held for the bank stating that the bank may pay checks in any order.

However, in *Arrow Industries, Inc. v. Zions First National Bank, 9 UCC Rep Serv 2d 672*, the court held that a bank could not choose the order of paying checks if it had agreed to pay other items. In this case, Zion took checks for collection from Arrow and agreed to pay Arrow's checks whenever the funds became available. After three days, and after paying other checks, the bank returned the checks to Arrow. The bank claimed that it could pay checks in any order that it wanted to. The court held that the bank had agreed to pay the checks and therefore was bound to do so.

10.5 PAYOR BANK'S RIGHT TO SUBROGATION ON IMPROPER PAYMENT

The payor bank may only charge a customer's account for a check that is properly payable. However, this does not mean that the bank must sustain the loss. Typically, when a customer complains to a bank that the bank has paid a check over a stop payment order, the bank's first reaction is that the bank must automatically refund the amount of the check to the customer. While this may make for good customer relations, the bank may be unnecessarily sustaining a loss. Section 4-407 states that if the bank pays an item over a valid stop payment order, or pays an item after an account has been closed, or otherwise pays an item under circumstances giving a basis for objection by the drawer or maker, the bank is subrogated to the rights of several different parties discussed below. The bank is only subrogated to the rights of these parties to prevent unjust enrichment and only to the extent necessary to prevent loss to the bank for the improper payment. The rationale behind this section is that some party should not gain from the bank's mistake. A customer issues a stop payment order either because he feels that he has not received the anticipated value for the amount of the check or because the customer is attempting not to pay for an obligation for which the customer is liable. In either case, some party will benefit by the bank's improper payment of the item unless the bank is subrogated to the rights of the parties listed below.

(a) SUBROGATED TO THE RIGHTS OF A HOLDER IN DUE COURSE

If the bank makes an improper payment as described above, the bank is subrogated to the rights of any holder in due course on the item against the drawer or maker. A stop payment order does not protect a customer from his or her liability on the instrument to a holder in due course even if the customer has a valid defense on the underlying transaction. For example, assume a customer stops payment on a check because the payee did not render the agreed upon services for which the check was issued. Assume further that the payee negotiates the check to a holder in due course and the check is dishonored by the payor bank. The holder in due course took the item free of the customer's defenses against the payee and the customer would be required to pay the holder in due course the amount of the check. Since the customer would be required to pay a holder in due course if the bank had honored the stop payment, the customer should not be allowed to avoid liability on the instrument because the bank made a mistake and paid the item over the stop payment order. The customer would be unjustly enriched if the bank were required to sustain the loss. Therefore, under Section 4-407(1), the bank is subrogated to the rights of any holder in due course on the item against the drawer or maker.

The fact that the item could have ended up in the hands of a holder in due course is not sufficient under this section. The item must have actually ended up in the hands of a holder in due course. For example, Bill Wiltshire issues a check to Joel Converse for an automobile. Joel misrepresented the condition of the car. It has defects that Bill was not aware of at the time he issued the check. Bill calls his bank and issues a stop payment order on the check. In the meantime, Joel cashes the check at the Check Cashing Service, Inc. (CCSI) who is a holder in due course on the instrument. The check is presented for payment, the payor bank mistakenly pays the check over Bill's stop payment order and Bill demands a refund. The payor bank would not be required to refund the money to Bill because the bank is subrogated to the rights of CCSI, who was a holder in due course of the check.

The bank must react quickly to a demand for refund if it has made an improper payment. If the customer is due a refund for the improper payment, the bank could be liable for wrongful dishonor for other items as provided for under Section 4-403(c). For example, a customer makes demand on a bank for payment of a check over a valid stop payment order on May 15. The bank begins its investigation and on May 20 determines that a refund is due the customer. In the meantime, the bank has returned several checks because the balance in the customer's account has been reduced by the amount of the check on which the stop payment was placed. The bank could be liable to the customer for wrongful dishonor of those items. For this reason, the bank should quickly determine its rights and respond quickly.

(b) SUBROGATED TO THE RIGHTS
OF THE PAYEE AGAINST THE DRAWER

A bank that improperly pays an item is also subrogated to the rights "of the payee or any other holder of the item against the drawer or maker either on the item or under the transaction out of which the item arose," according to Section 4-407(2). Not every item will end up in the hands of a holder in due course, so the bank may not be able to enforce the item against the customer as a holder in due course. Under this section, the bank may be able to enforce the item against the drawer or maker as the payee of the item. Enforcement of the item will be subject to any defenses that the customer may have against the payee. The payee may be entitled to the entire amount of the item, in which case the bank will not be required to make a refund to the customer. For example, Bill hires Joel to paint his house for an agreed upon amount. Joel paints the house and Bill issues Joel a check. Without justification, Bill orders his bank to stop payment on the check but through an error, the check is paid over the stop payment order. Bill then demands that the bank refund the amount of the check. Upon investigation, the bank determines that Joel had performed the agreed upon consideration and the money was justly due him. The bank is subrogated to Joel's rights against Bill on the check and on the underlying obligation and since Joel was due the money, the bank is not required to make a refund to Joel.

Here again, the bank must quickly perform an investigation and makes its decision. The problem that the bank is likely to encounter is a valid determination of the facts. In most disputed situations, each side will either have different facts or a different view of the same facts. If the facts are not easily determined, the bank may find itself in a situation of making a refund to the customer and then instigate litigation to collect from the customer. In many cases, the cost of litigation will outweigh the benefit and the bank will have to absorb the loss as a cost of doing business.

(c) SUBROGATED TO THE RIGHTS OF THE DRAWER AGAINST THE PAYEE

The bank is also subrogated to the rights "of the drawer or maker against the payee or any other holder of the item with respect to the transaction out of which the item arose," according to Section 4-407(3). The other two scenarios described above pitted the bank against its customer. This provision allows the bank to be subrogated to the rights of its customer. This option is by far the best for customer relations. The drawer may be completely justified in issuing a stop payment to the bank because of lack of consideration. The payee, for example, may have failed to perform the agreed upon service or may have failed to deliver the goods for which the instrument was issued. In that case, the bank would be subrogated to the rights of the drawer or maker against the payee and could enforce the rights that the drawer or maker had against the payee on the underlying obligation. Here again, the cost of litigation to collect the amount of the item may exceed the benefit, in which case the bank would sustain the loss. Not only may the bank bring an action under 4-407, but the court, in *Bryan v. Citizens National Bank in Abilene, 32 UCC Rep Serv, 225*, held that a bank that pays an item by mistake may also recover under Section 3-418. In this case, the bank paid the item over a valid stop payment by mistake and the payee was not entitled to the proceeds.

The drawee bank is not required to select just one of the parties to which it is subrogated under whose rights it brings the action. The court, in *Professional Savings Bank v. Galloway Farm Nursery Inc., 5 UCC Rep Serv 2d, 138*, allowed the bank that paid a check over a valid stop payment to bring an action against both the drawer and the payee of a check. In that case, the drawer of a check was a tenant of the payee. A dispute arose over that rent payment and the drawer stopped payment on the check. With knowledge of the stop payment, the payee presented the check and through mistake was paid. The bank filed suit against both the drawer and the payee because it was not sure which party would be unjustly enriched.

CHAPTER 11

CUSTOMER'S DUTY TO
EXAMINE BANK STATEMENT

The former version of Article 4 contained the requirement that the customer must examine the statement and checks made available by the bank and report forgeries and alterations to the bank in a timely manner. If the customer failed to comply with this duty, the customer was precluded from denying the signature or from asserting the alterations. On the other hand, if the bank failed to exercise ordinary care, the bank was precluded from raising the defense against the customer. Section 4-406 of the revised version of Article 4 also contains a requirement that the customer examine the bank statement and items made available by the bank; however, several of the provisions have been changed. The following sections will address each of the provisions of the revised Section 4-406.

11.1 BANK MUST MAKE STATEMENT
OF ACCOUNT AVAILABLE

Section 4-406(a) requires a bank to make a statement and the items or a statement that describes the items available to the customer. That sections states, "A bank that sends or makes available to a customer a statement of account showing payment of items for the account shall either return or make available to the customer the items paid or provide information in the statement of account sufficient to allow the customer reasonably to identify the items paid. The statement of account provides sufficient information if the item is described by item number, amount, and date of payment." There are several points in this subsection that are worthy of analysis. First of all, the section does not require the bank to send or make a statement of account available to the customer. If it does send a statement, the provision does require that the items paid either be returned with the bank statement or adequately identified. The court, in *Florida Federal Savings & Loan Assoc. v. Martin, 33 UCC Rep Serv 1427*, held that the bank could not raise the defenses under 4-406 requiring the customer to examine the statement and items if the bank does not make the items available to the customer and the customer did not request that the bank hold the items for the customer. The court in the Lichtenstein case discussed later came to the opposite conclusion. As discussed below, the new version of this section allows the bank to identify the items paid and does not require that the actual items be returned with the statement. This case would have turned out differently if this new section had been in place. If the bank does not send or make the statement available, then the balance of Section 4-406 will not apply and the bank would have no recourse against a negligent customer. The court, in *Bank of Thomas County v. Dekle, 6 UCC Rep Serv 756*, held that the prerequisite to eliminate the bank's liability is to show that the bank furnished the depositor the items paid, or notified the depositor that the statement or items paid were available for examination.

The second point is that the section does not require that the customer actually receive the statement. The exact wording is that "a bank that sends or makes available to a customer." The customer may have asked the bank to send the statement to a branch to be held for the customer. Holding the statement for the customer is making it available to the customer. The court in the Martin case cited above stated that Section 4-406 would apply if the customer requested that the bank hold the items. The bank evidently meets its obligation if it sends the statement to the customer regardless of whether the customer actually receives the statement or not. The customer provided the bank with the customer's address and nothing in the section requires the bank to make sure that the statement is received by the customer.

In *Cooley v. First National Bank of Little Rock, Arkansas, 33 UCC Rep Serv 1736*, the court held that where the bank statements are mailed to the address provided by the depositors as reflected on the signature card, they are available to the customer within the meaning of Section 4-406. In that case, the checks and bank statement were mailed to a P. O. Box provided by the customer. The court in *Kiernan v. Union Bank, 18 UCC Rep Serv 1026* also held that the statement of account is "made available" by the bank when the bank mailed the statement with the appropriate postage. In *Jensen v. Essexbank, 41 UCC Rep Serv 1366,* the court held that the statement was made available to the customer when they were mailed to the customer's attorney in accordance with the customer's instructions. In that case, the customer's attorney forged two checks on the customer's account. Since the statements were mailed to the attorney, the customer did not discover the forgeries for over a year. Another possibility is that the customer may move and not change the address on the account. Statements may be returned to the bank and unless the bank takes some action to correct the address, the statements will continue to be returned. It would appear that the customer would have the responsibility of notifying the bank of a change of address and of the fact that the customer has not been receiving the statements. It would also appear that the customer would be bound by the requirement to promptly report forgeries and alterations to the bank if the bank sent the statement even if the customer did not receive the statement.

If the bank sends the statement or makes it available, the bank must either return the items along with the bank statement or provide information to the customer that will identify the items that paid. As stated above, the last sentence of Subsection (a) states that the information is sufficient if it describes the item by number, amount, and date paid. This is a new provision that was not included in the former version of Section 4-406. This Subsection recognizes the fact that many banks are beginning to truncate checks, that the checks are not returned with the bank statement, and that the account statement describes the items by date paid, amount, and the check number. This provision reverses the decision of the court in the Martin case cited earlier. This section codifies the holding of the court in *Lichtenstein v. Kidder, Peabody & Co., Inc., 10 UCC Rep Serv 2d 1321.* In that case, the court held that the bank complied with 4-406 by sending its customer a monthly statement of account listing all account transactions. The court further stated while the actual checks were not returned to the customer, sufficient information was available to the customer to discover the unauthorized transactions. The customer could obtain a copy of the checks upon request to the bank, although a charge was assessed for copies in excess of three.   While

the section does not specifically provide for or allow image statements, return of an image of the check certainly sufficiently describes
an item to allow the customer reasonably to identify the items paid.

Savings accounts are included in the definition of account in Section 4-104. Therefore, Section 4-406 also applies to savings accounts.
Most banks neither return savings withdrawal slips nor describe withdrawals by item number. However, since a savings account is typically
not a high volume transaction type of account and most customers
know when they make withdrawals, it would appear that describing
the withdrawal from a savings account by amount and the date would
sufficiently describe the item even if there is no item number. The court,
in *Tally v. American Security Bank, 35 UCC Rep Serv 215*, held that Section 4-406 applies to savings account since the bank mails the statement
of the account activity to the customer and holds the withdrawal slips
at the bank for examination by the customer. The court held that the
bank made the statement and items available to the customer and the
customer had a duty to examine them and report the unauthorized
withdrawals.

11.2 CHECK SAFEKEEPING AND TRUNCATION

Subsection (b) specifically addresses the nonreturn of checks. That Subsection states that if the items are not returned to the customer, the
bank is either required to keep the actual items or, if the items are destroyed, to maintain the capacity to furnish legible copies of the items.
This requirement applies only to items that are not returned to the customer and would also apply to image statements. "Image statements"
refers to the process where the check is digitized and an electronically
produced image of the check is retuned to the customer. If the items are
returned to the customer, this section does not apply. The storage media for production of the copy is not dictated in the section. In other
words, the bank may either utilize a traditional film record of the item
or the bank could digitize the item and electronically store an image of
the item. The bank could then send the customer either a traditional
microfilm copy of the check or an electronically produced image of the
check. The bank must maintain the capacity to furnish copies of the
items for a period of seven years from the date the bank receives the
items. And while the Subsection does not specifically state that the copy
must also include a copy of the back of the item, it is reasonable to

assume that the back will also have to be produced. Because of the current cost of electronic storage of an image, most banks will most likely film the items for archival purposes.

This Subsection requires that the person retaining the item must either keep the originals or have the ability to furnish a copy of the item. The nonreturn of the check may be the result of a check safekeeping product offered by the payor bank or the result of a check truncation program where the items are kept by a collecting bank. The requirement to retain the item or to produce a copy is on the person that retains the check. However, the customer is going to look to the payor bank if the customer needs a copy of the item. If the copies are retained by the payor bank, then the payor bank can produce the copies itself. On the other hand, if the checks are kept by a collecting bank as the result of a check truncation program where the checks are presented electronically, the payor bank will have to rely on the bank keeping the checks to produce the copy. The electronic check presentment agreement between the participating banks should contain a provision that requires the bank keeping the checks to maintain the capacity to produce a copy of the check for the statutory period of seven years. The agreement should require that the copy must be a legible copy and that it must be produced within a specified period of time. Subsection (b) requires that the copy must be legible and that it must be produced within a reasonable time. Reasonable period of time is not defined but may be established by agreement.

As pointed out in the Official Comments to this section, the Act is silent as to whether a bank may charge a customer for a copy of the item. Since there is no restriction against the bank charging for production of a copy, it would appear that such a charge is justifiable and would be allowed. The bank's normal service charge structure will most likely differentiate pricing between accounts that have the checks returned and those that do not. The accounts that do not have the checks returned may incur less service charge than an account that does have the checks returned. Regardless of the service charge structure, it would appear that a bank would be justified in assessing a fee for production of the copy. The court in the Lichtenstein v. Kidder, Peabody case stated that the bank made the items available to the customer because the customer could request a copy even though the bank assessed a fee for producing the item. The bank should include a provision in the customer account agreement that addresses this issue and specifically allows the bank to charge for the production of copies of items. If the bank has entered into an electronic check presentment agreement, that agreement should likewise address the issue of charges for the production of copies.

The Official Comments to this section also points out that the Act does not specify sanctions for failure to furnish the items or copies upon request by the customer and that this is left to other laws regulating banks.

11.3 CUSTOMER'S DUTY TO EXAMINE BANK STATEMENT

Section 4-406(c) requires the customer to examine the bank statement and items that are made available to the customer by the bank. The customer must "exercise reasonable promptness in examining the statement or the items to determine whether any payment was not authorized because of an alteration of an item or because a purported signature by or on behalf of the customer was not authorized." If an examination of the statement or items would reveal the unauthorized payment, the customer must "promptly notify" the bank of the relevant facts. Under this section, the customer must promptly examine the statement or items and promptly notify the bank of the relevant facts. The impact of the customer's failure to examine the statement and notify the bank is provided for in Subsection (d), which is discussed below.

There are several points under Subsection (c) worthy of discussion. The requirement that the customer "exercise reasonable promptness" in examining the bank statement is not defined. A time period in which the customer must examine the bank statement is not listed or provided for anywhere in the UCC. Each set of circumstances will be different and what may be reasonable under one set of facts may not be reasonable under another scenario. The period of time that is reasonable to examine a bank statement with five items sent to an individual would be less than the period of time to examine a corporate bank account with thousands of checks. The individual with only five items should be able to determine if an item contains an unauthorized forgery or an alteration in a relatively short period of time. The corporation's account with thousands of items will obviously take much longer to examine and reconcile to determine an unauthorized payment.

Based on the literal interpretation of Subsection (c), the examination of the statement or items is limited to a search for the unauthorized signature of the customer or the alteration of an item. This section does not require the customer to discover a forged or missing indorsement, or an encoding error, or an item paid over a stop payment order, or any other erroneous payment of an item. The apparent purpose of the section is to require the customer to examine the statement or items to discover forgeries or alterations and to promptly notify the discovery of those items.

After discovery of the payment of an unauthorized item, the customer must promptly notify the bank. Here again, the period of time is not established by the Act. Each case must be determined on its own based on the particular circumstances of each case. The method of notification is likewise not addressed in this section. Apparently, any type of notification would be sufficient. The customer could notify the bank orally, in writing, electronically, by returning the item, by sending the bank a copy of the item, or by any other method. The specific wording of Subsection (c) is that "the customer must promptly notify the bank of the relevant facts." It would appear that the relevant facts would include the amount of the item, the date the item paid, a description of the item (such as date, check number, payee) and why the payment was improper. That is, whether the item was altered or contained an unauthorized signature of the drawer. The purpose of the prompt notification is to allow the bank to take whatever action is required under the circumstances to prevent any further unauthorized items from paying on the account. The timely notification should also assist the bank in recouping its losses. The more promptly the bank is notified, the more likely the bank will be to recover the losses from the wrongdoer.

If the customer fails to examine the bank statement or items and promptly notify the bank, then Subsection (d) applies. Subsection (d) states the following:

> If the bank proves that the customer failed, with respect to an item, to comply with the duties imposed on the customer by Subsection (c), the customer is precluded from asserting against the bank:
>
> (1) The customer's unauthorized signature or any alteration on the item, if the bank also proves that it suffered a loss by reason of the failure; and
>
> (2) The customer's unauthorized signature or alteration by the same wrongdoer on any other item paid in good faith by the bank if the payment was made before the bank received notice

from the customer of the unauthorized signature or alteration
and after the customer had been afforded a reasonable period
of time, not exceeding 30 days, in which to examine the item
or statement of account and notify the bank.

Under Subsection (d)(1), the bank must show that it sent or made
available to the customer the bank statement and items as described
above and the customer must have failed to promptly examine the bank
statement and notify the bank of the unauthorized payment. In addition, the bank must prove that the customer failed to exercise the required standard of care and that such failure on the part of the
customer caused the bank to suffer a loss. If the bank fails to meet the
required burden of proof, then the bank must sustain the loss. If the
bank does meet the burden of proof, and the bank meets the standard
of care required under Subsection (e), then the customer is precluded
from denying his forged signature or asserting the alteration. Subsection (e) is discussed below.

In the case of a single forged signature or even multiple forged
signatures in the same bank statement, the bank normally would have a
difficult time proving that the failure to discover and notify the bank on
the part of the customer caused the loss. Unless a prior transferor had
knowledge of the forged signature, the bank would not have any recourse against a prior transferor. Under the presentment warranties,
any prior transferor warrants that he has no knowledge of the drawer's
or maker's forgery. Even if the bank did have recourse, the bank would
have to prove that had the customer timely notified the bank of the
forged signature that the bank could have recovered from the prior
transferor. If the bank could prove the identity of the person who
forged the item and that the bank could have recovered from the forger
if the bank had been given prompt notification, then the bank may be
able to shift the loss to the customer.

For example, assume that Joel forges Bill's name on a check and
deposits the check to his own account maintained at the First Deposit
Bank (FDB). Assume further that FDB, which is also Bill's bank, sends
the bank statement and checks that also contains the forged check to
Bill. Bill receives the statement on May 15, but does not even open the
envelope until June 20, at which time he discovers the check containing
the forged signature. Bill finally notifies the bank of the forgery on June
25. Upon investigation, the bank determines that the check was deposited to Joel's account. Based on information supplied by Bill and based
on the examination of the check by a documents expert, the bank deter-

mines that Joel had forged Bill's name to the check. The bank also determines that the balance in Joel's account was not withdrawn until June 18. Had the bank been promptly notified of the forgery, the bank could have charged Joel's account for the amount of the check. Under this set of facts, a court could find that Bill did not promptly discover the forgery and notify the bank and that the failure to do so caused the loss.

The same burden of proof is also required on an instrument that has been altered. However, if an item is altered, the drawee may have recourse against a prior transferor for breach of presentment warranty under Sections 3-417 and 4-208. According to those sections, the warrantor may defend by proving that the drawer is precluded from asserting the alteration against the drawee under Section 4-406. If the customer failed to comply with Subsection (c), and the delay caused a loss, the warrantor could disclaim liability. For example, assume that Bill wrote a check to Joel for $10 and Joel altered the check by raising the amount to $100. Joel then deposits the check to his account with the First Deposit Bank (FDB). The check is then presented for payment and paid by Bill's bank. The statement and checks are sent to Bill but he does not reconcile the statement. Eight months later as Bill is preparing his income tax return he discovers the alteration and contacts his bank and asks for a refund. The payor bank, without giving Bill credit, sends the item back upstream to the FDB and demands a refund. Upon investigation, FDB determines that Joel's account had just been closed a week earlier. The bank also concluded that it could have recovered the amount of the loss from Joel if Bill had examined his bank statement and promptly notified the payor bank. The court could conclude that Bill's failure caused the loss and therefore he is precluded from asserting the alteration.

The bank can only avoid liability under Subsection (d)(1) when the right factual situations exist. The customer must fail to examine the bank statement and the failure must cause the loss. Subsection (d)(1) applies to the specific item in question that is the subject of the loss. Subsection (d)(2) applies to other items that are paid on the customer's account that are improper because of an unauthorized signature or an alteration. That section provides that if the bank proves that the customer failed to comply with Subsection (c), the customer is precluded from asserting against the bank the customer's unauthorized signature or alteration by the same wrongdoer on any other item paid in good faith by the bank. Another requirement is that the payment must have been made before the bank received notice from the customer of the unauthorized payment or the alteration. The customer must also have been given a reasonable period of time, not exceeding 30 days, in which to examine the item or statement of account and notify the bank.

An example of the application of Subsections (d)(1) and (d)(2) are as follows. Cindy, the bookkeeper for Flashback Music, Inc., forged the name of the president on check #123 made payable to herself. The check paid on the account of Flashback on May 15, and was included in the bank statement sent on May 31. Cindy had total responsibility for reconcilement of the bank statement so the forgery went unnoticed. Cindy laid low for the month of June to make sure that she had gotten away with her scheme. On July 15, however, she forged the name of the president to check #232, and thereafter she made forgeries on several more checks in the month of July. Upon receipt of the bank statement, Cindy once again covered up her theft. Cindy kept her scheme up, issuing 10 to 15 checks per month to herself, until the month of December when the checking account became overdrawn and a bank officer called the president of Flashback.

In this example, Subsection (d)(1) would apply to the first check, check #123, and Subsection (d)(2) would apply to the other checks. As to check #123, the bank would have to prove that the failure of Flashback to discover and report the forgery was the cause of the loss. As to the other checks, Flashback had a responsibility to examine the statement or items within a reasonable time, not to exceed 30 days, and to detect the improper payment of the forged check. This 30-day period of time affords the customer the opportunity to discover the improper payment and to notify the bank to prevent any further losses. The former version of this section contained a 14-day period of time in which the customer was required to examine the statement and notify the bank. The purpose of this section is to put the responsibility on the customer to examine the statement and to give the customer the incentive to do so. The customer is in the best position to prevent such a loss as this. As discussed in Chapter 3 of this book, the customer should also have in place procedures to prevent an employee or other unauthorized person from perpetuating such a scheme.

The following are several cases addressing the customer's duty to examine the bank statement and to promptly notify the bank of the forgery or alteration. In *Westport Bank & Trust Co. v. Lodge*, 12 UCC Rep Serv 450, an employee of the bank wrote a letter to the bank requesting the address on the account to be changed to that of the employee and forged the name of the customer. The forgery was a very good forgery and looked like the customer's signature. Some period after the employee changed the address, the employee forged the customer's signature on checks for a period of 26 months. During this period of time, the customer never complained to the bank about not receiving the bank statements. In fact, the customer knew that the employee was receiving the bank statements at her address. When the customer finally complained about the forgeries, the bank raised the defense under Section 4-406 claiming that the customer failed to examine the statement and promptly notify the bank of the forgeries. The customer contends that since it never received the statements, 4-406 did not apply and the customer had no duty to examine the statements. The court held that the statement and items were made available to the customer even though the dishonest employee was actually receiving the statements. The customer had a duty to inquire as to why she had not received statements from the bank. The court further held that had the customer exercised ordinary care in examining the statements, she would have detected the forgeries and could have prevented the loss.

In *Simcoe & Erie General Insurance Co. v. Chemical Bank*, 15 UCC Rep Serv 2d 1269, the customer's employee forged checks on customer's account for a period of 12 months. The customer did not examine the statement and checks supplied to the customer by the bank during this time and discover the forgeries. The court held that the bank was not liable to the customer for any of the forgeries committed after 14 days from the day that the statement and checks were made available to the customer. The bank refunded the amount of the checks that were paid during the 14-day period.

The obligations of the customer may be provided for in an agreement, so held the court in *Parent Teacher Association, Public School 72 v. Manufacturers Hanover Trust Co. v. Messina*, 5 UCC Rep Serv 2d 679. In that case, the husband of a bookkeeper forged checks on the customer's account and hid the forgery for three months. The bank refused to refund the money and the customer filed suit against the bank over a year after the customer had notice of the forgeries. The customer account agreement contained two provisions relevant to this case that were addressed by the court. The agreement required the customer to report any errors to the bank within 14 calendar days of delivery or mailing of any statement and that the customer must instigate legal proceedings against the bank for improperly paying an item within one year from the date that the statement is delivered or made available to the customer. The court held that the provisions of the agreement were not an attempt on the part of the bank to disclaim its responsibility for lack of good faith or failure to exercise ordinary care. The court also held that the statement was made available to the customer despite the fact that the statements were intercepted by the bookkeeper's husband.

The court in *Kiernan v. Union Bank, 18 UCC Rep Serv 1026* held that the time period for notification requirement begins to run from the time that the statement is made available to the customer. In this case, the specific question was whether items contained in the May bank statement were within the one year statute of limitations. The customer contended that items contained the May 1 statement were not received by the customer by May 11 which was one year from the date on which the case was filed. The court held that the statute begins to run from the date the statement is made available to the customer, i.e., the date on which the statement is mailed by the bank to the customer, not the date that the customer received the statement. The testimony of the bank employees was that the May 1 statement would have been mailed no later than May 6.

The court in *Zenith Syndicate, Inc. v. Marine Midland Bank Of New York, 28 UCC Rep Serv 483,* held that the customer was under an obligation to examine the cancelled checks and the statements forwarded by the bank and to notify the bank promptly of any irregularity. The court also held that the customer failed to meet its obligation and that the loss occurred as a result of the customer's failure.

The discussion above concerning Section 4-406(d)(1) states that the failure of the customer to notify the bank of the forgery or alteration within the 14-day period must be the cause of the loss. The court addressed this issue in *Schoenfelder v. Arizona Bank, 12 UCC Rep Serv 2d, 469.* In that case, the customer did not discover four forged checks that were included in the June statement until September. The bank defended on the grounds that the customer failed to discover the forgeries within the 14-day period required by Section 4-406. The court held that the bank had the burden of proof that the loss was the result of the customer's failure to notify the bank of the forgeries within that time frame. The bank did not meet the burden of proof so the customer was allowed to recover from the bank.

(a) BANK'S RESPONSIBILITY TO EXERCISE ORDINARY CARE

The customer is not given the total responsibility for a loss under Subsection (d). Subsection (e) states the following:

If Subsection (d) applies, and the customer proves that the bank failed to exercise ordinary care in paying the item and that the failure substantially contributed to loss, the loss is allocated between the customer precluded and the bank asserting the preclusion according to the extent to which the failure of the customer to comply with Subsection (c) and the failure of the bank to exercise ordinary care contributed to the loss. If the customer proves that the bank did not pay the item in good faith, the preclusion under Subsection (d) does not apply.

This section, along with Sections 3-404, 3-405, and 3-406, have adopted a form of comparative negligence. Under the previous version of this section, the bank was precluded from avoiding liability if the bank did not exercise ordinary care. The customer was precluded from denying forged signatures made by the same wrongdoer if the customer was negligent in examining the statement and reporting forgeries. However, the loss was shifted totally to the bank if the bank failed to exercise ordinary care in paying the item. Under the revised version of Section 4-406, the loss is allocated based on the negligence of both the bank and the customer. For example, if the court found that both the bank and the customer were equally negligent, the loss could be split equally between them.

The customer has the burden of proof under Subsection (e). The customer must first prove that the bank failed to exercise ordinary care in paying the item. "Ordinary care" is defined in Section 3-103(a)(7) as the following:

In the case of a person engaged in business means observance of reasonable commercial standards, prevailing in the area in which the person is located, with respect to the business in which the person is engaged. In the case of a bank that takes an instrument for processing for collection or payment by automated means, reasonable commercial standards do not require the bank to examine the instrument if failure to examine does not violate the bank's prescribed procedures and the bank's procedures do not vary unreasonably from general banking usage not disapproved by this Article or Article 4.

This definition of "ordinary care" is adopted by Article 4 through Section 4-104(c).

This definition of "ordinary care" should give the court specific direction on the issue of whether a bank has exercised ordinary care. The definition specifically states that "reasonable commercial standards do not require the bank to examine the instrument." Many courts, under the previous versions of Articles 3 & 4, have held that the failure to examine the signature on every check was a failure to exercise ordinary care. However, in recent decisions, the courts have recognized the fact that in order to reduce the cost of processing items, banks must automate many of the manual processes that they currently perform.

The court in *Rhode Island Hosp. Trust Nat'l Bank v. Zapata Corp.*, 6 UCC Rep. 2d 1, held that the bank had exercised ordinary care in paying checks that contained forgeries of the drawer's signature. The bank's procedure was to examine all checks of $1,000 or more, and to randomly examine one percent of checks between $100 and $1,000. The court held that the bank's procedures were not unreasonable even though the checks that contained the forged signatures were for amounts between $150 and $800. The court in *Wilder Binding Co. v. Oak Park Trust Savings Bank, 7 UCC Rep Serv 2d 134*, came to the opposite conclusion. In that case, the bank did not verify signatures on checks in the amount of $1,000 or below. A number of checks in amounts less than $1,000 were paid on a customer's account over a period of time. The court held that while the customer may have been negligent, the bank failed to exercise ordinary care in paying the items. The court specifically stated the failure to examine every check is not the exercise of ordinary care. As discussed below, the definition of "ordinary care" under the revisions states that failure to examine checks is not considered lack of ordinary care.

In view of the definition of "ordinary care" and the general practice among banks not to examine signatures, it would appear that the courts in the future will hold that failure to examine the signatures on checks is not a failure to exercise ordinary care. In fact, it would appear that the commercially reasonable standard in the banking industry is to not examine signatures on every item. With the advent of electronic check presentment, the actual item may never be presented to the payor bank. Therefore, the bank will not have the opportunity to examine the signature.

Even if the customer proves that the bank failed to exercise ordinary care in paying the item, the customer must also prove that the failure substantially contributed to loss. Merely proving that the bank failed to exercise ordinary care is not sufficient to allocate the loss. For example, assume that a bank's procedure did not require that checks be examined and the court held that failure to examine was not the exercise of ordinary care. Assume further that the forgeries on the checks were expertly done and that the forgeries could not be distinguished from the authorized signature. In this case, even if the bank had examined the signatures, the forgeries would not have been discovered by the bank. Therefore, the failure to exercise ordinary care did not substantially contribute to the loss. Given the definition of "ordinary care" and the requirement that the failure of the bank "substantially contribute" to the loss, it appears that the drafters did not intend for the loss to be easily allocated to the bank in this situation. The determination as to whether the failure substantially contributed to the loss is a question of fact to be determined by the trier of the fact. In *Westport Bank & Trust Co. v. Lodge* discussed above, the court held that the customer has the burden of proof that the bank did not exercise ordinary care. The customer failed to meet this burden of proof. The customer did not have a handwriting expert testify, did not produce the originals or copies of the forged items, and did not produce the signature card to show the authorized signatures. Having failed to meet the burden of proof, the court held for the bank.

The last sentence of Subsection (e) states, "If the customer proves that the bank did not pay the item in good faith, the preclusion under Subsection (d) does not apply. If the bank fails to exercise good faith in paying the items, the loss is shifted to the bank." "Good faith" is defined in Section 3-103(a)(4) to mean "honesty in fact and the observance of reasonable commercial standards of fair dealing." This definition is the same definition as found in Articles 2, 2A, and 4A and in Federal Reserve Regulation CC. This definition is a change from the previous versions of Articles 3 & 4 which required only honesty in fact. The definition now requires the "observance of reasonable commercial standards of fair dealing." At first glance, there appears to be a conflict within Subsection (e). The first part of Subsection (e) states that the loss is allocated between the bank and the customer if the bank fails to exercise ordinary care, and the last sentence states that the loss is shifted to the bank if the bank did not pay the item in good faith. The definitions of both "ordinary care" and "good faith" contain the requirement of the exercise of "reasonable commercial standards". The "reasonable commercial standards" in the definition of "good faith" applies to the requirement of "fair dealing." As pointed out in Official Comment #4 to Section 3-103, "Although fair dealing is a broad term that must be defined in context, it is clear that it is concerned with the fairness of conduct rather than the care with which an act is performed. Failure to exercise ordinary care in conducting a transaction is an entirely different concept than failure to deal fairly in conduction the transaction."

The observance of reasonable commercial standards in the definition of "ordinary care" goes to the act being performed. Specifically, as discussed above, the question of whether a bank examines a signature on a check is a question of the exercise of ordinary care. The question of whether a bank paid an item in good faith would refer to whether the bank knew or should have known the items contained a forged signature. If the customer is able to prove that the bank did not pay the item in good faith, then the bank is precluded from raising the defenses provided for in Subsection (d). The court in *Vending Chattanooga, Inc. v. American National Bank & Trust Co.* held that the customer has the burden of proof that the bank failed to exercise ordinary care in paying an item and that the failure of the bank to exercise ordinary care is the cause of the loss. The court held that a bank exercises ordinary care when it pays a check in good faith and in accordance with the reasonable commercial standards of the banking industry. Such a rule does not require the bank to be a handwriting expert on the signature of each check. More courts should follow the rulings by the court in this case and the Zapata case cited above. The majority of the banks establish dollar limits and do not check signatures under the dollar limit. This is the reasonable commercial standard of the industry and this fact should be recognized by the courts.

(b) CUSTOMER'S DUTY TO REPORT IMPROPER PAYMENT WITHIN ONE YEAR

Section 4-406(f) establishes a time limit within which the customer must report an unauthorized signature or the alteration of an item. Subsection (f) states the following:

> Without regard to care or lack of care of either the customer or the bank, a customer who does not within one year after the statement or items are made available to the customer (Subsection (a)) discover and report the customer's unauthorized signature on or any alteration on the item is precluded from asserting against the bank the unauthorized signature or alteration. If there is a preclusion under this Subsection, the payor bank may not recover for breach of warranty under Section 4-208 with respect to the unauthorized signature or alteration to which the preclusion applies.

This Subsection establishes the one-year period of time as the period of time in which the customer must report his or her unauthorized signature or an alteration. Time is the only requirement. This section is not concerned with the standard of care exercised by either the customer or the bank. If the customer does not report the unauthorized signature or alteration within the one-year period, then the bank is not required to make a refund to the customer for the improperly paid items.

The only issue of standard of care under this Subsection is whether the bank has met the requirements of Subsection (a). If the items are not returned with the statement or described by date paid, amount, and item number, the one year period would not apply. Another issue that could arise under Subsection (a) is when was the statement sent or made available to the customer? As discussed in the section on Subsection (a), the bank has met its obligation when it sends the statement to the customer whether the customer receives it or not. For example, if someone is stealing the customer's bank statement, the customer would have a duty to notify the bank that he or she has not received the statement. If the customer is out of the country and has not advised the bank of a forwarding address, the bank has met its obligation if it mails the statement to the address supplied by the customer. The point here is that Subsection (f) only requires that the bank send the statement or makes it available to the customer. If the bank has done that, it has met its obligation and the customer must then report the improper payment within the one-year period of time.

This Subsection applies only to the customer's unauthorized signature and to alterations. It does not apply to unauthorized indorsements as did the previous version of this section. Under the previous version, the customer was required to report an unauthorized indorsement, which also included a missing indorsement, within three years. Subsection (f) does not require the customer to examine the indorsement on an item. Most customers will not know if the indorsement is the indorsement of the payee unless the customer is familiar with the payee's indorsement. Therefore, it does not make much sense to require the customer to report an unauthorized indorsement. The payee or other person entitled to enforce the item will normally discover the unauthorized indorsement and report it to the customer. The customer must then notify the payor bank within the statutory period of time of three years as provided for in Section 4-111. That section requires that any action to enforce an obligation under Article 4 must be commenced within three years after the cause of action accrues.

Section 4-208, which is discussed in Chapter 2 of this book, establishes certain presentment warranties made by any person who presents an item that is paid in good faith. Two of the warranties made are that the warrantor has no knowledge that the signature of the purported drawer of an item is unauthorized and that the item has not been altered. If the customer is precluded from asserting the unauthorized signature or an alteration against the payor bank, the payor bank may not recover from the warrantor.

For example, assume that a check is issued by Customer for $10 but the amount of the check is altered to $100. The check is paid on Customer's account on May 15, 1991 and the statement and checks are mailed to Customer by the payor bank on May 20, 1991. Customer discovers the alteration on June 10, 1992, and demands a refund from the payor bank. Customer was required to report the alteration to the payor bank within one year from the date the statement was sent or made available or, in this case, no later than May 20, 1992. Since Customer did not report the alteration until June 10, 1992, Customer is precluded from asserting the alteration against the payor bank. Because of this preclusion, the payor bank may not recover from a warrantor that gave the warranty under Section 4-208 that the item had not been altered. The purpose of this section is to require the payor bank to raise any defenses that it has against its customer. The natural tendency of a payor bank is to protect its customer and to pass the loss on to some other party. Subsection (f) prevents this from happening. Sections 3-417 and 4-208 contain similar provisions that state that the warrantor may defend an action by a drawee based on a claim for breach of warranty if the drawer is precluded under Section 4-406.

CITATIONS

TABLE OF ARTICLE 3

Article 3 Sections	Publication Sections	Article 3 Sections	Publication Sections
1-201(10)	2.8	3-105(b)	1.3
1-201(14)	1.3	3-105(c)	1.3
1-201(20)	1.4(b)	3-106	1.2(a)
1-201(20)	4.1, 6.1	3-107	1.2(b)
1-201(24)	1.2(b)	3-108(a)	1.2(c)
1-201(38)	8.6(c)	3-108(b)	1.2(c)
1-201(39)	3.1	3-108(c)	1.2(c)
1-201(41)	5.6(a)	3-109	6.1
1-201(43)	3.2	3-109(a)	1.2(e)
1-207	2.8, 9.6	3-109(a)2	1.2(e)
3-102(a)	1.0	3-109(a)3	1.2(e)
3-102(b)	1.0	3-109(b)	1.2(e)
3-102(c)	1.0	3-109(c)	1.2(e)
3-103(a)(2)	2.2	3-110	1.4, 1.4(a), 5.1(b), 5.2, 5.3(a), 5.7(b), 5.7(c)
3-103(a)(3)	2.1		
3-103(a)(4)	3.3(b), 6.4(g), 11.3(a)	3-110(a)	1.4(a), 2.6(a), 5.1(a)
3-103(a)(5)	1.3, 2.1, 7.8	3-110(b)	1.4(a)
3-103(a)(6)	2.1	3-110(c)	1.4(b)
3-103(a)(7)	3.3(b), 5.7(a), 11.3(a)	3-110(c)(1)	1.4(b)
3-104	1.3(a)	3-110(c)(2)(i)	1.4(c)
3-104(a)	1.2(b)	3-110(c)(2)(ii)	1.4(c)
3-104(a)(1)	1.2(e)	3-110(c)(2)(iii)	1.4(c)
3-104(b)	1.3, 2.1	3-110(c)(2)(IV)	1.4(c)
3-104(e)	1.3, 2.1	3-110(d)	1.4(d)
3-104(f)	2.1	3-110(g)	2.9(b)
3-104(f)(i)(ii)	1.2(e)	3-111	7.1(a)
3-104(g)	2.5(a)	3-113(a)	1.2(d)
3-104(h)	2.5(a)	3-113(b)	1.2(d)
3-105	1.4(a)	3-114	1.3(b)
3-105(a)	1.3	3-115	1.3(a)

273

Article 3 Sections	Publication Sections	Article 3 Sections	Publication Sections
3-115(c)	1.3(a)	3-304	6.4(h)
3-115(d)	1.3(a)	3-305(a)	7.1
3-116(a)	2.6	3-305(b)	6.5
3-116(b)	2.6	3-305(c)	2.5(a)
3-117	1.1(a)	3-306	4.5, 9.2, 5.6(c)
3-141(d)	2.1	3-307	5.3(d)
3-201	5.6	3-307(b)	6.4(i)
3-201(a)	4.1, 4.3	3-308	6.5
3-201(b)	4.1, 5.2	3-309(a)	6.3
3-202(a)	4.2	3-309(b)	6.3
3-202(b)	4.2	3-310(b)	2.7(b)
3-203	4.3	3-310(b)(3)	2.7(b)
3-203(a)	4.3, 6.2(b)	3-310(b)(4)	2.7(b)
3-203(b)	4.3, 6.7	3-310(c)	2.7(b)
3-203(d)	4.3	3-311	2.8, 9.6
3-204	5.1	3-311(a)	2.8, 9.6
3-204(a)	5.1	3-311(b)	2.8, 9.6
3-204(b)	2.3, 5.1	3-311(c)	2.8, 9.6
3-204(c)	5.1	3-311(c)(1)	2.8
3-204(d)	1.4(a), 5.1(a)	3-311(c)(2)	2.8
3-205	5.1, 5.3	3-311(d)	9.6
3-205(a)	1.2(e), 5.3(a)	3-312	2.5(b)
3-205(b)	1.2(e), 5.3(b)	3-312(b)	2.5(b)
3-205(c)	5.3(b)	3-312(b)(1)	2.5(b)
3-205(d)	5.3(c)	3-312(b)(2)	2.5(b)
3-206	5.1, 5.3, 5.3(d), 5.5	3-312(b)(3)	2.5(b)
3-206(a)	5.3(d)	3-312(b)(4)	2.5(b)
3-206(b)	5.3(d)	3-312(c)	2.5(b)
3-206(c)	5.3(d)	3-401	1.3
3-206(d)	5.3(d)	3-401(a)	3.1
3-206(e)	5.3(d)	3-402(a)	3.1(a)
3-206(f)	5.3(d)	3-402(b)	3.1(a)
3-207	4.4	3-402(c)	3.1(a)
3-301	2.1, 2.3, 6.2, 6.2(a)	3-403	5.1
3-302	6.4	3-403(a)	3.2, 5.6(a), 5.7(b)
3-302(a)	6.4	3-403(b)	10.1, 3.1(b)
3-302(a)(2)	6.4(g), 6.4(h), 6.4(i)	3-403(c)	3.2(b)
3-302(b)	6.5	3-404	5.1, 2.9(d)
3-302(c)	6.6	3-404(a)	5.7(c)
3-302(d)	6.3(a)	3-404(b)	5.7(c)
3-302(e)	6.4(b)	3-404(c)	5.7(c)
3-303	6.4(a)	3-405	5.1, 2.9(d), 5.7(d)
3-303(a)	6.4(a)	3-405(a)	5.7(d)
3-303(a)(3)	6.4(c)	3-405(b)	5.7(d)
3-303(a)(4)	6.4(d)	3-405(c)	5.7(d)
3-303(a)(5)	6.4(e)	3-406	2.9(d), 10.1(d)
3-303(b)	6.4(f)	3-406(a)	3.3(b), 5.7(a)

Article 3 Sections	Publication Sections	Article 3 Sections	Publication Sections
3-406(b)	3.3(b), 5.7(a), 10.1(d)	3-418	9.2(c)
3-407	1.3(a), 10.1(d)	3-419	5.3
3-408	2.2, 2.4	3-419(d)	5.2
3-409	2.4	3-419(e)	2.6
3-409(a)	2.4	3-420	4.5
3-409(b)	2.4	3-420(a)	5.6(b)
3-409(c)	2.4	3-420(b)	2.9(b), 5.6(b)
3-409(d)	2.4, 2.5(a)	3-420(c)	5.6(b)
3-410	2.4	3-501	5.2
3-411	2.5(a), 2.5(b)	3-501(a)(1)	8.1(a)
3-411(b)	2.5(a)	3-501(a)(2)	8.1(b)
3-411(c)	2.5(a)	3-501(b)(1)	7.1(a), 7.1(d), 7.2, 7.3
3-412	2.5	3-501(b)(2)	7.1(d)
3-413	2.4	3-501(b)(3)	7.1(d)
3-413(a)	2.4	3-501(b)(4)	7.2
3-413(a)(ii)	2.4	3-502(b)(1)	8.2(a), 8.2(b)
3-413(a)(iii)	2.4	3-502(b)(2)	8.2(b)
3-413(b)	2.4	3-502(b)(3)	8.2(c), 8.4
3-414(a)	2.1	3-502(b)(4)	8.2(c), 8.4
3-414(b)	2.1	3-502(c)	8.2(d)
3-414(c)	2.1	3-502(d)	8.2(e)
3-414(d)	2.1, 8.5	3-502(e)	8.3
3-414(e)	2.1	3-502(f)	8.4
3-414(f)	2.1, 2.3(a)	3-503	5.2
3-415	5.1, 8.5	3-503(b)	8.5(a)
3-415(a)	5.2, 2.1, 2.3	3-503(c)	8.5(b)
3-415(b)	5.2	3-504(a)	7.6
3-415(c)	5.2, 2.1, 2.3(a)	3-504(b)	8.5, 8.5(c)
3-415(d)	5.2, 2.3(a)	3-504(c)	8.5(c)
3-415(e)	5.2, 2.3(a)	3-505	8.5(d)
3-416	4.6, 2.9, 2.9(a)	3-601(a)	9.1
3-416(a)	2.9(a)	3-601(b)	9.1
3-416(a)(1)	2.9(a)	3-602(a)	9.2(a)
3-416(a)(2)	2.9(a)	3-602(b)	9.2(b)
3-416(a)(3)	2.9(a)	3-602(c)	9.2(c)
3-416(a)(4)	2.9(a)	3-603(b)	9.3
3-416(a)(5)	2.9(a)	3-604(a)	9.4
3-416(b)	2.9(b)	3-604(b)	9.4
3-416(c)	2.9(c)	3-604(c)	9.5
3-416(d)	2.9(c)	3-604(d)	9.5
3-417	2.9, 2.9(d), 9.2(c)	3-605	5.1
3-417(b)	2.9(d)	3-605(b)	9.4
3-417(c)	2.9(d)	3-605(e)	9.5
3-417(d)	2.9(d)	3-605(f)	9.5
3-417(e)	2.9(d)	3-605(g)	9.5
3-417(f)	2.9(d)		

TABLE OF ARTICLE 4

Article 4 Sections	Publication Sections	Article 4 Sections	Publication Sections
4-101	1.0	4-207(d)	2.9(c)
4-102(a)	1.0	4-207(e)	2.9(c)
4-103	1.1(a), 10.3(b)	4-208	2.9, 2.9(d), 8.6(d), 11.3(b)
4-103(a)	1.1	4-208(b)	2.9(d)
4-103(b)	1.1	4-208(f)	2.9(d)
4-103(c)	1.1	4-209	7.11(a), 7.11(c)
4-103(e)	1.1	4-209(b)	7.11(b)
4-104	11.1	4-210	6.4(b)
4-104(12)	7.14	4-210(b)	6.4(b)
4-104(a)(10)	7.8	4-210(c)	6.4(b)
4-104(a)(11)	7.12, 7.13(a)	4-211	7.12, 6.4(b), 5.2, 7.5, 7.1(c)
4-104(a)(12)	2.5(a)	4-213	7.13(b)
4-104(a)(3)	7.2	4-213(a)(b)	7.13
4-105(5)	8.11(b)	4-214(b)	8.6(b)
4-106	7.3	4-215	9.2(a), 7.13, 7.13(b)
4-107	7.1(c)	4-215(e)	7.13(c)
4-108	7.2	4-216	7.14
4-109(a)	7.1(e)	4-301	7.13, 10.4, 7.3, 8.2(a), 8.6(c)
4-109(b)	7.1(e)	4-302	2.2, 7.3, 8.2(a), 8.6(c), 8.6(d)
4-110	7.5	4-302(a)(1)	2.5(b)
4-110(c)	7.11(a), 7.11(b)	4-303	10.4, 10.3(c)
4-201	7.7	4-303(a)	10.4
4-201(a)	7.7, 7.13(a)	4-303(b)	10.4(a)
4-201(b)	5.3(d), 5.5	4-401	7.7, 10.1
4-202	7.11(c), 8.6(a)	4-401(a)	10.1(a)
4-202(a)	8.6(a)	4-401(b)	10.1(a)
4-202(b)	8.6(a)	4-401(c)	1.2(d), 10.1(b)
4-203	7.9	4-401(d)	10.1(d)
4-204(a)	2.3, 7.1(e), 7.8	4-402	7.3, 10.1(b), 8.11(a), 10.3(e), 10.4
4-204(c)	7.1(a)	4-403	10.3
4-205	2.3, 5.1, 5.4, 5.7(c)	4-403(a)	10.3(a), 10.3(b), 10.3(c)
4-205(1)	7.11	4-403(b)	10.3(d)
4-205(2)	7.11	4-403(c)	10.3(e), 10.5(a)
4-205(a)	5.7(c)	4-404	10.1(c)
4-205(c)	5.7(c)	4-405(a)	10.2
4-205(d)	5.7(c)	4-405(b)	10.2
4-206	7.10	4-406	2.9(d), 7.5(a)
4-207	4.6, 2.9, 2.9(a)	4-406(a)	11.1
4-207(b)	5.2, 2.9(b)	4-406(b)	11.2

Article 4 Sections	Publication Sections	Article 4 Sections	Publication Sections
4-406(c)	11.3, 3.3(c)	4-407	10.5, 9.2(c)
4-406(d)	11.3	4-407(1)	10.5(a)
4-406(d)(1)	3.3(c)	4-407(2)	10.5(b)
4-406(d)(2)	3.3(c)	4-407(3)	10.5(c)
4-406(e)	11.3, 11.3(a)	4.202	7.8
4-406(f)	3.3(c), 11.3(b)		

APPENDIX:
ARTICLES 3 AND 4

ARTICLE 3

NEGOTIABLE INSTRUMENTS

PART 1

GENERAL PROVISIONS AND DEFINITIONS

§ 3-101. SHORT TITLE.

This Article may be cited as Uniform Commercial Code—Negotiable Instruments.

§ 3-102. SUBJECT MATTER.

(a) This Article applies to negotiable instruments. It does not apply to money, to payment orders governed by Article 4A, or to securities governed by Article 8.

(b) If there is conflict between this Article and Article 4 or 9, Articles 4 and 9 govern.

(c) Regulations of the Board of Governors of the Federal Reserve System and operating circulars of the Federal Reserve Banks supersede any inconsistent provision of this Article to the extent of the inconsistency.

§ 3-103. DEFINITIONS.

(a) In this Article:

(1) "Acceptor" means a drawee who has accepted a draft.

(2) "Drawee" means a person ordered in a draft to make payment.

(3) "Drawer" means a person who signs or is identified in a draft as a person ordering payment.

(4) "Good faith" means honesty in fact

and the observance of reasonable commercial standards of fair dealing.

(5) "Maker" means a person who signs or is identified in a note as a person undertaking to pay.

(6) "Order" means a written instruction to pay money signed by the person giving the instruction. The instruction may be addressed to any person, including the person giving the instruction, or to one or more persons jointly or in the alternative but not in succession. An authorization to pay is not an order unless the person authorized to pay is also instructed to pay.

(7) "Ordinary care" in the case of a person engaged in business means observance of reasonable commercial standards, prevailing in the area in which the person is located, with respect to the business in which the person is engaged. In the case of a bank that takes an instrument for processing for collection or payment by automated means, reasonable commercial standards do not require the bank to examine the instrument if the failure to examine does not violate the bank's prescribed procedures and the bank's procedures do not vary unreasonably from general banking usage not disapproved by this Article or Article 4.

(8) "Party" means a party to an instrument.

(9) "Promise" means a written undertaking to pay money signed by the person under-

taking to pay. An acknowledgment of an obligation by the obligor is not a promise unless the obligor also undertakes to pay the obligation.

(10) "Prove" with respect to a fact means to meet the burden of establishing the fact (Section 1-201(8)).

(11) "Remitter" means a person who purchases an instrument from its issuer if the instrument is payable to an identified person other than the purchaser.

(b) Other definitions applying to this Article and the sections in which they appear are:

"Acceptance"	Section 3-409
"Accommodated party"	Section 3-419
"Accommodation party"	Section 3-419
"Alteration"	Section 3-407
"Anomalous indorsement"	Section 3-205
"Blank indorsement"	Section 3-205
"Cashier's check"	Section 3-104
"Certificate of deposit"	Section 3-104
"Certified check"	Section 3-409
"Check"	Section 3-104
"Consideration"	Section 3-303
"Draft"	Section 3-104
"Holder in due course"	Section 3-302
"Incomplete instrument"	Section 3-115
"Indorsement"	Section 3-204
"Indorser"	Section 3-204
"Instrument"	Section 3-104
"Issue"	Section 3-105
"Issuer"	Section 3-105
"Negotiable instrument"	Section 3-104
"Negotiation"	Section 3-201
"Note"	Section 3-104
"Payable at a definite time"	Section 3-108
"Payable on demand"	Section 3-108
"Payable to bearer"	Section 3-109
"Payable to order"	Section 3-109
"Payment"	Section 3-602
"Person entitled to enforce"	Section 3-301
"Presentment"	Section 3-501
"Reacquisition"	Section 3-207
"Special indorsement"	Section 3-205
"Teller's check"	Section 3-104
"Transfer of instrument"	Section 3-203
"Traveler's check"	Section 3-104
"Value"	Section 3-303

(c) The following definitions in other Articles apply to this Article:

"Bank"	Section 4-105
"Banking day"	Section 4-104
"Clearing house"	Section 4-104
"Collecting bank"	Section 4-105
"Depositary bank"	Section 4-105
"Documentary draft"	Section 4-104
"Intermediary bank"	Section 4-105
"Item"	Section 4-104
"Payor bank"	Section 4-105
"Suspends payments"	Section 4-104

(d) In addition, Article 1 contains general definitions and principles of construction and interpretation applicable throughout this Article.

§ 3-104. NEGOTIABLE INSTRUMENT.

(a) Except as provided in subsections (c) and (d), "negotiable instrument" means an unconditional promise or order to pay a fixed amount of money, with or without interest or other charges described in the promise or order, if it:

(1) is payable to bearer or to order at the time it is issued or first comes into possession of a holder;

(2) is payable on demand or at a definite time; and

(3) does not state any other undertaking or instruction by the person promising or ordering payment to do any act in addition to the payment of money, but the promise or order may contain (i) an undertaking or power to give, maintain, or protect collateral to secure payment, (ii) an authorization or power to the holder to confess judgment or realize on or dispose of collateral, or (iii) a waiver of the benefit of any law intended for the advantage or protection of an obligor.

(b) "Instrument" means a negotiable instrument.

(c) An order that meets all of the requirements of subsection (a), except paragraph (1), and otherwise falls within the definition of "check" in subsection (f) is a negotiable instrument and a check.

(d) A promise or order other than a check is not an instrument if, at the time it is issued or first comes into possession of a holder, it contains a conspicuous statement, however expressed, to the effect that the promise or order is not negotiable or is not an instrument governed by this Article.

(e) An instrument is a "note" if it is a promise and is a "draft" if it is an order. If an instrument falls within the definition of both "note" and "draft," a person entitled to enforce the instrument may treat it as either.

(f) "Check" means (i) a draft, other than a documentary draft, payable on demand and drawn on a bank or (ii) a cashier's check or teller's check. An instrument may be a check even though it is described on its face by another term, such as "money order."

(g) "Cashier's check" means a draft with respect to which the drawer and drawee are the same bank or branches of the same bank.

(h) "Teller's check" means a draft drawn by a bank (i) on another bank, or (ii) payable at or through a bank.

(i) "Traveler's check" means an instrument that (i) is payable on demand, (ii) is drawn on or payable at or through a bank, (iii) is designated by the term "traveler's check" or by a substantially similar term, and (iv) requires, as a condition to payment, a countersignature by a person whose specimen signature appears on the instrument.

(j) "Certificate of deposit" means an instrument containing an acknowledgment by a bank that a sum of money has been received by the bank and a promise by the bank to repay the sum of money. A certificate of deposit is a note of the bank.

§ 3-105. ISSUE OF INSTRUMENT.

(a) "Issue" means the first delivery of an instrument by the maker or drawer, whether to a holder or nonholder, for the purpose of giving rights on the instrument to any person.

(b) An unissued instrument, or an unissued incomplete instrument that is completed, is binding on the maker or drawer, but nonissuance is a defense. An instrument that is conditionally issued or is issued for a special purpose is binding on the maker or drawer, but failure of the condition or special purpose to be fulfilled is a defense.

(c) "Issuer" applies to issued and unissued instruments and means a maker or drawer of an instrument.

§ 3-106. UNCONDITIONAL PROMISE OR ORDER.

(a) Except as provided in this section, for the purposes of Section 3-104(a), a promise or order is unconditional unless it states (i) an express condition to payment, (ii) that the promise or order is subject to or governed by another writing, or (iii) that rights or obligations with respect to the promise or order are stated in another writing. A reference to another writing does not of itself make the promise or order conditional.

(b) A promise or order is not made conditional (i) by a reference to another writing for a statement of rights with respect to collateral, prepayment, or acceleration, or (ii) because payment is limited to resort to a particular fund or source.

(c) If a promise or order requires, as a condition to payment, a countersignature by a person whose specimen signature appears on the promise or order, the condition does not make the promise or order conditional for the purposes of Section 3-104(a). If the person whose specimen signature appears on an instrument fails to countersign the instrument, the failure to countersign is a defense to the obligation of the issuer, but the failure does not prevent a transferee of the instrument from becoming a holder of the instrument.

(d) If a promise or order at the time it is issued or first comes into possession of a holder contains a statement, required by applicable statutory or administrative law, to the effect that the rights of a holder or transferee are subject to claims or defenses that the issuer could assert against the original payee, the promise or order is not thereby made conditional for the purposes of Section 3-104(a); but if the promise or order is an instrument, there cannot be a holder in due course of the instrument.

§ 3-107. INSTRUMENT PAYABLE IN FOREIGN MONEY.

Unless the instrument otherwise provides, an instrument that states the amount payable in foreign money may be paid in the foreign money or in an equivalent amount in dollars calculated by using the current bank-offered spot rate at the place of payment for the purchase of dollars on the day on which the instrument is paid.

§ 3-108. PAYABLE ON DEMAND OR AT
        DEFINITE TIME.

(a) A promise or order is "payable on demand" if it (i) states that it is payable on demand or at sight, or otherwise indicates that it
is payable at the will of the holder, or (ii) does
not state any time of payment.

(b) A promise or order is "payable at a definite time" if it is payable on elapse of a definite
period of time after sight or acceptance or at a
fixed date or dates or at a time or times readily
ascertainable at the time the promise or order is
issued, subject to rights of (i) prepayment, (ii)
acceleration, (iii) extension at the option of the
holder, or (iv) extension to a further definite
time at the option of the maker or acceptor or
automatically upon or after a specified act or
event.

(c) If an instrument, payable at a fixed date,
is also payable upon demand made before the
fixed date, the instrument is payable on demand until the fixed date and, if demand for
payment is not made before that date, becomes
payable at a definite time on the fixed date.

§ 3-109. PAYABLE TO BEARER OR TO OR-
        DER.

(a) A promise or order is payable to bearer
if it:

(1) states that it is payable to bearer or to
the order of bearer or otherwise indicates that
the person in possession of the promise or order is entitled to payment;

(2) does not state a payee; or

(3) states that it is payable to or to the
order of cash or otherwise indicates that it is
not payable to an identified person.

(b) A promise or order that is not payable to
bearer is payable to order if it is payable (i) to
the order of an identified person or (ii) to an
identified person or order. A promise or order
that is payable to order is payable to the identified person.

(c) An instrument payable to bearer may become payable to an identified person if it is
specially indorsed pursuant to Section 3-205(a).
An instrument payable to an identified person
may become payable to bearer if it is indorsed
in blank pursuant to Section 3-205(b).

§ 3-110. IDENTIFICATION OF PERSON TO
        WHOM INSTRUMENT IS PAYABLE.

(a) The person to whom an instrument is initially payable is determined by the intent of
the person, whether or not authorized, signing
as, or in the name or behalf of, the issuer of the
instrument. The instrument is payable to the
person intended by the signer even if that person is identified in the instrument by a name or
other identification that is not that of the intended person. If more than one person signs in
the name or behalf of the issuer of an instrument and all the signers do not intend the same
person as payee, the instrument is payable to
any person intended by one or more of the
signers.

(b) If the signature of the issuer of an instrument is made by automated means, such as a
check-writing machine, the payee of the instrument is determined by the intent of the person
who supplied the name or identification of the
payee, whether or not authorized to do so.

(c) A person to whom an instrument is payable may be identified in any way, including by
name, identifying number, office, or account
number. For the purpose of determining the
holder of an instrument, the following rules apply:

(1) If an instrument is payable to an account and the account is identified only by
number, the instrument is payable to the person to whom the account is payable. If an instrument is payable to an account identified by
number and by the name of a person, the instrument is payable to the named person,
whether or not that person is the owner of the
account identified by number.

(2) If an instrument is payable to:

(i) a trust, an estate, or a person described as trustee or representative of a trust or
estate, the instrument is payable to the trustee,
the representative, or a successor of either,
whether or not the beneficiary or estate is also
named;

(ii) a person described as agent or
similar representative of a named or identified
person, the instrument is payable to the represented person, the representative, or a successor
of the representative;

(iii) a fund or organization that is not
a legal entity, the instrument is payable to a
representative of the members of the fund or
organization; or

(iv) an office or to a person described

as holding an office, the instrument is payable to the named person, the incumbent of the office, or a successor to the incumbent.

(d) If an instrument is payable to two or more persons alternatively, it is payable too any of them and may be negotiated, discharged, or enforced by any or all of them in possession of the instrument. If an instrument is payable to two or more persons not alternatively, it is payable to all of them and may be negotiated, discharged, or enforced only by all of them. If an instrument payable to two or more persons is ambiguous as to whether it is payable to the persons alternatively, the instrument is payable to the persons alternatively.

§ 3-111. PLACE OF PAYMENT.

Except as otherwise provided for items in Article 4, an instrument is payable at the place of payment stated in the instrument. If no place of payment is stated, an instrument is payable at the address of the drawee or maker stated in the instrument. If no address is stated, the place of payment is the place of business of the drawee or maker. If a drawee or maker has more than one place of business, the place of payment is any place of business of the drawee or maker chosen by the person entitled to enforce the instrument. If the drawee or maker has no place of business, the place of payment is the residence of the drawee or maker.

§ 3-112. INTEREST.

(a) Unless otherwise provided in the instrument, (i) an instrument is not payable with interest, and (ii) interest on an interest-bearing instrument is payable from the date of the instrument.

(b) Interest may be stated in an instrument as a fixed or variable amount of money or it may be expressed as a fixed or variable rate or rates. The amount or rate of interest may be stated or described in the instrument in any manner and may require reference to information not contained in the instrument. If an instrument provides for interest, but the amount of interest payable cannot be ascertained from the description, interest is payable at the judgment rate in effect at the place of payment of the instrument and at the time interest first accrues.

§ 3-113. DATE OF INSTRUMENT.

(a) An instrument may be antedated or postdated. The date stated determines the time of payment if the instrument is payable at a fixed period after date. Except as provided in Section 4-401(c), an instrument payable on demand is not payable before the date of the instrument.

(b) If an instrument is undated, its date is the date of its issue or, in the case of an unissued instrument, the date it first comes into possession of a holder.

§ 3-114. CONTRADICTORY TERMS OF INSTRUMENT.

If an instrument contains contradictory terms, typewritten terms prevail over printed terms, handwritten terms prevail over both, and words prevail over numbers.

§ 3-115. INCOMPLETE INSTRUMENT.

(a) "Incomplete instrument" means a signed writing, whether or not issued by the signer, the contents of which show at the time of signing that it is incomplete but that the signer intended it to be completed by the addition of words or numbers.

(b) Subject to subsection (c), if an incomplete instrument is an instrument under Section 3-104, it may be enforced according to its terms if it is not completed, or according to its terms as augmented by completion. If an incomplete instrument is not an instrument under Section 3-104, but, after completion, the requirements of Section 3-104 are met, the instrument may be enforced according to its terms as augmented by completion.

(c) If words or numbers are added to an incomplete instrument without authority of the signer, there is an alteration of the incomplete instrument under Section 3-407.

(d) The burden of establishing that words or numbers were added to an incomplete instrument without authority of the signer is on the person asserting the lack of authority.

§ 3-116. JOINT AND SEVERAL LIABILITY; CONTRIBUTION.

(a) Except as otherwise provided in the instrument, two or more persons who have the same liability on an instrument as makers, drawers, acceptors, indorsers who indorse as joint payees, or anomalous indorsers are jointly and severally liable in the capacity in which they sign.

(b) Except as provided in Section 3-419(e) or by agreement of the affected parties, a party having joint and several liability who pays the instrument is entitled to receive from any party having the same joint and several liability contribution in accordance with applicable law.

(c) Discharge of one party having joint and several liability by a person entitled to enforce the instrument does not affect the right under subsection (b) of a party having the same joint and several liability to receive contribution from the party discharged.

§ 3-117. OTHER AGREEMENTS AFFECTING INSTRUMENT.

Subject to applicable law regarding exclusion of proof of contemporaneous or previous agreements, the obligation of a party to an instrument to pay the instrument may be modified, supplemented, or nullified by a separate agreement of the obligor and a person entitled to enforce the instrument, if the instrument is issued or the obligation is incurred in reliance on the agreement or as part of the same transaction giving rise to the agreement. To the extent an obligation is modified, supplemented, or nullified by an agreement under this section, the agreement is a defense to the obligation.

§ 3-118. STATUTE OF LIMITATIONS.

(a) Except as provided in subsection (e), an action to enforce the obligation of a party to pay a note payable at a definite time must be commenced within six years after the due date or dates stated in the note or, if a due date is accelerated, within six years after the accelerated due date.

(b) Except as provided in subsection (d) or (e), if demand for payment is made to the maker of a note payable on demand, an action to enforce the obligation of a party to pay the note must be commenced within six years after the demand. If no demand for payment is made to the maker, an action to enforce the note is barred if neither principal nor interest on the note has been paid for a continuous period of 10 years.

(c) Except as provided in subsection (d), an action to enforce the obligation of a party to an unaccepted draft to pay the draft must be commenced within three years after dishonor of the draft or 10 years after the date of the draft, whichever period expires first.

(d) An action to enforce the obligation of the acceptor of a certified check or the issuer of a teller's check, cashier's check, or traveler's check must be commenced within three years after demand for payment is made to the acceptor or issuer, as the case may be.

(e) An action to enforce the obligation of a party to a certificate of deposit to pay the instrument must be commenced within six years after demand for payment is made to the maker, but if the instrument states a due date and the maker is not required to pay before that date, the six-year period begins when a demand for payment is in effect and the due date has passed.

(f) An action to enforce the obligation of a party to pay an accepted draft, other than a certified check, must be commenced (i) within six years after the due date or dates stated in the draft or acceptance if the obligation of the acceptor is payable at a definite time, or (ii) within six years after the date of the acceptance if the obligation of the acceptor is payable on demand.

(g) Unless governed by other law regarding claims for indemnity or contribution, an action (i) for conversion of an instrument, for money had and received, or like action based on conversion, (ii) for breach of warranty, or (iii) to enforce an obligation, duty, or right arising under this Article and not governed by this section must be commenced within three years after the [cause of action] accrues.

§ 3-119. NOTICE OF RIGHT TO DEFEND ACTION.

In an action for breach of an obligation for which a third person is answerable over pursuant to this Article or Article 4, the defendant may give the third person written notice of the litigation, and the person notified may then give similar notice to any other person who is answerable over. If the notice states (i) that the person notified may come in and defend and (ii) that failure to do so will bind the person notified in an action later brought by the person giving the notice as to any determination of fact common to the two litigations, the person notified is so bound unless after seasonable receipt of the notice the person notified does come in and defend.

PART 2

NEGOTIATION, TRANSFER, AND INDORSEMENT

§ 3-201. NEGOTIATION.

(a) "Negotiation" means a transfer of possession, whether voluntary or involuntary, of an instrument by a person other than the issuer to a person who thereby becomes its holder.

(b) Except for negotiation by a remitter, if an instrument is payable to an identified person, negotiation requires transfer of possession of the instrument and its indorsement by the holder. If an instrument is payable to bearer, it may be negotiated by transfer of possession alone.

§ 3-202. NEGOTIATION SUBJECT TO RESCIS-
SION.

(a) Negotiation is effective even if obtained (i) from an infant, a corporation exceeding its powers, or a person without capacity, (ii) by fraud, duress, or mistake, or (iii) in breach of duty or as part of an illegal transaction.

(b) To the extent permitted by other law, negotiation may be rescinded or may be subject to other remedies, but those remedies may not be asserted against subsequent holder in due course or a person paying the instrument in good faith and without knowledge of facts that are a basis for rescission or other remedy.

§ 3-203. TRANSFER OF INSTRUMENT;
RIGHTS ACQUIRED BY TRANSFER.

(a) An instrument is transferred when it is delivered by a person other than its issuer for the purpose of giving to the person receiving delivery the right to enforce the instrument.

(b) Transfer of an instrument, whether or not the transfer is a negotiation, vests in the transferee any right of the transferor to enforce the instrument, including any right as a holder in due course, but the transferee cannot acquire rights of a holder in due course by a transfer, directly or indirectly, from a holder in due course if the transferee engaged in fraud or illegality affecting the instrument.

(c) Unless otherwise agreed, if an instru-ment is transferred for value and the transferee does not become a holder because of lack of indorsement by the transferor, the transferee has a specifically enforceable right to the unqualified indorsement of the transferor, but negotiation of the instrument does not occur until the indorsement is made.

(d) If a transferor purports to transfer less than the entire instrument, negotiation of the instrument does not occur. The transferee obtains no rights under this Article and has only the rights of a partial assignee.

§ 3-204. INDORSEMENT.

(a) "Indorsement" means a signature, other than that of a signer as maker, drawer, or acceptor, that alone or accompanied by other words is made on an instrument for the purpose of (i) negotiating the instrument, (ii) restricting payment of the instrument, or (iii) incurring indorser's liability on the instrument, but regardless of the intent of the signer, a signature and its accompanying words is an indorsement unless the accompanying words, terms of the instrument, place of the signature, or other circumstances unambiguously indicate that the signature was made for a purpose other than indorsement. For the purpose of determining whether a signature is made on an instrument, a paper affixed to the instrument is a part of the instrument.

(b) "Indorser" means a person who makes an indorsement.

(c) For the purpose of determining whether the transferee of an instrument is a holder, an indorsement that transfers a security interest in the instrument is effective as an unqualified indorsement of the instrument.

(d) If an instrument is payable to a holder under a name that is not the name of the holder, indorsement may be made by the holder in the name stated in the instrument or in the holder's name or both, but signature in both names may be required by a person paying or taking the instrument for value or collection.

§ 3-205. SPECIAL INDORSEMENT; BLANK
INDORSEMENT; ANOMALOUS IN-
DORSEMENT.

(a) If an indorsement is made by the holder of an instrument, whether payable to an identified person or payable to bearer, and the indorsement identifies a person to whom it makes the instrument payable, it is a "special indorsement." When specially indorsed, an instrument becomes payable to the identified person and may be negotiated only by the indorsement of that person. The principles stated in Section 3-110 apply to special indorsements.

(b) If an indorsement is made by the holder of an instrument and it is not a special indorsement, it is a "blank indorsement." When indorsed in blank, an instrument becomes payable to bearer and may be negotiated by transfer of possession alone until specially indorsed.

(c) The holder may convert a blank indorsement that consists only of a signature into a special indorsement by writing, above the signature of the indorser, words identifying the person to whom the instrument is made payable.

(d) "Anomalous indorsement" means an indorsement made by a person who is not the holder of the instrument. An anomalous indorsement does not affect the manner in which the instrument may be negotiated.

§ 3-206. RESTRICTIVE INDORSEMENT.

(a) An indorsement limiting payment to a particular person or otherwise prohibiting further transfer or negotiation of the instrument is not effective to prevent further transfer or negotiation of the instrument.

(b) An indorsement stating a condition to the right of the indorsee to receive payment does not affect the right of the indorsee to enforce the instrument. A person paying the instrument or taking it for value or collection may disregard the condition, and the rights and liabilities of that person are not affected by whether the condition has been fulfilled.

(c) If an instrument bears an indorsement (i) described in Section 4-201(b), or (ii) in blank or to a particular bank using the words "for deposit," "for collection," or other words indicating a purpose of having the instrument collected by a bank for the indorser or for a particular account, the following rules apply:

(1) A person, other than a bank, who purchases the instrument when so indorsed converts the instrument unless the amount paid

for the instrument is received by the indorser or applied consistently with the indorsement.

(2) A depositary bank that purchases the instrument or takes it for collection when so indorsed converts the instrument unless the amount paid by the bank with respect to the instrument is received by the indorser or applied consistently with the indorsement.

(3) A payor bank that is also the depositary bank or that takes the instrument for immediate payment over the counter from a person other than a collecting bank converts the instrument unless the proceeds of the instrument are received by the indorser or applied consistently with the indorsement.

(4) Except as otherwise provided in paragraph (3), a payor bank or intermediary bank may disregard the indorsement and is not liable if the proceeds of the instrument are not received by the indorser or applied consistently with the indorsement.

(d) Except for an indorsement covered by subsection (c), if an instrument bears an indorsement using words to the effect that payment is to be made to the indorsee as agent, trustee, or other fiduciary for the benefit of the indorser or another person, the following rules apply:

(1) Unless there is notice of breach of fiduciary duty as provided in Section 3-307, a person who purchases the instrument from the indorsee or takes the instrument from the indorsee for collection or payment may pay the proceeds of payment or the value given for the instrument to the indorsee without regard to whether the indorsee violates a fiduciary duty to the indorser.

(2) A subsequent transferee of the instrument or person who pays the instrument is neither given notice nor otherwise affected by the restriction in the indorsement unless the transferee or payor knows that the fiduciary dealt with the instrument or its proceeds in breach of fiduciary duty.

(e) The presence on an instrument of an indorsement to which this section applies does not prevent a purchaser of the instrument from becoming a holder in due course of the instrument unless the purchaser is a converter under subsection (c) or has notice or knowledge of breach of fiduciary duty as stated in subsection (d).

(f) In an action to enforce the obligation of a party to pay the instrument, the obligor has a defense if payment would violate an indorsement to which this section applies and the payment is not permitted by this section.

§ 3-207. REACQUISITION.

Reacquisition of an instrument occurs if it is transferred to a former holder, by negotiation or otherwise. A former holder who reacquires the instrument may cancel indorsements made after the reacquirer first became a holder of the instrument. If the cancellation causes the instrument to be payable to the reacquirer or to bearer, the reacquirer may negotiate the instrument. An indorser whose indorsement is canceled is discharged, and the discharge is effective against any subsequent holder.

PART 3

ENFORCEMENT OF INSTRUMENTS

§ 3 - 301. PERSON ENTITLED TO ENFORCE INSTRUMENT.

"Person entitled to enforce" an instrument means (i) the holder of the instrument, (ii) a nonholder in possession of the instrument who has the rights of a holder, or (iii) a person not in possession of the instrument who is entitled to enforced the instrument pursuant to Section 3-309 or 3-418(d). A person may be a person entitled to enforce the instrument even though the person is not the owner of the instrument or is in wrongful possession of the instrument.

§ 3-302. HOLDER IN DUE COURSE.

(a) Subject to subsection (c) and Section 3-106(d), "holder in due course" means the holder of an instrument if:

(1) the instrument when issued or negotiated to the holder does not bear such apparent evidence of forgery or alteration or is not otherwise so irregular or incomplete as to call into question its authenticity; and

(2) the holder took the instrument (i) for value, (ii) in good faith, (iii) without notice that the instrument is overdue or has been dishonored or that there is an uncured default with respect to payment of another instrument issued as part of the same series, (iv) without no-

tice that the instrument contains an unauthorized signature or has been altered, (v) without notice of any claim to the instrument described in Section 3-306, and (vi) without notice that any party has a defense or claim in recoupment described in Section 3-305(a).

(b) Notice of discharge of a party, other than discharge in an insolvency proceeding, is not notice of a defense under subsection (a), but discharge is effective against a person who became a holder in due course with notice of the discharge. Public filing or recording of a document does not of itself constitute notice of a defense, claim in recoupment, or claim to the instrument.

(c) Except to the extent a transferor or predecessor in interest has rights as a holder in due course, a person does not acquire rights of a holder in due course of an instrument taken (i) by legal process or by purchase in an execution, bankruptcy, or creditor's sale or similar proceeding, (ii) by purchase as part of a bulk transaction not in ordinary course of business of the transferor, or (iii) as the successor in interest to an estate or other organization.

(d) If, under Section 3-303(a)(1), the promise of performance that is the consideration for an instrument has been partially performed, the holder may assert rights as a holder in due course of the instrument only to the fraction of the amount payable under the instrument equal to the value of the partial performance divided by the value of the promised performance.

(e) If (i) the person entitled to enforce an instrument has only a security interest in the instrument and (ii) the person obliged to pay the instrument has a defense, claim in recoupment, or claim to the instrument that may be asserted against the person who granted the security interest, the person entitled to enforce the instrument may assert rights as a holder in due course only to an amount payable under the instrument which, at the time of enforcement of the instrument, does not exceed the amount of the unpaid obligation secured.

(f) To be effective, notice must be received at a time and in a manner that gives a reasonable opportunity to act on it.

(g) This section is subject to any law limiting status as a holder in due course in particular classes of transactions.

§ 3-303. VALUE AND CONSIDERATION.

(a) An instrument is issued or transferred for value if:

(1) the instrument is issued or transferred for a promise of performance, to the extent the promise has been performed;

(2) the transferee acquires a security interest or other lien in the instrument other than a lien obtained by judicial proceeding;

(3) the instrument is issued or transferred as payment of, or as security for, an antecedent claim against any person, whether or not the claim is due;

(4) the instrument is issued or transferred in exchange for a negotiable instrument; or

(5) the instrument is issued or transferred in exchange for the incurring of an irrevocable obligation to a third party by the person taking the instrument.

(b) "Consideration" means any consideration sufficient to support a simple contract. The drawer or maker of an instrument has a defense if the instrument is issued without consideration. If an instrument is issued for a promise of performance, the issuer has a defense to the extent performance of the promise is due and the promise has not been performed. If an instrument is issued for value as stated in subsection (a), the instrument is also issued for consideration.

§ 3-304. OVERDUE INSTRUMENT.

(a) An instrument payable on demand becomes overdue at the earliest of the following times:

(1) on the day after the day demand for payment is duly made;

(2) if the instrument is a check, 90 days after its date; or

(3) if the instrument is not a check, when the instrument has been outstanding for a period of time after its date which is unreasonably long under the circumstances of the particular case in light of the nature of the instrument and usage of the trade.

(b) With respect to an instrument payable at a definite time the following rules apply:

(1) If the principal is payable in installments and a due date has not been accelerated, the instrument becomes overdue upon default under the instrument for nonpayment of an installment, and the instrument remains overdue until the default is cured.

(2) If the principal is not payable in installments and the due date has not been accelerated, the instrument becomes overdue on the day after the due date.

(3) If a due date with respect to principal has been accelerated, the instrument becomes overdue on the day after the accelerated due date.

(c) Unless the due date of principal has been accelerated, an instrument does not become overdue if there is default in payment of interest but no default in payment of principal.

§ 3-305. DEFENSES AND CLAIMS IN RE-COUPMENT.

(a) Except as stated in subsection (b), the right to enforce the obligation of a party to pay an instrument is subject to the following:

(1) a defense of the obligor based on (i) infancy of the obligor to the extent it is a defense to a simple contract, (ii) duress, lack of legal capacity, or illegality of the transaction which, under other law, nullifies the obligation of the obligor, (iii) fraud that induced the obligor to sign the instrument with neither knowledge nor reasonable opportunity to learn of its character or its essential terms, or (iv) discharge of the obligor in insolvency proceedings;

(2) a defense of the obligor stated in another section of this Article or a defense of the obligor that would be available if the person entitled to enforce the instrument were enforcing a right to payment under a simple contract; and

(3) a claim in recoupment of the obligor against the original payee of the instrument if the claim arose from the transaction that gave rise to the instrument; but the claim of the obligor may be asserted against a transferee of the instrument only to reduce the amount owing on the instrument at the time the action is brought.

(b) The right of a holder in due course to enforce the obligation of a party to pay the instrument is subject to defenses of the obligor stated in subsection (a)(1), but is not subject to defenses of the obligor stated in subsection (a)(2) or claims in recoupment stated in subsection (a)(3) against a person other than the holder.

(c) Except as stated in subsection (d), in an action to enforce the obligation of a party to pay the instrument, the obligor may not assert against the person entitled to enforce the instrument a defense, claim in recoupment, or claim to the instrument (Section 3-306) of another person, but the other person's claim to the instrument may be asserted by the obligor if the other person is joined in the action and personally asserts the claim against the person entitled to enforce the instrument. An obligor is not obliged to pay the instrument if the person seeking enforcement of the instrument does not have rights of a holder in due course and the obligor proves that the instrument is a lost or stolen instrument.

(d) In an action to enforce the obligation of an accommodation party to pay an instrument, the accommodation party may assert against the person entitled to enforce the instrument any defense or claim in recoupment under subsection (a) that the accommodated party could assert against the person entitled to enforce the instrument except the defenses of discharge in insolvency proceedings, infancy, and lack of legal capacity.

§ 3-306. CLAIMS TO AN INSTRUMENT.

A person taking an instrument, other than a person having rights of a holder in due course, is subject to a claim of a property or possessory right in the instrument or its proceeds, including a claim to rescind a negotiation and to recover the instrument or its proceeds. A person having rights of a holder in due course takes free of the claim to the instrument.

§ 3-307. NOTICE OF BREACH OF FIDUCI-
ARY DUTY.

(a) In this section:

(1) "Fiduciary" means an agent, trustee, partner, corporate officer or director, or other representative owing a fiduciary duty with respect to an instrument.

(2) "Represented person" means the principal, beneficiary, partnership, corporation, or other person to whom the duty stated in paragraph (1) is owed.

(b) If (i) an instrument is taken from a fiduciary for payment or collection or for value, (ii) the taker has knowledge of the fiduciary status of the fiduciary, and (iii) the represented person makes a claim to the instrument or its proceeds on the basis that the transaction of the fiduciary is a breach of fiduciary duty, the following rules apply:

(1) Notice of breach of fiduciary duty by the fiduciary is notice of the claim of the represented person.

(2) In the case of an instrument payable to the represented person or the fiduciary as such, the taker has notice of the breach of fiduciary duty if the instrument is (i) taken in payment of or as security for a debt known by the taker to be the personal debt of the fiduciary, (ii) taken in a transaction known by the taker to be for the personal benefit of the fiduciary, or (iii) deposited to an account other than an account of the fiduciary, as such, or an account of the represented person.

(3) If an instrument is issued by the represented person or the fiduciary as such, and made payable to the fiduciary personally, the taker does not have notice of the breach of fiduciary duty unless the taker knows of the breach of fiduciary duty.

(4) If an instrument is issued by the represented person or the fiduciary as such, to the taker as payee, the taker has notice of the breach of fiduciary duty if the instrument is (i) taken in payment of or as security for a debt known by the taker to be the personal debt of the fiduciary, (ii) taken in a transaction known by the taker to be for the personal benefit of the fiduciary, or (iii) deposited to an account other than an account of the fiduciary, as such, or an account of the represented person.

§ 3-308. PROOF OF SIGNATURES AND
STATUS AS HOLDER IN DUE
COURSE.

(a) In an action with respect to an instrument, the authenticity of, and authority to make, each signature on the instrument is admitted unless specifically denied in the pleadings. If the validity of a signature is denied in the pleadings, the burden of establishing validity is on the person claiming validity, but the signature is presumed to be authentic and authorized unless the action is to enforce the liability of the purported signer and the signer is dead or incompetent at the time of trial of the issue of validity of the signature. If an action to enforce the instrument is brought against a person as the undisclosed principal of a person who signed the instrument as a party to the instrument, the plaintiff has the burden of establishing that the defendant is liable on the instrument as a represented person under Section 3-402(a).

(b) If the validity of signatures is admitted or proved and there is compliance with subsection (a), a plaintiff producing the instrument is entitled to payment if the plaintiff proves entitlement to enforce the instrument under Section 3-301, unless the defendant proves a defense or claim in recoupment. If a defense or claim in recoupment is proved, the right to payment of the plaintiff is subject to the defense or claim, except to the extent the plaintiff proves that the plaintiff has rights of a holder in due course which are not subject to the defense or claim.

§ 3-309. ENFORCEMENT OF LOST, DESTROYED, OR STOLEN INSTRUMENT.

(a) A person not in possession of an instrument is entitled to enforce the instrument if (i) the person was in possession of the instrument and entitled to enforce it when loss of possession occurred, (ii) the loss of possession was not the result of a transfer by the person or a lawful seizure, and (iii) the person cannot reasonably obtain possession of the instrument because the instrument was destroyed, its whereabouts cannot be determined, or it is in the wrongful possession of an unknown person or a person that cannot be found or is not amenable to service of process.

(b) A person seeking enforcement of an instrument under subsection (a) must prove the terms of the instrument and the person's right to enforce the instrument. If that proof is made, Section 3-308 applies to the case as if the person seeking enforcement had produced the instrument. The court may not enter judgment in favor of the person seeking enforcement unless it finds that the person required to pay the instrument is adequately protected against loss that might occur by reason of a claim by another person to enforce the instrument. Adequate protection may be provided by any reasonable means.

§ 3-310. EFFECT OF INSTRUMENT ON OBLIGATION FOR WHICH TAKEN.

(a) Unless otherwise agreed, if a certified check, cashier's check, or teller's check is taken for an obligation, the obligation is discharged to the same extent discharge would result if an amount of money equal to the amount of the instrument were taken in payment of the obligation. Discharge of the obligation does not affect any liability that the obligor may have as an indorser of the instrument.

(b) Unless otherwise agreed and except as provided in subsection (a), if a note or an uncertified check is taken for an obligation, the obligation is suspended to the same extent the obligation would be discharged if an amount of money equal to the amount of the instrument were taken, and the following rules apply:

(1) In the case of an uncertified check, suspension of the obligation continues until dishonor of the check or until it is paid or certified. Payment or certification of the check results in discharge of the obligation to the extent of the amount of the check.

(2) In the case of a note, suspension of the obligation continues until dishonor of the note or until it is paid. Payment of the note results in discharge of the obligation to the extent of the payment.

(3) Except as provided in paragraph (4), if the check or note is dishonored and the obligee of the obligation for which the instrument was taken is the person entitled to enforce the instrument, the obligee may enforce either the instrument or the obligation. In the case of an instrument of a third person which is negotiated to the obligee by the obligor, discharge of the obligor on the instrument also discharges the obligation.

(4) If the person entitled to enforce the instrument taken for an obligation is a person other than the obligee, the obligee may not enforce the obligation to the extent the obligation is suspended. If the obligee is the person entitled to enforce the instrument but no longer has possession of it because it was lost, stolen, or destroyed, the obligation may not be enforced to the extent of the amount payable on the instrument, and to that extent the obligee's rights against the obligor are limited to enforcement of the instrument.

(c) If an instrument other than one described in subsection (a) or (b) is taken for an obligation, the effect is (i) that stated in subsection (a) if the instrument is one on which a bank is liable as maker or acceptor, or (ii) that stated in subsection (b) in any other case.

§ 3-311. ACCORD AND SATISFACTION BY USE OF INSTRUMENT.

(a) If a person against whom a claim is asserted proves that (i) that person in good faith tendered an instrument to the claimant as full satisfaction of the claim, (ii) the amount of the claim was unliquidated or subject to a bona fide dispute, and (iii) the claimant obtained payment of the instrument, the following subsections apply.

(b) Unless subsection (c) applies, the claim is discharged if the person against whom the claim is asserted proves that the instrument or an accompanying written communication contained a conspicuous statement to the effect that the instrument was tendered as full satisfaction of the claim.

(c) Subject to subsection (d), a claim is not discharged under subsection (b) if either of the following applies:

(1) The claimant, if an organization, proves that (i) within a reasonable time before the tender, the claimant sent a conspicuous statement to the person against whom the claim is asserted that communications concerning disputed debts, including an instrument tendered as full satisfaction of a debt, are to be sent to a designated person, office, or place, and (ii) the instrument or accompanying communication was not received by that designated person, office, or place.

(2) The claimant, whether or not an organization, proves that within 90 days after payment of the instrument, the claimant tendered repayment of the amount of the instrument to the person against whom the claim is asserted. This paragraph does not apply if the claimant is an organization that sent a statement complying with paragraph (1)(i).

(d) A claim is discharged if the person against whom the claim is asserted proves that within a reasonable time before collection of the instrument was initiated, the claimant, or an agent of the claimant having direct responsibility with respect to the disputed obligation, knew that the instrument was tendered in full satisfaction of the claim.

PART 4

LIABILITY OF PARTIES

§ 3-401. SIGNATURE.

(a) A person is not liable on an instrument unless (i) the person signed the instrument, or (ii) the person is represented by an agent or representative who signed the instrument and the signature is binding on the represented person under Section 3-402.

(b) A signature may be made (i) manually or by means of a device or machine, and (ii) by the use of any name, including a trade or assumed name, or by a word, mark, or symbol executed or adopted by a person with present intention to authenticate a writing.

§ 3-402. SIGNATURE BY REPRESENTATIVE.

(a) If a person acting, or purporting to act, as a representative signs an instrument by signing either the name of the represented person or the name of the signer, the represented person is bound by the signature to the same extent the represented person would be bound if the signature were on a simple contract. If the represented person is bound, the signature of the representative is the "authorized signature of the represented person" and the represented person is liable on the instrument, whether or not identified in the instrument.

(b) If a representative signs the name of the representative to an instrument and the signature is an authorized signature of the represented person, the following rules apply:

(1) If the form of the signature shows unambiguously that the signature is made on behalf of the represented person who is identified in the instrument, the representative is not liable on the instrument.

(2) Subject to subsection (c), if (i) the form of the signature does not show unambiguously that the signature is made in a representative capacity or (ii) the represented person is not identified in the instrument, the representative is liable on the instrument to a holder in due course that took the instrument without notice that the representative was not intended to be liable on the instrument. With respect to any other person, the representative is liable on the instrument unless the representative proves that the original parties did not intend the rep-

resentative to be liable on the instrument.

(c) If a representative signs the name of the representative as drawer of a check without indication of the representative status and the check is payable from an account of the represented person who is identified on the check, the signer is not liable on the check if the signature is an authorized signature of the represented person.

§ 3-403. UNAUTHORIZED SIGNATURE.

(a) Unless otherwise provided in this Article or Article 4, an unauthorized signature is ineffective except as the signature of the unauthorized signer in favor of a person who in good faith pays the instrument or takes it for value. An unauthorized signature may be ratified for all purposes of this Article.

(b) If the signature of more than one person is required to constitute the authorized signature of an organization, the signature of the organization is unauthorized if one of the required signatures is lacking.

(c) The civil or criminal liability of a person who makes an unauthorized signature is not affected by any provision of this Article which makes the unauthorized signature effective for the purposes of this Article.

§ 3-404. IMPOSTORS; FICTITIOUS PAYEES.

(a) If an impostor, by use of the mails or otherwise, induces the issuer of an instrument to issue the instrument to the impostor, or to a person acting in concert with the impostor, by impersonating the payee of the instrument or a person authorized to act for the payee, an indorsement of the instrument by any person in the name of the payee is effective as the indorsement of the payee in favor of a person who, in good faith, pays the instrument or takes it for value or for collection.

(b) If (i) a person whose intent determines to whom an instrument is payable (Section 3-110(a) or (b)) does not intend the person identified as payee to have any interest in the instrument, or (ii) the person identified as payee of an instrument is a fictitious person, the following rules apply until the instrument is negotiated by special indorsement:

(1) Any person in possession of the instrument is its holder.

(2) An indorsement by any person in the name of the payee stated in the instrument is effective as the indorsement of the payee in favor of a person who, in good faith, pays the instrument or takes it for value or for collection.

(c) Under subsection (a) or (b), an indorsement is made in the name of a payee if (i) it is made in a name substantially similar to that of the payee or (ii) the instrument, whether or not indorsed, is deposited in a depositary bank to an account in a name substantially similar to that of the payee.

(d) With respect to an instrument to which subsection (a) or (b) applies, if a person paying the instrument or taking it for value or for collection fails to exercise ordinary care in paying or taking the instrument and that failure substantially contributes to loss resulting from payment of the instrument, the person bearing the loss may recover from the person failing to exercise ordinary care to the extent the failure to exercise ordinary care contributed to the loss.

§ 3-405. EMPLOYER'S RESPONSIBILITY FOR FRAUDULENT INDORSEMENT BY EMPLOYEE.

(a) In this section:

(1) "Employee" includes an independent contractor and employee of an independent contractor retained by the employer.

(2) "Fraudulent indorsement" means (i) in the case of an instrument payable to the employer, a forged indorsement purporting to be that of the employer, or (ii) in the case of an instrument with respect to which the employer is the issuer, a forged indorsement purporting to be that of the person identified as payee.

(3) "Responsibility" with respect to instruments means authority (i) to sign or indorse instruments on behalf of the employer, (ii) to process instruments received by the employer for bookkeeping purposes, for deposit to an account, or for other disposition, (iii) to prepare or process instruments for issue in the name of the employer, (iv) to supply information determining the names or addresses of payees of instruments to be issued in the name of the employer, (v) to control the disposition of instruments to be issued in the name of the employer, or (vi) to act otherwise with respect to instruments in a responsible capacity. "Responsibility" does not include authority that merely allows an employee to have access to instru-

ments or blank or incomplete instrument forms that are being stored or transported or are part of incoming or outgoing mail, or similar access.

(b) For the purpose of determining the rights and liabilities of a person who, in good faith, pays an instrument or takes it for value or for collection, if an employer entrusted an employee with responsibility with respect to the instrument and the employee or a person acting in concert with the employee makes a fraudulent indorsement of the instrument, the indorsement is effective as the indorsement of the person to whom the instrument is payable if it is made in the name of that person. If the person paying the instrument or taking it for value or for collection fails to exercise ordinary care in paying or taking the instrument and that failure substantially contributes to loss resulting from the fraud, the person bearing the loss may recover from the person failing to exercise ordinary care to the extent the failure to exercise ordinary care contributed to the loss.

(c) Under subsection (b), an indorsement is made in the name of the person to whom an instrument is payable if (i) it is made in a name substantially similar to the name of that person or (ii) the instrument, whether or not indorsed, is deposited in a depositary bank to an account in a name substantially similar to the name of that person.

§ 3-406. NEGLIGENCE CONTRIBUTING TO FORGED SIGNATURE OR ALTERATION OF INSTRUMENT.

(a) A person whose failure to exercise ordinary care substantially contributes to an alteration of an instrument or to the making of a forged signature on an instrument is precluded from asserting the alteration or the forgery against a person who, in good faith, pays the instrument or takes it for value or for collection.

(b) Under subsection (a), if the person asserting the preclusion fails to exercise ordinary care in paying or taking the instrument and that failure substantially contributes to loss, the loss is allocated between the person precluded and the person asserting the preclusion according to the extent to which the failure of each to exercise ordinary care contributed to the loss.

(c) Under subsection (a), the burden of proving failure to exercise ordinary care is on the person asserting the preclusion. Under subsec-

tion (b), the burden of proving failure to exercise ordinary care is on the person precluded.

§ 3-407. ALTERATION.

(a) "Alteration" means (i) an unauthorized change in an instrument that purports to modify in any respect the obligation of a party, or (ii) an unauthorized addition of words or numbers or other change to an incomplete instrument relating to the obligation of a party.

(b) Except as provided in subsection (c), an alteration fraudulently made discharges a party whose obligation is affected by the alteration unless that party assents or is precluded from asserting the alteration. No other alteration discharges a party, and the instrument may be enforced according to its original terms.

(c) A payor bank or drawee paying a fraudulently altered instrument or a person taking it for value, in good faith and without notice of the alteration, may enforce rights with respect to the instrument (i) according to its original terms, or (ii) in the case of an incomplete instrument altered by unauthorized completion, according to its terms as completed.

§ 3-408. DRAWEE NOT LIABLE ON UNACCEPTED DRAFT.

A check or other draft does not of itself operate as an assignment of funds in the hands of the drawee available for its payment, and the drawee is not liable on the instrument until the drawee accepts it.

§ 3-409. ACCEPTANCE OF DRAFT; CERTIFIED CHECK.

(a) "Acceptance" means the drawee's signed agreement to pay a draft as presented. It must be written on the draft and may consist of the drawee's signature alone. Acceptance may be made at any time and becomes effective when notification pursuant to instructions is given or the accepted draft is delivered for the purpose of giving rights on the acceptance to any person.

(b) A draft may be accepted although it has not been signed by the drawer, is otherwise incomplete, is overdue, or has been dishonored.

(c) If a draft is payable at a fixed period after sight and the acceptor fails to date the acceptance, the holder may complete the acceptance by supplying a date in good faith.

(d) "Certified check" means a check accepted by the bank on which it is drawn. Acceptance may be made as stated in subsection (a) or by a writing on the check which indicates that the check is certified. The drawee of a check has no obligation to certify the check, and refusal to certify is not dishonor of the check.

§ 3-410. ACCEPTANCE VARYING DRAFT.

(a) If the terms of a drawee's acceptance vary from the terms of the draft as presented, the holder may refuse the acceptance and treat the draft as dishonored. In that case, the drawee may cancel the acceptance.

(b) The terms of a draft are not varied by an acceptance to pay at a particular bank or place in the United States, unless the acceptance states that the draft is to be paid only at that bank or place.

(c) If the holder assents to an acceptance varying the terms of a draft, the obligation of each drawer and indorser that does not expressly assent to the acceptance is discharged.

§ 3-411. REFUSAL TO PAY CASHIER'S CHECKS, TELLER'S CHECKS, AND CERTIFIED CHECKS.

(a) In this section, "obligated bank" means the acceptor of a certified check or the issuer of a cashier's check or teller's check bought from the issuer.

(b) If the obligated bank wrongfully (i) refuses to pay a cashier's check or certified check, (ii) stops payment of a teller's check, or (iii) refuses to pay a dishonored teller's check, the person asserting the right to enforce the check is entitled to compensation for expenses and loss of interest resulting from the nonpayment and may recover consequential damages if the obligated bank refuses to pay after receiving notice of particular circumstances giving rise to the damages.

(c) Expenses or consequential damages under subsection (b) are not recoverable if the refusal of the obligated bank to pay occurs because (i) the bank suspends payments, (ii) the obligated bank asserts a claim or defense of the bank that it has reasonable grounds to believe is available against the person entitled to enforce the instrument, (iii) the obligated bank has a reasonable doubt whether the person demanding payment is the person entitled to enforce the instrument, or (iv) payment is prohibited by law.

§ 3-412. OBLIGATION OF ISSUER OF NOTE OR CASHIER'S CHECK.

The issuer of a note or cashier's check or other draft drawn on the drawer is obliged to pay the instrument (i) according to its terms at the time it was issued or, if not issued, at the time it first came into possession of a holder, or (ii) if the issuer signed an incomplete instrument, according to its terms when completed, to the extent stated in Sections 3-115 and 3-407. The obligation is owed to a person entitled to enforce the instrument or to an indorser who paid the instrument under Section 3-415.

§ 3-413. OBLIGATION OF ACCEPTOR.

(a) The acceptor of a draft is obliged to pay the draft (i) according to its terms at the time it was accepted, even though the acceptance states that the draft is payable "as originally drawn" or equivalent terms, (ii) if the acceptance varies the terms of the draft, according to the terms of the draft as varied, or (iii) if the acceptance is of a draft that is an incomplete instrument, according to its terms when completed, to the extent stated in Sections 3-115 and 3-407. The obligation is owed to a person entitled to enforce the draft or to the drawer or an indorser who paid the draft under Section 3-414 or 3-415.

(b) If the certification of a check or other acceptance of a draft states the amount certified or accepted, the obligation of the acceptor is that amount. If (i) the certification or acceptance does not state an amount, (ii) the amount of the instrument is subsequently raised, and (iii) the instrument is then negotiated to a holder in due course, the obligation of the acceptor is the amount of the instrument at the time it was taken by the holder in due course.

§ 3-414. OBLIGATION OF DRAWER.

(a) This section does not apply to cashier's checks or other drafts drawn on the drawer.

(b) If an unaccepted draft is dishonored, the drawer is obliged to pay the draft (i) according to its terms at the time it was issued or, if not issued, at the time it first came into possession of a holder, or (ii) if the drawer signed an incomplete instrument, according to its terms when completed, to the extent stated in Sections 3-115 and 3-407. The obligation is owed to a person entitled to enforce the draft or to an indorser who paid the draft under Section 3-415.

(c) If a draft is accepted by a bank, the drawer is discharged, regardless of when or by whom acceptance was obtained.

(d) If a draft is accepted and the acceptor is not a bank, the obligation of the drawer to pay the draft if the draft is dishonored by the acceptor is the same as the obligation of an indorser under Section 3-415(a) and (c).

(e) If a draft states that it is drawn "without recourse" or otherwise disclaims liability of the drawer to pay the draft, the drawer is not liable under subsection (b) to pay the draft if the draft is not a check. A disclaimer of the liability stated in subsection (b) is not effective if the draft is a check.

(f) If (i) a check is not presented for payment or given to a depositary bank for collection within 30 days after its date, (ii) the drawee suspends payments after expiration of the 30-day period without paying the check, and (iii) because of the suspension of payments, the drawer is deprived of funds maintained with the drawee to cover payment of the check, the drawer to the extent deprived of funds may discharge its obligation to pay the check by assigning to the person entitled to enforce the check the rights of the drawer against the drawee with respect to the funds.

§ 3-415. OBLIGATION OF INDORSER.

(a) Subject to subsections (b), (c), and (d) and to Section 3-419(d), if an instrument is dishonored, an indorser is obliged to pay the amount due on the instrument (i) according to the terms of the instrument at the time it was indorsed, or (ii) if the indorser indorsed an incomplete instrument, according to its terms when completed, to the extent stated in Sections 3-115 and 3-407. The obligation of the indorser is owed to a person entitled to enforce the instrument or to a subsequent indorser who paid the instrument under this section.

(b) If an indorsement states that it is made "without recourse" or otherwise disclaims liability of the indorser, the indorser is not liable under subsection (a) to pay the instrument.

(c) If notice of dishonor of an instrument is required by Section 3-503 and notice of dishonor complying with that section is not given to an indorser, the liability of the indorser under subsection (a) is discharged.

(d) If a draft is accepted by a bank after an indorsement is made, the liability of the indorser under subsection (a) is discharged.

(e) If an indorser of a check is liable under subsection (a) and the check is not presented for payment, or given to a depositary bank for collection, within 30 days after the day the indorsement was made, the liability of the indorser under subsection (a) is discharged.

§ 3-416. TRANSFER WARRANTIES

(a) A person who transfers an instrument for consideration warrants to the transferee and, if the transfer is by indorsement, to any subsequent transferee that:

(1) the warrantor is a person entitled to enforce the instrument;

(2) all signatures on the instrument are authentic and authorized;

(3) the instrument has not been altered;

(4) the instrument is not subject to a defense or claim in recoupment of any party which can be asserted against the warrantor; and

(5) the warrantor has no knowledge of any insolvency proceeding commenced with respect to the maker or acceptor or, in the case of an unaccepted draft, the drawer.

(b) A person to whom the warranties under subsection (a) are made and who took the instrument in good faith may recover from the warrantor as damages for breach of warranty an amount equal to the loss suffered as a result of the breach, but not more than the amount of the instrument plus expenses and loss of interest incurred as a result of the breach.

(c) The warranties stated in subsection (a) cannot be disclaimed with respect to checks. Unless notice of a claim for breach of warranty is given to the warrantor within 30 days after the claimant has reason to know of the breach and the identity of the warrantor, the liability of the warrantor under subsection (b) is discharged to the extent of any loss caused by the delay in giving notice of the claim.

(d) A [cause of action] for breach of warranty under this section accrues when the claimant has reason to know of the breach.

§ 3-417. PRESENTMENT WARRANTIES.

(a) If an unaccepted draft is presented to the drawee for payment or acceptance and the drawee pays or accepts the draft, (i) the person obtaining payment or acceptance, at the time of presentment, and (ii) a previous transferor of the draft, at the time of transfer, warrant to the drawee making payment or accepting the draft in good faith that:

(1) the warrantor is, or was, at the time the warrantor transferred the draft, a person entitled to enforce the draft or authorized to obtain payment or acceptance of the draft on behalf of a person entitled to enforce the draft;

(2) the draft has not been altered; and

(3) the warrantor has no knowledge that the signature of the drawer of the draft is unauthorized.

(b) A drawee making payment may recover from any warrantor damages for breach of warranty equal to the amount paid by the drawee less the amount the drawee received or is entitled to receive from the drawer because of the payment. In addition, the drawee is entitled to compensation for expenses and loss of interest resulting from the breach. The right of the drawee to recover damages under this subsection is not affected by any failure of the drawee to exercise ordinary care in making payment. If the drawee accepts the draft, breach of warranty is a defense to the obligation of the acceptor. If the acceptor makes payment with respect to the draft, the acceptor is entitled to recover from any warrantor for breach of warranty the amounts stated in this subsection.

(c) If a drawee asserts a claim for breach of warranty under subsection (a) based on an unauthorized indorsement of the draft or an alteration of the draft, the warrantor may defend by proving that the indorsement is effective under Section 3-404 or 3-405 or the drawer is precluded under Section 3-406 or 4-406 from asserting against the drawee the unauthorized indorsement or alteration.

(d) If (i) a dishonored draft is presented for payment to the drawer or an indorser or (ii) any other instrument is presented for payment to a party obliged to pay the instrument, and (iii) payment is received, the following rules apply:

(1) The person obtaining payment and a prior transferor of the instrument warrant to the person making payment in good faith that the warrantor is, or was, at the time the warrantor transferred the instrument, a person entitled to enforce the instrument or authorized to obtain payment on behalf of a person entitled to enforce the instrument.

(2) The person making payment may recover from any warrantor for breach of warranty an amount equal to the amount paid plus expenses and loss of interest resulting from the breach.

(e) The warranties stated in subsections (a) and (d) cannot be disclaimed with respect to checks. Unless notice of a claim for breach of warranty is given to the warrantor within 30 days after the claimant has reason to know of the breach and the identity of the warrantor, the liability of the warrantor under subsection (b) or (d) is discharged to the extent of any loss caused by the delay in giving notice of the claim.

(f) A [cause of action] for breach of warranty under this section-accrues when the claimant has reason to know of the breach.

§ 3-418. PAYMENT OR ACCEPTANCE BY MISTAKE.

(a) Except as provided in subsection (c), if the drawee of a draft pays or accepts the draft and the drawee acted on the mistaken belief that (i) payment of the draft had not been stopped pursuant to Section 4-403 or (ii) the signature of the drawer of the draft was authorized, the drawee may recover the amount of the draft from the person to whom or for whose benefit payment was made or, in the case of acceptance, may revoke the acceptance. Rights of the drawee under this subsection are not affected by failure of the drawee to exercise ordinary care in paying or accepting the draft.

(b) Except as provided in subsection (c), if an instrument has been paid or accepted by mistake and the case is not covered by subsection (a), the person paying or accepting may, to the extent permitted by the law governing mistake and restitution, (i) recover the payment from the person to whom or for whose benefit payment was made or (ii) in the case of acceptance, may revoke the acceptance.

(c) The remedies provided by subsection (a)

or (b) may not be asserted against a person who took the instrument in good faith and for value or who in good faith changed position in reliance on the payment or acceptance. This subsection does not limit remedies provided by Section 3-417 or 4-407.

(d) Notwithstanding Section 4-215, if an instrument is paid or accepted by mistake and the payor or acceptor recovers payment or revokes acceptance under subsection (a) or (b), the instrument is deemed not to have been paid or accepted and is treated as dishonored, and the person from whom payment is recovered has rights as a person entitled to enforce the dishonored instrument.

§ 3-419. INSTRUMENTS SIGNED FOR ACCOMMODATION.

(a) If an instrument is issued for value given for the benefit of a party to the instrument ("accommodated party") and another party to the instrument ("accommodation party") signs the instrument for the purpose of incurring liability on the instrument without being a direct beneficiary of the value given for the instrument, the instrument is signed by the accommodation party "for accommodation."

(b) An accommodation party may sign the instrument as maker, drawer, acceptor, or indorser and, subject to subsection (d), is obliged to pay the instrument in the capacity in which the accommodation party signs. The obligation of an accommodation party may be enforced notwithstanding any statute of frauds and whether or not the accommodation party receives consideration for the accommodation.

(c) A person signing an instrument is presumed to be an accommodation party and there is notice that the instrument is signed for accommodation if the signature is an anomalous indorsement or is accompanied by words indicating that the signer is acting as surety or guarantor with respect to the obligation of another party to the instrument. Except as provided in Section 3-605, the obligation of an accommodation party to pay the instrument is not affected by the fact that the person enforcing the obligation had notice when the instrument was taken by that person that the accommodation party signed the instrument for accommodation.

(d) If the signature of a party to an instrument is accompanied by words indicating unambiguously that the party is guaranteeing collection rather than payment of the obligation of another party to the instrument, the signer is obliged to pay the amount due on the instrument to a person entitled to enforce the instrument only if (i) execution of judgment against the other party has been returned unsatisfied, (ii) the other party is insolvent or in an insolvency proceeding, (iii) the other party cannot be served with process, or (iv) it is otherwise apparent that payment cannot be obtained from the other party.

(e) An accommodation party who pays the instrument is entitled to reimbursement from the accommodated party and is entitled to enforce the instrument against the accommodated party. An accommodated party who pays the instrument has no right of recourse against, and is not entitled to contribution from, an accommodation party.

§ 3-420. CONVERSION OF INSTRUMENT.

(a) The law applicable to conversion of personal property applies to instruments. An instrument is also converted if it is taken by transfer, other than a negotiation, from a person not entitled to enforce the instrument or a bank makes or obtains payment with respect to the instrument for a person not entitled to enforce the instrument or receive payment. An action for conversion of an instrument may not be brought by (i) the issuer or acceptor of the instrument or (ii) a payee or indorsee who did not receive delivery of the instrument either directly or through delivery to an agent or a copayee.

(b) In an action under subsection (a), the measure of liability is presumed to be the amount payable on the instrument, but recovery may not exceed the amount of the plaintiff's interest in the instrument.

(c) A representative, other than a depositary bank, who has in good faith dealt with an instrument or its proceeds on behalf of one who was not the person entitled to enforce the instrument is not liable in conversion to that person beyond the amount of any proceeds that it has not paid out.

PART 5

DISHONOR

§ 3-501. PRESENTMENT.

(a) "Presentment" means a demand made by or on behalf of a person entitled to enforce an instrument (i) to pay the instrument made to the drawee or a party obliged to pay the instrument or, in the case of a note or accepted draft payable at a bank, to the bank, or (ii) to accept a draft made to the drawee.

(b) The following rules are subject to Article 4, agreement of the parties, and clearing-house rules and the like:

(1) Presentment may be made at the place of payment of the instrument and must be made at the place of payment if the instrument is payable at a bank in the United States; may be made by any commercially reasonable means, including an oral, written, or electronic communication; is effective when the demand for payment or acceptance is received by the person to whom presentment is made; and is effective if made to any one of two or more makers, acceptors, drawees, or other payors.

(2) Upon demand of the person to whom presentment is made, the person making presentment must (i) exhibit the instrument, (ii) give reasonable identification and, if presentment is made on behalf of another person, reasonable evidence of authority to do so, and (iii) sign a receipt for the instrument for any payment made or surrender the instrument if full payment is made.

(3) Without dishonoring the instrument, the party to whom presentment is made may (i) return the instrument for lack of a necessary indorsement, or (ii) refuse payment or acceptance for failure of the presentment to comply with the terms of the instrument, an agreement of the parties, or other applicable law or rule.

(4) The party to whom presentment is made may treat presentment as occurring on the next business day after the day of presentment if the party to whom presentment is made has established a cut-off hour not earlier than 2 p.m. for the receipt and processing of instruments presented for payment or acceptance and presentment is made after the cut-off hour.

§ 3-502. DISHONOR.

(a) Dishonor of a note is governed by the following rules:

(1) If the note is payable on demand, the note is dishonored if presentment is duly made to the maker and the note is not paid on the day of presentment.

(2) If the note is not payable on demand and is payable at or through a bank or the terms of the note require presentment, the note is dishonored if presentment is duly made and the note is not paid on the day it becomes payable or the day of presentment, whichever is later.

(3) If the note is not payable on demand and paragraph (2) does not apply, the note is dishonored if it is not paid on the day it becomes payable.

(b) Dishonor of an unaccepted draft other than a documentary draft is governed by the following rules:

(1) If a check is duly presented for payment to the payor bank otherwise than for immediate payment over the counter, the check is dishonored if the payor bank makes timely return of the check or sends timely notice of dishonor or nonpayment under Section 4-301 or 4-302, or becomes accountable for the amount of the check under Section 4-302.

(2) If a draft is payable on demand and paragraph (1) does not apply, the draft is dishonored if presentment for payment is duly made to the drawee and the draft is not paid on the day of presentment.

(3) If a draft is payable on a date stated in the draft, the draft is dishonored if (i) presentment for payment is duly made to the drawee and payment is not made on the day the draft becomes payable or the day of presentment, whichever is later, or (ii) presentment for acceptance is duly made before the day the draft becomes payable and the draft is not accepted on the day of presentment.

(4) If a draft is payable on elapse of a period of time after sight or acceptance, the draft is dishonored if presentment for acceptance is duly made and the draft is not accepted on the day of presentment.

(c) Dishonor of an unaccepted documentary draft occurs according to the rules stated in subsection (b)(2), (3), and (4), except that payment or acceptance may, be delayed without dishonor until no later than the close of the third business day of the drawee following the day on which payment or acceptance is required by those paragraphs.

(d) Dishonor of an accepted draft is governed by the following rules:

(1) If the draft is payable on demand, the draft is dishonored if presentment for payment is duly made to the acceptor and the draft is not paid on the day of presentment.

(2) If the draft is not payable on demand, the draft is dishonored if presentment for payment is duly made to the acceptor and payment is not made on the day it becomes payable or the day of presentment, whichever is later.

(e) In any case in which presentment is otherwise required for dishonor under this section and presentment is excused under Section 3-504, dishonor occurs without presentment if the instrument is not duly accepted or paid.

(f) If a draft is dishonored because timely acceptance of the draft was not made and the person entitled to demand acceptance consents to a late acceptance, from the time of acceptance the draft is treated as never having been dishonored.

§ 3-503. NOTICE OF DISHONOR.

(a) The obligation of an indorser stated in Section 3-415(a) and the obligation of a drawer stated in Section 3-414(d) may not be enforced unless (i) the indorser or drawer is given notice of dishonor of the instrument complying with this section or (ii) notice of dishonor is excused under Section 3-504(b).

(b) Notice of dishonor may be given by any person; may be given by any commercially reasonable means, including an oral, written, or electronic communication; and is sufficient if it reasonably identifies the instrument and indicates that the instrument has been dishonored or has not been paid or accepted. Return of an instrument given to a bank for collection is sufficient notice of dishonor.

(c) Subject to, Section 3-504(c), with respect to an instrument taken for collection by a collecting bank, notice of dishonor must be given (i) by the bank before midnight of the next banking day following the banking day on which the bank receives notice of dishonor of the instrument, or (ii) by any other person within 30 days following the day on which the

person receives notice of dishonor. With respect to any other instrument, notice of dishonor must be given within 30 days following the day on which dishonor occurs.

§ 3-504. EXCUSED PRESENTMENT AND NOTICE OF DISHONOR.

(a) Presentment for payment or acceptance of an instrument is excused if (i) the person entitled to present the instrument cannot with reasonable diligence make presentment, (ii) the maker or acceptor has repudiated an obligation to pay the instrument or is dead or in insolvency proceedings, (iii) by the terms of the instrument presentment is not necessary to enforce the obligation of indorsers or the drawer, (iv) the drawer or indorser whose obligation is being enforced has waived presentment or otherwise has no reason to expect or right to require that the instrument be paid or accepted, or (v) the drawer instructed the drawee not to pay or accept the draft or the drawee was not obligated to the drawer to pay the draft.

(b) Notice of dishonor is excused if (i) by the terms of the instrument notice of dishonor is not necessary to enforce the obligation of a party to pay the instrument, or (ii) the party whose obligation is being enforced waived notice of dishonor. A waiver of presentment is also a waiver of notice of dishonor.

(c) Delay in giving notice of dishonor is excused if the delay was caused by circumstances beyond the control of the person giving the notice and the person giving the notice exercised reasonable diligence after the cause of the delay ceased to operate.

§ 3-505. EVIDENCE OF DISHONOR.

(a) The following are admissible as evidence and create a presumption of dishonor and of any notice of dishonor stated:

(1) a document regular in form as provided in subsection (b) which purports to be a protest;

(2) a purported stamp or writing of the drawee, payor bank, or presenting bank on or accompanying the instrument stating that acceptance or payment has been refused unless reasons for the refusal are stated and the reasons are not consistent with dishonor;

(3) a book or record of the drawee, payor

bank, or collecting bank, kept in the usual course of business which shows dishonor, even if there is no evidence of who made the entry.

(b) A protest is a certificate of dishonor made by a United States consul or vice consul, or a notary public or other person authorized to administer oaths by the law of the place where dishonor occurs. It may be made upon information satisfactory to that person. The protest must identify the instrument and certify either that presentment has been made or, if not made, the reason why it was not made, and that the instrument has been dishonored by nonacceptance or nonpayment. The protest may also certify that notice of dishonor has been given to some or all parties.

PART 6

DISCHARGE AND PAYMENT

§ 3-601. DISCHARGE AND EFFECT OF DIS-
       CHARGE.

(a) The obligation of a party to pay the instrument is discharged as stated in this Article or by an act or agreement with the party which would discharge an obligation to pay money under a simple contract.

(b) Discharge of the obligation of a party is not effective against a person acquiring rights of a holder in due course of the instrument without notice of the discharge.

§ 3-602. PAYMENT.

(a) Subject to subsection (b), an instrument is paid to the extent payment is made (i) by or on behalf of a party obliged to pay the instrument, and (ii) to a person entitled to enforce the instrument. To the extent of the payment, the obligation of the party obliged to pay the instrument is discharged even though payment is made with knowledge of a claim to the instrument under Section 3-306 by another person.

(b) The obligation of a party to pay the instrument is not discharged under subsection (a) if:

(1) a claim to the instrument under Section 3-306 is enforceable against the party receiving payment and (i) payment is made with knowledge by the payor that payment is prohibited by injunction or similar process of a court of competent jurisdiction, or (ii) in the

case of an instrument other than a cashier's check, teller's check, or certified check, the party making payment accepted, from the person having a claim to the instrument, indemnity against loss resulting from refusal to pay the person entitled to enforce the instrument; or

(2) the person making payment knows that the instrument is a stolen instrument and pays a person it knows is in wrongful possession of the instrument.

§ 3-603. TENDER OF PAYMENT.

(a) If tender of payment of an obligation to pay an instrument is made to a person entitled to enforce the instrument, the effect of tender is governed by principles of law applicable to tender of payment under a simple contract.

(b) If tender of payment of an obligation to pay an instrument is made to a person entitled to enforce the instrument and the tender is refused, there is discharge, to the extent of the amount of the tender, of the obligation of an indorser or accommodation party having a right of recourse with respect to the obligation to which the tender relates.

(c) If tender of payment of an amount due on an instrument is made to a person entitled to enforce the instrument, the obligation of the obligor to pay interest after the due date on the amount tendered is discharged. If presentment is required with respect to an instrument and the obligor is able and ready to pay on the due date at every place of payment stated in the instrument, the obligor is deemed to have made tender of payment on the due date to the person entitled to enforce the instrument.

§ 3-604. DISCHARGE BY CANCELLATION
       OR RENUNCIATION.

(a) A person entitled to enforce an instrument, with or without consideration, may discharge the obligation of a party to pay the instrument (i) by an intentional voluntary act, such as surrender of the instrument to the party, destruction, mutilation, or cancellation of the instrument, cancellation or striking out of the party's signature, or the addition of words to the instrument indicating discharge, or (ii) by agreeing not to sue or otherwise renouncing rights against the party by a signed writing.

(b) Cancellation or striking out of an indorsement pursuant to subsection (a) does not affect the status and rights of a party derived from the indorsement.

§ 3-605. DISCHARGE OF INDORSERS AND ACCOMMODATION PARTIES.

(a) In this section, the term "indorser" includes a drawer having the obligation described in Section 3-414(d).

(b) Discharge, under Section 3-604, of the obligation of a party to pay an instrument does not discharge the obligation of an indorser or accommodation party having a right of recourse against the discharged party.

(c) If a person entitled to enforce an instrument agrees, with or without consideration, to an extension of the due date of the obligation of a party to pay the instrument, the extension discharges an indorser or accommodation party having a right of recourse against the party whose obligation is extended to the extent the indorser or accommodation party proves that the extension caused loss to the indorser or accommodation party with respect to the right of recourse.

(d) If a person entitled to enforce an instrument agrees, with or without consideration, to a material modification of the obligation of a party other than an extension of the due date, the modification discharges the obligation of an indorser or accommodation party having a right of recourse against the person whose obligation is modified to the extent the modification causes loss to the indorser or accommodation party with respect to the right of recourse. The loss suffered by the indorser or accommodation party as a result of the modification is equal to the amount of the right of recourse unless the person enforcing the instrument proves that no loss was caused by the modification or that the loss caused by the modification was an amount less than the amount of the right of recourse.

(e) If the obligation of a party to pay an instrument is secured by an interest in collateral and a person entitled to enforce the instrument impairs the value of the interest in collateral, the obligation of an indorser or accommodation party having a right of recourse against the obligor is discharged to the extent of the impairment. The value of an interest in collateral is impaired to the extent (i) the value of the interest is reduced to an amount less than the amount of the right of recourse of the party asserting discharge, or (ii) the reduction in value of the interest causes an increase in the amount by which the amount of the right of recourse exceeds the value of the interest. The burden of proving impairment is on the party asserting discharge.

(f) If the obligation of a party is secured by an interest in collateral not provided by an accommodation party and a person entitled to enforce the instrument impairs the value of the interest in collateral, the obligation of any party who is jointly and severally liable with respect to the secured obligation is discharged to the extent the impairment causes the party asserting discharge to pay more than that party would have been obliged to pay, taking into account rights of contribution, if impairment had not occurred. If the party asserting discharge is an accommodation party not entitled to discharge under subsection (e), the party is deemed to have a right to contribution based on joint and several liability rather than a right to reimbursement. The burden of proving impairment is on the party asserting discharge.

(g) Under subsection (e) or (f), impairing value of an interest in collateral includes (i) failure to obtain or maintain perfection or recordation of the interest in collateral, (ii) release of collateral without substitution of collateral of equal value, (iii) failure to perform a duty to preserve the value of collateral owed, under Article 9 or other law, to a debtor or surety or other person secondarily liable, or (iv) failure to comply with applicable law in disposing of collateral.

(h) An accommodation party is not discharged under subsection (c), (d), or (e) unless the person entitled to enforce the instrument knows of the accommodation or has notice under Section 3-419 (c) that the instrument was signed for accommodation.

(i) A party is not discharged under this section if (i) the party asserting discharge consents to the event or conduct that is the basis of the discharge, or (ii) the instrument or a separate agreement of the party provides for waiver of discharge under this section either specifically or by general language indicating that parties waive defenses based on suretyship or impairment of collateral.

BANK DEPOSITS AND COLLECTIONS

Conforming and Miscellaneous Amendments to Uniform Commercial Code

§4-101. SHORT TITLE.

This Article may be cited as Uniform Commercial Code — Bank Deposits and Collections.

§4-102. APPLICABILITY.

(a) To the extent that items within this Article are also within Articles 3 and 8, they are subject to those Articles. If there is conflict, this Article governs Article 3, but Article 8 governs this Article.

(b) The liability of a bank for action or non-action with respect to an item handled by it for purposes of presentment, or payment, or collection is governed by the law of the place where the bank is located. In the case of actio nor non-action by or at a branch or separate office of a bank, its liability is governed by the law of the place where the branch or separate office is located.

§4-103. VARIATION BY AGREEMENT; MEASURE OF DAMAGES; ACTION CONSTITUTING ORDINARY CARE.

(a) The effect of the provisions of this Article may be varied by agreement but the parties to the agreement cannot disclaim a bank's responsibility for its lack of good faith or failure to exercise ordinary care of limit the measure of damages for the lack or failure. However, the parties may determine by agreement the standards by which the bank's responsibility is to be measured if those standards are not manifestly unreasonable.

(b) Federal Reserve regulations and operating circulars, clearing-house rules, and the like have the effect of agreements under subsection (a), whether or not specifically assented to by all parties interest in items handled.

(c) Action or non-action approved by this Article or pursuant to Federal Reserve regulations or operating circulars is the exercise of ordinary care and, in the absence of special instructions, action or non-action consistent with clearing-house rules and the like or with a general banking usage not disapproved by this Article, is prima facie the exercise of ordinary care.

(d) The specification or approval of certain procedures by this Article is not disapproval of other procedures that may be reasonable under the circumstances.

(e) The measure of damages for failure to exercise ordinary care in handling an item is the amount of the item reduced by an amount

305

that could not have been realized by the exercise of ordinary care. If there is also bad faith it includes any other damages the party suffered as a proximate consequence.

§4-104. DEFINITIONS AND INDEX OF DEFINITIONS.

(a) In this Article, unless the context otherwise requires:

(1) "Account" means any deposit or credit account with a bank including a demand, time, savings, passbook, share draft, or like account, other than an account evidenced by a certificate of deposit;

(2) "Afternoon" means the period of a day between noon and midnight;

(3) "Banking day" means the part of a day on which a bank is open to the public for carrying on substantially all of its banking functions;

(4) "Clearing house" means an association of banks or other payors regularly clearing items;

(5) "Customer" means a person having an account with a bank or for whom a bank has agreed to collect items including a bank that maintains an account at another bank;

(6) "Documentary draft" means a draft to be presented for acceptance or payment if specified documents, certificated securities (Section 8-102) or instructions for uncertificated securities (Section 8-308), or other certificates, statements or the like are to be received by the drawee or other payor before acceptance or payment of the draft;

(7) "Draft" means a draft as defined in Section 3-104 or an item, other than an instrument, that is an order.

(8) "Drawee" means a person ordered in a draft to make payment.

(9) "Item" means an instrument or a promise or order to pay money handled by a bank for collection or payment. The term does not include a payment order governed by Article 4A or a credit or debit card slip;

(10) "Midnight deadline" with respect to a bank is midnight on its next banking day following the banking day on which it receives the relevant item or notice or from which the time for taking action commences to run, whichever is later;

(11) "Settle" means to pay in cash, by clearing-house settlement, in a charge or credit or by remittance, or otherwise as agreed. A settlement may be either provisional or final.

(12) "Suspends payments" with respect to a bank means that it has been closed by order of the supervisory authorities, that a public officer has been appointed to take it over, or that it ceases or refuses to make payments in the ordinary course of business.

(b) Other definitions applying to this Article and the sections in which they appear are:

"Agreement for electronic presentment"	Section 4-110.
"Bank"	Section 4-105.
"Collecting bank"	Section 4-105.
"Depositary bank"	Section 4-105.
"Intermediary bank"	Section 4-105.
"Payor bank"	Section 4-105.
"Presenting bank"	Section 4-105.
"Presentment notice"	Section 4-110.

(c) The following definitions in other Articles apply to this Article:

"Acceptance"	Section 3-409.
"Alteration"	Section 3-407.
"Cashier's check"	Section 3-104.
"Certificate of deposit"	Section 3-104.
"Certified check"	Section 3-409.
"Check"	Section 3-104.
"Good faith"	Section 3-103.
"Holder in due course"	Section 3-302.
"Instrument"	Section 3-104.
"Notice of dishonor"	Section 3-503.
"Order"	Section 3-103.
"Ordinary care"	Section 3-103.
"Person entitled to enforce"	Section 3-301.
"Presentment"	Section 3-501.
"Promise"	Section 3-103.
"Prove"	Section 3-103.
"Teller's check"	Section 3-104.
"Unauthorized signature"	Section 3-403.

(d) In addition, Article 1 contains general definitions and principles of construction and interpretation applicable throughout this Article.

§4-105. "BANK"; "DEPOSITARY BANK"; "PAYOR BANK"; "INTERMEDIARY BANK"; "COLLECTING BANK"; "PRESENTING BANK";

In this Article:

(1) "Bank" means a person engaged in the business of banking, including a savings bank, savings and loan association, credit union, or trust company.

(2) "Depositary bank" means the first bank to take an item even though it is also the payor bank, unless the item is presented for immediate payment over the counter;

(3) "Payor bank" means a bank that is the drawee of a draft;

(4) "Intermediary bank" means a bank to which an item is transferred in course of collection except the depositary or payor bank;

(5) "Collecting bank" means a bank handling an item for collection except the payor bank;

(6) "Presenting bank" means a bank presenting an item except a payor bank.

§4-106. PAYABLE THROUGH OR PAYABLE AT BANK: COLLECTING BANK.

(a) If an item states that it is "payable through" a bank identified in the item, (i) the item designates the bank as a collecting bank and does not by itself authorize the bank to pay the item, and (ii) the item may be presented for payment only by or through the bank.

Alternative A

(b) If an item states that it is "payable at" a bank identified in the item, the item is equivalent to a draft drawn on the bank.

Alternative B

(b) If an item states that it is "payable at" a bank identified in the item, (i) the item designates the bank as a collecting bank and does not by itself authorize the bank to pay the item, and (ii) the item may be presented for payment only by or through the bank.

(c) If a draft names a nonbank drawee and it is unclear whether a bank named in the draft is a co-drawee or a collecting bank, the bank is a collecting bank.

§4-107. SEPARATE OFFICE OF BANK.

A branch or separate office of a bank is a separate bank for the purpose of computing the time within which and determining the place at or to which action may be taken or notice or orders must be given under this Article and under Article 3.

§4-108. TIME OF RECEIPT OF ITEMS.

(a) For the purpose of allowing time to process items, prove balances, and make the necessary entries on its books to determine its position for the day, a bank may fix an afternoon hour of 2 P.M. or later as a cutoff hour for the handling of money and items and the making of entries on its books.

(b) An item or deposit of money received on any day after a cutoff hour so fixed or after the close of the banking day may be treated as being received at the opening of the next banking day.

§4-109. DELAYS.

(a) Unless otherwise instructed, a collecting bank in a good faith effort to secure payment of a specific item drawn on a payor other than a bank, and with or without the approval of any person involved, may waive, modify, or extend time limits imposed or permitted by this [Act] for a period not exceeding two additional banking days without discharge of drawers or indorser or liability to its transferor or a prior party.

(b) Delay by a collecting bank or payor bank beyond time limits prescribed or permitted by this [Act] or by instructions is excused if (i) the delay is caused by interruption of communication or computer facilities, suspension of payments by another bank, war, emergency conditions, failure of equipment, or other circumstances beyond the control of the bank and (ii) the bank exercises such diligence as the circumstances require.

§4-110. ELECTRONIC PRESENTMENT.

(a) "Agreement for electronic presentment" means an agreement, clearing-house rule, or Federal Reserve regulation or operating circular, providing that presentment of an item may be made by transmission of an image of an item or information describing the item ("presentment notice") rather than delivery of the item itself. The agreement may provide for procedures governing retention, presentment, payment, dishonor, and other matters concerning items subject to the agreement.

(b) Presentment of an item pursuant to an agreement for presentment is made when the presentment notice is received.

(c) If presentment is made by presentment notice, a reference to "item" or "check" in this Article means the presentment notice unless the context otherwise indicates.

§4-111. STATUTE OF LIMITATIONS.

An action to enforce an obligation, duty, or right arising under this Article must be commenced within three years after the (cause of action) accrues.

§4-201. STATUS OF COLLECTING BANK AS AGENT AND PROVISIONAL STATUS OF CREDITS; APPLICABILITY OF ARTICLE; ITEM INDORSED "PAY ANY BANK".

(a) Unless a contrary intent clearly appears and before the time that a settlement given by a collecting bank for an item is or becomes final, the bank with respect to the item, is an agent or sub-agent of the owner of the item and any settlement given for the item is provisional. This provision applies regardless of the form of indorsement or lack of indorsement and even though credit give for the item is subject to immediate withdrawal as of right or is in fact withdrawn; but the continuance of ownership of an item by its owner and any rights of the owner to proceeds of the item are subject to rights of a collecting bank, such as those resulting from outstanding advances on the item and rights of recoupment or setoff. If an item is handled by banks for purposes of presentment, payment, collection, or return, the relevant provisions of this Article apply even though action of the parties clearly establishes that a particular bank has purchased the item and is the owner of it.

(b) After an item has been indorsed with the words "pay any bank" or the like, only a bank may acquire the rights of a holder until the item has been:

(1) returned to the customer initiating collection; or

(2) specially indorsed by a bank to a person who is not a bank.

§4-202. RESPONSIBILITY FOR COLLECTION OR RETURN; WHEN ACTION TIMELY.

(a) A collecting bank must exercise ordinary care in:

(1) presenting an item or sending it for presentment;

(2) sending notice of dishonor or nonpayment or returning an item other than a documentary draft to the bank's transferor after learning that the item has not been paid or accepted, as the case may be;

(3) settling for an item when the bank receives final settlement; and

(4) notifying its transferor of any loss or delay in transit within a reasonable time after discovery thereof.

(b) A collecting bank exercises ordinary care under subsection (a) by taking proper action before its midnight deadline following receipt of an item, notice, or settlement. Taking proper action within a reasonably longer time may constitute the exercise of ordinary care, but the bank has the burden of establishing timeliness.

(c) Subject to subsection (a)(1), a bank is not liable for the insolvency, neglect, misconduct, mistake, or default of another bank or person or for loss or destruction of an item in the possession of others or in transit.

§4-203. EFFECT OF INSTRUCTIONS.

Subject to Article 3 concerning conversion of instruments (Section 3-420) and restrictive indorsements (Section 3-206), only a collecting bank's transferor can give instructions that affect the bank or constitute notice to it, and a collecting bank is not liable to prior parties for any action taken pursuant to the instructions or in accordance with any agreement with its transferor.

§4-204. METHODS OF SENDING AND PRESENTING; SENDING DIRECTLY TO PAYOR BANK.

(a) A collecting bank shall send items by a reasonably prompt method, taking into consideration relevant instructions, the nature of the item, the number of those items on hand, the cost of collection involved, and the method generally used by it or others to present those items.

(b) A collecting bank may send:

(1) an item directly to the payor bank;

(2) an item to a nonbank payor if authorized by its transferor; and

(3) an item other than documentary

drafts to a nonbank payor, if authorized by Federal Reserve regulation or operating circular, clearing-house rule, or the like.

(c) Presentment may be made by a presenting bank at a place where the payor bank or other payor has requested that presentment be made.

§4-205. DEPOSITARY BANK HOLDER OF UNINDORSED ITEM.

If a customer delivers an item to a depositary bank for collection:

(1) the depositary bank becomes a holder of the item at the time it receives the item for collection if the customer at the time of delivery was a holder of the item, whether or not the customer indorses the item, and, if the bank satisfies the other requirements of Section 3-302, it is a holder in due course; and

(2) the depositary bank warrants to collecting banks, the payor bank or other payor, and the drawer that the amount of the item was paid to the customer or deposited to the customer's account.

§4-206. TRANSFER BETWEEN BANKS.

Any agreed method that identifies the transferor bank is sufficient for the item's further transfer to another bank.

§4-207. TRANSFER WARRANTIES.

(a) A customer or collecting bank that transfers an item and receives a settlement or other consideration warrants to the transferee and to any subsequent collecting bank that:

(1) the warrantor is a person entitled to enforce the item;

(2) all signatures on the item are authentic and authorized;

(3) the item has not been altered;

(4) the item is not subject to a defense or claim in recoupment (Section 3-305(a)) of any party that can be asserted against the warrantor; and

(5) the warrantor has no knowledge of any insolvency proceeding commenced with respect to the maker or acceptor or, in the case of unaccepted draft, the drawer.

(b) If an item is dishonored, a customer or collecting bank transferring the item and receiving settlement or other consideration is obliged to pay the amount due on the item (i) according to the terms of the item at the time it was transferred, or (ii) if the transfer was of an incomplete item, according to its terms when completed as stated in Sections 3-115 and 3-407. The obligation of a transferor is owed to the transferee and to any subsequent collecting bank that takes the item in good faith. A transferor cannot disclaim its obligation under this subsection by an indorsement stating that it is made "without recourse" or otherwise disclaiming liability.

(c) A person to whom the warranties under subsection (a) are made and who took the item in good faith may recover from the warrantor as damages for breach of warranty an amount equal to the loss suffered as a result of the breach, but not more than the amount of the item plus expenses and loss of interest incurred as a result of the breach.

(d) The warranties stated in subsection (a) cannot be disclaimed with respect to checks. Unless notice of a claim for breach of warranty is given to the warrantor within 30 days after the claimant has reason to know of the breach and the identity of the warrantor, the warrantor is discharged to the extent of any loss caused by the delay in giving notice of the claim.

(e) A cause of action for breach of warranty under this section accrues when the claimant has reason to know of the breach.

§4-208. PRESENTMENT WARRANTIES.

(a) If an unaccepted draft is presented to the drawee for payment or acceptance and the drawee pays or accepts the draft, (i) the person obtaining payment or acceptance, at the time of presentment, and (ii) a previous transferor of the draft, at the time of transfer, warrant to the drawee that pays or accepts the draft in good faith that:

(1) the warrantor is, or was, at the time the warrantor transferred the draft, a person entitled to enforce the draft or authorized to obtain payment or acceptance of the draft on behalf of a person entitled to enforce the draft;

(2) the draft has not been altered; and

(3) the warrantor has no knowledge that the signature of the purported drawer of the draft is unauthorized.

(b) A drawee making payment may recover from a warrantor damages for breach of warranty equal to the amount paid by the drawee less the amount the drawee received or is entitled to receive from the drawer because of the payment. In addition, the drawee is entitled to compensation for expenses and loss of interest resulting from the breach. The right of the drawee to recover damages under this subsection is not affected by any failure of the drawee to exercise ordinary care in making payment. If the drawee accepts the draft (i) breach of warranty is a defense to the obligation of the acceptor, and (ii) if the acceptor makes payment with respect to the draft, the acceptor is entitled to recover from a warrantor for breach of warranty the amounts stated in this subsection.

(c) If a drawee asserts a claim for breach of warranty under subsection (a) based on an unauthorized indorsement of the draft or an alteration of the draft, the warrantor may defend by proving that the indorsement is effective under Section 3-404 or 3-405 or the drawer is precluded under Section 3-406 or 4-406 from asserting against the drawee the unauthorized indorsement or alteration.

(d) If (i) a dishonored draft is presented for payment to the drawer or an indorser or (ii) any other item is presented for payment to a party obliged to pay the item, and the item is paid, the person obtaining payment and a prior transferor of the item warrant to the person making payment in good faith that the warrantor is, or was, at the time the warrantor transferred the item, a person entitled to enforce the item or authorized to obtain payment on behalf of a person entitled to enforce the item. The person making payment may recover from any warrantor for breach of warranty an amount equal to the amount paid plus expenses and loss of interest resulting from the breach.

(e) The warranties stated in subsections (a) and (d) cannot be disclaimed with respect to checks. Unless notice of a claim for breach of warranty is given to the warrantor within 30 days after the claimant has reason to know of the breach and the identity of the warrantor, the warrantor is discharged to the extent of any loss caused by the delay in giving notice of the claim.

(f) A cause of action for breach of warranty under this section accrues when the claimant has reason to know of the breach.

§4-209. ENCODING AND RETENTION WARRANTIES.

(a) A person who encodes information on or with respect to an item after issue warrants to any subsequent collecting bank and to the payor bank or other payor that the information is correctly encoded. If the customer of a depositary bank encodes, that bank also makes the warranty.

(b) A person who undertakes to retain an item pursuant to an agreement for electronic presentment warrants to any subsequent collecting bank and to the payor bank or other payor that retention and presentment of the item comply with the agreement. If a customer of a depositary bank undertakes to retain an item, that bank also makes this warranty.

(c) A person to whom warranties are made under this section and who took the item in good faith may recover from the warrantor as damages for breach of warranty an amount equal to the loss suffered as a result of the breach, plus expenses and loss of interest incurred as a result of the breach.

§4-210. SECURITY INTEREST OF COLLECTING BANK IN ITEMS, ACCOMPANYING DOCUMENTS AND PROCEEDS.

(a) A collecting bank has a security interest in an item and any accompanying documents or the proceeds of either:

(1) in case of an item deposited in an account, to the extent to which credit given for the item has been withdrawn or applied;

(2) in case of an item for which it has given credit available for withdrawal as of right, to the extent of the credit given, whether or not the credit is drawn upon or there is a right of charge-back; or

(3) if it makes an advance on or against the item.

(b) If credit given for several items received at one time or pursuant to a single agreement is withdrawn or applied in part, the security interest remains upon all the items, any accompanying documents or the proceeds of either. For the purpose of this section, credits first given are first withdrawn.

(c) Receipt by a collecting bank of a final settlement for an item is a realization on its security interest in the item, accompanying documents, and proceeds. So long as the bank does not receive final settlement for the item or give up possession of the item or accompanying documents for purposes other than collection, the security interest continues to that extent and is subject to Article 9, but:

(1) no security agreement is necessary to make the security interest enforceable (Section 9-203(1)(a));

(2) no filing is required to perfect the security interest; and

(3) the security interest has priority over conflicting perfected security interests in the item, accompanying documents, or proceeds.

§4-211. WHEN BANK GIVES VALUE FOR PURPOSES OF HOLDER IN DUE COURSE.

For purposes of determining its status as a holder in due course, a bank has given value to the extent it has a security interest in an item, if the bank otherwise complies with the requirements of Section 3-302 on what constitutes a holder in due course.

§4-212. PRESENTMENT BY NOTICE OF ITEM NOT PAYABLE BY, THROUGH, OR AT BANK; LIABILITY OF DRAWER OR INDORSER.

(a) Unless otherwise instructed, a collecting bank may present an item not payable by, through, or at a bank by sending to the party to accept or pay a written notice that the bank holds the item for acceptance or payment. The notice must be sent in time to be received on or before the day when presentment is due and the bank must meet any requirement of the party to accept or pay under Section 3-501 by the close of the bank's next banking day after it knows of the requirement.

(b) If presentment is made by notice and payment, acceptance, or request for compliance with a requirement under Section 3-501 is not received by the close of business on the day after maturity or, in the case of demand items, by the close of business on the third banking day after notice was sent, the presenting bank may treat the item as dishonored and charge any drawer or indorser by sending it notice of facts.

§4-213. MEDIUM AND TIME OF SETTLEMENT BY BANK.

(a) With respect to settlement by a bank, the medium and time of settlement may be prescribed by Federal Reserve regulations or circulars, clearing-house rules, and the like, or agreement. In the absence of such prescription:

(1) the medium of settlement is cash or credit to an account in a Federal Reserve bank of or specified by the person to receive settlement; and

(2) the time of settlement, is:

(i) with respect to tender of settlement by cash, a cashier's check, or teller's check, when the cash or check is sent or delivered;

(ii) with respect to tender of settlement by credit in an account in a Federal Reserve Bank, when the credit is made;

(iii) with respect to tender of settlement by a credit or debit to an account in a bank, when the credit or debit is made or, in the case of tender of settlement by authority to charge an account, when the authority is sent or delivered; or

(iv) with respect to tender of settlement by a funds transfer, when payment is made pursuant to Section 4A-406(a) to the person receiving settlement.

(b) If the tender of settlement is not by a medium authorized by subsection (a), no settlement occurs until the tender of settlement is accepted by the person receiving settlement.

(c) If settlement for an item is made by cashier's check or teller's check and the person receiving settlement, before its midnight deadline.:

(1) presents or forwards the check for collection, settlement is final when the check is finally paid; or

(2) fails to present or forward the check for collection, settlement is final at the midnight deadline of the person receiving settlement.

(d) If settlement for an item is made by giving authority to charge the account of the bank giving settlement in the bank receiving settlement, settlement is final when the charge is made by the bank receiving settlement if there are funds available in the account for the amount of the item.

§4-214. RIGHT OF CHARGE-BACK OR REFUND; LIABILITY OF COLLECTING BANK; RETURN OF ITEM.

(a) If a collecting bank has made provisional

settlement with its customer for an item and fails by reason of dishonor, suspension of payments by a bank, or otherwise to receive settlement for the item which is or becomes final, the bank may revoke the settlement give by it, charge back the amount of any credit given for the item to its customer's account, or obtain refund from its customer, whether or not it is able to return the item, if by its midnight deadline or within a longer reasonable time after it learns the facts it returns the item or sends notification of the facts. If the return or notice is delayed beyond the bank's midnight deadline or a longer reasonable time after it learns the facts, the bank may revoke the settlement, charge back the credit, or obtain refund from its customer, but it is liable for any loss resulting from the delay. These rights to revoke, charge back, and obtain refund terminate if and when a settlement for the item received by the bank is or becomes final.

(b) A collecting bank returns an item when it is sent or delivered to the bank's customer or transferor or pursuant to its instructions.

(c) A depository bank that is also the payor may charge back the amount of an item to its customer's account or obtain refund in accordance with the section governing return of an item received by a payor bank for credit on its books (Section 4-301).

(d) The right to charge back is not affected by:

(1) previous use of a credit given for the item; or

(2) failure by any bank to exercise ordinary care with respect to the item, but a bank so failing remains liable.

(e) A failure to charge back or claim refund does not affect other rights of the bank against the customer or any other party.

(f) If credit is given in dollars as the equivalent of the value of an item payable in foreign money, the dollar amount of any charge-back or refund must be calculated on the basis of the bank-offered spot rate for the foreign money prevailing on the day when the person entitled to the charge-back or refund learns that it will not receive payment in ordinary course.

§4-215. FINAL PAYMENT OF ITEM BY PAYOR BANK; WHEN PROVISIONAL DEBITS AND CREDITS BECOME FINAL; WHEN CERTAIN CREDITS BECOME AVAILABLE FOR WITHDRAWAL.

(a) An item is finally paid by a payor bank when the bank has first done any of the following:

(1) paid the item in cash;

(2) settled for the item without having a right to revoke the settlement under statute, clearing-house rule, or agreement; or

(3) made a provisional settlement for the item and failed to revoke the settlement in the time and manner permitted by statute, clearing-house rule, or agreement.

(b) If provisional settlement for an item does not become final, the item is not finally paid.

(c) If provisional settlement for an item between the presenting and payor banks is made through a clearing-house or by debits or credits in an account between them, then to the extent that provisional debits or credits for the item are entered in accounts between the presenting and payor banks or between the presenting and successive prior collecting banks seriatim, they become final upon final payment of the items by the payor bank.

(d) If a collecting bank receives a settlement for an item which is or becomes final, the bank is accountable to its customer for the amount of the item and any provisional credit given for the item in an account with its customer becomes final.

(e) Subject to (i) applicable law stating a time for availability of funds and (ii) any right of the bank to apply the credit to an obligation of the customer, credit given by a bank for an item in a customer's account becomes available for withdrawal as of right:

(1) if the bank has received a provisional settlement for the item, when the settlement becomes final and the bank has had a reasonable time to receive return of the item and the item has not been received within that time;

(2) if the bank is both the depositary bank and the payor bank, and the item is finally paid, at the opening of the bank's second banking day following receipt of the item.

(f) Subject to applicable law stating a time for availability of funds and any right of a bank to apply a deposit to an obligation of the depositor, a deposit of money becomes available for withdrawal as of right at the opening of the bank's next banking day after receipt of the deposit.

§4-216. INSOLVENCY AND PREFERENCE.

(a) If an item is in or comes into the possession of a payor or collecting bank that suspends payment and the item has not been finally paid, the item must be returned by the receiver, trustee, or agent in charge of the closed bank to the presenting bank or the closed bank's customer.

(b) If a payor bank finally pays an item suspends payments without making a settlement for the item with its customer or the presenting bank which settlement is or becomes final, the owner of the item has a preferred claim against the payor bank.

(c) If a payor bank gives or a collecting bank gives or receives a provisional settlement for an item and thereafter suspends payments, the suspension does not prevent or interfere with the settlement's becoming final if the finality occurs automatically upon the lapse of certain time or the happening of certain events.

(d) If a collecting bank receives from subsequent parties settlement for an item, which settlement is or becomes final and the bank suspends payments without making a settlement for the item with its customer which settlement is or becomes final, the owner of the item has a preferred claim against the collecting bank.

§4-301. DEFERRED POSTING;RECOVERY OF PAYMENT BY RETURN OF ITEMS; TIME OF DISHONOR; RETURN OF ITEMS BY PAYOR BANK.

(a) If a payor bank settles for a demand item other than a documentary draft presented otherwise than for immediate payment over the counter before midnight of the banking day of receipt, the payor bank may revoke the settlement and recover the settlement if, before it has made final payment and before its midnight deadline, it

(1) returns the item; or

(2) sends written notice of dishonor or nonpayment if the item is unavailable for return.

(b) If a demand item is received by a payor bank for credit on its books, it may return the item or send notice of dishonor and may revoke any credit given or recover the amount thereof withdrawn by its customer, if it acts within the time limit an din the manner specified in subsection (a).

(c) Unless previous notice of dishonor has been sent, an item is dishonored at the time when for purposes of dishonor it is returned or notice sent in accordance with this section.

(d) An item is returned:

(1) as to an item presented through a clearing-house, when it is delivered to the presenting or last collecting bank or to the clearing-house or is sent or delivered in accordance with clearing-house rules; or

(2) in all other cases, when it is sent or delivered to the bank's customer or transferor or pursuant to instructions.

§4-302. PAYOR BANK'S RESPONSIBILITY FOR LATE RETURN OF ITEM.

(a) If an item is presented to and received by a payor bank, the bank is accountable for the amount of:

(1) a demand item, other than a documentary draft, whether properly payable or not, if the bank, in any case in which it is not also the depositary bank, retains the item beyond midnight of the banking day of receipt without settling for it or, whether or not it is also the depositary bank, does not pay or return the item or send notice of dishonor until after its midnight deadline; or

(2) any other properly payable item unless, within the time allowed for acceptance or payment of that item, the bank either accepts or pays the item or returns it and accompanying documents.

(b) The liability of a payor bank to pay an item pursuant to subsection (a) is subject to defenses based on breach of a presentment warranty (Section 4-208) or proof that the person seeking enforcement of the liability presented or transferred the item for the purpose of defrauding the payor bank.

§4-303. WHEN ITEMS SUBJECT TO NOTICE, STOP-PAYMENT ORDER, LEGAL PROCESS, OR SETOFF; ORDER IN WHICH ITEMS MAY BE CHARGED OR CERTIFIED.

(a) Any knowledge, notice, or stop-payment

order received by, legal process served upon, or setoff exercised by a payor bank comes too late to terminate, suspend, or modify the bank's right or duty to pay an item or to charge its customer's account for the item if the knowledge, notice, stop-payment order, or legal process is received or served and a reasonable time for the bank to act thereon expires or the setoff is exercised after the earliest of the following:

(1) the bank accepts or certifies the item;

(2) the bank pays the item in cash;

(3) the bank settles for the item without having a right to revoke the settlement under statute, clearing-house rule, or agreement;

(4) the bank becomes accountable for the amount of the item under Section 4-302 dealing with the payor bank's responsibility for late return of items; or

(5) with respect to checks, a cutoff hour no earlier than one hour after the opening of the next banking day after the banking day on which the bank received the check and no later than the close of that next banking day or, if no cutoff hour is fixed, the close of the next banking day after the banking day on which the bank received the check.

(b) Subject to subsection (a), items may be accepted, paid, certified, or charged to the indicated account of its customer in any order.

§4-401. WHEN BANK MAY CHARGE CUSTOMER'S ACCOUNT.

(a) A bank may charge against the account of a customer an item that is properly payable from that account even though the charge creates an overdraft. An item is properly payable if it is authorized by the customer and is in accordance with any agreement between the customer and bank.

(b) A customer is not liable for the amount of an overdraft if the customer neither signed the item nor benefited from the proceeds of the item.

(c) A bank may charge against the account of a customer a check that is otherwise properly payable from the account, even though payment was made before the date of the check, unless the customer has given notice to the bank of the postdating describing the check with reasonable certainty. The notice is effective for the period stated in Section 4-403(b) for

stop-payment orders, and must be received at such time and in such manner as to afford the bank a reasonable opportunity to act on it before the bank takes any action with respect to the check described in Section 4-303. If a bank charges against the account of a customer a check before the dates stated in the notice of postdating, the bank is liable for damages for the loss resulting from its act. The loss may include damages for dishonor of subsequent items under Section 4-402.

(d) A bank that in good faith makes payment to a holder may charge the indicated account of its customer according to:

(1) the original terms of the altered item; or

(2) the terms of the completed item, even though the bank knows the item has been completed unless the bank has notice that the completion was improper.

§4-402. BANK'S LIABILITY TO CUSTOMER FOR WRONGFUL DISHONOR; TIME OF DETERMINING INSUFFICIENCY OF ACCOUNT.

(a) Except as otherwise provided in this Article, a payor bank wrongfully dishonors an item if it dishonors an item that is properly payable, but a bank may dishonor an item that would create an overdraft unless it has agreed to pay the overdraft.

(b) A payor bank is liable to its customer for damages proximately caused by the wrongful dishonor of an item. Liability is limited to actual damages proved and may include damages for an arrest or prosecution of the customer or other consequential damages. Whether any consequential damages are proximately caused by the wrongful dishonor is a question of fact to be determined in each case.

(c) A payor bank's determination of the customer's account balance on which a decision to dishonor for insufficiency of available funds is based may be made at any time between the time the item is received by the payor bank and the time that the payor bank returns the item or gives notice in lieu of return, and no more than one determination need be made. If, at the election of the payor bank, a subsequent balance determination is made for the purpose of reevaluating the bank's decision to dishonor the item, the account balance at that time is determinative of whether a dishonor for insufficiency of available funds is wrongful.

§4-403. CUSTOMER'S RIGHT TO STOP PAYMENT; BURDEN OF PROOF OF LOSS.

(a) A customer or any person authorized to draw on the account if there is more than one person may stop payment of any item drawn on the customer's account or close the account by an order to the bank describing the item or account with reasonable certainty received at a time and in a manner that affords the bank a reasonable opportunity to act on it before any action by the bank with respect to the item described in Section 4-303. If the signature of more than one person is required to draw on an account, any of these persons may stop payment or close the account.

(b) A stop-payment order is effective for six months, but it lapses after 14 calendar days if the original order was oral an was not confirmed in writing within that period. A stop-payment order may be renewed for additional six-month periods by a writing given to the bank within a period during which the stop-payment order is effective.

(c) The burden of establishing the fact and amount of loss resulting from the payment of an item contrary to a stop-payment order or order to close an account is on the customer. The loss from payment of an item contrary to a stop-payment order may include damages for dishonor of subsequent items under Section 4-402.

§4-404. BANK NOT OBLIGED TO PAY CHECK MORE THAN SIX MONTHS OLD.

A bank is under no obligation to a customer having a checking account to pay a check, other than a certified check, which is presented more than six months after its date, but it may charge its customer's account for a payment made thereafter in good faith.

§4-405. DEATH OR INCOMPETENCE OF CUSTOMER.

(a) A payor or collecting bank's authority to accept, pay, or collect an item or to account for proceeds of its collection, if otherwise effective, is not rendered ineffective by incompetence of a customer of either bank existing at the time the item is issued or its collection is undertaken if the bank does not know of an adjudication of incompetence. Neither death nor incompetence of a customer revokes the authority to accept, pay, collect, or account until the bank knows of the fact of death or of an adjudication of incompetence and has reasonable opportunity to act on it.

(b) Even with knowledge, a bank may for 10 days after the date of death pay or certify checks drawn on or before that date unless ordered to stop payment by a person claiming an interest in the account.

§4-406. CUSTOMER'S DUTY TO DISCOVER AND REPORT UNAUTHORIZED SIGNATURE OR ALTERATION.

(a) A bank that sends or makes available to a customer a statement of account showing payment of items for the account shall either return or make available to the customer the items paid or provide information in the statement of account sufficient to allow the customer reasonably to identify the items paid. The statement of account provides sufficient information if the item is described by item number, amount, and date of payment.

(b) If the items are not returned to the customer, the person retaining the items shall either retain the items or, if the items are destroyed, maintain the capacity to furnish legible copies of the items until the expiration of seven years after receipt of the items. A customer may request an item from the bank that paid the item, and that bank must provide in a reasonable time either the item or, if the item has been destroyed or is not otherwise obtainable, a legible copy of the item.

(c) If a bank sends or makes available a statement of account or items pursuant to subsection (a), the customer must exercise reasonable promptness in examining the statement or the items to determine whether any payment was not authorized because of an alteration of an item or because a purported signature by or on behalf of the customer was not authorized. If, based on the statement or items provided, the customer should reasonably have discovered the unauthorized payment, the customer must promptly notify the bank of the relevant facts.

(d) If the bank proves that the customer failed, with respect to an item, to comply with the duties imposed on the customer by subsection (c), the customer is precluded from asserting against the bank:

(1) the customer's unauthorized signature or any alteration on the item, if the bank also proves that it suffered a loss by reason of the failure; and

(2) the customer's unauthorized signature or alteration by the same wrongdoer on any other item paid in good faith by the bank if the payment was made before the bank received notice from the customer of the unauthorized signature or alteration and after the customer had been afforded a reasonable period of time, not exceeding 30 days, in which to examine the item or statement of account and notify the bank.

(e) If subsection (d) applies and the customer proves that the bank failed to exercise ordinary care in paying the item and that the failure substantially contributed to loss, the loss is allocated between the customer precluded and the bank asserting the preclusion according to the extent to which the failure of the customer to comply with subsection (c) and the failure of the bank to exercise ordinary care contributed to the loss. If the customer proves that the bank did not pay the item in good faith, the preclusion under subsection (d) does not apply.

(f) Without regard to care or lack of care of either the customer or the bank, a customer who does not within one year after the statement or items are made available to the customer (subsection (a)) discover and report the customer's unauthorized signature on or any alteration on the item is precluded from asserting against the bank the unauthorized signature or alteration. If there is a preclusion under this subsection, the payor bank may not recover for breach of warranty under Section 4-208 with respect to the unauthorized signature or alteration to which the preclusion applies.

§4-407. PAYOR BANK'S RIGHT TO SUBROGATION ON IMPROPER PAYMENT.

If a payor bank has paid an item over the order of the drawer or maker to stop payment, or after an account has been closed, or other-

wise under circumstances giving a basis for objection by the drawer or maker, to prevent unjust enrichment and only to the extent necessary to prevent loss to the bank by reason of its payment of the item, the payor bank is subrogated to the rights

(1) of any holder in due course on the item against the drawer or maker;

(2) of the payee or any other holder of the item against the drawer or maker either on the item or under the transaction out of which the item arose; and

(3) of the drawer or maker against the payee or any other holder of the item with respect to the transaction out of which the item arose.

§4-501. HANDLING OF DOCUMENTARY DRAFTS; DUTY TO SEND FOR PRESENTMENT AND TO NOTIFY CUSTOMER OF DISHONOR.

A bank that takes a documentary draft for collection shall present or send the draft and accompanying documents for presentment and, upon learning that the draft has not been paid or accepted in due course, shall seasonably notify its customer of the fact even though it may have discounted or bought the draft or extended credit available for withdrawal as of right.

§4-502. PRESENTMENT OF "ON ARRIVAL" DRAFTS.

If a draft or the relevant instructions require presentment "on arrival", "when goods arrive" or the like, the collecting bank need not present until in its judgment a reasonable time for arrival of the goods has expired. Refusal to pay or accept because the goods have not arrived is not dishonor; the bank must notify its transferor of the refusal but need not present the draft again until it is instructed to do so or learns of the arrival of the goods.

§4-503. RESPONSIBILITY OF PRESENTING BANK FOR DOCUMENTS AND GOODS; REPORT OF REASONS FOR DISHONOR; REFEREE IN CASE OF NEED.

Unless otherwise instructed and except as provided in Article 5, a bank presenting a documentary draft:

(1) must deliver the documents to the drawee on acceptance of the draft if it is payable more than three days after presentment; otherwise, only on payment; and

(2) upon dishonor, either in the case of presentment for acceptance or presentment for payment, may seek and follow instructions from any referee in case of need designated in the draft or, if the presenting bank does not choose to utilize the referee's services, it must use diligence and good faith to ascertain the reason for dishonor, must notify its transferor of the dishonor and of the results of its effort to ascertain the reasons therefor, and must request instructions.

However, the presenting bank is under no obligation with respect to goods represented by the documents except to follow any reasonable instructions seasonably received; it has a right to reimbursement for any expense incurred in following instructions and to prepayment of or indemnity for those expenses.

§4-504. PRIVILEGE OF PRESENTING BANK TO DEAL WITH GOODS; SECURITY INTEREST FOR EXPENSES.

(a) A presenting bank that, following the dishonor of a documentary draft, has seasonably requested instructions but does not receive them within a reasonable time may store, sell, or otherwise deal with the goods in any reasonable manner.

(b) For its reasonable expenses incurred by action under subsection (a), the presenting bank has a lien upon the goods or their proceeds, which may be foreclosed in the same manner as an unpaid seller's lien.

INDEX

About the Publisher

PROBUS PUBLISHING COMPANY

Probus Publishing Company fills the informational needs of today's business professional by publishing authoritative, quality books on timely and relevant topics, including:

- Investing
- Futures/Options Trading
- Banking
- Finance
- Marketing and Sales
- Manufacturing and Project Management
- Personal Finance, Real Estate, Insurance and Estate Planning
- Entrepreneurship
- Management

Probus books are available at quantity discounts when purchased for business, educational or sales promotional use. For more information, please call the Director, Corporate/Institutional Sales at 1-800-PROBUS-1, or write:

Director, Corporate/Institutional Sales
Probus Publishing Company
1925 N. Clybourn Avenue
Chicago, Illinois 60614
FAX (312) 868-6250